VIEW FROM THE UN

VIEW FROM THE UN

U THANT

DOUBLEDAY & COMPANY, INC.
GARDEN CITY, NEW YORK 1978

Library of Congress Cataloging in Publication Data

Thant U, 1909–74.
  View from the UN.

  1. Thant, U, 1909–74. 2. United Nations—
Biography. 3. Statesmen—Biography. I. Title.
D839.7.T5A35   341.23'3'0924 [B]
ISBN: 0-385-11541-5
Library of Congress Catalog Card Number 76–57517

To all who strive for peace, justice, and progress

FOREWORD

The publication of this book marks a happy moment for the author's family, which at the same time is saddened by the thought that the late Secretary General has not lived to see his memoirs published. He painstakingly completed the final chapter of the memoirs in April 1974, thus accomplishing his great desire to write the history of the ten turbulent years of his office at the United Nations. His last days were filled with deep emotion, however, for he had begun, but was unable to continue, writing a second book, which was to have been about his life and the many friends who so generously helped him in his ceaseless search for world peace.

The original manuscript has been edited with the sole purpose of facilitating an uninterrupted reading; hence, many important—but lengthy—documents have been appended at the end of the book, some passages shortened, and still others summarized, while always retaining as much of the original text as possible. For the skillful completion of this difficult task, the author's family is deeply grateful to Mr. Kenneth McCormick of Doubleday and his editorial staff.

Particular thanks are due to Robert A. Gravallese for his untiring editorial work on this book. The author's family particularly acknowledges his invaluable help.

Finally, inasmuch as U Thant was so public a figure and his writings of such historical importance, the family has decided to deposit the original unedited text with the United Nations Dag Hammarskjöld Library.

TYN MYINT-U

ACKNOWLEDGMENTS

I am deeply indebted to the Adlai Stevenson Institute of International Affairs for honoring me with a senior fellowship, and for facilitating my work in writing these memoirs by providing an administrative secretary and a research assistant. My debt to the president of the Institute, Dr. William R. Polk, and to Miss Barbara Ward (Lady Jackson), chairman of the Institute's finance committee, cannot be adequately expressed. Even before my retirement from the service of the United Nations, they both gave me their enthusiastic support.

According to Dr. Polk, the following have given generous support to the Institute on my behalf: former Governor Edmund G. Brown (of California), the Marie G. Dennett Foundation, Mrs. Lyle Ramsey, and Morrison Ward. To all of them I am most grateful.

I must also express my sincere thanks to my former colleagues in the United Nations Secretariat for their most valuable advice and assistance. Special mention must be made of C. V. Narasimhan, Constantin A. Stavropoulos, Bohdan Lewandowski, Bruce Turner, Brian E. Urquhart, Robert Muller, William Powell, and Yasushi Akashi.

I am deeply in debt to my former secretary, Mrs. Estella Mira. She did everything a determined, dedicated, and efficient secretary could do to assist me in compiling, classifying, and indexing all my personal files. I must also add a word of appreciation to my daughter Aye Aye (Mrs. Tyn Myint-U) for going over my diaries and confidential papers and suggesting useful material for incorporation into this book. The contribution of my two research assistants—C. Y. Chai (formerly of the United Nations Political and Security Council Affairs Department) and Max Harrelson (formerly head of the Associated Press Bureau at the United Nations)—has been most meticulous, and they deserve my very special thanks. I am also greatly indebted to my very efficient administrative secretary, Mrs. Theresa K. Sullivan, for her general administrative assistance and flawless typing.

My deeply felt appreciation must also go to Richard J. Walton, my editorial consultant, whose wide experience in the writing of books and commentaries and whose sound editorial advice were of inestimable assistance.

U THANT

CONTENTS

xiv

INTRODUCTION

From 1961 to 1971, I witnessed—and often actively mediated—the bitter controversies and tragic confrontations that took place in the world during that turbulent decade: the series of crises in the Congo, the Arab-Israeli war of 1967, and the Cuban missile crisis, to name only a few. I viewed these and other conflicts from a unique vantage point, that of the Secretary General of the United Nations. This book is an assessment of my decade of experience in that cockpit of world tensions.

My account of those years is not intended to be a book of memoirs in the traditional sense of the term; nor is it an autobiography. Rather, it reflects the wide range of ideas, interests, and events that came before the vision of the man occupying the office on the thirty-eighth floor of the UN building. It attempts to answer the questions: What did I observe during that decade? How did I view my responsibilities? How did I react to my opportunities and challenges? And what did I think about the personalities and problems that moved before me as Secretary General?

As each conflict I dealt with ran its course, and as events unfolded day by day through the news media, the member states of the United Nations deliberated and conducted negotiations, while behind the scenes, many individuals engaged in activities, often in secret, that had a significant and often determining impact on the outcome. On numerous occasions, for example, I was called upon to exercise my good offices, again often in secret, to settle a dispute or mediate it. In my view, many of these activities are historically important; yet they could not be disclosed during my tenure of office. Certainly, the story of what occurred behind the scenes needs to be told, and the Secretary General is the only person who can tell it.

This book is therefore not only an account of events as they unfolded at the United Nations; it is also my intention to reveal some important features of my private conversations with heads of state and heads of government, as well as with leading thinkers and personalities of international repute.

I have mentioned that the Secretary General of the United Nations has a singular perspective. I was called upon to view each dispute, not from one side or the other of the argument, but as a deeply concerned moderator standing in an absolutely unique position. Because of this perspective, the Secretary General can see what is happening so much more objectively than those who confront each other. And for that reason, many of the events related in these pages will have at times an astonishingly different meaning from that conveyed at the time they occurred, as reported by a section of the press or other public media. For press reports are often necessarily based on only a few of the facts—often distorted facts—then known.

There were many instances, to be discussed at length in these pages, in which the facts of a situation as they confronted me were suppressed or ignored or distorted in a section of the news media. The Cuban missile crisis of 1962 was one such instance: the view from the thirty-eighth floor was, during those crucial days, a very different one from that of the contestants and the public at large. I was suddenly called upon to act as a go-between, so as to gain time for the main contestants to save face and, incidentally, to help save humanity from imminent nuclear annihilation. The public—in the United States, in the Soviet Union, in Cuba, the world over—did not know how much it owed to the United Nations for being involved at that decisive moment. Not only was the United Nations the only spot on the globe in which the three contestants could and did literally face each other without a resulting catastrophe. The man in the street, lined up behind one side or the other, did not realize how much his survival depended on what the United Nations *did* to help the rival factions gain the time they both needed to effect the compromise that eventually came about.

Another instance is the story leading to my withdrawal of the United Nations Emergency Force from Sinai and Gaza in May 1967, just before the Six-Day War—an action for which I was widely criticized in the press and other quarters. But it made all the difference in the world as to how I saw the issues at the time and why I acted as I did. This dramatic episode, and the account of the missile crisis, form two of the major chapters in this book. There are many other untold stories: the secret search for peace in Vietnam and the role of the United Nations in bringing about the cease-fire in the Indo-Pakistani War of 1965 are two examples.

Has the time come for these things—some painful, some glorious—to be said at all? Would it not be wiser to leave where they were the mistakes and tragedies of yesterday? One of my problems in compiling this record was deciding *how much* to reveal, without wounding or embarrassing some high government leader, official, or national spokesman. The demarcation line between what should and should not be disclosed is very thin, however, and I believe that it will be in the public interest if I go as far as I can in the disclosure of facts and my own assessment of those facts. The only limit, perhaps, should be revelations that might affect the future—the future of human society. For is not tomorrow more important than today? As Santayana has said: "Those who will not learn the lessons of history will live to repeat its mistakes." My main concern, therefore, is tomorrow. What is past is past. Only the lessons of the past can spur us on to work for a better future.

Although this book is not meant to be a historical object lesson, it is a historical record. In recording and reporting the events of those dramatic ten years, I have tried to be impartial and believe in retrospect that I have largely succeeded. Yet I inevitably had a point of view as a man, as a Burmese, as an Asian. I would not be writing from my heart, from the depth of my religious faith, and from the unique experience I gained during my tenure, if I confined my account merely to the things that *happened*. I must attempt to distill as much as I can of the essence of the moral values and humanism that have inspired me in the discharge of my responsibilities. It is really my credo—my beliefs and philosophy—that dominates. So perhaps this book is an apologia, too, for an apologia can be made only after the restraints of public office have been laid aside.

Partly because of my faith and philosophy, and partly because of my special vantage point, I am apt to moralize, from time to time, on the issues facing the human community, and am inclined to remind man of those attributes of spirit and mind that can yet spare him from the scourge of another world war, by creating the conditions for a peaceful and just society under law. I have before me a vision of a unified mankind living in peace under a just world order.

With the advent of the atomic age, the nature of interdependence and the imperative need to change our old concepts become more apparent. It is a fact of life, however, that both politically and psychologically, most governments remain conditioned by *pre*-atomic and *pre*-global traditions that prevent them from taking fresh, new approaches on a planetary basis.

In a world that demands the full application of human intelligence and the spirit of unity, mankind still remains tragically divided, because national foreign policies tend to stay as they were formulated a generation or more ago. Foreign policies are notoriously conservative. Nationalistic claims and slogans are repeated by statesmen year after year—as though nothing had changed in the international scene around them. But the truth is that since the Second World War, the whole matrix of international relations between sovereign governments has been broken into pieces and recast in an altogether different pattern.

Surely it must have become plain by this time that the swift growth of scientific discovery—especially the splitting of the atom and the interlocking of all countries through instantaneous communication—together with the collapse of colonial empires and the "revolution of rising expectations," have transformed the prewar era beyond recall.

Many orthodox policies are therefore quite irrelevant to the world situation today, if not completely disastrous to the countries that are still pursuing them as though history had stood still. Hence, some of the topics surveyed in the following chapters—the crises in Cuba and the Dominican Republic, the invasion of Czechoslovakia, the Middle East dispute—are set within the purview of the international politician, not that of the national politician. As such, their presentation is likely to be more proximate to reality than the web of self-delusion that—as is the case of the Vietnam war, for instance—has so frequently snared the best-meaning national leaders and dragged their peoples into division and disaster.

At the end of my survey of the ten dramatic years of my tenure, I look into the decade we have entered—the 1970s—and beyond. The concluding section of this book contains my assessment of world conditions at the present time, an analysis of the characteristics of the postatomic era in which we live, and an evaluation of the United Nations as an instrument of worldwide change. In it I also make a plea for that new quality of planetary imagination— a component of my vision of unified man—which, in my view, is demanded from all of us as the price of human survival.

It is my hope, therefore, to present these memoirs not merely as one person's private story, but also as a world peace program— a proposal for the future global society.

U THANT

Harrison, New York
May 1974

PART I

THE
SEARCH
FOR A
SECRETARY
GENERAL

CHAPTER I

TROIKA

It was a cloudy Monday morning on September 18, 1961, when, just as I was about to leave for my office, news came on the radio that Dag Hammarskjöld, while en route to a crucial meeting concerning the former Belgian Congo, had died the day before in a plane crash near Ndola in Northern Rhodesia (now Zambia). I was stunned with shock and disbelief. Only a few days before, I had received a letter from him sent via Paris conveying his thoughts on a one-act play written by the then Prime Minister of Burma, U Nu, entitled *The Wages of Sin.* My first thoughts on hearing the news were centered on the United Nations and the future of the Congo operations. The sixteenth session of the United Nations General Assembly was scheduled to convene on the next day, September 19.

Dag Hammarskjöld's sudden death not only threw a pall of sorrow and confusion over the opening of the sixteenth session of the Assembly, but revived with full force Chairman Nikita Khrushchev's year-old proposal of a *troika* administration of the United Nations.

For the past twelve months, the Soviet Union had been boycotting the Secretary General, treating him as functioning illegally, mainly because of Mr. Hammarskjöld's interpretation and active implementation of the Security Council resolutions on the

Congo. As we shall see in Part III, Chairman Khrushchev believed that the Secretary General was acting in the Congo on behalf of Western interests, and that the United Nations had no business in the Congo after the death of Prime Minister Patrice Lumumba, who first requested UN military involvement in the Congo. The Soviet Chairman had insisted that the Secretary General should be replaced by a *troika:* three equal Secretaries General—one representing the East, one the West, and one representing nonaligned countries. (*Troika* is the Russian word for a carriage drawn by three horses.) The basis for his demand was his conviction that "while there are neutral countries, there are no neutral men."

Mr. Khrushchev's position had very little support at the United Nations. First of all, it was obvious to most governments that the uncommitted or nonaligned nations could be divided into further subcategories: for example, the pro-Western neutrality of country A could be contrasted with pro-Soviet neutrality of country B and with the genuine neutrality of country C. The truth of such differing ideological orientations came out clearly at the Conference of Heads of State of Nonaligned Countries, held in Belgrade from September 1 to 6, 1961, which I attended as a member of the Burmese delegation. Prime Minister Jawaharlal Nehru of India, who had been the de facto leader of the nonaligned countries for years, again played a leading role at Belgrade in the formulation of policies, and he emerged as a genuine neutral, while some other heads of state or government demonstrated pro-Western or pro-Eastern leanings. Thus the Belgrade conference, held just a few weeks before the opening of the General Assembly, implicitly rejected the concept of "three main currents" in international affairs. Besides, many delegates who attended the conference felt that the *troika* concept was against the letter and spirit of the Charter of the United Nations, and if put into practice, would have rendered the whole United Nations system ineffective and impotent. As a simple practical matter, it would be difficult, perhaps impossible, to administer the United Nations with three chiefs of equal rank who would have to agree before anything could be done. And with two of the three representing conflicting sides in the Cold War, such agreement would seldom be possible. In any case, the Charter is quite specific on the election of a Secretary General. It says in Article 97: "The Secretary-General shall be appointed by the General Assembly upon the recommendation of the Security Council." And it is plain that the appointment of a *troika* would have required an amendment to the Charter, for Article 97 also specifies a *single* Secretary General: "He shall be the chief administrative officer of the Organization."

Against this background, Prime Minister Nehru's statement of September 18 on Dag Hammarskjöld's death carried a special significance. Although he avoided the *troika* issue, he left no doubt about his support of the Secretary General's actions in the Congo, and thus, by implication, also supported the concept of a single Secretary General. On the same day, President Kennedy, in a statement broadcast over radio and television networks, came out strongly for a single, independent Secretary General.

Behind-the-scenes discussions and negotiations in search of Mr. Hammarskjöld's successor, from September 18 to November 2, provide ample material for a separate book. His death at first seemed to put an end to any hope of peace in the Congo. Only a few weeks before, things had looked brighter in that embattled country. Parliament was reconvened, and a new national unity government under Mr. Cyrille Adoula was formed. The second Conciliation Commission for the Congo, established on April 15, 1961, was immediately convened under my chairmanship on August 28, and noted with satisfaction the encouraging developments in the Congo, in particular the reconvening of parliament and the institution of a national unity government.

But within two weeks, the situation in the Congo had seriously deteriorated. As we shall see, United Nations troops, who were attempting to eject the mercenaries operating in Katanga, were hard-pressed; an Irish contingent had been completely cut off and captured in Jadotville.

With the background of this confused and critical situation in the Congo, negotiations at the United Nations on the appointment of Mr. Hammarskjöld's successor were proceeding, and the Big Four—the United States, the Soviet Union, the United Kingdom, and France—played a leading role in those negotiations.

On Tuesday, September 19, when the Assembly opened, Mongi Slim of Tunisia was unanimously elected its president. (On the next day, incidentally, tributes were paid to the late Secretary General, and in the course of my tribute I proposed that Mr. Hammarskjöld, "who fell in his unrelenting fight for peace," should be posthumously awarded the Nobel Peace Prize.)

But it was the choice of a successor that occupied the minds of all delegations. Three names were freely mentioned as possible candidates: Ambassador Slim of Tunisia, who was the only elected official of the session; Ambassador Frederick H. Boland of Ireland, president of the previous session; and Ambassador Ralph Enckell of Finland. All three were very able diplomats, highly respected in United Nations circles and close to the late Secretary General. I was among the first to suggest these names to several delegates. Therefore, to my surprise—and I believe to the surprise of everybody else—the New York *Herald Tribune* came out on the morning of September 20 with a story that I had emerged as the leading candidate to succeed Dag Hammarskjöld. It added: "U Thant was considered by some as an ideal candidate enjoying the support of Asians and Africans and many other smaller countries and who, at the same time, had not been involved in Hammarskjöld's Secretariat." Even now I have no firm knowledge of the basis for the *Herald Tribune* story. It might have been based on a report in the *London Observer* on September 3, 1961, describing me as "a Crippsian-like Socialist and . . . a typically cool Civil Servant, a charmer, a man of infinite discretion, and the embodiment of non-alignment." The report went on to say that "with Mr. Khrushchev holding his view that only God is 'neutral,' it will be interesting to see what line he takes if U Thant should one day emerge as the choice of the non-aligned for the Secretary-General's job."

To all who asked me, I expressed no interest in the post. My only concern at that time was to help in the choice of a successor to Dag Hammarskjöld, and to bring about political reconciliation in the Congo as the chairman of its Conciliation Commission.

On September 19, before the opening of the General Assembly, Foreign Minister Andrei Gromyko of the Soviet Union had sent one of his senior advisers, Mr. Alexei Nesterenko (who later became an undersecretary at the United Nations) to my office to explain the policy of the Soviet government regarding the appointment of Mr. Hammarskjöld's successor. His government, he said, would still insist on *troika,* but as an interim measure it would like to have an interim Secretary General and three undersecretaries acting collectively at the second level. The Soviet Union would oppose any one nominee, without agreement on the three undersecretaries who would act as a team, irrespective of nationality or political affiliation. He told me that if my name were proposed by some government or governments, without naming the three deputies and defining their functions, the Soviet Union's opposition should not be misunderstood. I told him that my government was opposed to the concept of a *troika* at any level, and I assured him that, at any rate, I was not at all interested in the post. On the basis of the *Tribune* article, however, several delegates asked me if I was interested; I replied in the negative to all such enquiries.

On September 21, the *Herald Tribune* reported again that "U Thant remains the favorite." I had to spend a good deal of time that day in explaining that I was *not* a candidate, and that my government was not even contemplating offering my name as one. On the previous night, several delegations had met and considered a formula whereby the Security Council would be urged to nominate Dag Hammarskjöld's successor as early as possible. In the light of the Soviet Union's strong insistence on a *troika* administration and the majority opposition to that proposal, the group felt that an early Security Council action was not in sight, and so, pending such a recommendation, the General Assembly should appoint a temporary chief executive to run the Secretariat. All the delegates attending that meeting were reported to have referred that formula to their respective governments for instruction.

On that day (September 21), I had a meeting with Ambassador Adlai Stevenson of the United States, who was accompanied by Ambassador Charles Yost. Mr. Stevenson told me that the United States would fight the *troika* concept "tooth and nail," since it had no support whatsoever outside the Eastern European group. I told him that my government was also opposed to it.

After my meeting with Ambassadors Stevenson and Yost, I attended a meeting of twenty-three Belgrade conference participants. The Foreign Minister of Ghana, Ako Ajei, and Ambassador Alex Quaison-Sackey formally proposed a new Secretariat, set up with an individual Secretary General assisted by three advisers, each representing the East, the West, and nonaligned groups. The actual functions of the three deputies were not clearly defined, but the Ghanaian Foreign Minister suggested that a united front should be presented by the group to break the deadlock. No decision was reached, and each of us stated that the proposal would be referred back to our respective governments for consideration.

It was a day of extraordinary activity. In the evening, several delegations met and considered a draft resolution to be tabled before the General Assembly. The text was as follows:

> Considering that it is urgently important to provide due direction to the operation of the Secretariat pending the resolution of problems created by the death of Mr. Dag Hammarskjöld,
>
> Appoints (Mr. X) to supervise for the time being the direction of the Secretariat.[1]

Ambassador Stevenson told me that the United States would not favor such a resolution since the functions of the appointee were not specified. He told me that the United States strongly maintained its position that the Secretary General must function independently and without restraint, as envisaged in the Charter. Ambassador Zorin said that he had no immediate reaction to the draft resolution.

I reported the developments by cable to my government, for now, despite my expressed disinterest, it was clear that I was a leading candidate, and I received the views of Prime Minister U Nu through the Foreign Office. In effect, he wanted to see me appointed Secretary General, but only on a permanent and regular basis. He was opposed to my accepting any interim appointment for two reasons: first, it would be illegal; and second (since the Soviet Union would withhold its co-operation), my position would be undermined from the beginning. He agreed with me that I should not offer myself as a candidate in that confused situation. He added that, if I thought it would help, the Burmese government was prepared to put out a statement on those lines.

---

[1] Given to me by Mongi Slim (but not necessarily drafted by him).

The next day, I replied to U Nu through the Foreign Office, expressing my total agreement with his views. I advised him, however, against putting out any official statement at that juncture, for several reasons. Many delegations felt that—mainly because of Afro-Asian feelings—the Soviet Union was beginning to soften its stand on *troika*. In addition, the Burmese government's conception of illegality regarding an interim arrangement would be questioned by most delegations, especially the United States, which maintained that the General Assembly was competent to decide on temporary measures to ensure the continuity of Secretariat operations, pending the appointment of a new Secretary General. Another development was that Ambassadors Stevenson and Zorin were to confer on Tuesday (September 26), when an agreed formula was likely to emerge. I also reported to the Prime Minister that I had been privately informing many delegations that my government would not release me for any interim appointment.

In the light of my categorical stand, a strong move was initiated on Monday, September 25, to name Mongi Slim as an interim chief executive. The permanent representatives of Ireland, Norway, and Argentina showed me a revised draft to be tabled the next day.

In the afternoon, Ambassadors Boland of Ireland, Nielsen of Norway, Amadeo of Argentina, and I saw Ambassador Slim and discussed the draft, expressing our strong desire that he should make himself available. He said that he was prepared to quit the presidency of the Assembly if such a resolution was adopted by a two-thirds majority. I assured the sponsors that I would vote for the resolution if my government agreed, and I immediately cabled to the Foreign Office for instructions.

On September 29, further interesting developments took place. Ambassador Gideon Rafael, a member of the Israeli delegation (later Israel's permanent representative to the United Nations and director general of its Foreign Office) told me that I should announce my candidacy without delay and that Israel would give it full support. On the same day, Ambassador Omar Loutfi of the United Arab Republic—who later became an undersecretary in the United Nations—and Ambassador Adnan Pachachi of Iraq, a very close colleague of mine, saw me separately and informed me that their governments would support my candidacy if I were available. They said that their governments appreciated my work as chairman of the Afro-Asian Standing Committee on Algerian Independence for three years, and my active participation in matters related to colonialism and imperialism. Canadian Foreign Minister Howard G. Green also told me that the Soviet Union would not withhold co-operation if I were in charge. I disagreed and told him that I had already committed myself to support Ambassador Slim and that I was awaiting instructions from my government.

Although I supported Ambassador Slim, it began to become apparent that he did not have enough support to be named Secretary General; Third World and communist-bloc nations thought he was too close to the West, and France opposed him because of the French-Tunisian conflict over the base France maintained at Bizerte, despite Tunisian objections.

Meanwhile, however, Mr. Gromyko had proposed a new interim formula whereby a *four*-man team would be appointed, each representing the East, the West, Asia, and Africa. He stressed that those representing Asia and Africa must be nonaligned, and that one of them was "to preside over" the team of four. He did not mention veto power, but stressed that all four should work "as a team" and "with mutual understanding." When I told him that, apart from other considerations, Latin Americans would not like it, he replied, "Are not Latin Americans allied to the United States?"

Although the new formulation was very vague, the Soviet position had perceptibly softened. It was also significant that Mr. Gromyko did not mention the word *troika* in his address before the General Assembly on that day. But Mr. Stevenson told me that evening that he had also talked to Gromyko, who gave him the same formulation, and that the Big-Four permanent representatives had just met; the United States, the United Kingdom, and France, he said, had found the Soviet formula unacceptable. For the first time, Mr. Stevenson also told me that, because of the very strained relations between France and Tunisia, France would not agree to the appointment of Mr. Slim even for an interim period. He doubted that France would support my candidacy, if put forward, because of my "active role" in the Algerian independence movement as chairman of the Afro-Asian committee on Algerian independence. I assured him that I would not offer myself as a candidate for an interim period, and that my government's position on this matter was firm.

On the same day, Mrs. Golda Meir, then Foreign Minister of Israel, told me that Israel would strongly oppose the candidacy of Mr. Slim. Tunisia, of course, was an Arab state.

On September 27, I received a cable from my Foreign Office informing me that President Kwame Nkrumah of Ghana had suggested to Presidents Tito, Nasser, and Sukarno, and to Prime Minister Nehru, that the nonaligned powers should take the initiative in proposing a suitable candidate from one of the nonaligned countries as the next Secretary General, to be assisted by three deputy secretaries general, of whom one would be from the United States, one from the Soviet Union, and one from a neutral country. President Nkrumah added that a candidate from Burma, in his view, should be proposed for the Secretary Generalship. Prime Minister Nehru had replied that Nkrumah's proposal, including the choice of a Burmese candidate, had much virtue in it and that he would be happy if it were generally agreed upon. In reply, Prime Minister U Nu had supported President Nkrumah's proposal and expressed appreciation for the latter's selection of Burma as the country to fill the post of Secretary General. President Nkrumah's proposal was made public in Accra, and it received wide coverage in the New York press on Thursday, September 28.

It was at this point that a long, frustrating deadlock developed at the United Nations over the appointment of Dag Hammarskjöld's successor. The Soviet Union continued to insist on a four-man team, representing the East, the West, Asia, and Africa, with one member "presiding over" the team of four. Since veto power was implied in the Soviet formula, the Western European delegations continued to oppose it.

Then the United States and the United Kingdom decided to by-pass the Security Council altogether and bring the matter up before the General Assembly. A Soviet veto was, of course, probable in the Council, and in their view, interim measures could legitimately be taken by the Assembly. But the Soviet Union maintained that action by the Security Council was, as Mr. Gromyko insisted, "absolutely necessary." India and Burma also thought the Security Council must not be by-passed.

At this time, I was in almost daily communication with my government, which felt that any solution must have the support, or at least the acquiescence, of the Soviet Union. Otherwise, it feared that the new Secretary General would not function properly and that the Cold War would be intensified within the United Nations. As to the deadlock, Burma informed me (on October 5) that it would go along neither with by-passing the Security Council, nor with the *troika* idea, nor with any formula based on bloc representation. My government believed that veto power would make *troika* unworkable and that the entire conception of a division of the world into blocs "does not accord with reality." In order to break the deadlock, however, Burma would be prepared to go along with a formula whereby three or more deputies are appointed to assist the Secretary General, provided:

(1) That there is no question of the exercise by them of veto powers;
(2) It is clearly understood that the deputies are not bloc representatives but representatives of their respective countries or possibly of geographical regions;
(3) That such a formula is accepted by both East and West.

The last message added: "Government would be happy to see you fill the top post under such an arrangement which is accepted by both the East and the West blocs. All the best of luck."[2]

On the same day, the situation at the United Nations became —temporarily—clearer. Since October 2, several delegations had been working on a compromise formula, and were in contact with both the United States and the Soviet Union. Agreement was reached on the appointment of a single, interim Secretary General, who would serve until April 1963; on the need for the Security Council to recommend the appointment; and on the need to have top advisers. There was no agreement yet, however, on the *num-*

---

[2] Burma Foreign Office Code Cable No. BUN 340/HTA, October 5, 1961.

ber of advisers or the character of consultations between them and the interim head.

There now followed what Mr. Stevenson called "the numbers game." The United States and the West preferred five advisers, appointed on the basis of geographical regions and not on ideological groupings. Their five advisers would comprise the United States (North America), the Soviet Union (East Europe), one European country (West Europe), Africa, and Latin America. This position was based on the assumption that the interim head would come from Asia.

The Soviet Union and its allies stuck to four: i.e., the United States, the Soviet Union, Africa, and Latin America, a position also based on the same assumption that the interim head would come from Asia.

Regarding prospective candidates, Golda Meir, the Israeli Foreign Minister, was vigorously campaigning against Mr. Slim, and a New York *Times* editorial of Saturday, September 30, ruled out Mr. Slim, since "the Tunisian Government will not speak to the Israelis." It also ruled me out, since "Burmese friendship with Israel would displease Arab states."

On Tuesday, October 3, I attended a luncheon given by Dr. Mahmoud Fawzi, Foreign Minister of the United Arab Republic. Foreign Minister Gromyko was also among those who attended. Dr. Fawzi, who in my opinion is one of the ablest and most decent diplomats ever to attend the General Assembly sessions, told me in front of Mr. Gromyko that his country "sees eye to eye with Burma on all issues except one"—and he smiled. He did not elaborate, but apparently he meant Burma's close relationship with Israel.

On the night of October 4, Foreign Minister Ako Ajei of Ghana told me that I was Ghana's choice for the top post. He also said that both Mr. Gromyko and Mr. Stevenson had told him that they agreed on my appointment, but that "other matters" remained to be solved.

Meanwhile, Afro-Asian pressures for an urgent solution were intensified. Delegates became restless. Both on October 5 and October 6, the Afro-Asians, joined by many Latin Americans, met informally. On October 6, several Arab delegates informed me that they would support me despite my close association with Israel. On the same day, some Latin-American delegates also expressed their support for me, and it was later confirmed by Ambassador Gideon Rafael of Israel, who had sounded out most of them.

Meanwhile, the United States and the Soviet Union had been trying to work out their differences over the number of advisers the new Secretary General was to have. On October 9, the U.S.S.R. agreed to five advisers (the number proposed by the U.S.), but now the two powers disagreed on the region the fifth adviser was to represent: the U.S. wanted Western Europe, while the U.S.S.R. wanted Eastern Europe. Disagreement also persisted over the nature of consultation between the Secretary General and his advisers, the U.S.S.R. wanting compulsory consultation and the U.S. opposing it. The Soviets, moreover, wanted the nominee to state in advance, to the Security Council, the names of the advisers he would appoint, while the United States objected that a statement should be made only in the Assembly, and that the advisers need not be named.

By October 11, Mr. Zorin softened his position: he would not insist on my naming the advisers, but would be satisfied with my announcing the regions from which they would be appointed; he also agreed to consultation "on the basis of mutual understanding." But the Soviets still insisted on Eastern European representation in the panel if Western Europe was to be represented, and still insisted on a statement in the Council.

To make matters worse, the Indian ambassador told me that his government would insist on Asian representation in the panel if both Western and Eastern European regions were represented.

Thus, "the numbers game" persisted. No agreement was in sight. On October 13, the Soviet position softened once again. At a dinner given by the Foreign Minister of Bulgaria, Carlo Lukanov, Mr. Zorin told me that if there was no agreement on four or five, the Soviet Union would go along with seven (the U.S., the U.S.S.R., Western Europe, Eastern Europe, Africa, Latin America, and Asia), provided that a Western European was not made chef de cabinet. He also told me that he had clarified the Soviet position at a long press conference early that day, when he had said that the Acting Secretary General must be given full powers, but that "he should listen to the views of his principal advisers before he acts. If his views differ from those of any of his advisers, he is the one responsible and he can act as he feels necessary." It was the most conciliatory statement ever made by Mr. Zorin, almost identical with the views expressed by Mr. Stevenson, Mr. Godber, Sir Patrick Dean, and others. Only the "numbers game" remained unresolved.

On October 14, Ambassador Stevenson announced on a television interview: "U Thant is acceptable to the Soviet Union and highly acceptable to the United States." He went on to say, however, that the Big Powers still had to agree on the number of principal advisers, their functions, and the procedures to be adopted both in the Security Council and the General Assembly. On the same day, I reported to my government that it was probable that agreement on all points would be reached late that week or early the following week, and requested the government to urgently consider temporary arrangements regarding my successor as permanent representative.

On the afternoon of October 17, Ambassador Stevenson told me that "the numbers game" was still unresolved, and in view of the very serious deterioration of the Congo situation, his government felt the extreme urgency of appointing an interim Secretary General. He said that he would talk very seriously both with the Soviet delegation and the Western Europeans. Earlier that day, the latter had issued a statement rejecting any arrangement whereby Western Europe was excluded from the list of principal advisers. On the same day, Ambassador Armand Bérard of France told me that the Western European statement was based on rumors to the effect that the United States was contemplating four principal advisers without Western European representation, and for the first time, he confided to me that his government would not oppose my appointment. (A few days later, however, a French diplomat was reported to have told a correspondent that I was a short man, and did not even speak French. When a correspondent brought the remark to my attention for comment, I told him that I was taller than Napoleon, and that he did not even speak English!)

By October 18, the two powers were no nearer a solution. Ambassador Stevenson told me that he still stood for five advisers, while Mr. Zorin still wanted four or seven. At this point I decided to change my tactics. On the night of October 19, I informed both the United States and the Soviet Union that if negotiations continued to stall by the following week, I proposed to present my own views and formula on a "take-it-or-leave-it" basis. This seemed to have some effect, for on the afternoon of October 20, a very frustrated Stevenson saw me and outlined a different U.S. position. The new U.S. proposal would have the Security Council recommend me for appointment without any conditions or prior agreement regarding the advisers.

After Ambassador Stevenson left, Hans Engen, the Norwegian undersecretary of state, conveyed to me the same plan to break the deadlock. He agreed with Ambassador Stevenson that the Soviet Union would not oppose it, since it had agreed to my nomination and since the whole Afro-Asian group was behind me. But that same night, Ambassador Zorin told me that if the West were to go ahead with the "no strings" proposal, the Soviet Union would not merely abstain, but definitely vote against it. I reported to the Foreign Office the same night.

On October 23, I received instructions from the Prime Minister of Burma that I should "wield positive support of both East and West blocs for any formula." When I informed Ambassador Stevenson of that new instruction, he was visibly distressed. On the same day, I was informed by many Afro-Asian delegates that they were inclined toward the Soviet formulation of four or seven principal advisers, as against the U.S. and Western formula of five.

My statement to the press on October 26—that I might come out with my own formula the following week, if the deadlock still persisted—received mixed reactions. Most Afro-Asians thought that it might break the deadlock, particularly in view of the fact that there was no other candidate acceptable to both East and West. All the Big Four dissuaded me from taking that course, however, since it could create another crisis. Ambassador Stevenson saw me on the morning of October 28 and informed me that he was putting out a statement on Monday (October 30) to the effect that the United States would like to see me elected without strings attached.

At 3:30 P.M. on Sunday, October 29, I appeared on the television program "Adlai Stevenson Reports," moderated by Mr. Arnold Michaelis, a very gifted and enterprising commentator. In the course of that appearance, I attempted to present my concept of the Secretary General's functions.

In reply to a question put by Mr. Michaelis, I said that whoever occupies the office of Secretary General must be impartial, but not necessarily neutral. In regard to moral issues, the Secretary General cannot, and should not, remain neutral or passive. I cited the functions of a judge who must try to be impartial, but who cannot be neutral when it comes to the question of "who is the criminal and who is the person on whom a crime has been committed." Ambassador Stevenson agreed with me.

At last the long, difficult deadlock began to break when, on November 1, the United States and the United Kingdom came out with public statements that, in effect, would leave the question of advisers in my hands. France followed suit, though in more cautious terms. Ambassador Zorin told me on the same day that he would like to follow suit, but would prefer to wait until the next day. On November 2, he came out with the promised statement that paved the way for the Security Council and General Assembly meeting on November 3. According to that statement, I was given a free hand to come out with my own formula, both in regard to the number of principal advisers and the nature of my consultations with them.

The Security Council met at 11:00 A.M. in a closed session and unanimously recommended me as Acting Secretary General. The General Assembly met at 3:30 P.M., when by a secret ballot of the entire membership, I was unanimously appointed to serve the unexpired term of Mr. Dag Hammarskjöld (until April 1963).

From the beginning of the negotiations, it was apparent that the third Secretary General of the United Nations would not be from Europe. NATO and Warsaw Pact countries were understandably out of consideration. Of the militarily nonaligned countries of Europe, Sweden had already contributed the second Secretary General. No diplomat from Austria, Cyprus, Finland, Ireland, or Yugoslavia was considered for the post, although at first the names of Ambassadors Boland and Enckell, respectively of Ireland and Finland, were mentioned. The Afro-Asian countries felt that it was the turn of the Third World, and the Latin Americans joined hands. So, from the middle of October, no other name besides mine was ever mentioned, and only the question of principal advisers occupied the attention of the member states, particularly the Big Powers.

My acceptance speech did not conform either to the Western or the Eastern formulation in regard to the number of principal advisers. In it I said:

> It is my intention to invite a limited number of persons who are at present undersecretaries, or to be appointed as undersecretaries, to act as my principal advisers on important questions pertaining to the performance of functions entrusted to the Secretary General by the United Nations Charter.
>
> In extending this invitation, I am fully conscious of the paramount consideration of securing the highest standards of efficiency, competence, and integrity, and with due regard to the importance of as wide a geographical basis as possible, as laid down in Article 101 of the Charter. I intend to include among these advisers Dr. Ralph J. Bunche and Mr. Georgi Petrovitch Arkadev.
>
> It is also my intention to work together with these colleagues in close collaboration and consultation in a spirit of mutual understanding. I am sure that they will seek to work with me in the same manner.

Among the first messages of congratulation I received that night was one from my own government, a few hours after my appointment. The message also stated that the Burmese Cabinet had decided to confer on me one of the highest titles ever awarded. After a hurried consultation with Mr. C. V. Narasimhan of India, who was to continue as chef de cabinet (head of the executive office of the Secretary General), I sent a cable to my government thanking them for the very kind congratulations and gracious award of high honors. I had to point out, however, that in accordance with the Charter of the United Nations, and based on Article 100, a tradition had been established that the Secretary General does not accept any award or title conferred by any government. So I had to decline the award.

CHAPTER II

HOW DID I CONCEIVE MY ROLE?

Many people have asked me how I felt at the time of my appointment as Acting Secretary General. They have been invariably surprised to learn that I did not feel the way most people would have felt in similar circumstances. To understand my feelings—and my conception of the role of Secretary General—the nature of my religious and cultural background must first be understood. I should therefore like to outline not only my religious beliefs, but also my conception of human institutions and of the human situation itself.

As a Buddhist, I was trained to be tolerant of everything except intolerance. I was brought up not only to develop the spirit of tolerance, but also to cherish moral and spiritual qualities, especially modesty, humility, compassion, and, most important, to attain a certain degree of emotional equilibrium. I was taught to control my emotions through a process of concentration and meditation. Of course, being human, and not yet having reached the stage of *arahant* or *arhat* (one who attains perfect enlightenment), I cannot completely "control" my emotions, but I must say that I am not easily excited or excitable.

To understand my religious background, a brief explanation of certain ethical aspects of Buddhism will be necessary. Among the teachings of the Buddha are four features of meditation, the primary purpose of which is the attainment of moral and spiritual excellence: *metta* (good will or kindness), *karuna* (compassion), *mudita* (sympathetic joy), and *upekka* (equanimity or equilibrium).

A true Buddhist practices his *metta* to all, without distinction; Buddhists need to apply in their daily lives the teachings of *metta* even to those whom they have never seen before, and will not see afterwards. "Just as the sun shines on all, or the rain falls on all, without distinction," *metta* embraces all beings impartially and spontaneously, expecting nothing in return, not even appreciation. *Metta* is impersonal love or good will, the opposite of sensuous craving or a burning, sensual fire that can turn into wrath, hatred, or revenge when not requited. A true Buddhist has to practice *metta* to friends and foes alike.

Karuna (compassion) is the second aspect of Buddhist meditation that all true Buddhists are expected to practice. This quality of compassion is deeply rooted in the Buddhist concept of suffering. Human life is one of suffering; hence, it is the duty of a good Buddhist to mitigate the suffering of others, not only in his thoughts but also in practice. He shows his compassion or pity to all, be they living in this or in another world. (Buddhism believes in life after death.) Buddhist charity is best seen during the feasts or *dana* given to the poor or to homeless monks, who are provided with almsfood with a view to the donor's attaining a higher order of bliss in the other world. The regular practice of compassion opens one's mind to the "Noble Truth of Suffering" and its origin. For the Buddha has taught us that suffering originates in craving and ignorance. Hatred, for instance, is the root of all evil.

Mudita (sympathetic joy) can best be defined as one's expression of sympathy with other people's joy. The happiness of others generates happiness in the mind of a good Buddhist. Melancholy and pessimism have no place in the *Buddha-dhamma* or *dharma* (the cosmic and moral law governing the world, as formulated by the Buddha in his teachings). One's life gains in joy by sharing in the happiness of others, as if that happiness were one's own. The person who cultivates altruistic joy radiates it over everyone in his surroundings, and thus everyone enjoys working and living with him. The practice of *mudita* not only dispels worry and frustrations but strengthens our moral fiber. Thus, a true Buddhist is expected to pray for the happiness of all human beings. By practicing *mudita,* one automatically renders an important service to the entire community.

Upekka (equanimity or equilibrium or detachment) connotes the acquisition of a balance of mind, whether in triumph or tragedy. This balance is achieved only as a result of deep insight into the nature of things, and primarily by contemplation and meditation. If one understands how unstable and impermanent all worldly things and conditions are, one learns to bear lightly even the greatest misfortune that befalls one or the greatest reward that is bestowed on one. This lofty quality of even-mindedness or emotional equilibrium is the most difficult of all ethical virtues to practice and apply in our hectic world. To contemplate life, but not to be enmeshed in it, is the law of the Buddha.

To achieve *upekka,* one has to meditate. The Buddha's teaching regarding meditation aims at producing a state of perfect mental health, emotional equilibrium, and tranquillity. But this concept of Buddhist meditation is very much misunderstood, both by Buddhists and non-Buddhists. The word "meditation" is generally associated with a particular posture, or musing on some kind of mystic or mysterious thought, or going into a trance. Such misunderstanding is mainly due to the lack of a suitable English word for the original term *bhavana,* which means mental culture or mental development. The Buddhist *bhavana* aims at cleansing the mind of impurities, such as ill will, hatred, and restlessness; it aims at cultivating such qualities as concentration, awareness, intelligence, confidence, and tranquillity, leading finally to the attainment of the highest wisdom.

In other words, through meditation I seek inner peace. I heartily agree with Father Dominique Georges Pire, winner of the Nobel Peace Prize, when he says: "I still think that to be a peacemaker, that is to say a man of peace, one must first be at peace with oneself. One must first achieve inner peace. This involves getting to know oneself and learning to control one's impulses. Only then can a peaceful being approach the immense task of creating harmoney between groups and between individuals."[1]

It is far from my intention to claim that I have reached a very high stage on the path to attainment of the highest wisdom, or that I have attained complete "inner peace." I can claim, however, that I practice *bhavana* every day. I try to cultivate the ethical aspects of Buddhism, and I believe that I have attained a greater degree of emotional equilibrium than most people. This explains why I received the tragic news of the sudden death (in a traffic accident) of my only son, Tin Maung Thant, on May 21, 1962, with minimal emotional reaction. For are not birth and death the two phases of the same life process? According to the Buddha, birth is followed by death, but death, in turn, is followed by rebirth.

The same minimal emotional reaction applied to the news brought to me on September 23, 1965, by the Norwegian permanent representative, Ambassador Sivert Nielsen, that it was the intention of the Nobel Peace Committee in Oslo to award me the coveted prize for 1965. He showed me the letter addressed to him by the Nobel Peace Committee. My response was: is not the Secretary General merely doing his job when he works for peace? After Ambassador Nielsen left my office, my thoughts wandered to those who were more deserving of that prize than myself—those whose lifelong preoccupation had been the peace of the world, the welfare of mankind, and the unity of the human community: people like Paul Hoffman, Dr. S. Radhakrishnan, and many others. In any event, it was most gratifying to learn (on October 25) that UNICEF (the United Nations Children's Fund), whose accomplishments in the humanitarian field no one questions, was the recipient of that prize.

In the course of my statement made on that day, I said:

> UNICEF originally came into existence as an emergency fund for children. It lost its emergency character long ago and has now become established as one of the most meritorious agencies of the United Nations which has earned the unstinted support of men

---

[1] *Building Peace*, p. 108.

and women all over the world. Its devotion to the welfare of children and mothers everywhere reflects a concern for the younger generation which we all must share. If Maurice Pate had been alive today, this would surely have gladdened his heart, because, in a sense, this is a posthumous tribute to his selfless work as Executive Director of UNICEF for so many years.[2]

My religious belief and practice alone, of course, did not constitute the sole basis of my actions as Secretary General of the United Nations. My personal conception of human society also had something to do with the way I functioned. First of all, I am always conscious of the fact that I am a member of the human race, and I am very jealous of my membership. This consciousness prompts me to work for a great human synthesis, which is the implicit goal of the World Organization I had the privilege of serving.

The ideal of human synthesis has been developed by almost all great religions. In regard to the ethical concepts of life that help bring such an ideal to realization, Albert Schweitzer and Pierre Teilhard de Chardin, among Western thinkers, had powerful ideas and have been important influences on me.

In his *Philosophy of Civilization,* Schweitzer first presented the ethic of "reverence for life"—a theme consistently featured in his life and thought, and the central core of most of his speeches and conversations. Although from time to time he met resistance to his philosophy from a section of the religious establishment, he stubbornly pressed to drive home his point, and developed the theme to encompass wider horizons. Man, he said, must not limit life to the affirmation of man alone; man's ethics must not end with man, but should extend to the universe. He must regain the consciousness of the great chain of life from which he cannot be separated. Schweitzer preached the necessity of "the will to live an ethical life," which should be the primary motivation of man, and he said life should be for a higher value and purpose—not spent in merely selfish or thoughtless actions. What then results for man is

---

[2] *United Nations Press Release SG/SM/388,* October 25, 1965.

not only a deepening of relationships, but a widening of relationships.[3]

Pierre Teilhard de Chardin was a Jesuit priest as well as an eminent biologist and a profound thinker. I do not know whether he ever used the phrase "reverence for life," but his writings leave no doubt in my mind that he perfectly understood it, for he shared with Schweitzer the same prayers and hopes for a troubled world. Like Schweitzer, he called for an assertion of a new ethical imperative in man as well as within the churches. In an address on New Year's Day, 1932, he said, "May joy dwell in our hearts and all around us. May what sorrow cannot be spared us be transfigured into a finer joy, the joy of knowing that we have occupied each his own station in the universe, and that, in that station, we have done as we ought." In *The Phenomenon of Man,* he wrote, "Love alone is capable of uniting living beings in such a way as to complete and fulfill them, for it alone takes them and joins them by what is deepest in themselves." He said further, "A universal love is not only psychologically possible; it is the only complete and final way in which we are able to love."[4] This concept of universal or planetary man is of course not new. It has been the central theme of great religious leaders and philosophers for thousands of years.

Long before I was appointed Secretary General, I used to dwell at some length in my public statements, as well as in private conversations, on the oneness of the human community. If there is one thing that I find objectionable, it is generalizing about whole peoples—saying, for instance, that all Asians or Africans or Europeans or Latin Americans are good or bad, brave or timid, cultured or wild. When we apply such adjectives to nations or groups of nations, what we are in fact doing is describing our own emotional reactions to those who have our approval or disapproval. The plain fact is that no single group of people can be categorized in general terms.

It is generally assumed that there is one civilization in the East and quite a different one in the West, resulting in seeds of

---

[3] George Marshall and David Poling, *Schweitzer: a Biography* (New York: Doubleday & Company, Inc., 1971), p. 201.

[4] (New York: Harper & Row, 1959), p. 265.

tension or conflict between the peoples of these different geographical regions. This concept is a fallacy. The distinction of civilization into Eastern and Western types seems to me almost mean-
ingless. As I noted in a public speech many years ago,[5] I seriously
question whether tension or conflict between one people and another ever arises from conflicting viewpoints in their respective
cultures or civilizations. England and France, or France and Germany, may be said to share the same civilization and profess the
same Christianity, yet they had been at war off and on for centuries. Conflicts between nations or individuals generally arise, not
out of different viewpoints in their civilizations, not from reasons
of their traditions and history, but from uncivilized elements in
their character.

To me, civilization connotes a mental and spiritual excellence, just as health means a certain physical excellence. Health
does not mean one thing for an American and another for a Burmese. Similarly, civilization should mean one and the same thing
for all. To me, there is no difference between the civilization of
the American Adlai Stevenson and that of the Russian V. V. Kuznetsov, nor between the civilization of the Israeli Michael Comay
and that of the Egyptian Omar Loutfi.

When we speak of the civilization of a country, we are apt to
suppose that all the people of that country are civilized in more or
less the same way, but in reality the different individuals of the
same country are not civilized in the same way or to the same extent. A Burmese of mental and spiritual excellence will not differ
essentially from an American of such excellence, but they will
differ widely from their relatively uncivilized compatriots in their
own countries. This principle applies equally to Americans, Russians, Chinese, or Burmese.

With this background and this conviction, I learned to cherish tolerance long before I came to New York. And tolerance is
the principal foundation on which the United Nations Charter
rests. Without the spirit of tolerance, one cannot understand,
much less appreciate, the Charter. "To practice tolerance and live

---

[5] Address delivered at the University of Wisconsin, July 6, 1961.

together in peace with one another as good neighbours"[6] is the actual language of the Charter, and one of the primary functions of the Secretary General is not only to practice tolerance in his personal dealings, but also to extend this concept of tolerance to international relations. In other words, my conception of the Secretary General's role is to build bridges between peoples, governments, and states. This is why my main preoccupation during my tenure of office was not only to bring about a détente between differing nations, but also to eliminate the obstacles to such a détente.

In some cases, I have succeeded in building bridges or in eliminating tensions and conflicts between nations. Major examples of such successes—which will be elaborated in subsequent chapters—were my efforts to mediate the conflicts between Cuba and the United States in 1962, and between India and Pakistan in 1965. Some of the minor ones might be mentioned here: the conflicts between the Netherlands and Indonesia, the Philippines and Malaysia, and between Egypt and Saudi Arabia. I also successfully mediated disputes between Yemen and Saudi Arabia, Spain and Equatorial Guinea, Algeria and Morocco, and Morocco and Mauretania. In addition, I could claim success in disputes between Nigeria and some of the African states, between Ruanda and Burundi, and Thailand and Cambodia.

In other cases I have not succeeded: instances of relations that have not improved are those between Israel and the Arab nations, the United States and (as of this writing) North Vietnam, Cyprus and Turkey, South Africa and most of the African states, Southern Rhodesia and most of the rest of Africa, and last but far from least, China and the rest of the international community.

Some of the successes and failures can be attributed to what is generally called the exercise of the good offices of the Secretary General. Others are attributive to the deliberative organs of the United Nations, such as the Security Council and the General Assembly. There were occasions when the Secretary General could act without the guidance of the principal deliberative organs; there

---

[6] United Nations, *Charter,* Preamble.

were other occasions when the Secretary General could not act alone. In all cases, the Secretary General can never exercise his good offices without the consent of the parties primarily involved. This brings me to my concept of the Secretary General's role, which has its basis, of course, not only in my cultural and religious background, but in the Charter, and in the experience and practices of my two predecessors.

CHAPTER III

WHAT IS THE SECRETARY GENERAL?

Almost everybody knows what a secretary is and what a general is. Only a few, however, really know what the Secretary General of the United Nations is.

Under the Charter, the Secretary General is the chief administrative officer of the United Nations. In that capacity, he is responsible for securing the highest standards of efficiency, competence, and integrity throughout the Secretariat. He should be regarded as the head of a staff of international civil servants, who are not to be influenced in the performance of their duties by national, ideological, or personal considerations of any kind. Once a member of the Secretariat is influenced in any way by any authority external to the Organization, he ceases to be a truly international civil servant.

The Secretary General is more than the chief administrative officer of the United Nations. Under Article 99 of the Charter, he is also a high political officer. In that capacity, he may take the lead in dealing with matters that may threaten the maintenance of international peace and security. In this respect, the Secretary General of the United Nations has far greater political powers than his counterpart in the League of Nations had. According to Article 99, "The Secretary-General may bring to the attention of the Security Council any matter which in his opinion may threaten the maintenance of international peace and security." Article 99 is both far-reaching and vague. In its report submitted in 1945, the Preparatory Commission of the United Nations elaborated on Article 99 as follows:

> The Secretary-General may have an important role to play as a mediator and as an informal adviser of many Governments, and will undoubtedly be called upon from time to time, in the exercise of his administrative duties, to take decisions which may justly be called political. Under Article 99 of the Charter, moreover, he has been given a quite special right which goes beyond any power previously accorded to the head of an international organization, viz., to bring to the attention of the Security Council any matter (not merely any dispute or situation) which, in his opinion, may threaten the maintenance of international peace and security. It is impossible to foresee how this Article will be applied; but the responsibility it confers upon the Secretary-General will require the exercise of the highest qualities of political judgment, tact and integrity.

This, in fact, is the only official guidance available to the Secretary General on the implications of Article 99, which, according to records, was adopted with very little debate in San Francisco. The right to bring matters to the attention of the Security Council implies that the Secretary General can use his own discretion, without the guidance or authorization of the Security Council or the General Assembly, to conduct inquiries or to engage in diplomatic activity in regard to matters relating to the maintenance of international peace and security. In this connection, Article 33 of the Charter is also relevant. It says:

> The parties to any dispute, the continuance of which is likely to endanger the maintenance of international peace and security, shall, first of all, seek a solution by negotiation, enquiry, mediation, conciliation, arbitration, judicial settlement, resort to regional agencies or arrangements, or other peaceful means of their own choice.

When these two Articles are taken together, the Secretary General enjoys special powers of political or diplomatic initiative that no Secretary General of the League of Nations enjoyed. Article 99 has been specifically invoked only once, however, when

Dag Hammarskjöld used it to call the Security Council into session over the Congo, in May 1960. At that time, as we shall see, not one single member state opposed the Secretary General's action. It was only much later that the Secretary General was criticized by the East European nations and many Afro-Asian states for his interpretation of the Security Council resolutions, and the manner in which he discharged his responsibilities.

There are, of course, many ways of carrying out the wide but imprecise responsibilities of the Secretary General under Article 99. In 1961, I saw these responsibilities in the broader context of the nature of the Secretary Generalship as it had developed over the years, both under Trygve Lie and Dag Hammarskjöld. It is worth recalling that in the early stages of drafting the Charter, President Roosevelt suggested that the chief officer of the United Nations should be called "Moderator," and I know of no better single word to describe my own conception of this office. Partly because of my training and background, and partly because of my experience of the United Nations in action, I have always felt that the most important political duty of the Secretary General is to concentrate on the harmonizing function of the United Nations, as set out in Article 1 (4) of the Charter. It defines one of the purposes of the United Nations "to be a centre for harmonizing the actions of nations." President Roosevelt's suggestion exactly fitted my idea and conception of the Secretary General's role, but it was not accepted by the framers of the Charter.

With Article 33 in mind, I foresaw, in 1961, the need to exercise my good offices in the settlement of disputes or difficulties, even without specific authorization from the Security Council or the General Assembly, when the states concerned requested it. As I have stated in the preceding pages, I exercised my good offices in a large number of disputes or difficulties. In doing so, I was merely following the previously established practice of taking action and keeping the Security Council informed of what I was doing. I believed at that time, and I still believe in retrospect, that preventive diplomacy of this kind is far more effective—and incidentally much cheaper—than attempting to resolve a conflict that has been allowed to reach an acute stage. It of course requires total discretion on the part of the Secretary General, and the co-operation, restraint, and good will of the parties concerned. I shall describe some such instances in subsequent pages.

In the exercise of the good offices of the Secretary General, the less publicity there is during these efforts, the more successful they are likely to be. This quiet method of forestalling conflict seems to me to be a part of the Secretary General's role. There are good reasons why Article 99 has been specifically invoked only once. Nothing could be more divisive and useless than for the Secretary General to bring a situation publicly to the Security Council when there is no practical possibility of the Council's agreeing on effective or useful action. On the other hand, a quiet approach that avoids a public confrontation may often hold some hope of success.

Great problems usually come to the United Nations because governments have been unable to think of anything else to do about them. The United Nations is a last-ditch, last-resort affair, and it is not surprising that the Organization should often be blamed for failing to solve problems that have already been found to be insoluble by governments. More often than not, the United Nations is criticized for failing to resolve a crisis or to enforce an action. It is not generally realized that the failure of the United Nations is the failure of the international community, and the failure to enforce an action is due to the refusal of the party or parties concerned to comply with the Organization's decisions. Unlike its constituents, the Organization lacks the attributes of sovereignty, and its Secretary General has to work by persuasion, argument, negotiation, and a persistent search for consensus.

There is a widespread illusion that the Secretary General is comparable to the head of a government. He is often criticized for failure to take an action—when over 130 sovereign member states collectively fail to act. The plain fact is that the United Nations, and the Secretary General, have none of the attributes of sovereignty and no independent power, although the Secretary General has, and must maintain, his independence of judgment, and must never become the agent of any particular government or group of governments. No parliament enacts for the Secretary General the *enforceable* legislation that provides a prime minister with precise directives. No clear-cut policy illuminates his course of action. He is supported by none of the great permanent establishments of a state, and often lacks the first-hand sources of information upon which governments can base their plans. More often than not, he faces the conflicts of the present or the problems of the future with vague or nonexistent directives, with an inadequate budget, and, in the case of some peace-keeping operations or of vast relief problems, with resources based solely on voluntary contributions. These are some of the limitations of the Secretary General.

In matters relating to international peace and security, however, two simple considerations are inescapable. First, the Secretary General must always be prepared to take an initiative, no matter what the consequences to his office or to him personally may be, if he sincerely believes that it might mean the difference between peace and war. In such a situation, the personal prestige of a Secretary General—and even the position of his office—must be considered to be expendable. The second cardinal consideration must be the maintenance of the Secretary General's independent position, as set out in Article 100 of the Charter, which alone can give him the freedom to act, without fear or favor, in the interests of world peace. Such independence does not imply any disrespect for the wishes or opinions of member governments. On the contrary, his independence is an insurance that the Secretary General will be able to serve, in full accordance with his oath of office, the long-term interest in peace of *all* members of the Organization.

I felt in 1961, and I still feel very strongly, that the United Nations will not become the effective instrument its founders intended it to be until its members abide by its rules and give real attention to its decisions and resolutions. Any Secretary General, irrespective of his personal views on any issue, is obliged to stand by every resolution or decision of the main deliberative organs of the United Nations. All resolutions of the Security Council must be implemented. This necessity is reinforced when such resolutions are adopted unanimously. In all such cases, the failure to reach a solution is not so much the failure of the United Nations to take decisions as the failure of its members to abide by those decisions. The Secretary General must take a categorical stand in support of such resolutions. He has no option whatsoever in this regard, whatever may be the temporary effect on his relations with individual member states. To cite an extreme case as an illustration, if my own country Burma were involved in an international problem, and if this problem were brought to the Security Council, and if the Security Council adopted a resolution asking Burma to take a certain course of action, I would want my country to comply with that resolution. If it did not, then I would side with the United Nations, not with Burma.

Since it is important to understand the nature of Security Council resolutions, some observations on the constitution of the Council will be relevant. (Incidentally, a shift in the balance of power within the Council that occurred, for reasons we shall see, after 1955, accounted for a corresponding change in the role of the Secretary General, which thereafter became more important.)

The record of the proceedings of the Preparatory Commission at San Francisco in 1945 shows that the original plan of action in the United Nations called for the leadership of the five major powers with permanent seats in the Security Council, acting by the method of consensus. At that time, it was assumed that major decisions on problems involving threats to international peace and security could be made only with the unanimous agreement of these five. Although that assumption was realistic in 1945, the emergence of the Cold War destroyed the prospects for a united leadership of the five powers. Competitive military alliances appeared, and the solidarity of the major powers ended.

In the early years of the United Nations, it was obvious that whenever the Security Council was deadlocked over a question because of Big-Power disagreement, the United States was able to muster the required majority in the General Assembly. For a decade, when the membership of the United Nations did not exceed sixty, there were more than forty members that generally supported the United States position on major issues. I was a member of the Burmese delegation to the seventh session of the General Assembly in 1952, and I very well remember that although important decisions in the General Assembly require a two-thirds majority, the United States could generally muster such a majority. It was like a one-party system functioning in the Assembly, and the political role of the Secretary General was not considered to be of major importance.

With subsequent growth of membership in the United Nations, a United States-dominated one-party system no longer held good. After 1955, the United States could no longer always muster the required two-thirds majority in the General Assembly, and, since 1960, the United States and its traditional allies no longer wield even a majority. The balance of power has fallen into the hands of the newly admitted nonaligned and uncommitted states. Most of these new member states sided with neither one bloc nor the other on major issues, and thus a multiparty system—not a two-party system—of international policies emerged in the General Assembly. The political role of the Secretary General therefore became more important, particularly in his role of representing the philosophy he shares with almost all of the small and medium states. Most of the new members, who are nonaligned and uncommitted, are motivated by the one major objective of preserving the United Nations as the guardian of their rights and liberties. The major support received by Dag Hammarskjöld in his Congo policies from these nonaligned and uncommitted states was due principally to their agreement with the Secretary General's interpretation of the relevant Security Council resolutions, and to their agreement with his actions, and not because they endorsed United States policies in general. India, for instance, generally regarded as the leading neutralist at that time, invariably supported Dag Hammarskjöld in the General Assembly on the Secretary General's Congo policies. Successive votes of confidence in Dag Hammarskjöld in the Assembly serve as a barometer of the growing importance of the Secretary General in the performance of his political functions. It has always been my belief that the fears of those who question the qualifications of newly independent states for active participation in United Nations activities are unwarranted. They have increasingly shown an independent policy, and have brought to its deliberations a deep devotion to the UN, as well as a strong faith in its principles.

These facts were borne out at the Belgrade conference that took place during the first week of September 1961. It was attended by twenty-eight nations that claimed to be nonaligned. The fact that it received a good press neither in the East nor in the West was the true measure of its nonalignment. First of all, every aligned power was excluded from the conference—a decision that succeeded in irritating both the Soviet Union and the People's Republic of China. The West was rebuffed when the conference failed to condemn the U.S.S.R. for restricting access to West Berlin, and the United States was especially unhappy that Guantanamo base in Cuba was specifically mentioned in the final declaration. The conference also urged that China's seat at the UN be given to the People's Republic of China. While there was a strong endorsement of anticolonialism, the conference refused to set a date after which all remaining colonies should be free.

My participation at the Belgrade conference and my personal contacts with the leaders of the nonaligned countries no doubt influenced my political thinking. I shall be less than honest if I say that such experience and contacts had no impact on me. In the fifties, I found myself increasingly identified with the cause of small nations, poor nations, newly independent nations, and nations struggling for independence. So my conception of the United Nations was primarily from the vantage point of the Third World.

I came from one of the newly independent countries that was not one of the original fifty-one members of the United Nations. Burma won her independence only in January 1948, and became a member of the United Nations three months later. The outstanding difference that distinguished me from all other Secretaries General of the League of Nations or of the United Nations lay in the fact that I was the first non-European to occupy that post. Burma had been a colony of Great Britain for almost a century. Both the League of Nations and the United Nations up to 1961 had been Western-oriented. In fact, the League was almost exclusively a European club. Not only do I have my own set of values, which are different from those of all my predecessors, but I also had first-hand experience of colonialism at work. I know what hunger, poverty, disease, illiteracy, and human suffering really mean.

Although I have been trained to be tolerant, it is difficult for me to shake off unhappy memories of servitude. I cannot forget the fact, for instance, that even an officiating lieutenant governor of Burma, the highest officeholder in the country, could not become a member of any of the three prestigious clubs in Rangoon, simply because he was a Burmese and the clubs were exclusively European. Such memories no doubt influence my approach to colonial problems, and even long before my appointment as Secretary General, I was deeply involved in national and international meetings in the discussion of colonialism. Thus, in formulating my conception of the role of the Secretary General, the question of colonialism was very much on my mind.

That is, no doubt, why I became such an admirer of George Orwell.[1] Orwell served for some years in Burma as a police officer. In his inimitable style and with extraordinary pungency, he described his mood, and the mood of the Burmese people, when he was in the service of the British government in Lower Burma in the late twenties. He wrote:

> I was hated by large numbers of people—the only time in my life that I have been important enough for this to happen to me. I was sub-divisional police officer of the town, and in an aimless, petty kind of way anti-European feeling was very bitter. No one had the guts to raise a riot, but if a European woman went through the bazaars alone, somebody would probably spit betel juice over her dress. As a police officer I was an obvious target and was baited whenever it seemed safe to do.
>
> All this was perplexing and upsetting. For at that time I had already made up my mind that imperialism was an evil thing and the sooner I chucked up my job and got out of it the better. Theoretically—and secretly of course—I was all for the Burmese and all against their oppressors, the British. As for the job I was doing, I hated it more bitterly than I can perhaps make clear. In a job like that you see the dirty work of Empire at close quarters. The wretched prisoners huddling in the stinking cages of the lock-ups, the grey, cowed faces of the long-term convicts, the scarred buttocks of the men who had been flogged with bamboos—all these oppressed me with an intolerable sense of guilt. But I could get nothing into perspective. . . . I did not know that the British Empire is dying, still less did I know that it is a great deal better than the younger empires that are going to supplant it.[2]

---

[1] Penname for Eric Blair.
[2] *Shooting an Elephant and Other Essays* (London: Secker & Warburg, 1950), p. 79.

This sums up the feeling of a highly intelligent and seriously introspective British official serving in a colony. His later works—*Burmese Days, The Road to Wigan Pier,* and *Homage to Catalonia*—are full of such emotional, though extremely literate, observations on imperialism.

I refer to George Orwell's writings just to present one aspect of colonialism—strong resentment on the part of the governed. In the late forties and early fifties, as a free-lance political journalist, I used to assess and evaluate the colonial system that had already left Burma. The colonial record can claim, with some justification, to have controlled or eliminated some of the worst aspects of primitive life in certain parts of the world. It has introduced hospitals and better sanitation; it has brought improved methods of transport and communication. Many other material accomplishments can be enumerated.

Nevertheless, against these substantial benefits must be reckoned many features and tendencies that have countered such progressive influences. Chief among them is the fact that, in the past at any rate, the primary motive of the colonial power in developing the natural resources of a colony was its own commercial profit. Consequently, the greater part of the wealth obtained from the colony went into the pockets of the colonial investors. Further, the colonies remained essentially as primary producers, with very little industrial development. The result is that when the colonial powers left the scene, the colonies remained poor. To me, this titanic problem of development must be one of the principal concerns of the United Nations system.

In the relations between the newly independent countries and the rest of the world, two main factors clearly emerge: the elemental desire for independence, and the desperate need for outside help. After the departure of the colonial authority, something must take its place—an authority that is not only capable of assuring order, but of maintaining and strengthening independence. Freedom is not enough. Economic and social development of the less-developed countries is an urgent need. In formulating my concept of the role of the Secretary General, I had very much in mind the central role to be played by the United Nations system in bringing this about. I became increasingly convinced that the division of the world into the rich and the poor, the master race and the abject poor, is much more important, much more fundamental, and in the long run much more explosive, than the division of the world based on differing political ideologies. In narrowing this gap, the United Nations system can, and must, play a leading role.

PART II
THE
SECRETARY
GENERAL
AS MEDIATOR

CHAPTER IV

EFFORTS FOR PEACE

There were so many crises during my decade as Secretary General that it is sometimes difficult to recall all of them. Even the casual reader of newspaper headlines will remember the major ones: the Cuban missile crisis, the Arab-Israeli war of 1967, the invasions of Czechoslovakia and the Dominican Republic—all of which are discussed in detail in subsequent chapters. Even while these major crises were erupting, however, I had to deal with lesser ones. In terms of world public interest, these were relatively minor disputes, but to the peoples and nations concerned, they were of vital importance. In addition, the lesser crises demonstrate the constant overlapping of problems a Secretary General has to face and the conflicting ideals and interests he constantly must keep in mind, and, if possible, try to reconcile. They also illustrate the variety of ways the good offices of a Secretary General can be used, sometimes successfully and sometimes not, as an instrument of preventive diplomacy.

One of the most important things I learned during my tenure was that the Secretary General's world has two poles: at one extreme the idealism and global objectives of the Charter, and at the other, the pragmatic and, if I may say so, the unconcealed selfish nature of national sovereignty. Working between these poles, he cannot afford to lose touch with either. In every critical situation, whatever action the Secretary General takes will seem to some governments excessive and an interference, but to others, weak and passive. He must tread his way through this jungle of conflicting national policies with the Charter as his only compass and, perhaps, a general directive from one of the deliberative organs of the UN as his only guide. If he does not have such a directive, and a conflict or potential conflict is brought to his attention, he has the duty to do whatever he can, in whatever way seems most helpful, so long as his action does not violate the Charter. Sometimes this action breaks a new diplomatic path.

The exercise of the Secretary General's good offices can be a useful method of preventing differences between states from developing into major crises or of getting results on sensitive problems before they reach the insoluble stage. Preventive diplomacy of this kind is far more effective and, no less important, much cheaper in money and human lives than attempting to settle a conflict that has been allowed to reach an acute stage. As I mentioned earlier, however, it requires the total co-operation, restraint, and good will of the parties concerned. It also requires from them courage and vision, as well as confidence in the discretion and integrity of the Secretary General. When these conditions are present, much can be done quietly. When they are absent, little can be done, and the United Nations has little or no effect.

Unhappy examples of the latter instance were the series of disputes that took place in southern Africa and in Cyprus during the 1960s, the years that included most of my tenure as Secretary General. The seemingly intractable problems of those years in South Africa, Southern Rhodesia, and South-West Africa deeply disturbed me because of the racism and exploitation that are at their root.

In regard to race relations, South Africa is a unique country. *Apartheid* is a denial of *all* political rights to nonwhites in the so-called white areas of South Africa; the government openly admits this. Any African man or woman, for example, can be exiled within the country, and many have been sent to strange, desolate areas for indefinite periods. No trial and no explanation are necessary. The question of *apartheid* had been before the General Assembly since the UN's earliest days, and it had made repeated appeals to South Africa to revise its racial policies to conform with the principles of the UN Charter. South Africa has consistently argued, however, that the matter was within its domestic jurisdiction and that, thus, the UN had no authority to consider it.

But after the "Sharpeville massacre" of March 21, 1960 (in which police fired on thousands of demonstrators, killing 70 and wounding 170), the Security Council declared that *apartheid* was a matter of international, not merely domestic, concern. In November, the General Assembly established a special committee to consider the question of *apartheid;* and the following month, the Council asked me to establish a group of recognized experts to examine methods of resolving the situation. The result was a recommendation that a national convention be held in South Africa to set a new course for the future. In June, the Security Council invited South Africa to submit its views on the proposed convention. I was not surprised when, in November, South Africa rejected the Council's invitation and asserted that it was seeking the abdication of South Africa's sovereignty in favor of the United Nations. Thus, the Security Council found itself powerless.

In 1961, the Council found itself equally powerless in a dispute between South Africa and its neighbor, South-West Africa (Namibia). After World War II, South Africa wanted to annex South-West Africa, a proposal rejected by the General Assembly. In December of that year, six weeks after I became Acting Secretary General, the Assembly proclaimed the right of the people of South-West Africa to independence. And as South Africa moved toward extending its policy of *apartheid* to its neighbor, the Assembly (in October 1966) declared that the territory was henceforth under the direct sovereignty of the United Nations. South Africa not only ignored these declarations, however; it also refused to permit the United Nations to enter the territory. Thus the goal of independence, which had been projected for June 1968, was not met. It is painful to report that *all* the UN resolutions and initiatives have had little practical effect on the abhorrent situation in South Africa and Namibia. As of this writing, similar situations exist in Southern Rhodesia, Angola, and the Portuguese territories. Despite UN resolutions almost beyond number, there has been little practical improvement.

The United Nations had somewhat more success in Cyprus: it succeeded, at least, in establishing a peace-keeping force on the island. The very success of the force, however, had the ironic result that it encouraged a postponement of the difficult question underlying the crisis.

To understand this unique problem, a little background is necessary. Cyprus, the third-largest island in the Mediterranean, is largely Greek in population (about 80 per cent Greek Orthodox) yet lies only 40 miles off the Turkish coast and 400 miles from Greece. Most of the rest of the population is ethnically Turkish and of the Moslem faith. For more than three hundred years it had been a province of Turkey, but in 1878, with the weakening of the Ottoman Empire, it came under British rule and remained so until it gained its independence in 1960. After World War II, however, a movement for union with Greece (*enosis*) had grown in intensity among the Greek Cypriots, with vehement opposition from the Turkish Cypriots. This conflict led to widespread violence. Worst of all, Greek and Turkish army units joined in the fighting.

In December 1963, Cyprus called for an urgent meeting of the Security Council, charging Turkey with aggression and intervention in the internal affairs of Cyprus. The root of the problem was the divisive provisions of the constitution, which split the people into hostile camps. For President [Archbishop] Makarios had proposed that the constitution be amended. The Greek Cypriots argued that the original constitution was unworkable, while the Turkish Cypriots argued that their communal safety depended on the constitution as originally written. Turkey denied the charges of aggression and accused the Greek Cypriots of a campaign of annihilation aimed at the Turkish Cypriots. It was in March 1963 that the Security Council adopted a resolution creating a UN peace-keeping force in Cyprus, the commander of which was to be appointed by me. It also called on me to designate a mediator in the dispute. This essentially dumped the problem in my lap.

Although there were sporadic outbreaks of fighting from time to time that placed the UN troops in difficult and dangerous situations, the force did succeed in maintaining general calm. Meanwhile, the mediator I appointed also submitted his report, which indicated that *enosis* was the most divisive and potentially explosive aspect of the problem; it would be viewed by the Turkish side as tantamount to annexation. On the other hand, the report also rejected partition, which would be utterly unacceptable to the majority of Greek Cypriots. The mediator thought that a balance could have been found, through discussion, between the right of the political majority to rule and the rights of the minority. In a word, he suggested that the Greeks and the Turks should get together and settle their own problems. The Turkish government rejected this report out of hand and declared the mediator's services at an end.

During 1966 and most of 1967, the situation in Cyprus remained tense but relatively calm. Then in November 1967, war seemed imminent between Greece and Turkey. Heavy fighting between Greek and Turkish Cypriots broke out, and it appeared that Turkey would send troops to the island to support its outnumbered compatriots. But war was averted once again as a result of strenuous negotiations conducted by myself in New York and by the UN force on Cyprus. In this connection I must pay particular tribute to Cyrus Vance, U.S. undersecretary of state, for his energetic role in Ankara, Athens, and Nicosia in averting the war.

In 1968, I exercised my good offices in an attempt to improve the situation on the island. A number of normalization measures were introduced by the government, including substantial freedom of movement for Turkish Cypriots.

But by the end of 1971, shortly before I left office, there was a marked deterioration in conditions on Cyprus. Communal tension had increased, and there had been a number of incidents. The task of the UN force was becoming more difficult as each side continued to improve its military position. As of this writing, there still has not been a settlement, and the UN peace-keeping force is still on the island maintaining the truce, its mandate being extended routinely each six months. Thus the impasse gave rise to the criticism that the UN presence has consolidated an abnormal status quo and reduced the sense of urgency felt by both sides. That may be so. I wonder, however, whether that situation is not to be preferred to the bloody fighting that only the UN presence has prevented.

The disputes described above are examples of how little the United Nations can do without the co-operation of the parties concerned. They also illustrate the multiplicity of problems a Secretary General has to deal with, sometimes simultaneously. It must be remembered that even as I was seeking solutions to such relatively minor disputes, the more dangerous and complex crises of my tenure were developing: the Congo in 1961, the Cuban crisis in 1962, the invasion of the Dominican Republic in 1965, the war in the Middle East in 1967, to name only a few.

In December 1961, for instance, I had been Acting Secretary General barely a month and was preoccupied with the latest in a series of crises in the Congo. I nevertheless had to divert some of my attention to the situation in New Guinea, where fighting had broken out between troops of the Netherlands and Indonesia. The dispute concerned the territory of West Irian (also called West New Guinea), which, with Indonesia, had been governed as part of the Netherlands East Indies until Indonesia gained its independence in 1949. President Sukarno's government promptly asserted that West New Guinea was an integral part of Indonesia, while the Netherlands argued that the territory should be allowed to determine its own future. Although the dispute was often brought before the General Assembly, no resolution was possible. It became a genuine threat to peace when the Netherlands sent reinforcements and President Sukarno received from the Soviet Union supersonic fighters, naval craft, and other weapons.

As a result of a series of appeals I made to both governments, informal talks, in which Ellsworth Bunker and Robert F. Kennedy were involved, were held during the winter and spring of 1962. In August, it was agreed that the administration of the territory would be transferred to the UN temporarily, with eventual transfer to Indonesia. This was achieved peacefully and without incident. It was a unique experience that proved the capacity of the United Nations to undertake its function, provided it received adequate support from the member states.

The agreement was historic in that for the first time, the UN itself was to administer a territory, which it did (under an administrator appointed by me) from October 1962, to May 1963, when full administrative authority was handed over to Indonesia.

The agreement also provided that Indonesia would conduct a plebiscite to determine whether the population of West Irian wanted to retain ties with Indonesia or cut them. In July 1969, it decided to remain with Indonesia. It should be noted that in the same month as the West Irian situation was sorting itself out, the crisis in the Congo was approaching its final spasm, and, in the Western Hemisphere, the frightening days of the Cuban missile crisis were rapidly approaching.

During the same period, there was yet another problem in an equally remote part of the world: Yemen, where (in September 1962) the Imam Al-Badr was deposed by a coup d'état. Space permits only the briefest account of the conflict, the details of which are, however, readily available. Suffice it to say that the crisis threatened to split the Arab world and had immediate repercussions at the UN, for the United Arab Republic recognized the new republican regime, while King Saud of neighboring Saudi Arabia declared his support of the Imam. In addition, several major powers were involved. The British, still occupying Aden on the southern tip of Yemen, were blaming President Nasser of the U.A.R., who was pouring troops into Yemen. The U.S.S.R. fully backed Nasser. Meanwhile, because of the great cost of the Congo operation, the UN was on the verge of financial bankruptcy, a problem I will return to in a later chapter.

I sent Ralph Bunche on a peace-keeping mission to Yemen in February; President Kennedy sent Ambassador Bunker. After consultations that lasted into April, the parties accepted terms I had proposed for a disengagement in Yemen, and a demilitarized zone was established, with UN observers stationed on both sides between Yemen and Saudi Arabia. It was not until August 1965, that King Faisal and President Nasser signed a peace agreement and ended the lingering crisis.

The above instances demonstrate that the exercise of good offices—one of the major elements in what Dag Hammarskjöld liked to call quiet diplomacy—constitutes a substantial part of the Secretary General's workload. Like my predecessor, I was convinced that the Secretary General not only had the authority but also the duty to assist in the settlement of disputes when the states concerned requested it—or agreed to it. According to my interpretation, this was implicit in Article 99 of the Charter, which gives the Secretary General certain political responsibilities in addition to his administrative duties. I had no doubt but that the Secretary General had powers, including those of inquiry, to reach a seasoned and independent opinion on whether or not a particular matter might threaten international security, and that he could, and should, endeavor, through the exercise of good offices, to play a part in preventive diplomacy designed to ensure that a matter did not become a threat to peace.

My part in a dispute between Britain and Iran in 1970 is a case in point. This concerned Bahrain, an archipelago of some thirty islands in the Persian Gulf. Iran claimed Bahrain as part of its territory, asserting that only the protection of Britain had prevented Iran from exercising her legitimate rights there. The United Kingdom, on the other hand, argued that Bahrain was a sovereign Arab state with which they were in "special treaty relations." Through my mediation, the dispute was settled before it broke into armed conflict. More than that, it was the first time in the history of the United Nations that the parties to a dispute entrusted it to the Secretary General's good offices *by giving a prior pledge* to accept without reservation the findings or conclusions of his personal representative, provided that the conclusions were endorsed by the Security Council.

With the wise assistance of Ralph Bunche, I discussed the matter over a period of many months with Ambassador Medhi Vakil of Iran and Lord Caradon, the British ambassador. In March 1970, I received a formal request from Iran asking me to exercise my good offices with a view to ascertaining the true wishes of the people of Bahrain with respect to the future status of the islands, and to appoint a personal representative to carry out the mission. After I informed Britain of the request, the British government also asked me to mediate the question, and I subsequently chose as my personal representative Vittorio Winspeare Guicciardi, undersecretary general and director general of the UN office in Geneva.

Mr. Guicciardi visited Bahrain from March to April 1970, and the inquiry was conducted throughout in a peaceful and orderly manner and without disturbances or demonstrations. He reported that almost all of those consulted were explicit in hoping that the Iranian claim would be removed once and for all, although there was no bitterness or hostility toward Iran. On the contrary, once the question of the claim had been settled, closer relations with other states in the Gulf, including Iran, were expected to follow. The decision, which granted Bahrain independence, was accepted by both sides in an equally amicable spirit. My confidence in Mr. Guicciardi was borne out by his meticulous method of carrying out his task and, what is more important, by the unanimous endorsement of his report by the Security Council, which had been a principal condition for acceptance by the two parties.

There was an air of jubilation in the Council after the unanimous adoption of the resolution accepting Mr. Guicciardi's report. Lord Caradon broke into verse:

> The play is over. Witness now
> The actors come to make their bow.
> Praise first the Shah; what joy to see
> Imperial magnanimity.
> Cheer next U Thant who never tires
> In harmonizing our desires.
> Next the Italian wins applause
> For Roman justice is his cause.
> In gratitude we cry, "Long live
> The Special Representative!"
> The people made their wishes plain,
> Their independence they retain.
> Good luck, God Speed to Bahrain.

Another instance of a dispute in which the parties agreed in advance that my findings and conclusions would be binding was related to the formation of the Federation of Malaysia. The issue was whether the peoples of North Borneo and Sarawak wished to be included in the proposed enlargement of the Federation in 1961. (The Federation of Malaya became independent in 1957, ending a long period of British rule, but the United Kingdom was still the administering power for North Borneo, Sarawak, and Singapore. The enlarged Federation was to consist of Malaya, together with the three states just mentioned.)

The association of Borneo and Sarawak with Malaysia was opposed by both Indonesia and the Philippines. In 1963, the Foreign Ministers of those two states, and the Foreign Minister of Malaya, asked me to ascertain the wishes of the peoples of North Borneo and Sarawak.

For the first time in the history of the United Nations, the Secretary General was asked by three member states to arbitrate a dispute: I was asked not only to undertake a fact-finding job but also to make a political judgment. I accepted this unusual mandate only on condition that my findings and decisions would in fact be binding, and did so without the authorization of the General Assembly or the Security Council.

The task was carried out in August 1963 by the UN Malaysian Mission, consisting of eight members of the Secretariat. My conclusions, based on the mission's report, were that the peoples of North Borneo and Sarawak did wish to join the Federation. The Federation of Malaysia was proclaimed on September 16, 1963, two days after the publication of my report.

Indonesia and the Philippines refused to accept my conclusions, however, and there were armed clashes on the borders of North Borneo and Sarawak. Indonesia asserted that the United Kingdom was using Malaysia as a base from which to subvert the Indonesian revolution—a charge denied, of course, by Britain. When the Federation of Malaysia was elected to membership in the Security Council in January 1965, I received the shocking news that the government of Indonesia had decided to withdraw from the UN. Despite my repeated appeals to President Sukarno to reconsider his decision, Indonesia did not participate in any activity of the United Nations for nearly two years. It was only on September 19, 1966, that Indonesia announced its decision to resume full co-operation with the UN and to resume participation in its activities, starting with the twenty-first session of the General Assembly in 1966. Thus the dispute was settled, and from that time onward the three countries enjoyed excellent relations.

A list of all the instances in which the good offices of the Secretary General have played a role would certainly be a long one; it would also be difficult to make because the interventions often were made in complete secrecy—only the parties themselves were aware of them.

During my term as Secretary General, I used my good offices, either personally or through personal representatives, numerous times and, as has been seen, with varying degrees of success. In addition, I had to refuse a number of requests because they were incompatible with the office of Secretary General, or were impractical. There were occasions, for example, when governments asked me to present warnings or even threats to other governments, or to hold them up for judgment before the bar of world opinion. In 1966 and again in 1967, I felt unable to meet requests from the government of South Vietnam to provide UN observers to the elections that were to be held in that country. My reasons were both practical and constitutional. From a practical point of view, I saw no possibility in the circumstances and in the time available of setting up the necessary machinery. From the constitutional point of view, I felt that I could not send UN observers to South Vietnam without the authorization of the Security Council, since the question of Vietnam was formally on the Council's agenda.

It was similarly impossible for me to act during one of the most tragic events of the decade of my tenure: the civil war in Nigeria in 1967. In May of that year, the eastern region of Nigeria declared its secession, proclaiming itself the Republic of Biafra. Although I was deeply concerned by the incredible human suffering and starvation in Biafra, there was never any doubt in my mind that the conflict was strictly an internal matter and, therefore, outside the jurisdiction of the United Nations. This was the position taken by the Organization of African Unity (OAU).

As a result, there was an unbelievable amount of misunderstanding concerning the lack of a UN role in seeking a political settlement. Both the United Nations and other organizations, such as the International Committee of the Red Cross, were often criticized unjustly, chiefly because of obstructionist attitudes of those bearing responsibility in the areas of conflict, and I found myself under violent attack in the Western press.

But although Biafra gained wide public sympathy during the three-year war, partly because of the grim pictures of starving children appearing in the world press, the so-called Biafran government never won any substantial recognition from other governments. In Africa, for example, only four countries—Gabon, the Ivory Coast, Tanzania, and Zambia—officially recognized the secessionist government. Thus the major UN effort was directed at trying to get food and supplies to the starving Biafrans—an effort that turned out to be a frustrating experience. Biafra was landlocked, and relief supplies could be sent in only by highly risky airlifts or by overland access corridors from seaports in federally controlled territory. There were also widespread fears in Biafra that the federal authorities would poison foods entering through the overland corridors. This was one of the difficulties we faced and one of the contributing factors to the continued starvation in Biafra. Even though the International Committee of the Red Cross was the agreed channel for relief supplies, I dispatched a personal representative, Nils-Goran Gussing of Sweden, to Nigeria to assist in humanitarian activities for victims of hostilities.

Another factor was that Biafra was receiving military supplies and weapons from a number of countries, including France, Portugal, South Africa, and the People's Republic of China. The Lagos government, on the other hand, was getting most of its military equipment from the United Kingdom and the U.S.S.R. The United States, which was opposed to the "Balkanization" of Nigeria, refused to supply arms to either side. The civil war officially came to an end in January 1970, and the Republic of Biafra ceased to exist.

After the war, some correspondents came out with more blistering attacks on me. Needless to say, I was very much upset by what I considered to be unfair conclusions based upon distorted information. I am convinced to this day that I had no choice but to go along with the Organization of African Unity and the member states of the United Nations. Neither the OAU nor any member states ever moved to bring the Biafra conflict before the UN. I firmly believed that the OAU was the most appropriate instrument for promoting peace in Nigeria and that the United Nations should not intervene until all possible regional resources had been exhausted.

In addition to those cases in which a Secretary General finds himself unable to act in a dispute for legal or practical reasons, there are times when his good offices are respectfully declined. Such was the case with regard to Northern Ireland, that tragic land where there seems no end of troubles. At about the time I was discussing Bahrain, the government of Ireland was in constant contact with me about the situation in Northern Ireland. I met with the Irish ambassador and Foreign Minister several times in 1969 and offered to mediate the dispute. Specifically, I proposed that if both London and Dublin agreed, the question could be looked into by a third party, with or without my involvement. I had in mind the names of two statesmen who were universally recognized to be impartial: Lester Pearson, former Prime Minister of Canada, and Earl Warren, former Chief Justice of the United States. While Dublin appeared receptive to the idea, however, London remained silent. And later, while not referring directly to my proposal, London many times reiterated its position that "the matter does not lend itself to intervention from outside."

The exercise of good offices can be initiated by the parties to a dispute, by the Secretary General himself, or by the initiative of a third party. An example of the latter was the dispute between Guinea and the Ivory Coast, in 1967, over diplomatic immunities. In June, the Foreign Minister of Guinea and the Guinean permanent representative to the UN were arrested when the plane on which they were returning home from an emergency session of the General Assembly made an unscheduled stop at Abidjan, Ivory Coast. Relations between Guinea and the Ivory Coast had been strained, and I later found out that the detention of the Guineans was a consequence of the earlier arrest in Guinea of several nationals of the Ivory Coast. That, however, was no justification for the detention by the Ivory Coast of the Guinean diplomats, particularly when they were returning from a General Assembly session. In this instance, a third party, namely the Organization of African Unity, asked me to intervene to obtain the release of the detained diplomats.

After my initial appeals to the Foreign Minister of the Ivory Coast were rejected, I realized that we were faced with a potentially dangerous dispute that would require on-the-scene negotiations, and I dispatched a personal representative to the area. He returned to New York without a solution. At this point, I took matters into my own hands. In a letter to the Foreign Minister of the Ivory Coast, I formally requested the immediate release of the Guineans, stating that his government had established a grave precedent by ignoring the diplomatic immunities that should have been enjoyed by the detained diplomats. This got results. But even when word came that the two governments had unilaterally acted to release the detained nationals of the other country, I was not ready to drop the matter, for I felt that important questions of principle had been raised by the dispute. I therefore brought the question before the General Assembly at its twenty-second session in September. The result was the adoption of a resolution by the General Assembly deploring "all departures from the rules of international law governing diplomatic privileges and immunities" and urging member states that had not done so to accede to the Convention on Privileges and Immunities.

There were scores of such instances in which I was asked by member states or other organizations to use my good offices to settle disputes or ease tensions—all examples of what can be done through quiet diplomacy. They demonstrate that the good offices of the Secretary General are indeed flexible and can be used in many ways, some of which no doubt are yet to be devised as circumstances demand innovation. I have always felt and still feel that the Secretary General's competence to use his good offices, and his decision to do so, depend upon his own judgment as to whether his action would be appropriate, useful, and, above all, not counterproductive. This sphere of the Secretary General's activities is potentially one of the most useful but least understood possibilities of the United Nations.

CHAPTER V

THE SECRET
SEARCH FOR PEACE
IN VIETNAM

In the preceding pages I have dealt with disputes I was able to mediate (or attempted to mediate) in my capacity as Secretary General, sometimes without the participation of the major organs of the United Nations; and in subsequent chapters of this book I shall examine events in which the United Nations was deeply involved, both through my efforts at mediation and through actions taken in the Security Council and the General Assembly. There were other conflicts, however—some of them posing the gravest threat to international peace and security—in which the United Nations did not take part, and in which I was involved only indirectly. One such case was the tragic war in Vietnam.

At the time I assumed office as Acting Secretary General, the United Nations was not involved directly in the political and military conflicts in Southeast Asia. As permanent representative of Burma, I had watched the frustrating experiences of the Security Council and Dag Hammarskjöld in connection with Laos during 1959 and 1960, and was more convinced than ever that, because of disagreement among the Big Powers, the United Nations could not play a major role in the Indo-Chinese situation. Peking, ostracized by the international community, had been denouncing the United Nations as a stooge of Washington. Moscow and Paris did not favor United Nations involvement in the Vietnam war because Hanoi did not want it.

Thus when the Geneva Conference on Vietnam was held in 1954, no nation attempted to bring the matter before the United Nations. And in May 1961, when the Geneva Conference on Laos began (with the Soviet Union and Britain as cochairmen), no one even thought aloud that the matter should be dealt with by the United Nations. Nevertheless, during the first weeks of my tenure, I privately discussed the question of Vietnam with several permanent representatives, but found a total lack of enthusiasm on their part to bring the matter to the United Nations.

The reluctance of the member states to involve the United Nations, however, was no measure of my own feelings about the war in Vietnam. I had held all along that the real issue of the war was not whether the political aims of U.S. policy were right or wrong; the issue was the American *conduct* of the war. Even if the United States were right politically, it was, in my view, immoral to wage a war of this kind. One does not have to be a pacifist to condemn the napalming and dropping of antipersonnel bombs on hamlets from 35,000 feet above. All wars are basically alike, but modern war is nothing less than mass murder. Though the murderers today are not intrinsically more wicked than their grandfathers, their new weapons now change their status in the business of killing from the retail to the wholesale category.

One peculiar feature of the Vietnam war was that there were no decisive military actions. There were only the jungle, the guerrillas, the regular troops with mass formations overrunning first this town and then that village, the endless carnage, and the devastation of everything that can be destroyed.

As the months rolled by without producing a ray of hope, I was becoming increasingly concerned about the escalation of the fighting. I started to speak out against the war. At a press conference in Paris on April 29, 1964, I said: "Military methods have failed to solve the problem. They did not solve it in 1954, and I do not see any reason why they would succeed ten years later. As I see the problem in Southeast Asia, it is not essentially military, it is political; and, therefore, political and diplomatic means alone, in my view, can solve it."[1]

---

[1] *United Nations Press Release SG/T/17/Add. 1,* April 30, 1964.

From this time on my personal involvement in the Vietnam war was intensified. I began private discussions with a number of individuals, including Ambassador Adlai Stevenson. Privately, he was very sympathetic to my views on Vietnam, but it was obvious that his influence on the formulation of policy in Washington was minimal. I also had private discussions with Nikita Khrushchev, President de Gaulle, and President Johnson. Mr. Khrushchev was candid. He told me that Vietnam was "thousands of miles away" from the Soviet Union and that there was nothing very much Moscow could do. He said he would appreciate my personal involvement "as an Asian" in seeking an end to the war.

Although General de Gaulle was highly critical of U.S. military actions in Vietnam, he was not clear about the nature of the solution. He stressed the need to leave it to the Vietnamese themselves to work out a solution. My first two meetings with him were devoted mainly to the Congo and the financial crisis of the United Nations, a subject I deal with in the next chapter.

President Johnson was deeply concerned with "communist aggression" in Southeast Asia. He did not encourage me to discuss the Vietnam war, but he relished talking about our personal lives. I was charmed by his well-researched revelations about me. He told me that although he was five months older, both he and I went to college about the same time, left college the same time, and became teachers the same time! The most surprising research material was that both he and I were married on the same day—November 17, 1934![2]

In retrospect I found President Johnson one of the warmest, most informal, and congenial men to talk to—so long as you did not take up international affairs. I felt that he had a liking for me. During many of his visits to New York, he would phone me from a hotel, after his official function was over, to tell me that he was on his way to the UN to see me! The UN security people had less than ten minutes to make arrangements for his arrival and his flight to the thirty-eighth floor. I do not remember having met any head of state or head of government so informal and so warm toward me, and at the same time so juvenile in his concept of inter-

---

[2] He died on January 22, 1973, my sixty-fourth birthday.

national developments. He once told me that if South Vietnam were to fall to the communists, then the next target would be Hawaii!

It is interesting to contrast President Johnson with Chairman Khrushchev—the one tall and imposing, the other stocky, with a peasant look and earthy manners, both the most congenial but at the same time the most temperamental of men.

I first met Mr. Khrushchev during the summer of 1962, when I paid my first official visits to London, Paris, Moscow, and Washington. Of those visits, the one with Chairman Khrushchev was the most memorable. It was on August 28, in his country house near Yalta on the Black Sea. His reception was the most informal and the least conventional ever given me by a head of government in my tenure as Secretary General. First, he was waiting for my car at the gate of his garden, while his two infant grandsons, Ivan and Sergeyevich, were frolicking around him. (Ivan is the son of Mr. Khrushchev's daughter Rada, whose husband Alexei Adzhubei was then editor of *Izvestia;* Sergeyevich is the son of Mr. Khrushchev's son Sergei.) I stopped the car at the gate, and after shaking hands with the Chairman, I took Ivan in my arms, and both of us walked across the lawn to his country house. Eugeny Kiselev (the undersecretary for political and security affairs who accompanied me on that trip) walked behind us holding Sergeyevich's hand.

The country house has an idyllic rural setting with a sweeping view of the vast Black Sea. The Soviet Chairman wore a somewhat rumpled light suit. His peasant figure and manners brought back to me memories of my youth in Pantanaw, the small town in Burma in which I was born and brought up. When I was about seven or eight years old, my father on Sunday mornings used to take my second brother Khant and myself to his farm, about three miles from town. I remember vividly the head farmer, U Myat Thin, coming to town at dawn in his bullock cart; soon we would all leave for the paddy field, taking with us eatables for the day. We would spend the whole day playing with the head farmer's children, plucking fruits and wild flowers. Now, at Yalta, I was in no mood to talk business: how I wished I could play with the two little blond boys instead! I felt much more at home in Khru-

shchev's *dacha,* which is closer to my roots, than the heavily
chandeliered Élysée Palace with its resplendent *garde républicain.*

At the time, the problems uppermost in my mind were the
Congo and the UN's financial difficulties. When we finally began
our serious discussions, it was the Chairman who did most of the
talking. He reiterated his government's position on the Congo and
the financial crisis, and I did not detect any sign of even a slight
shift. When I asked him if his government was likely to make a
voluntary contribution to ease the financial strain of the United
Nations, he looked at me and said in effect, "Don't worry. The
Americans will pay. They pushed the United Nations into the
Congo, and the Congo is shaping up according to their wish. At
the last moment they will pay."

While the talks were in progress, the two little children were
crawling in and out of their grandfather's chair legs. Mr. Kiselev,
who was present at the talks, took copious notes of the conversation; I also jotted down some points he raised. However, what
interested me more was Mr. Khrushchev the man, not Mr.
Khrushchev the Chairman of the Council of Ministers of the
Union of Soviet Socialist Republics. Talking to me was a man
with genuine emotional, temperamental, and verbal links with
working-class people.

After the talks, we sat down to lunch in the large dining room
poised on the edge of the sea. What a lunch! Besides Mr. Kiselev
and an interpreter, there was no one outside Mr. Khrushchev's
immediate family. Those present were Mrs. Khrushchev, their
daughter Rada and her husband Alexei Adzhubei, and their son
Sergei and his wife Nina. That was all. Mr. Khrushchev enlivened
the lunch with his peasant tales and jokes.

Immediately after lunch, Mr. Khrushchev invited me to swim
in the Black Sea. I mildly protested with the plea that it might
cause indigestion. He was sure, however, that swimming in the sea
immediately after lunch was very good for digestion! I yielded.
We walked a short distance along the coast to a small cabana in
which we changed into swimming trunks. What trunks! The ones
he gave me would fit a Japanese heavyweight Somo wrestler with
a fifty-inch waist. In fact, Mr. Khrushchev's waist could not have
been less than fifty inches. I somehow managed to tuck the trunks

around my waist as I would a Burmese *longyi*. Before he waded
into the sea, Mr. Khrushchev put an inflated rubber ring under his
arms to keep him afloat. I was sure that with his rotund barrel-like
figure he would be afloat anyway, without the help of the rubber
ring. I swam without the help of any float. Those thirty minutes in
the Black Sea were the most memorable, and at the same time the
most boring, I had ever spent with a head of state. I do not speak
one word of Russian and Mr. Khrushchev did not speak any English except his famous "very o.k." He just hummed what sounded
to me a Russian tune. Meanwhile, my security and press aides,
and Mr. Khrushchev's aides, were watching us with amusement
from the shore. They must have been wondering how we were
communicating. After the swim I found out that Mr. Khrushchev
was right: I had no indigestion.

During the summer of 1964, I again made a round of visits to
various capitals, including Cairo, Paris, London, Rangoon, and
Moscow. This time, the war in Vietnam featured in all my talks
with world leaders. Premier Khrushchev and General Ne Win of
Burma particularly encouraged me to exert my utmost to contribute toward a peaceful solution of the Vietnam problem.

I returned to New York on July 31, and visited Washington
on August 6 at the invitation of President Johnson. The White
House reception for me was the most unforgettable in my ten-year
experience as Secretary General. On that trip, I was accompanied
by Ralph Bunche and Osgood Caruthers, my press officer. A helicopter set us down near the White House. On the south lawn of
the Executive Mansion, the U. S. Marine Corps band played.
There were ceremonial speeches in the Rose Garden and a talk in
the Oval Office of the President. Over two hundred guests attended the President's formal dinner. There were senators and
representatives, leaders of religion, leaders of business, industry,
and labor, the diplomatic corps, prominent actors and actresses,
and leaders of the mass media. I was deeply moved. It was not
only the President who showered me with kindness and affection;
Lady Bird Johnson was equally gracious and warm. I had had an
opportunity to talk with Mrs. Johnson earlier in the day on the
White House lawn, and I was greatly impressed by her intelligence, sensitivity to beauty, and fondness for nature. No doubt in

her own right, she deserved the title First Lady of the land. Earlier in the day, there was a working luncheon at the State Department, given by Dean Rusk, which was attended by Averell Harriman, William Bundy, Adlai Stevenson, Charles Yost, and Ralph Bunche. Clark Clifford, a friend of the President who later became Secretary of Defense, joined us for coffee.

It was at this luncheon that my search for peace in Vietnam began—an initiative that was to be rejected by the United States without the President's knowledge.

After I presented my views on the nature of the Vietnam war, I indicated to Mr. Rusk and the others that it would be very useful if emissaries of the United States and North Vietnam could get together for private conversations, without any publicity whatsoever. I also informed my luncheon companions that I knew Ho Chi Minh; that I had been in Hanoi in November 1954 and had had talks with the Vietnamese leaders. I did not make any specific proposals, but simply stressed the advisability of the two emissaries getting together for a heart-to-heart talk, without any third-party participation. I felt that Mr. Rusk and his colleagues were receptive to the idea. Ambassador Harriman seemed to be enthusiastic, and Mr. Bundy made no comment.

Back in New York, I decided to contact Hanoi. The greatest danger was the possibility of Peking's hearing of such a contact. At that time, the People's Republic of China was against Hanoi's accommodating Washington in any way. To Peking, the United Nations was just the tool of the United States. (I had been somewhat encouraged, however, to see the Chinese ambassador attending the Burmese Foreign Minister's reception given for me in Rangoon on July 27. Was it a thaw in the Chinese attitude toward the United Nations?) In any case, I decided to use Moscow as a channel of communication with Hanoi. Since my relations with Ambassador Fedorenko were cool, I asked Vladimir Suslov, undersecretary for political and Security Council affairs, to transmit an oral message from me to President Ho Chi Minh. The message was that, in my view, it would be in the interest of peace if an emissary of Hanoi would have a face-to-face talk with one from Washington, without any publicity and without the participation of any third party. Mr. Suslov, who assured me that he had his own means of communication with Moscow, told me in late September that he had received, through Moscow, a positive response from Hanoi to my proposal.

On September 23, I told Mr. Stevenson of the good news. He said he was favorably surprised and promised to report immediately to Washington. I told him that the direct exploratory talks should be secret and at the ambassadorial level. I saw him every two or three days and kept inquiring about a response from Washington. At the same time, I informed Mr. Suslov that I had conveyed Hanoi's positive response to Washington through Mr. Stevenson.

On October 15, Mr. Stevenson told me that the President was heavily occupied with the election campaign against Senator Barry Goldwater and advised me to shelve the initiative for some time. After the election, I began to get impatient and kept asking Mr. Stevenson about Washington's response. He told me in November that Washington, checking through its own channels, had not got the impression that Hanoi was willing to talk seriously. When I asked him to identify the channel, I was told that it was the Canadian representative on the International Control Commission. On November 30, I checked with Paul Martin, the Canadian Foreign Minister, when he came to New York for the General Assembly meeting. Mr. Martin told me that the Canadian member of the ICC, J. Blair Seaborn, had no access to any member of the North Vietnamese Cabinet. His only official contact in Hanoi was with an official of the Foreign Office. In any case, no member of the North Vietnamese government was likely to confide to a Canadian that it was interested in secret face-to-face talks with a representative of Washington.

On the next day, I told Vladimir Suslov about Washington's initial reaction and Mr. Seaborn's possible contacts in Hanoi. He was worried that if Hanoi's positive initiative were leaked to the press, either in the United States or Canada, Hanoi would come out with a public denial. I agreed with him, particularly in view of Peking's aversion to Hanoi-Washington contacts.

Before I saw Mr. Martin, I had checked with two other members of the ICC—Poland and India—to see if their representatives had direct access to Ho Chi Minh's government. They told me, as Mr. Martin told me later, that the members of the ICC had access only to the officials of the Foreign Office. The Indian representative, who was the chairman of the ICC, had occasional contacts with the members of the Cabinet, and I believed that the Polish member also, on account of ideological identity and Polish military support of Hanoi, could be presumed to have a similar privilege.

On December 1, I told Mr. Gromyko, who had arrived in New York two days earlier to attend the General Assembly, that I had used Mr. Suslov for the transmittal of a message to Hanoi. He simply nodded and made no comment. At that time, there were unconfirmed reports that Fedorenko and Suslov were not on speaking terms, and I wondered if Suslov's secret assignment was known to Fedorenko.

On December 4, I entered a hospital for treatment of a stomach ulcer, and I lost contact with Mr. Stevenson for two weeks. After my discharge from the hospital on December 18, I talked to Mr. Stevenson, but there were no new developments. On the advice of my doctors, I departed for a week's vacation on December 31, and when I returned to New York, Mr. Stevenson was away on holiday. I asked Charles Yost, Mr. Stevenson's deputy, if he had heard anything from Washington on the initiative. To my utter surprise, Mr. Yost not only had not heard anything from Washington, he did not even know what I was talking about! Then I knew for the first time that Mr. Stevenson did not let anyone in the U.S. mission know of the initiative, and more surprisingly, that there was nothing in writing: he used to report to someone in Washington on the phone. Both Ralph Bunche and I were amazed at the new discovery because whenever Mr. Stevenson came to see me, he made copious notes on pieces of paper on what transpired at the meeting, and both of us were under the impression that he must have reported to Washington in writing.

Mr. Stevenson saw me on January 13, and, apparently on his own, asked me to suggest a suitable meeting place for the two emissaries in case Washington decided to send one. I named five countries where both the United States and North Vietnam maintained either diplomatic or consular missions—Cambodia, Burma, Pakistan, Switzerland, and France. I told Mr. Stevenson that I had not sounded out other countries, but in my view, General Ne Win of Burma would be most co-operative in guaranteeing the secrecy of the meetings. He wanted me to sound out Rangoon.

On the next day, January 14, I asked the permanent representative of Burma to convey my request to the Burmese government to make the necessary arrangements for the secret meeting. On January 18, he brought me the government's reply that it would be happy to be the host. I telephoned Mr. Stevenson the same day about the Burmese government's willingness to make the arrangements. On the phone, I suggested that if the two governments agreed, for the sake of absolute secrecy, the United States ambassador in Burma, Henry Byroade, should be authorized to initiate exploratory talks with the North Vietnamese emissary, who could be either the resident consul general in Burma or someone to be sent from Hanoi for the purpose. Mr. Stevenson said he would convey this to Washington.

On the morning of Saturday, January 30, a disappointed Stevenson saw me and advised me that Washington would not agree to such a meeting. According to him, Washington felt such a meeting could not be kept secret, and that if the news leaked out, it would demoralize the Saigon government, and that it would fall. I told him that four or five Saigon governments had fallen in the past five years, and what was essential was to bring peace to a land that had not seen any for a quarter-century. He agreed, but said there was nothing he could do about it. On Monday, February 1, I told Mr. Suslov about Washington's negative response, and asked him to transmit it to Hanoi through his own channels.

I mentioned this episode to some close friends, including Walter Lippmann, perhaps one of the wisest journalists of our time. His theory was that, almost imperceptibly, Washington had been planning an enlargement of the war, including the bombing of North Vietnam. Mr. Lippmann believed that the Johnson Administration did not like to bargain from a position of relative weakness, and that a convincing military superiority had to be established before serious negotiations could be considered.

On February 7, the United States bombed North Vietnam, ostensibly in retaliation for a Vietcong raid on the Pleiku American barracks in South Vietnam. From then on, Hanoi declared publicly that it would not consider any talks with Washington while the bombing of North Vietnam was going on.

At my press conference on February 24, in reply to a question, I said:

> I am sure that the great American people, if only they knew the true facts and the background to the developments in South Vietnam, will agree with me that further bloodshed is unnecessary. The political and diplomatic method of discussion and negotiation alone can create conditions which will enable the United States to withdraw gracefully from that part of the world. As you know, in times of war and of hostilities, the first casualty is truth.[3]

With those words, whatever utility I might have as a prospective go-between came to an end, as far as Washington was concerned.

Although men like Adlai Stevenson and Ralph Bunche knew the background to those words, President Johnson did not know why I had said them. Only on June 25 did I find out that the President had been completely in the dark about my initiative and Mr. Stevenson's messages to Washington.

On that day, both President Johnson and I delivered speeches in the San Francisco Opera House, commemorating the twentieth anniversary of the United Nations. After the ceremony, the President told me that he wanted to have a word with me. We walked to a small room adjoining the Opera Hall, and he asked his elder daughter, Lynda Bird Johnson, to join us. Much to the dismay of Mr. Stevenson, the President told him that he wanted a private chat with me alone. The conversation started at 12:00 noon and was over at 1:10 P.M.

The President was in a serious, even sour, mood. He said that because of his esteem and affection for me as well as his support of the United Nations, his dinner for me in August 1964 was the biggest ever held in the White House. He had wanted to tell the whole world that he regarded me as a man of peace and that the United Nations was the only hope for peace. He was distressed, however, at my criticism of his Vietnam policies and the general attitude of the United Nations in that matter.

---

[3] *United Nations Note 3075*, February 24, 1965.

At that point, I explained to him my initiative, Mr. Stevenson's reports to Washington, and Washington's final rejection of my initiative. There was no sign of surprise on the President's face, but I got the impression that he had not been informed of the initiative while it was alive, but had checked on it when the newspapers reported it in February, after my press conference. He just repeated the argument Mr. Stevenson had relayed to me on January 30, 1964, that if the news of the secret meeting were to leak, then the government in Saigon might fall.

Then he mused on Adlai Stevenson. He said Stevenson had lost twice in the presidential race; he had no sense of correct judgment of public opinion; his evaluation of events, both domestic and foreign, usually turned out to be incorrect. In the President's opinion, Mr. Stevenson was just an idealist with his head in the clouds. He said that, in making important decisions, he had to take public opinion into account. He then told me that Ambassador Harriman was ready to go anywhere and would talk to anybody on Vietnam. He had already put a plane at his disposal, and Mr. Harriman was prepared to leave Washington at twenty-four hours' notice. I told the President that to my knowledge, Hanoi's position had changed since February. Now Hanoi was insisting that the Vietcong must be involved in any talks on the war. He did not comment.

After a short pause, the President said that he had always wanted a peaceful solution of the Vietnam problem. General LeMay, he pointed out, had strongly recommended the bombing of China. He would never do that, and he had assured General LeMay he never would. He disagreed with LeMay's "outdated" attitudes. That was why he had extended his service by only four months and then retired him.

Another brief pause. He then looked at me and said that he had earmarked one billion dollars for the rehabilitation of both North and South Vietnam, once a peaceful solution was reached. I reminded the President that I had publicly welcomed the move. He said he knew it, and that the decision had been conveyed to Hanoi, but there had been no response. Only the previous day, he had sent Eugene Black, former president of the World Bank, to Bangkok to pave the way for economic aid to both South and

North Vietnam. I told him that Eugene Black had seen me only the previous week to explain the purpose of his mission, but I was afraid that nothing would come out of it so long as the bombing of North Vietnam was going on. He said that he had issued orders to confine the bombing to military targets only, and again observed that the President of the United States had to take into account the public opinion prevailing in the country. According to him, there was an overwhelming opinion in this country in favor of bombing, as long as the Vietcong were committing acts of aggression in South Vietnam. He appeared to be very resolute on this, and I decided not to argue with him. I simply said that I knew public opinion in the United States was in favor of the bombing.

The President brightened up and said that public opinion was very important. Until a few days ago, he said, he had decided not to attend the twentieth anniversary celebrations in San Francisco, since "the United Nations" was very critical of his Vietnam policies. But of course the President knew that the United Nations as such was not critical of his Vietnam policies, since the question of Vietnam was not before the UN. It was the Secretary General who was critical. The President, however, diplomatically avoided any direct reference to me. He said that because of this criticism, many congressmen (such as Senator Dirksen) had advised him to stay away from the celebration. Dean Rusk and Adlai Stevenson had strongly advised him to attend it, however, and he decided to attend "only the other day."

Then the President took up the question of the Dominican Republic, his legislative measures for racial justice in the United States, and economic aid to India and Pakistan. By that time, he was relaxed and all smiles. We all then left the room and joined Governor Pat Brown, Ambassador Stevenson, Mr. Bunche, and others. The President waved to the photographers to come and take group photographs. He insisted on my standing on his right, while I insisted on his standing on my right. The President was now in an extremely good mood, and Mr. Stevenson, who looked ill at ease, must have been wondering what had changed the President's mood from sullen grimness to relaxed joviality.

Only a couple of weeks later, on July 4, 1965, Mr. Stevenson dropped dead on a London street. Two days before he died, he had a long and rambling talk with Eric Sevareid, an old friend, at the London residence of the American ambassador. Mr. Sevareid's account of that talk appeared in the November 30, 1965, issue of *Look* magazine, and it immediately created a sensation. Among other things, Stevenson talked of his despair over the course of the United States policy in Vietnam, of my initiative, and Washington's coolness toward it. Except in one instance, Mr. Sevareid's account was fairly accurate. Stevenson was reported to have told him that it was Robert McNamara who had opposed my initiative. But Stevenson had never once mentioned McNamara's name in the course of our innumerable meetings, and I had no reason to believe that Mr. McNamara would oppose such a move. When Mr. Sevareid saw me at my Riverdale residence on the night of December 11, I recounted the full story as far as I could recollect it.

Incidentally, in his memoirs President Johnson did not mention the Rangoon affair. Thus he did not clear up publicly what his own role, if any, was in the decision to drop the proposed talks. I personally do not believe that Johnson knew about the Rangoon arrangement while the issue was alive. Presidential press secretary William Moyers said later that he could find no evidence that the Rangoon matter had come to Johnson's attention. There was no doubt that the initiative had been rejected without the President's knowledge.

Almost a year after the Sevareid article, on October 7, 1966, the story took another interesting turn. The President, on a speechmaking visit to New York, accompanied by Dean Rusk, Arthur Goldberg, and others, called on me at the United Nations. Ralph Bunche was also present at the sixty-minute talk. Inevitably, the conversation turned to the 1964 initiative, and once again the President told me that he had not been informed of it. He said, "It was a new book to me," and turned to Dean Rusk with a look of inquiry. Mr. Rusk added a new twist. The Secretary of State told me that *Stevenson* had not been authorized to reject my approach. He added, to our utter amazement, "Stevenson had been asked to keep the door open." Both Ralph Bunche and I were stunned with disbelief. Was it conceivable that Stevenson would have taken it upon himself to cancel such an initiative? In any case, a chapter of the peace effort had come to an end, and the opportunity to use my good offices never came back.

My press conference statement of February 24, 1965, and Eric Sevareid's *Look* article of November 30, 1965, did not increase my popularity in Washington, which already was embarrassed and annoyed by the revelations. This feeling was perhaps best illustrated by an off-the-record speech Dean Rusk made on June 19, 1967, to a group of American educators. The speech was later put on the record by Senator Fulbright of Arkansas, a very staunch supporter of my peace initiatives. Rusk said in part:

> You have heard about the end-of-'64 beginning-of-'65 business when peace was about to break out in Rangoon. (Laughter.) The only contact there was a Russian member of the Secretariat. During that period, I had several talks with Mr. Gromyko. So it is not surprising that I would consider Mr. Gromyko more relevant than anything that came from a relatively junior member of the Secretariat. In any event, Hanoi denied there was ever any such contact, and other denials came into the picture. . . . Really, what happens on these matters is basically this: there are an awful lot of candidates for the Nobel Peace Prize running around the world these days. (Laughter.). . . . they don't understand what they hear. . . .[4]

It was not only Washington that was annoyed by my peace efforts and public statements. Peking was much more critical of my involvement in the Vietnam crisis. I was variously described by Hsin Hua News Agency dispatches as the "stooge" or "lackey" of Washington, and the United Nations as a "tool of the imperialists." In March 1965, I proposed a three-step peace proposal: cessation of the bombing of North Vietnam, de-escalation of all military activities in South Vietnam by all parties, and participation of all those who were fighting in South Vietnam in any discussions for a peaceful settlement.

Peking, not Hanoi, was the first to react. Ignoring the first two points, Peking radio said:

---

[4] United Nations Files.

How could U Thant ask for the scaling down of all military actions in South Vietnam? Why did he equate the American aggressors with the victims of the aggression? The Vietnamese people must continue to struggle for their liberation until all Americans are driven off Vietnamese soil.[5]

To my knowledge, Moscow had no public comment on my proposal. On March 21, Hanoi radio broadcast a brief reference to it: "U Thant should have demanded the withdrawal of American aggressors from Vietnamese soil."[6]

As for the United States, it rejected steps one and three, only to accept them five years later, after tens of thousands of more deaths and untold devastation.

In the course of my travels to Europe and Asia, I took advantage of my visits to the capitals by seeing North Vietnamese diplomats. One thing that struck me was their unwavering conviction that the Americans were sure to be defeated and driven out of Southeast Asia! Whether it was in Paris or Moscow, Rangoon or New Delhi, Hanoi representatives were so sure of their victory that the policy of give-and-take did not appeal to them. My most important meeting with the North Vietnamese representatives took place in Rangoon on March 2, 1967.

In arranging that meeting, which was to be a secret one, it was most important to choose an appropriate channel of communication with Hanoi. What I wanted was to meet with a top-level representative from Hanoi when I went to Rangoon, and to find out what the North Vietnamese really wanted. Whom to use as an envoy to set up such a meeting?

Since my 1964 initiative through Suslov, relations between him and Fedorenko had gone from bad to worse. Suslov was recalled to Moscow in 1965, and I appointed Alexei Nesterenko, Soviet ambassador to Pakistan, to succeed him as undersecretary for political and Security Council affairs. But I decided that as a channel of communication I should not use the Soviet undersecretary. I thought of more suitable channels, and considered the French ambassador, Roger Seydoux, to be the most appropriate.

[5] Hsin Hua news report, March 12, 1965.
[6] Hanoi radio broadcast, March 21, 1965.

Our relationship had become very close since he presented his credentials to me in August 1962, and it seemed there were no secrets between us. Besides, France had excellent relations with Hanoi, and General de Gaulle had repeatedly assured me of his government's full co-operation in my efforts for a peaceful solution of the Vietnam problem. Early in February 1967, I requested Mr. Seydoux to transmit an oral message to Hanoi to the effect that I would greatly appreciate talking to a high-level representative from North Vietnam during my projected visit to Burma in late February or early March. It was to be my second visit to my home country since my appointment as Secretary General in 1961, the first one being in July 1964. Mr. Seydoux readily agreed to comply with my request, and on February 20 informed me that the message had been relayed to Hanoi via Paris, and that Hanoi was sending a high-level representative to Rangoon to talk with me.

I arrived in Rangoon on February 24 and called on Generals Ne Win and San Yu on the next day. They told me that a delegation from Hanoi would arrive in Rangoon in a few days, and described to me the arrangements that had secretly been made for my meeting with the North Vietnamese delegation, whose arrival in Rangoon would not be announced, as requested by Hanoi. At 9 P.M. on March 2, a senior Burmese military officer took us from the government guest house to the residence of the North Vietnamese counsul general. Normally the drive would have taken about six or seven minutes, but since press cars were trailing us, we took a roundabout route to mislead the journalists. I arrived at the destination twenty minutes later, with no sign of any press cars in view.

The Hanoi delegation was led by Colonel Ha Van Lau, North Vietnamese chief representative to the International Control Commission and deputy chief of the Hanoi Foreign Office. Others with him were Nguyen Tu Huyen from the Hanoi Foreign Office (who served as interpreter), Le Tung Son, consul general, and Thai Thanh Nen, consul.

It was a very friendly meeting. Vietnamese delicacies were served, and the food reminded me of the meals I had in November 1954, during my two-day stop in Hanoi on the way to Peking.

A wide range of topics connected with the Vietnam war was covered; I took copious notes and so did Nguyen Tu Huyen.

After a couple of hours of talk, I summed up my proposals: a general standstill truce, preliminary talks between the United States and North Vietnam, and the reconvening of the Geneva Conference. These proposals were not intended to supplement my 1965 three-point proposal, but to adapt it to the circumstances as they existed in 1967.

Colonel Ha Van Lau wanted me to keep the proposals confidential since they needed thorough examination by his government. I understood the delicate nature of our meeting, for Peking had been advising Hanoi not to send a delegation to Rangoon to talk to me. Peking's attitude all along had been that the United States must negotiate with the South Vietnam National Liberation Front (the Vietcong). I also knew that Hanoi was ideologically closer to Moscow than to Peking, but for geographical and economic considerations, it could not ignore Peking.

The proposals I made regarding the participants in the projected Geneva Conference were later a subject of controversy. What I said was that the participants should be agreed to primarily by the United States and the Democratic Republic of Vietnam (North Vietnam). My proposals specifically included neither the Republic of Vietnam (South Vietnam) nor the Vietcong. The talks could take any of the following forms:

(1) Direct talks between the United States of America and the Democratic Republic of Vietnam (North Vietnam);

(2) Direct talks between the two governments mentioned above, with the participation of the two cochairmen of the Geneva Conference of 1954 (the United Kingdom and the Soviet Union);

(3) Direct talks between the two governments mentioned with the participation of the members of the International Control Commission (India, Canada, and Poland);

(4) Direct talks between the two governments mentioned, with the participation of the two cochairmen of the Geneva Conference of 1954 and the members of the International Control Commission.

As regards the participation of the Republic of Vietnam (South Vietnam), my views had been well known. I had said on several occasions that no fruitful discussions on ending the war in Vietnam could take place without involving *all* those who were actually fighting, including the government in Saigon, as well as the National Liberation Front of South Vietnam (the Vietcong). Saigon, however, had been insisting that it would not sit down at a table with representatives of the National Liberation Front. My proposal was designed to get around this problem, leaving it to be worked out between Washington and Hanoi in their preliminary talks. The objective of the conference should be the implementation of the Geneva agreement of 1954.

Of course it was difficult to keep a meeting like this a secret for very long. The mysterious arrival in Rangoon of some officials from Hanoi, and my 9:00 P.M. drive in an unmarked car from the government guest house to an unknown destination, stirred up all kinds of rumors in Rangoon. On the next day, the press asked the consul general about it, and he had to confirm that I had visited the consulate. "U Thant came here," he said; "I received him as an Asian, and we exchanged views on the Vietnamese problem." I avoided the press until the next day, when I was confronted at the airport as I prepared to leave for New York. The Hanoi mission had already left with my new proposals, and I carefully avoided any reference to the substance of our conversations. All I could say then and on my arrival in New York was that I had met the North Vietnamese representatives "in my private capacity, and not as the Secretary General of the United Nations," and that we had a "useful and friendly exchange of views."

After my return to New York, I had discussions with Ambassador Goldberg, Ambassador Seydoux, Ambassador Fedorenko, Lord Caradon, and Ambassador Nguyen Duy-Lien, permanent observer of South Vietnam to the United Nations. Since I did not hear from Hanoi as expected, I quietly circulated the new proposals on March 14 in the form of an aide-mémoire to the United States, North Vietnam, South Vietnam, and the National Liberation Front.

Within a few days, word leaked out that I had made some new proposals. The first public reaction was a broadcast on Hanoi radio on March 19, asserting that the United States government was trying to "use the United Nations to interfere in the Vietnamese question." Much more specific was a statement by a Foreign Ministry spokesman a few days later. He said: "To call on both sides to cease fire and hold unconditional negotiations, while the United States is committing aggression against Vietnam and taking serious steps in its military escalation in both zones in Vietnam, is to make no distinction between the aggressors and the victims of aggression, to depart from reality, and to demand that the Vietnamese people accept the conditions of the aggressors."[7]

Because of this and other comments, some of them based on erroneous and distorted reports of the proposals, I had no choice but to make the aide mémoire public, which I did at a press conference on March 28. In it I proposed a general standstill truce, including the cessation of bombing, preliminary talks (as outlined above), and the reconvening of the Geneva Conference. The aide mémoire is reproduced in full in Appendix A, Part II.

The United States and Saigon were pleased with the reciprocity implicit in the standstill truce, but were unhappy about my stress on the cessation of the bombing of North Vietnam and the limitation of the preliminary talks to representatives of the United States and North Vietnam. "We resent being treated as puppets," a South Vietnamese spokesman said. "It is unthinkable that the recognized government of South Vietnam should not be included in talks which so vitally affect its interests."[8] But I have already explained that the reason for this omission was Saigon's insistence that it would not negotiate with the National Liberation Front.

There was little cause for optimism on April 4, 1967, as I left headquarters for a trip to Geneva, after which I was to go on to Ceylon, India, Nepal, Afghanistan, and Pakistan—a trip that was to keep me away three weeks. I found the leaders of these Asian countries in complete agreement with me that the Vietnam problem could not be settled by military means and that the objective should be a return to the Geneva Conference.

I returned to New York firmly convinced that a halt in the

---

[7] Hanoi radio broadcast, March 22, 1967.
[8] United Nations Files.

bombing of North Vietnam would alone open the way for peace talks, and that little could be done except to continue pressing for such a halt. I had reluctantly concluded by then that my proposals of March 14 were not acceptable to either side, and, as I told a luncheon meeting of the UN Correspondents Association on May 11, "must therefore be regarded as no longer under consideration." "In my view," I said, "the only realistic approach is to focus our attention on only one aspect of the problem—that is, the cessation of the bombing of North Vietnam." I realized that a bombing halt entailed a certain amount of risk that Hanoi might take advantage of it to increase its infiltration below the demilitarized zone, but I agreed with the assessment of Secretary of Defense Robert McNamara that the bombing was more of a penalty than a deterrent to infiltration. I felt certain that whatever risk was involved was worth taking when one looked at the alternative— the risk that the possibility of a just and lasting peace might be jeopardized, as well as the détente between the United States and the Soviet Union.

After months of seeming intransigence on the part of the parties involved in the war, signs of movement began to appear around the beginning of 1968. The Foreign Minister of North Vietnam made a conciliatory statement on December 29, and President Johnson, in his State of the Union message on January 17, said he was still exploring the Hanoi statement. I myself began a new round of consultations, which included talks with the leaders of India, the Soviet Union, the United Kingdom, France, and the United States, as well as with the representatives of both North Vietnam and South Vietnam. In New Delhi, I met again with North Vietnam's consul general on February 8. He affirmed that his government "would hold talks with Washington on all relevant matters at an appropriate time, after the unconditional cessation of bombing and of all other acts of war" against his country. I put to him a series of questions that he promised to transmit to his government, assuring me that it would reply as soon as possible. A few days later, while I was in London, I was informed that Mai Van Bo, the North Vietnamese representative in France, had received a message from his government for transmittal to me. I flew to Paris immediately, and on February 14, I received the reply to my questions. I was told that talks could begin just as soon as the cessation of bombing and other acts of war became effective. I also was informed that either side could bring up any matter, including the reduction of fighting in South Vietnam and the reconvening of the Geneva Conference. In effect, Hanoi was agreeing to reconsider my proposals of March 14, 1967, which it had rejected at that time.

Upon my return to New York, I gave a full report to Ambassador Goldberg and to Nguyen Huu Chi, Saigon's United Nations observer. On February 21, I was received in Washington by President Johnson and Secretary of State Dean Rusk. The President reaffirmed both his desire to achieve a peaceful settlement and the continued validity of the "San Antonio formula," a set of proposals he had advanced in a speech in San Antonio, Texas, on September 29, in these words: "The United States is willing to stop all aerial and naval bombardment of North Vietnam when this will lead to productive discussions. We, of course, assume that while discussions proceed, North Vietnam would not take advantage of the bombing cessation or limitation." I felt certain at the conclusion of the consultations that if a bombing halt took place, meaningful talks could begin within a few days. I came back to New York with a definite impression that President Johnson was inclined toward a bombing halt, while the Secretary of State was not favorably disposed to it.

On March 31, President Johnson announced that the bombing of North Vietnam would cease "except in the area north of the demilitarized zone, where the continued enemy buildup directly threatens allied forward positions and where the movements of their troops and supplies are clearly related to that threat." This was not the total halt that Hanoi had been demanding, but on the morning of April 3, I was handed a Reuters news dispatch that said: "Hanoi radio said tonight that North Vietnam was ready to meet with American representatives to consider an end to the fighting."

At last, it appeared that the first positive steps were being taken. Difficulties developed immediately, however, over selection of a site for the preliminary talks. I was in contact with both Washington and Hanoi, trying to resolve the question. I suggested

Paris, Geneva, or Warsaw for the talks. If both sides agreed on Geneva, I assured them of providing necessary conference facilities in the Palais des Nations. On May 3, agreement was reached to begin the talks in Paris on May 10.

This was the breakthrough I had been hoping for since 1964. I knew, of course, that the end was not yet in sight and that the negotiations might be long and difficult. By July 1, prospects for the talks still had not moved perceptibly, so I decided to pause in Paris on my scheduled trip to Geneva for the summer session of the Economic and Social Council. I conferred with United States negotiators Averell Harriman and Cyrus Vance, and with the North Vietnamese representative, Xuan Thuy, in an effort to get their views on the outlook for the talks. Naturally, I was disappointed at the way the negotiations were going, but in my view, the very fact that the parties were continuing their efforts was a hopeful sign.

I continued to be deeply concerned with the heavy loss of life in Vietnam and with the bombing north of the demilitarized zone. Although the March 31 limitation had ended the bombing north of the twentieth parallel, there had been an increase in the total amount of bombing in North Vietnam. I had done all I could to get a total cessation, but the question of my personal role was raised again in Paris in mid-September, when the North Vietnamese delegation made a public appeal to me "to use my prestige and influence" to get a bombing halt. I was asked at my September 23 press conference whether this may not have been a way of saying Hanoi was interested in some sort of mediation by me. I replied: "I have been involved in the search for a solution regarding the Vietnam problem for the past three years or more. As regards the statement by the North Vietnamese spokesman in Paris last week that the Secretary General has influence and prestige, I am not sure whether I have both or either. But so long as the war in Vietnam goes on, it will be my constant endeavor to try to contribute toward a peaceful solution of the problem. I still feel very strongly that in this very tragic war, essential first steps are necessary, and without these essential first steps, I do not see how the stalemate can be broken. As a matter of fact, I must confess that I do not see the light at the end of the tunnel for another year or so."

On October 31, President Johnson ordered the cessation of all aerial, naval, and military bombardment of North Vietnam. I welcomed the decision in a statement as a "first and essential step toward peace that I and many others have been urging for nearly three years. . . ."[9]

I was able to welcome in the same statement the reported agreement on the participation of representatives of South Vietnam and the National Liberation Front in the Paris talks. With the cessation of bombing and the arrangements for formal negotiations by all the involved parties, my own role was drawing to an end. I felt that the Paris talks should be permitted to follow their course without outside interference.

Up to this point, I have concentrated on my various private initiatives. I was also concerned, however, not only as Secretary General but as a person and as an Asian. Although by nature and training, I tend to use mild language—that is why Ralph Bunche was so astonished when, in 1961, I called Moise Tshombe and his supporters "a bunch of clowns" (see page 140)—my personal view of the Vietnam war was clearly understood in Washington, where, if I may say so, I was less than popular in the State Department and the White House. And my views were clear to the press, at the United Nations, and to anyone who examined my words. As early as February 1965, when the antiwar movement in the United States was in its early stages, I was making public statements that, I am told and believe, angered Secretary of State Dean Rusk. It might be of value to the historical record to recall just a few of them.

On February 24, 1965, shortly after President Johnson began the bombing of North Vietnam, I implied (as I mentioned above) that the American people did not know the true facts about developments in South Vietnam. I said, perhaps quite undiplomatically, that in times of war the first casualty is truth. At that same press conference I also said:

> . . . I have never advocated the immediate withdrawal of United States troops from the Republic of Vietnam. I am fully conscious of the fact that such a step will naturally involve ques-

---

[9] *United Nations Press Release SG/SM/1030,* November 1, 1968.

tions of face and prestige, and questions of the abrogation of previous commitments, and so forth. But I feel that once diplomatic and political methods have been tried, if there is any perceptible improvement in the situation, and if some sort of stability can be restored in the country, then at that time, of course, the United States can withdraw its troops with dignity.

This is exactly what happened—eight years and many thousands of lives later. And I am sure that I am not the only Asian who found it ironic that, as it seemed to us, the United States stayed in Vietnam to save face, a characteristic that Westerners are fond of attributing to Asians.

Then, in a holiday message released at headquarters on December 22, 1965, I characterized the war in words equally unpleasing to Washington. I termed it "a war more violent, more cruel, more damaging to human life and property, more harmful to relations among the great powers, and more perilous to the whole world, than at any other time during the generation of conflict that country has known."

At a time when the concept of a nonaligned Vietnam was most unwelcome in Washington, I called for nonalignment, as I had earlier, at a speech in London on April 29, 1966. Soon after, on May 24, 1966, before the Amalgamated Clothing Workers in Atlantic City, New Jersey, this is what I said:

> In Vietnam, there is growing evidence that the so-called "fight for democracy" is no longer relevant to the realities of the situation. Twenty years of outside intervention and the presence of a succession of foreign armies have so profoundly affected Vietnamese political life that it seems illusory to represent it as a mere contest between communism and liberal democracy. Indeed, recent events have shown that the passion for national identity, perhaps one should say national survival, is the only ideology that may be left to a growing number of Vietnamese. Thus, the increasing intervention by outside powers in the conflict—involving their armies, their armaments and, above all, their prestige—has tended to alienate the people of Vietnam from their own destiny. And if, therefore, the issue in Vietnam is not a struggle between two different views of democracy, what is really at stake, unless an early end to the hostilities is brought about, is the independence, the identity, and the survival of the country itself.

During this period, I frequently called for three things that were anathema to the Johnson Administration: an end to the bombing of North Vietnam, a de-escalation of the fighting (at a time that the United States was stepping up its participation), and participation by the National Liberation Front (the Vietcong) in any negotiations. All three proved necessary before even a limited settlement was finally agreed to by the Nixon Administration, four years after his first election.

On December 30, 1966, I wrote to Ambassador Goldberg that I believed it was "a situation in which a powerful nation like the United States should take the initiative in the quest for peace and show an enlightened and humanitarian spirit." I believed that, in the circumstances, only action deliberately undertaken in such a spirit—which, because of its power and position, the United States could afford to undertake—could halt the escalation and enlargement of this war, and thus bring about a turning of the tide towards peace.

A few months later, on May 10, 1967, I made what I believed to be an important point: that Hanoi, as I knew from my own initiatives, was willing to talk before February 7, 1965. After February 7, it was not. The reason was obvious. Once the bombing started, Hanoi refused to talk. When finally the scope of the bombing was materially reduced, Hanoi did talk.

As was well known, the so-called domino theory was often advanced as the rationale for the massive American intervention in Indo-China. As I said during a press conference at headquarters in January 1967:

> . . . I do not subscribe to the generally held view that if South Vietnam falls, then country X, country Y, and country Z will follow. I do not agree with this so-called domino theory. In my view, the destiny of every country is shaped by its own peculiar circumstances, its national characteristics, its historical background, and its own political philosophy. What is true of country X is not necessarily true of country Y or country Z.

Neither did I subscribe to the view that South Vietnam was strategically vital to Western security, nor that the National Liberation Front was a "stooge of Hanoi." I knew the mood of the leaders in North Vietnam and was certain that they were very independent—obsessed, in fact, with the principle of nonalignment. If Vietnam were independent and militarily nonaligned, preferably with the guarantee of the Big Powers, as I had been advocating, then I did not see how it could pose a threat to international peace or could be strategically vital to the interests and security of the West.

On June 18, 1968, I was impelled by the continuing bloodshed, the continuing misery, to speak out once again against the savage conduct of the war:

> . . . I find it difficult to express adequately the strong sense of repugnance to all established standards and norms of civilized society that the continuance of this savage war evokes. I do not see how one can build a democratic government or a stable society over huge graveyards and with the participation of enormous refugee camps. I know that advocates of escalation prescribe more drastic and large-scale destruction, but such senseless escalation would only produce a cure that is infinitely worse than the disease; in the words of an eminent theologian, "the operation might be successful, but the patient would certainly be buried, and the hospital buried with him."

Once the peace talks began in Paris, I refrained from any substantive statements in order to avoid any risk of creating unnecessary difficulties for the negotiators. But with the American invasion of Cambodia, I felt I could no longer conceal my deep concern, and in May 1970, I issued a statement in which I said:

> . . . One country that had been trying very hard to keep itself neutral seems now to have been drawn into the conflict. Recent reports of a resumption of the bombing of North Vietnam have given further cause for grave anxiety. I would also like to make public the concern I have felt in recent months regarding the intensification of the fighting in Laos. I fear that, if the parties involved do not take urgent, decisive, and courageous measures toward peace, it will become increasingly difficult to end a war that constitutes a threat not only for the peoples of Indo-China but for the whole of mankind.

The staggering cost of the war, in human lives and materials, is well known: as of this writing, 53,813 Americans killed in South Vietnam alone, and 153,302 seriously wounded throughout Indo-

China. According to the Pentagon, 932,793 communists have been killed. The financial cost to the United States, again according to the Pentagon, is $108 billion.[10]

However, according to Senator Mike Mansfield, the overall cost of the Vietnam war would be around $676 billion, when ultimate veterans' costs are paid.[11] It is difficult to visualize what advantages the United States and the American taxpayer have achieved by these astronomical expenses both in manpower and money.

As of this writing, it is more than five years since the Paris peace talks have started, and an agreement of sorts has been reached, due primarily to the outstanding diplomatic initiatives of the United States Secretary of State, Dr. Henry Kissinger.

I can only hope that the negotiators in Paris will achieve an enduring peace in Vietnam, and that a truly national government will emerge in Saigon. Once peace and stability are restored, can we not expect that the energies and talents of all the people of Vietnam will be turned toward healing their divisions and the reconstruction and modernization of both parts of the country? Indeed, one may expect that Vietnam, given its natural resources and the intellectual capacity and vigor of its people, would at some future date become the moving spirit of a new co-operative effort among the countries of the region, irrespective of their overall political systems.

---

[10] *Time*, August 27, 1973.
[11] *The Christian Science Monitor*, May 17, 1974.

CHAPTER VI

THE FINANCIAL CRISIS

As the reader explores the more complex and dramatic crises that are described in detail in the later sections of this book—particularly those in the Congo and the Middle East—he should bear in mind one other dimension of the Secretary General's role: his responsibility for the solvency of the World Organization. I have already alluded to nagging financial problems in connection with peace-keeping operations in Cyprus and other trouble spots. Although two parties to a dispute would sometimes agree in advance to share the cost of the UN force stationed between them, more often (as was the case with Cyprus) the Security Council established peace-keeping forces in various parts of the world without also devising ways of paying for them, relying on voluntary contributions. This made any serious advance planning impossible and meant, inevitably, that the UN operated at a deficit, a deficit that continued to grow each year, despite my frequent appeals for contributions.

But the financial problem had its genesis long before my tenure as Secretary General, and was all the more difficult because it had grown out of serious political differences. The problem began with the creation of the UN peace-keeping force for the Middle East in 1956, after the Suez war. In 1957, some thirty countries, consisting mainly of the Soviet bloc and the Arab states, refused to pay their assessments on the ground that the governments responsible for the Suez conflict should pay the entire cost. By 1961, the deficit for the Middle East force alone was running $5 million a year out of a total assessment of $19 million. A total deficit of $29 million at the end of 1959 ballooned to $86.9 million by the end of 1960, as a result of the Congo operation and the continued nonpayment of assessments for the force in the Middle East. The prospect was that the deficit would pass $100 million by the end of 1961, and that by the end of 1962, it would amount to $170 million. This brought the Organization literally to the brink of bankruptcy.

The United Nations was therefore facing an acute financial crisis when I became Acting Secretary General on November 3, 1961. By 1964, it also became the most serious *internal* conflict in the history of the Organization, whose very existence was at stake. For as a result of the political dimension of the financial problem, the United States and the Soviet Union were moving toward a head-on collision that threatened the effective life of the UN: the United States was now insisting that the Soviet Union be deprived of its vote in the General Assembly, in accordance with Articles 17 and 19 of the UN Charter.

Article 17 says that the expenses of the Organization shall be borne by all members of the General Assembly, and Article 19, that a member falling in arrears by two years must be deprived of its vote in the Assembly, unless failure to pay is due to conditions beyond the control of the defaulting member, that is, inability to pay. Because the U.S.S.R. had refused to pay its assessments for the Congo and Middle East operations, it was behind two years in its payments; and France, which had refused to pay for the Congo operation, would also soon be sufficiently in arrears. The Soviet Union, as we have seen, maintained that the "aggressor" countries —and not the entire membership—must be made to bear the financial consequences of their actions; it also maintained that the Congo operation was "illegal," since the Security Council—not the Secretary General—must decide which states shall take part in carrying out its decisions relating to the maintenance of international peace and security. As for France, it agreed that the expenditure for the force in the Middle East fell within the meaning of Article 17, but France had not agreed to the Congo operations; it therefore regularly paid its share for the force in the Middle East, while it refused to pay for the one in the Congo. Clearly, however, any attempt by a group of nations headed by the United States to deprive the Soviet Union of its vote would precipitate a clash that would mean the effective end of the United Nations.

Such were the frightening dimensions of the problem by 1964. To go back a bit in time, I took steps to restore the financial solvency of the Organization just two days after my appointment in November of 1961. On November 5, I began consultations with the representatives of member states on possibilities of a solution. Such consultations took place almost daily, even while my attention was devoted primarily to the Congo, to complaints by Cuba of the imminent armed intervention by the United States in the Dominican Republic, and the mounting friction over Angola between Portugal and the African states. After considering various alternatives, I decided to seek approval of the Assembly for a special bond issue, and on December 20, 1961, the Assembly, over the opposition of eleven Soviet-bloc countries, plus France and Belgium, approved a resolution calling for the issuance of $200 million in United Nations bonds. The bonds, which bore interest at two per cent and were repayable in twenty-five equal annual installments, were to be offered to member states, UN specialized agencies, and—if the Secretary General so decided—to private nonprofit organizations.

Backers of the resolution, including the United States, pictured the bond issue as a one-time emergency measure to keep the Organization from collapsing in bankruptcy. The Soviet Union and France, on the other hand, argued that the proposal was a maneuver to enable the UN to engage in peace-keeping activities (like those in the Middle East and the Congo) whose financing was challenged as illegal.

It fell to me to sell the bonds. Early in 1962, President Kennedy sent a special message to Congress requesting an appropriation of $100 million for this purpose. After a prolonged debate, Congress passed a bill that permitted the United States to match purchases of other members of the UN up to $100 million. There were legislative battles in other countries, including the

United Kingdom, which pledged itself to purchase up to $12 million by the end of 1963. Although these purchases brought in enough money to ease the financial pressures threatening the Organization, they fell short of the $200 million authorized. Eventually, purchases reached $154.7 million. Had it not been for the bonds and the generous response of a surprisingly wide-ranging number of member states as well as nonmembers, the fate of the UN's primary peace-keeping function—and perhaps of the Organization itself—might well have been calamitous.

On December 20, 1961, the same day the Assembly approved the $200 million bond issue, it took another decision that was to play a significant role in the resolution of the political as well as the financial aspects of the crisis. This was its request to the International Court of Justice for an advisory opinion as to whether expenditures relating to the operations in the Middle East and the Congo constituted mandatory expenses of the United Nations within the meaning of Article 17 of the Charter. As we have noted, a number of states, including the Soviet Union and France, had taken the position that peace-keeping expenditures were a special category that did not fall within Article 17. In its advisory opinion, delivered on July 20, 1962, the Court rejected this contention and, by a vote of nine to five, held that the term "expenses of the Organization" meant *all* expenses approved by the General Assembly and not just administrative and other costs provided for under regular budgetary appropriations.

Despite the split decision, which generally reflected the divergent views of the United Nations membership itself, the Court's opinion was one of the most significant in its history. For one thing, it affirmed the right of the Assembly to establish machineries to maintain peace and security. It further asserted that the fiscal powers of the Assembly extended to all requirements of the Organization, including peace-keeping operations. But by holding that the expenditures for the forces in the Middle East and the Congo were expenses within the meaning of Article 17, the advisory opinion opened the door to possible sanctions under Article 19: the right to vote in the General Assembly could now be denied to defaulting members.

Thus the stage was set for the confrontation between the

United States and the Soviet Union. By the beginning of 1964, as I have mentioned, the crisis over Article 19 had reached an acute stage. Despite the bond issue, the Organization was still in debt by some $134 million, and no relief was in sight. It appeared inevitable that the opening of the nineteenth session of the Assembly in September would bring a disastrous clash between the United States and the U.S.S.R. On September 11, the Soviet Union argued that by threatening the application of Article 19 against the U.S.S.R., the United States was attempting to force it and other states to make a choice between either acquiescing in the actual destruction of the Charter or reviewing their attitude toward the United Nations. On October 8, the United States asserted that the opening of the nineteenth session of the Assembly would present the "inevitable and inescapable" issue of Article 19, unless requisite payments were made before that date. It went on to say that failure to apply Article 19 to a great power, because it was a great power, would undermine the integrity of the Organization.

The atmosphere at the United Nations in September and October 1964 was one of utter gloom. There was the general feeling that the Organization would find itself unable to meet on-going (including payroll) commitments. Several representatives were even predicting that the United Nations would have to shut down. To avert the crisis, the member states agreed to postpone the opening of the Assembly to November 10, and then to December. I was convinced, however, by the experience of the past three years, that a policy of drift, of improvisation, of ad hoc solutions, and of reliance on the generosity of the few rather than the collective responsibility of all, could not endure much longer.

In the light of the firmly and publicly declared attitude of the U.S.S.R., it seemed imperative that a way be found that would enable the Soviet Union to contribute to the strengthening of the Organization without abandoning its basic position, that is, the preservation of the principle that a member state is not obligated to pay for activities it considers to be illegal. Therefore, a device needed to be found that would in effect induce payment under protest. Such a device would also be useful for other member states, such as the Arab nations, which were withholding payments, not for financial reasons, but in order to preserve the principle that "the aggressor must pay." Accordingly, in September and October, I concentrated on the idea of a peace (solvency) fund. Under my proposal, a member state that, for reasons of principle, refused to pay its assessment for a peace-keeping operation, could—without prejudice to the principle involved—make a payment into the solvency fund, which was to be administered by the Secretary General. The contribution would be deducted from any payment due from that member state. This attempt bore no fruit, since no defaulting state wanted even to give the appearance of having defaulted in payment.

It was only at the last moment that we found a way to avert an immediate confrontation. On the eve of the opening of the nineteenth session, agreement was reached among the U.S., the U.S.S.R., France, and Britain on a formula that would permit the Assembly to transact essential and noncontroversial business by unanimous consent—that is, without taking a formal vote, thereby avoiding the issue of who was qualified to vote. When the Assembly opened, there was an understanding that issues other than those that could be disposed of without objection would not be raised in the general debates. The session proceeded without incident.

When the Assembly reconvened on January 18, 1965, the confrontation was again averted when Adlai Stevenson, the U.S. representative, declared that in order to prevent the will of the majority from being "frustrated by one member," the United States would not invoke Article 19. The threat of a confrontation was finally lifted altogether in August 1965, when Stevenson's successor, Arthur J. Goldberg, told the Special Committee on Peace-keeping that the United States had decided reluctantly to bow to the will of the majority and refrain from invoking Article 19.

However, it was still necessary to find a way to end the policy of improvisation that had been holding the line against outright bankruptcy. During the September session in 1965, the consensus was that the financial difficulties of the Organization should be solved through voluntary contributions by member states, with the highly developed countries making substantial contributions. I took the occasion to make an urgent appeal to all members to follow through with voluntary contributions as provided in the consensus. My major effort from then until I completed my second term was directed at trying to find a formula under which the Big Powers would make the voluntary contributions they were committed to in principle.

Meanwhile, the United Kingdom came out with a generous voluntary contribution of $10 million. It was a big boost to those of us who were concerned with the future solvency of the Organization. The United Kingdom's example was followed by other member states. Both Nikolay Fedorenko of the Soviet Union and Roger Seydoux of France took personal interest in restoring the financial solvency of the UN. Their governments agreed to make substantial voluntary contributions without prejudice to their stated positions, provided the United States would come out with a substantial contribution at the same time.

Nevertheless, after some five years of personal discussions with the governments concerned, including talks at the highest level, the situation in late 1971 was so serious that I was compelled to say in the introduction to my annual report that "the United Nations, after ten or more years of deficit financing . . . must very soon face the fact that it is a bankrupt organization."

Although in October 1971, French Foreign Minister Maurice Shumann announced that his government had decided to make a contribution of approximately $3.9 million, when I left office on December 31, 1971, unpaid regular budget assessments were in excess of $65 million, in addition to more than $50 million in debts incurred for past and continuing peace-keeping operations. The financial outlook of the Organization still remained bleak.

PART III

THE
POLITICS
OF
CONFRONTATION

CHAPTER VII

CRISIS IN THE CONGO

PRELUDE

On the morning of Friday, September 8, 1967, as I was about to leave for the office, my private telephone rang. When I picked up the receiver, a husky male voice asked, "Is it Mr. U Thant?" When I said yes, the unfamiliar voice continued, "If you go to Kinshasa, you will land in Bukavu." Then the caller hung up.

I was surprised and puzzled on several counts. My private phone was unlisted, and the number was known only to some of my senior colleagues in the Secretariat and a few close family friends. The practice had been for all calls to my Riverdale residence to be routed through the United Nations, with which my house had a direct tie line. The United Nations security screened calls from private individuals unconnected with the UN. Another cause for surprise was that nobody who knows me ever addressed me as "Mr. U Thant," since "U" means "Mr."

The more I thought of it, the more uneasy I became, for two days later I was to leave for Kinshasa (Léopoldville) in the Congo[1] to attend the fifth session of the Assembly of Heads of State and Government of the Organization of African Unity, as I had done for previous sessions of the OAU. Air flight to the Congo via Brussels had been booked well in advance for two aides and myself (under assumed names, as in most cases). For security and other reasons, the actual names were usually furnished to the airlines about twenty-four hours before the scheduled time for takeoff.

---

[1] Now the Republic of Zaire.

I discussed with Donald Thomas, as he drove me to the
United Nations, the very unusual telephone call I had received
only a few minutes earlier. Don was my chief security aide and administrative assistant, and a very dependable man. He accompanied me in all my foreign travels, and I came to regard him as a
member of my family. He and another security aide, George
Pogue, an equally reliable man, were to accompany me on the
projected trip to Kinshasa. In the course of the twenty-five minute
drive to my office, we talked about several possibilities regarding
that mysterious call. Of course, my phone number, though unlisted, could well be available from one of those who had it. What
was inexplicable was the motive of the call. It could well have
been made by a crank, but how did he know that I was going to
Kinshasa, and why did he mention Bukavu as my likely landing
place, instead of Kinshasa? At that time, Bukavu, a town in the
far-eastern corner of the Congo, was held by Congolese rebels.
According to news reports, from 150 to 200 foreign mercenaries
were with the rebels, and sporadic battles were taking place between the Congolese government forces and these mercenary-led
rebels. Don and I stretched our imaginations and recalled that Mr.
Moise Tshombe, who, seven years earlier, had led the prolonged
but unsuccessful secessionist movement of Katanga in the Congo
with the aid of foreign mercenaries, was a prisoner in Algeria. He
had been in exile in Madrid since November 1965, following the
seizure of power by Joseph Mobutu. On June 30, 1967, Tshombe
was hijacked over the Mediterranean by a Frenchman named
Francis Bodenan, reportedly an agent of the Congolese government, and brought to Algiers.

During his period as President of the secessionist province of
Katanga in the Congo, Tshombe had built up an enormous bank
account in Switzerland. He had also been in touch with major European financial interests that saw in him the greatest pro-Western
leader that Africa had ever produced. He was the number-one African hero in white-ruled Rhodesia and the super-racist state of
South Africa. During his Katanga regime, many of his white mercenaries had been recruited from these two countries.

Ironically, while he was in exile, Tshombe was systematically
planning for the overthrow of his greatest political enemy, President Joseph Mobutu, who himself was the darling of the United

States. His days in Madrid had therefore been marked with plot and counterplot. The visitors to his villa in Madrid included double agents working for him as well as for the government of the Congo. Francis Bodenan was working for Tshombe, while at the same time he was in the pay of the Congolese government.

Five days after Tshombe's seizure in Algiers, a Belgian, Major Jean Schramme, reportedly in the pay of Tshombe, was leading a group of white mercenaries and Congolese rebels in Bukavu in revolt against Mobutu's government. Could it be that Mr. Tshombe's supporters or sympathizers wanted his release from confinement in Algeria and were planning to use me as a hostage for an exchange? If this were the case, why did someone warn me of it in advance? Could it be that he wanted to dissuade me from going to Kinshasa? In that case, he might be a well-wisher who genuinely wanted me not to go. Or maybe the caller wanted to embarrass me with the Organization of African Unity or wanted to embarrass the OAU itself. We could not come to any conclusion, but both of us agreed that the risk was not worth taking. At the same time, the information should not be passed on to anybody, since the mass media would naturally and understandably make a sensational story out of it.

As soon as I got to the office, I told Mr. C. V. Narasimhan, an undersecretary as well as my chef de cabinet, about the mysterious call. He agreed that I should not take the risk. I immediately sent cables to Mr. Diallo Telli, secretary general of the OAU, and to the Congolese President, Joseph Mobutu, head of state of the host country, that due to extreme pressure of work at UN headquarters, I regretted that I would not be able to attend and address the plenary session of the OAU. On the same day, Donald Thomas cancelled the reserved flights.

Many African delegates as well as senior African officials of the United Nations Secretariat were understandably upset at my decision, and for the first time in my public career I found myself in a most embarrassing situation of not being able to offer a plausible excuse.

On Monday, September 11, I received a cable from the Foreign Minister of Tunisia, Mr. Habib Bourguiba, Jr., to the effect that my absence from the OAU meeting would be widely misunderstood, and that all the Foreign Ministers attending the conference requested me to reconsider my decision. The cable concluded that if I could not attend and address the opening session, the African Foreign Ministers would suggest that I attend and address one of the following plenary sessions. Since I had no valid official reasons to offer, I immediately cabled to Mr. Bourguiba that I would try to attend the second day of the conference. Air bookings via Dakar (in Senegal) were hurriedly made by Don, and we left for the Congo on the night of Tuesday, September 12, arriving in Kinshasa on September 13. After less than twenty-four hours' stay in the city, during which I addressed the gathering of African heads of state and government, we returned to New York by the same route.

It is far from my intention to insinuate that there was actually a move to hijack the plane in which I was traveling and make me a hostage. It is still more difficult to present any proof, even circumstantial, that anyone wanted to exchange me for Mr. Tshombe (who was still a prisoner in Algiers) after having been hijacked there. The phone call might well have been the work of a prankster—or was he someone who did not want me to identify myself too closely with the activities of OAU or the African states? As of this writing, I have no answer.

I have opened this chapter with this episode just to underline the serious difficulties and obstacles encountered for four years by the United Nations in its operations in the Congo, and to emphasize the unprecedented misunderstanding and confusion regarding that operation. So many political crosscurrents had added to its inherent complications. Beyond doubt, however, much of this misunderstanding and confusion resulted, among other things, from the deliberate, planned, and well-financed activities of the Katanga propaganda lobby, ably abetted by certain habitual detractors of the United Nations, disseminating falsehoods and distortions about the operation.

OVERVIEW

The United Nations went into the Congo in response to an urgent appeal from the government of the Republic of the Congo on July

12, 1960. The country had just received its independence from Belgium less than two weeks earlier, on June 30. At the time of independence, the province of Katanga was an integral part of the Congo. About a week after independence, the Congolese army mutinied. It was a heavily armed force of some 28,000 men. Because of this mutiny, and ostensibly to protect the considerable number of Belgian nationals in the country, Belgian paratroopers were redeployed in the Congo, against the wishes of the Congolese government. There were also tribal conflicts and threats of secession in several sections of the country.

Thus, this vast country was threatened with a complete breakdown of authority and resultant chaos. It was in these circumstances that the Congolese government had to seek outside assistance. It appealed first to the government of the United States, but President Eisenhower, to his eternal credit, advised that the appeal should be made to the United Nations rather than to any single country. This wise advice was followed.

The internal difficulties of the Congo were compounded by various types of interference from outside, for political and financial motives. This was particularly true with regard to the province of Katanga, which is very rich in minerals, especially copper, cobalt, and uranium.

The Security Council responded favorably to the appeal of the government of the Congo, in view of the potential danger to international peace and security from the confused situation in that country. The members recognized that a vacuum of authority in the Congo would invite foreign interference, and that this might well lead to a most dangerous confrontation there of the two superpowers, the United States and the Soviet Union—a confrontation they, as much as anyone, wanted to avoid. Although recognizing the political and financial difficulties involved, the Security Council had no choice but to respond to the appeal of the government.

To meet the vast and complex task with which the United Nations was confronted in the Congo, it was necessary to assemble, by UN standards, an extraordinarily large team of civilian and military personnel. At its peak strength, the United Nations force in the Congo totaled more than 18,000 officers and men, plus some 1,300 civilians.

It is noteworthy also that the United Nations military and civilian personnel went into Katanga with the full consent of the provincial authorities of Katanga. Provincial President Moise Tshombe himself and some of his ministers were at the airport in Elisabethville—capital of the Province of Katanga—to welcome Mr. Hammarskjöld and the first elements of the United Nations troops when they arrived in early August 1960.

I believe that a detailed account of the Congo crisis as seen from the United Nations will help the reader understand the complexity of the problem, the dilemmas faced both by Dag Hammarskjöld and myself, and the political currents and crosscurrents that compounded the maze of issues. Before embarking on this general survey, I should like to provide the following chronological outline, which will help the reader keep his bearings in a story of extraordinary complexity.

CHRONOLOGY

1960

June 23:   First Central Government of the Congo established with Joseph Kasavubu as President and Patrice Lumumba as Prime Minister.

June 30:   Republic of the Congo receives independence from Belgium.

July 5:   Mutiny of *Force Publique* in Léopoldville.

July 10:   Belgian troops intervene, occupying Léopoldville and Elisabethville.

July 11:   Moise Tshombe, President of the Katanga Provincial Government, proclaims secession of Katanga.

July 12:   Republic of the Congo requests intervention of UN.

July 14 and 22:	Security Council appeals for cease-fire and calls for immediate withdrawal of Belgian troops from Katanga.
August 30:	Rajeshwar Dayal (of India) appointed special UN representative in the Congo. Pending arrival of Dayal, Andrew Cordier takes interim charge of UN operations in the Congo.
September 5:	Kasavubu makes radio broadcast dismissing Lumumba; Lumumba in turn broadcasts dismissal of Kasavubu; Cordier orders Congo's airport closed to all but UN planes.
September 6:	Cordier orders national radio station closed, refusing Lumumba permission to broadcast again.
September 12:	Lumumba arrested on order of Col. Joseph Mobutu, but later released.
September 15:	Lumumba takes refuge in Ghanaian officers' mess of ONUC in Léopoldville.
November 27:	Lumumba mysteriously leaves residence in Léopoldville, probably in hope of reaching Stanleyville.
November 30:	Lumumba arrested at Mweka.

1961

January 17:	Lumumba and two other prisoners flown to Elisabethville.
February 12:	According to Katanga authorities, Lumumba and his companions are killed during an attempted escape.
February 21:	Security Council calls for withdrawal and evacuation of all Belgian troops and mercenaries; ONUC sets time limit for surrender of mercenaries.

September 13:   ONUC met by force; fighting in Elisabethville and Katanga.

September 12:   Hammarskjöld leaves N.Y., arrives Léopoldville September 13 amid fighting between ONUC and Congolese.

September 15:   Tshombe proposes meeting Hammarskjöld at Bancroft, Northern Rhodesia, on September 17; agrees to cease-fire.

September 17:   Hammarskjöld dies in plane crash near Ndola, Northern Rhodesia.

November 11:   U Thant appointed Acting Secretary General of UN.

November 24:   Security Council adopts resolution opposing secessionist activities in Katanga and for the first time authorizes Secretary General to use force to remove foreign mercenaries.

December 21:   Kitona agreement signed by Tshombe and Adoula recognizing authority of central government and ending secession of Katanga.

1962

December 24:   UN troops in Elisabethville and other towns fired upon.

December 28:   U Thant authorizes military action against Tshombe's forces.

1963

January 3:   ONUC crosses Lufira River and enters Jadotville without opposition; Tshombe flees to Rhodesia.

January 14:   Tshombe ends secession of Katanga.

June 30:   Withdrawal of UN forces completed.

1964

July 9:   Renewed conflict in Congo: Adoula resigns;
                 Tshombe heads transitional government, opposed
                 by insurgent forces.

1965

Fall: Tshombe deprived of seat in parliament; in fear
                 for his life, he flees to Europe, ending in Madrid.

1967

July 1:   Tshombe's plane hijacked to Algeria.

1969

June 30:   Tshombe dies in confinement in Algiers.

VIEW FROM THE UN

The crisis in the Congo was, in many ways, the culmination of a
series of events that had their cause and origin in the failure of the
former Belgian colonial administration to prepare the Congolese
adequately for the independence that was granted to them on June
30, 1960. There was an overwhelming opinion at the United Nations that under the Belgian administration a policy of paternalism
was consistently practiced. While the Congolese enjoyed a stand-
ard of living higher than that of most other African countries, the
Belgian authorities did not promote their political advancement.
The education of the African population was oriented to produce,
at best, clerks, skilled workers, and sergeants rather than man-
agers, administrators, engineers, educators, and officers. Not until
1957 were political activities tolerated in the territory. Arrangements for independence were made only at the beginning of 1960,
at a round-table conference in which Congolese leaders participated. The first legislative elections ever held in the Congo took
place in May 1960. Parliament met for the first time on June 17,

and the First Central Government, with Mr. Kasavubu as President and Mr. Patrice Lumumba as Prime Minister, was established on June 23, only a week before independence.

A consequence of this policy was that when the Congolese were given independence, they were ill-prepared for it. There were at that time only seventeen Congolese university graduates and not a single doctor or engineer. There were few political leaders with any experience and none with truly national experience, and there were no experienced African administrators.

In order to keep the administrative machinery and technical services running after independence, the Belgian government put at the disposal of the Congolese government, under the treaty of friendship, assistance and co-operation. The treaty was signed by the two governments but never ratified by their parliaments. At the time of independence, however, there were more than 10,000 Belgian administrators and technicians, and many army officers. Much hope was placed in the *Force Publique,* well-trained and armed, and entirely officered by Belgians.

On July 5, 1960, five days after the Congo attained independence, certain elements of the *Force Publique* in Léopoldville, dissatisfied over the failure of the authorities to Africanize their cadres, mutinied. The mutiny soon spread to other towns in the Congo, including Elisabethville. Some of the mutineers went on a rampage during which they manhandled Belgians in general and in some cases committed rape. These disturbances led to a mass exodus of the Belgian population, including almost all the administrators and technicians put at the disposal of the Congolese government under the friendship treaty. Their departure entailed a nearly complete breakdown of essential services and, in many parts of the country, the interruption of economic activities.

When the disturbances broke out, the Belgian government sought to impress upon Prime Minister Patrice Lumumba the need to invoke the Belgo-Congolese friendship treaty, and, to maintain law and order, to request the intervention, under that treaty, of the Belgian troops stationed in the military bases of Kamina and Kitona. This Mr. Lumumba adamantly refused to do, contending that his government was able to restore law and order without outside help. In this connection, Dr. Ralph J. Bunche, who had come to the Congo to attend the independence ceremonies as the representative of Secretary General Dag Hammarskjöld, warned the Belgian ambassador in Léopoldville of the serious consequences that could follow if the Belgian troops were called out without the consent of the Congolese government. He pointed out that the Belgian government could bring up the question of excesses before the Security Council.

Despite Dr. Bunche's warning, however, the Belgian government unilaterally decided to intervene. On the morning of July 10, 1960, Belgian troops, following an appeal by Moise Tshombe, President of the Katanga provincial government, moved into Elisabethville. Subsequently, other Belgian troops occupied several towns in the Congo, including the capital, Léopoldville. On July 11, one day after the arrival of Belgian troops in Elisabethville, Mr. Tshombe proclaimed the independence of Katanga. In proclaiming independence, Tshombe was not acting alone; the move was made with the unconcealed help of Belgian advisers, and was backed by Belgian troops. Thus from the outset, outside intervention became inextricably linked with the secession of Katanga. This posed a threat to international peace and security in the immediate area of the Congo and in Africa as a whole, a threat that was made more dangerous by the evident interest of certain groups in the riches of Katanga.

With the national independence and territorial integrity of its country threatened by foreign military intervention and secessionist activities, the government of the Congo, unable to maintain law and order and to ensure the operation of its essential services, first turned to the United States, as I have mentioned, and then, on the advice of President Eisenhower, brought the question to the United Nations.

THE UNITED NATIONS FORCE
AND ITS CRITICS

It is difficult for the general public to realize fully the magnitude of the task confronting the United Nations force (commonly known by its French initials as ONUC). With an area as large as the whole of Western Europe or eighty times the size of Belgium, its former ruler, a large part of the Congo (the bush) was still isolated from the outside world. Its African population, which numbered at that time about fourteen million, is composed of a great many tribes having different languages and customs; tribal animosities among them, moreover, were very strong at the time of independence. Many of the resident Europeans, most of whom were Belgian, did not fully understand the nature and principles of the United Nations operation in the Congo.

When the United Nations operation got underway in the Congo soon after the middle of July 1960, it found the country in a state of chaos. The administrative machinery of government and essential services had in a large measure collapsed. Economic life had almost completely stopped. There was an acute food shortage in many areas, not for lack of food, but because the food distribution system had broken down. Belgian military intervention had also raised among the Congolese intense feelings of hatred and fear. As the government was unable to assume its normal responsibilities, the tasks of maintaining law and order, of continuing essential services, and restoring normal economic activities, fell almost entirely upon ONUC.

The purposes and objectives of ONUC were defined by several resolutions of the Security Council. Stated briefly, they were: to assist the government in restoring and maintaining national unity and law and order; to protect the country from external interference in its internal affairs, particularly through the elimination of the mercenaries; to assist in the development of essential public services, especially health and communications; and to assist in economic and social development by a long-term program of training and technical assistance. In pursuit of these objectives, the United Nations operation adhered to the principle of avoiding any interference in the internal political affairs, national or provincial, of the Congo. It therefore never supported or opposed any Congolese personality or faction. Moreover, the United Nations force, while armed, operated under the strict principle of employing its arms only for self-defense.

Many critics of the United Nations operation in the Congo

argued, however, that it conflicted with the principle of self-determination, although both the Security Council and the General Assembly agreed that the operation was in no way in conflict with the principle of self-determination. Indeed, self-determination was, and still is, a fundamental United Nations principle. The fact is that there was no question of self-determination involved in the Congo or in Katanga. The Congo was admitted to the United Nations, following its independence, as a united state comprising several provinces, including the province of Katanga. This unified Congo had been agreed upon by all of the Congolese tribal and provincial leaders, including Mr. Tshombe, at a round-table conference in Brussels shortly before independence. Of his own free choice, Mr. Tshombe opted for unity at this conference.

As regards Katanga, it is important to note that the people of Katanga themselves had opposed secession. In February 1960, a few months before independence, the political parties of the Congo, including the Conakat Party of Mr. Tshombe, agreed that "the Congo within its actual frontiers shall constitute an independent state, the inhabitants of which possess one and the same nationality."[2] It is also important to note that no sovereign state in the world ever recognized the independence of Katanga—indeed, not a single state had even endorsed the secessionist effort.

In addition, Mr. Tshombe's provincial government was never able to exercise effective control over the northern half of the province. Mr. Tshombe himself on numerous occasions had repudiated secession and independence for Katanga. Even after my appointment as Acting Secretary General, he reiterated his attitude in his declaration signed at Kitona on December 21, 1961. In the period from March to June 1962, in the course of his formal talks in Léopoldville (now Kinshasa) with Cyrille Adoula, Mr. Tshombe reassured the Prime Minister of his total repudiation of the secession and independence of Katanga. When in September 1962 I offered a formal Plan of National Reconciliation, he accepted it without reservation, as did Prime Minister Adoula. On January 14, 1963, he made a voluntary declaration at Kolwezi that he would no longer engage in secessionist activities.

---

[2] *United Nations Official Records.*

I mention these specific dates and places because it was a peculiar trait of Mr. Tshombe's character that he *always* went back on his promises, assurances, and declarations.

MEETING THE CRITICS

The United Nations and its Secretaries General—Dag Hammarskjöld and myself—were targets of criticism from several sides, for completely different reasons. Many critics maintained that the United Nations should not have used force in the Congo, while others felt that the United Nations was perfunctory in ending the secession of Katanga.

I vividly remember an episode in Washington, D.C., on Thursday, September 13, 1962, when I was an official guest of President Kennedy. After the President's luncheon, undersecretary of state George Ball and Mrs. Ball gave me a reception in the John Quincy Adams Room in the State Department. At 5:00 P.M., I was standing in the reception line with Mr. and Mrs. Ball, when the guests started to arrive. A few minutes later, a very intense person entered the room, shook hands with the hosts and then with me. He looked straight into my face and said, "Don't send any more UN troops to the Congo." I was completely taken aback; while I was groping for words, he left the room without joining the other guests. I asked George Ball who he was, and he told me that the guest who came to the reception for a few seconds to convey a special message to me was Congressman Wayne Hays of Ohio.

This was not an isolated case. The late Senator Thomas Dodd of Connecticut was among the most vehement critics of the United Nations for using force in its operations in the Congo, and especially against "the most civilized African statesman—Mr. Moise Tshombe." He used to make long statements on the floor of the United States Senate in defense of Tshombe, and against the United Nations and the U. S. State Department. In the course of a two-hour speech in the Senate on August 3, 1962, for instance, he castigated the UN's "repeated threats of military action against Katanga, the cheap abuse of Katanga and the Katangese leaders by UN officials up to the rank of Secretary General U Thant, and our consistent unfriendliness and total lack of contact or rapport with Tshombe."

Dag Hammarskjöld once told me that during his tenure as Secretary General, he had never received as much hate mail on any issue as he had on the Congo. The explanation was not hard to find. Undersecretary Ball, in answering the critics, said on December 19, 1961: "It is the revenues Mr. Tshombe has been able to obtain by taxing the production under his control, the soldiers of fortune and writers of propaganda he has been able to mobilize with these revenues, and the encouragement he has received from outside financial interests, that have given the peculiar flavor to the Katangese attempt at secession."[3]

A few days later, the assistant secretary of state for African affairs, G. Mennen Williams, followed with a sharp attack on the "horrendous lies of indiscriminate mayhem by the UN troops"[4] fabricated by the Katanga propaganda machine. The deputy assistant secretary of state for public affairs, Carl T. Rowan (who later became a United States delegate to the United Nations) hit even harder, singling out for attack Michel Struelens, director general of the Katanga Information Office, "who operates out of some rather plush quarters in New York."[5] Mr. Rowan continued, "By spreading around at least $140,000 over the past year, Mr. Struelens has gotten some extremely vocal help in dispensing a string of myths and a stream of misinformation about Katanga and the Congo."

Where did his money come from? Mr. Rowan had the following revelations: "Despite all of the Congo's troubles, this Belgian-controlled firm (*Union Minière du Haut-Katanga*) had net profits of $47 million in 1960. *Union Minière* pays about 80 per cent of the tax revenues of Katanga—and I need not tell you any organization that contributes that much of a province's revenues is going to be a powerful force in the affairs of that province."[6]

Incidentally, an influential newspaper published in Rio De

---

[3] *U. S. Department of State Press Release,* December 19, 1961.
[4] *The New Republic,* January 8, 1962.
[5] Ibid.
[6] Ibid.

Janeiro, *Tribuna da Imprensa,* in its issue of December 12, 1961, reported that a million dollars had been deposited in a Zurich bank by Tshombe for use by Mr. Struelens. To my knowledge, that report was never denied.

Some explanation is called for to answer those critics who have maintained—and some still maintain—that the United Nations should not have used force in its operations in the Congo.

In the first place, the UN troops in the Congo used their arms only as a last resort and in self-defense under attack. The employment of force was thus severely limited. Under the resolutions of the Security Council, force could be used only under three conditions: namely, ultimate self-defense, as a last resort in the prevention of civil war, and as a last resort in the ejection of mercenaries. During their four years in the Congo, UN troops resorted to arms, in a significant way, only on three occasions:

The first was the attempt to round up foreign mercenaries, an operation that began peacefully on August 28, 1961, with the support (as I have already described) of Mr. Tshombe himself. By the middle of September, however, the UN effort encountered resistance from the mercenaries, who fired on the UN troops. The result was firing and skirmishing, mainly in Elisabethville, on several subsequent days.

The second conflict involving UN troops occurred a few weeks after my assumption of duties as Acting Secretary General, in December 1961. Incited by Mr. Tshombe and some of his associates, the mercenaries attacked UN personnel in Elisabethville and set up roadblocks to prevent the movement of UN troops and cut them off from the airport. The UN had to eliminate the roadblocks and re-establish its freedom of movement by resort to arms. This action, with its limited objectives, began on December 5 and was completed on December 19.

The third and last conflict was "Operation Grand Slam." This operation, which I discuss in detail on pages 143–45, established complete freedom of movement for all UN personnel in the whole of Katanga and led to the defeat of Mr. Tshombe and his renunciation of secession on January 9, 1963. Here I will only point out that the operation was provoked by Mr. Tshombe's forces. In December 1962, the Katangese *Gendarmerie,* commanded by its mercenary officers, opened fire on UN positions in Elisabethville —without any provocation—and continued sporadic firing at them for six days. In this situation, the UN troops displayed remarkable restraint, for they obeyed scrupulously their commander's orders not to return the Katangese fire, even though they suffered casualties.

In these three episodes of fighting there had been, inevitably, some casualties among the military and also among the civilian population. By any customary standards of military appraisal, however, the casualties among both civilians and military had been remarkably light, due principally to the severe restraint exercised by the United Nations troops, notwithstanding the almost continuous provocations to which they had been subjected.

Allegations of atrocities against civilians by UN troops were also made both during Mr. Hammarskjöld's tenure and mine. For the most part, they were wild and irresponsible. They were a deliberate product of the propaganda sponsored and paid for by the Katanga "information machine." There had been a few instances of apparently deplorable conduct attributed to one or another UN individual soldier. In every such instance, a prompt and thorough investigation ensued, with a view to establishing guilt and administering proper punishment, under the force's regulations.

The United States government, both under Presidents Eisenhower and Kennedy, along with the majority of member states, agreed not only with the purposes and objectives described above, but also with the manner in which these objectives were sought by the United Nations. Some historians and observers, however, believe that the United Nations and Secretary General Dag Hammarskjöld were merely serving U.S. interests in the Congo. In their view, U.S. policy was directed at eliminating leftist Congolese leaders like Lumumba and Gizenga from the political scene, and installing anticommunists like Kasavubu and Mobutu in power. To achieve this objective, they said, the United States, from time to time, helped the United Nations with the provision of transport airplanes and other supplies, and even endorsed the use of force, as authorized by the Security Council in November 1961.

The government of the United Kingdom, however, insisted from time to time that the United Nations should under no circumstances use force in the Congo, not even when its resolutions were being flouted. The British attitude was based on a multitude of factors. There was a very powerful Katanga lobby in both Houses of Parliament. The British press, by and large, supported Moise Tshombe, who was seen as the most reliable custodian of British mining interests in Katanga. Some influential members of Parliament openly supported the recruitment of mercenaries from Rhodesia and South Africa, to serve Tshombe.

France was still more emphatic against the use of force and all United Nations involvement "in the internal affairs" of any state. In the past, France had been against any UN involvement in what it considered to be purely domestic matters. The General Assembly consideration of the French-Algerian conflict was highly resented in France, and so was the UN consideration of, and Dag Hammarskjöld's personal involvement in, the French-Tunisian dispute. No doubt, another factor in shaping French policy toward the Congo was her sympathy for Belgian interests, both political and financial. The fact that there was a considerable number of French mercenaries (veterans of the Algerian war) in the pay of Tshombe prompted an influential section of the French press to espouse the cause of Katanga secession.

Among the great powers, the Soviet Union alone identified itself with the policies of Prime Minister Lumumba, who, until his arrest and assassination, saw the UN role as being merely to help the central government militarily in ending the Katanga secessionist movement. This attitude was shared by several Afro-Asian countries at that time, such as Ghana, Guinea, Morocco, Indonesia, and the United Arab Republic.

While Senator Thomas Dodd, Representative Wayne Hays, and many others, including many influential members of the U. S. Congress and the British Parliament, were strongly critical of the United Nations for its "strong-arm policies" against Katanga and Moise Tshombe, Chairman Khrushchev and some Afro-Asian governments were equally vehement in their criticism of the UN for "dragging its feet" in implementing the Security Council resolutions to end the secessionist movement of Katanga. In their view, ONUC should have served as an arm of the central government in putting an end to Katanga's secessionist movement.

HAMMARSKJÖLD AND THE CONGO TRAGEDY: THE FIRST PHASE

During the first anxious days of the Congo crisis, Ralph Bunche was the Secretary General's special representative in the Congo. Hammarskjöld appointed him not only because he was already on the scene but also because he had complete faith in his impartiality. As I learned from the nearly ten years we worked together after I became Secretary General, Bunche was an international civil servant in the true sense of the word, and I cannot think of anyone in the upper echelon of the Secretariat dealing with political matters who was less nationalistic in his concept and his approach to problems. This was not true, however, of his Soviet opposite number, undersecretary Georgi Arkadev, who, perhaps inevitably, represented his government's point of view. This difficult and crucial question of divided loyalty, between the UN and one's nation, among the members of the Secretariat, I will discuss in more detail later.

In any case, because of his great faith in Bunche's impartiality, Hammarskjöld gave him that delicate assignment in the Congo, where both the United States and the Soviet Union had strong interests. While the United States wanted to see a unified anticommunist, or at least noncommunist, Congo under leaders like Kasavubu or Mobutu, the Soviet Union wanted a unified procommunist, or "progressive," Congo under leaders like Lumumba or Gizenga. The only thing the two nations could agree on was that the Congo should be united, with Katanga as an integral part of the country. Hammarskjöld drew the wrath of the Soviet Union not only for his interpretation of the United Nations resolutions—which differed from the Soviet interpretation—but also for his increasing reliance on Bunche, an American, while completely ignoring Arkadev, a Russian, in formulating his Congo policies. Arkadev never sat in "the Congo club," the name given to a small inner group of advisers around Hammarskjöld. Originally, "the Congo club" comprised Bunche and undersecretary Andrew Cordier (another American), Major General Indar Jit Rikhye, military adviser to the Secretary General (Indian), Sir Alexander MacFarquhar, chief adviser on civilian operations in the Congo, and Heinz Wieschhoff, Arkadev's deputy. (Wieschhoff died with Hammarskjöld in the plane crash.)

Bunche, as mentioned earlier, had been in Léopoldville to represent Hammarskjöld at the Congo's independence ceremonies. Then, when widespread disorders erupted, Hammarskjöld asked Bunche to stay on as special representative. In the face of the mounting Soviet criticism of Hammarskjöld's handling of the Congo crisis, the Secretary General negotiated with the government of India for the appointment of Rajeshwar Dayal, the Indian high commissioner (ambassador) to Pakistan. Meanwhile, Bunche, conscious of the political difficulties caused by his assignment, and of the increasing friction with Prime Minister Lumumba, informed UN headquarters of his very strong desire to be replaced as soon as possible. Hammarskjöld decided to comply with this request. At the same time, however, he felt that, pending the arrival of Dayal, there should be someone to take charge of the Congo operations. He asked Cordier to go to the Congo, which he did immediately. When Dayal arrived in New York on August 30, 1960, he found that Cordier had left four days earlier.

Cordier's brief spell in the Congo was marked by dramatic developments. On September 5, President Kasavubu summoned him to the presidential palace and informed him of his plans to announce Lumumba's dismissal as Prime Minister that night. Dayal had arrived in Léopoldville the previous day but had not yet taken charge of ONUC. That night, September 5, President Kasavubu announced in a radio broadcast that Prime Minister Lumumba had failed in his duties; he dismissed the government with immediate effect. The President then entrusted Mr. Joseph Ileo, president of the Senate, with the task of forming a new government.

Mr. Lumumba violently opposed this proclamation and on the same night called a meeting of the Council of Ministers, which decided to depose Kasavubu on the ground that he had violated the Fundamental Law in dismissing the Prime Minister.

Soon afterward, Lumumba in turn made a radio broadcast, announcing that he had dismissed President Kasavubu. He also called on the Congolese people to decide which of the two actions should prevail. In this confused situation, Cordier ordered the Congo's airports closed to all but United Nations planes. On September 6, he ordered the national radio station closed, and did not give Lumumba permission to broadcast again. Although Lumumba had no means of communicating his views to the Congolese people, Kasavubu could broadcast his statements through the much more powerful Brazzaville transmitter across the river. (President Abbé Fulbert Youlou of the [French] Congo Republic, of which Brazzaville was the capital, was a kinsman of Kasavubu.) By that time, Cordier had already put a UN guard around the President's residence and another contingent around the Parliament building.

This action aroused angry protests not only from the Soviet Union but from several African states. The Afro-Asian group met at United Nations headquarters on Wednesday afternoon, September 7, to consider the situation. The consensus was that Lumumba should have been given the opportunity to appeal to Parliament for a decision as to whether the President or the Prime Minister should prevail. Cordier's action in closing down the national radio station was widely criticized. Rajeshwar Dayal, who was in Léopoldville waiting to take charge of the UN office from Cordier, was not happy at the latter's action. He even thought of flying to New York to express his misgivings to the Secretary General. In view of the fact that he was to assume duties in two days, however, he confined himself to dispatching his views in writing to Mr. Hammarskjöld.

As the following pages will reveal, Kasavubu's dismissal of Lumumba, and the latter's inability to appeal to the Congolese Parliament, generated a chain of events culminating in the death of the first Congolese Prime Minister.

Another tragic aspect of the UN's involvement in the Congo was the frequent differences that arose between ONUC and the

Congolese government. In order to carry out its extraordinary task, ONUC needed the full co-operation of the Congo government. Unfortunately, its relations with Prime Minister Patrice Lumumba became strained after the first few weeks of UN involvement in the Congo. That grave conflict was related mainly to the interpretation of the mandate of the United Nations. According to Ralph Bunche, who was highly critical of Mr. Lumumba's "arrogance," the clash of personalities between the Prime Minister and Dag Hammarskjöld was also a factor in the conflict.

To understand the differences between Prime Minister Lumumba and Secretary General Dag Hammarskjöld, it is necessary to revert to the nature of the Congolese government's appeal to the United Nations on July 12, 1960, and the Security Council's resolution adopted two days later. In its appeal to the United Nations, the Congo government specifically requested military assistance to end the secession of Katanga, but the Security Council resolution of July 14, 1960, contained no mention of this point. On July 22, the Council recognized that it had dealt with the Republic as a unit, and asked all states to refrain from any action that might undermine the territorial integrity and political independence of the Congo. In August, the Council called for the immediate withdrawal of Belgian troops from Katanga. It also made clear, however, as I have indicated, that the United Nations was not to take sides in Congolese internal conflicts, constitutional or otherwise; nor was the Organization to be used to influence the outcome of any such conflict.

But Patrice Lumumba never saw it that way. When he came to New York on Monday, July 25, shortly after independence, he made his intention clear in a meeting with Dag Hammarskjöld. After talking with the Secretary General, he addressed a meeting of the Afro-Asian group at 3:30 P.M. on the same day. As the permanent representative of Burma to the United Nations, I attended the meeting. Lumumba stressed the dangers of imperialism and the imperative need for the United Nations to eradicate it, especially in Africa. He did not refer to his meeting earlier with the Secretary General, but it was disclosed much later by the permanent representative of the Congo, Thomas Kanza, that there had been "a very heated exchange" between Lumumba and Hammarskjöld. Kanza, the son of the mayor of Léopoldville and the first Congolese graduate from Louvain University in Belgium, was an accomplished diplomat. In spite of his very brief assignment at the United Nations, he earned the esteem of his fellow ambassadors. He was responsible for the absence of fireworks in Lumumba's exposition of his case, both at the Afro-Asian group meeting and at the press conference he gave on the same day. Kanza tried his best to prepare the ground for a smooth Lumumba-Hammarskjöld meeting, but he failed. Lumumba was impetuous and proud; Hammarskjöld, equally proud and highly sensitive. The two never got along well, as Kanza had wished, and the difference was due more to the clash of personalities than to the divergence of political ideologies.

The sole purpose of Lumumba's visit to the United Nations was to get an assurance from Hammarskjöld that the Secretary General would extend UN military assistance to the Congolese government against the secessionist movement of Katanga. This the Secretary General refused firmly. He repeated what he had said only a few days before in his first report to the Security Council—that the UN could not be a party to any internal conflict. Lumumba found Hammarskjöld's position difficult to understand. To him the issue was simple: his government had asked the United Nations to end the secessionist movement of Katanga, and the UN had complied with its request. Why should ONUC not help Léopoldville to subdue Katanga by force? Hammarskjöld's view, which had the support of the vast majority of the member states, was that Katanga's secession was just an internal Congolese affair, and that the primary purpose of ONUC, as defined by the Security Council, was to evict foreign mercenaries from the Congo and restore law and order.

In the eyes of many small member states, the issue went beyond the simple question of UN military support of the Congolese central government, or the eviction of foreign mercenaries from the country. They saw the main UN role as that of counteracting the threat of direct United States-Soviet intervention in the Congo. My reports to the government of Burma at that time stressed the UN role in the Congo in that context.

One result of the Lumumba-Hammarskjöld split was Lumumba's request for direct unilateral Soviet aid. This request was promptly met by the Soviet Union, and trucks and airplanes started arriving in Léopoldville. The United States, in turn, tried to take countermeasures by encouraging Mobutu to take control of the government.

From August 1960, the Soviet government became increasingly condemnatory of United Nations operations in the Congo. Soviet criticism was extended to Mr. Hammarskjöld, who was alleged "to have collaborated with NATO" in presenting his plan for UN operations in the Congo. In an official note issued on August 6, 1960, the Soviet government asserted that the Security Council decisions of July 14 and 22, regarding the withdrawal of Belgian forces, were not being carried out. It proposed that if the UN command, "with NATO participation," remained unwilling to implement those resolutions, they should be replaced by troops from states prepared to carry them out. Prime Minister Patrice Lumumba of the Congo put his full weight behind the Soviet position. He held, as we have seen, that the UN forces should be used, by all possible means, to subdue the rebel government of Katanga.

Mr. Hammarskjöld, on the contrary, took the position that the terms of the resolution precluded the United Nations from influencing the course of the conflict between the central and provincial governments of Katanga, other than through the neutralization and withdrawal of all foreign mercenaries.

The extreme dissatisfaction of the Soviet Union was reflected in a proposal made in September 1960 to the Security Council to give the control of the UN operations to a group of representatives of countries already participating in the force. This group would act in conjunction with the Security Council; the role of Secretary General was not even mentioned in that proposal. The Soviet statement asserted that the real leaders of the Congolese people, such as Patrice Lumumba, were being "driven out by NATO agents," and that they were being replaced by "NATO hirelings," such as General Mobutu and Mr. Tshombe. Then the demand was made that the United Nations should establish a special commission of Afro-Asian representatives to investigate the sources from which General Mobutu's men were being financed and supplied with arms. Prominence was given in the Moscow press to reports from the Congo that General Mobutu and Mr. Tshombe were receiving military equipment from Belgian, French, South African, and NATO sources, although there was no direct evidence to confirm such reports.

The Soviet Union's condemnation of Hammarskjöld and ONUC thus grew more intense, until Dayal took over from Cordier the post of special representative of the Secretary General on September 8, four days after his arrival in the Congo.

Hammarskjöld's appointment of Dayal to that delicate and highly controversial post was a very shrewd political move on the part of the Secretary General. The hawk-nosed, sad-eyed Indian diplomat had shown his ability and sound political judgment as a member of the United Nations Observer Group in Lebanon in 1958. He had a vast administrative background as a senior member of the Indian Civil Service, and when Hammarskjöld chose him to succeed Bunche and Cordier, he was serving as his country's ambassador to Pakistan. The most significant factor in his choice, however, was that he came from Nehru's India, which had provided ONUC with the largest number of troops: 5,500, of 18,000 at ONUC's peak strength. Nehru had consistently supported Hammarskjöld in his interpretation of UN resolutions—and nobody had ever accused Nehru of being anti-Soviet! Another advantage of Dayal's appointment was that he knew Hammarskjöld's mind and way of thinking, and such understanding stood him in good stead in performing his functions with initiative and courage. Above all, he also understood Lumumba's political philosophy, which only an observant diplomat from a nonaligned country could understand. Understandably therefore, his first clash was not with Lumumba but with Ambassador Clare Timberlake of the United States and Ambassador Ian Scott of the United Kingdom, both serving in Léopoldville. Scott, who was also a member of the Indian Civil Service, was reported to be a pompous diplomat with a sneer for independent and nonwhite members of that service. During colonial days, there was a well-known witticism in India and Burma that the Indian Civil Service was neither Indian, nor civil, nor a service. Besides, Scott happened to be serving a government that was supported by a very powerful Katanga lobby both in the House of Lords and the

House of Commons. Dayal's appointment and his frequent clashes with Scott stilled Soviet criticism of Hammarskjöld and ONUC operations, at least for some time.

THE DEATH OF LUMUMBA

Dayal faced the first test of fire six days after his assumption of office. On September 14, Colonel Joseph Mobutu, chief of staff of the army, assumed control of the government, suspended Parliament, and issued warrants in the name of President Kasavubu to arrest Lumumba and some other ministers. Under the Congolese Fundamental Law (*Loi Fondamentale*), consent of Parliament was required to arrest the Prime Minister and other members of the Cabinet. Since the Parliament had been suspended, however, there was no means of ascertaining its views. Dayal, therefore, with the consent of Hammarskjöld, prevented the *Armée Nationale Congolaise* (Congolese National Army) from arresting Lumumba and other leaders.

On September 15, the day after Colonel Mobutu announced that the army had assumed control, Mr. Lumumba took refuge in the Ghanaian officers' mess of the ONUC detachment at the Congolese army's main camp at Léopoldville. On the afternoon of the same day, President Kasavubu and Prime Minister designate Ileo asked ONUC to arrest Mr. Lumumba, but Dayal firmly refused to accede to this request, pointing out that such a step was totally outside ONUC's powers. On the same day, Mr. Lumumba, feeling that he was in danger, asked the assistance of Ghanaian troops, who, with the help of some members of the national *Gendarmerie,* were able to escort Mr. Lumumba out of the camp at nightfall to a private residential building. Dayal then posted UN troops around their residences, thus incurring the hostility of the Kasavubu-Mobutu group. (Thus from the early days of his assignment, Dayal became persona non grata with the powerful Kasavubu-Mobutu group.)

Mr. Lumumba then received United Nations protection until November 27, 1960, when he left his house under mysterious circumstances, probably in the hope of reaching Stanleyville, which was his stronghold.

At this point, I must interrupt my narrative of these dramatic events to explain that about two months after Lumumba's assassination, the General Assembly established a commission to investigate the circumstances of his death. On May 21, 1961, the commission, which was composed of representatives of Burma, Ethiopia, Mexico, and Tago, requested permission to visit the Congo. But in a letter to Dag Hammarskjöld, J. M. Bomboko, Foreign Minister of the Congo, said that his government opposed the creation of the commission, and that in its view, the death of Lumumba was strictly an internal matter. The commission therefore attempted to collect all available evidence in Europe, and, in London, Brussels, and Geneva, held sixty-six meetings, of which sixteen were devoted to the hearing of witnesses. (While the commission was drafting its report, incidentally, it learned of the presence of Mr. Tshombe in Geneva and invited him to appear. Although the commission's letter was delivered to him personally, Mr. Tshombe did not acknowledge its receipt and did not appear.) The following pages are based on the commission's findings.

According to Dayal, Major General Indar Jit Rikhye, head of ONUC, and other witnesses who testified before the commission, the circumstances leading to Mr. Lumumba's death can be summarized as follows:

It appeared that on the night of November 27, 1960, the United Nations Moroccan guard on duty at the gate of Mr. Lumumba's residence saw a large black car drive toward them. As was customary, they stopped the car, which they recognized. No suspicion was raised, since they had seen that car, with the same driver, go in and out a number of times; it was a car that frequently came into the residence and left with various other passengers. So they let the car in, and after a short while it left with three passengers—all men.

General Rikhye explained that the ONUC guard only controlled the entry of people to the residence to "make sure that they were not carrying weapons, knives, daggers, bombs, or anything of that kind and thus prevent any personal danger to Mr.

Lumumba." He told the commission, "We never checked anybody who went out and . . . even if Mr. Lumumba had been recognized leaving his residence, he would not have been stopped because he was free to leave his house as and when he wished."

General Rikhye also told the commission that the Congolese authorities subsequently came to ask ONUC to help them find Mr. Lumumba. On that score, Mr. Dayal had issued very clear orders to the United Nations military command; these were the words: "ONUC will not under any circumstances provide intelligence or assistance to the pursuer or the pursued." General Rikhye assured the commission that "these instructions were rigidly obeyed."

From all information available, a certain Major Pongo was in charge of the search, and it was this officer who arrested Mr. Lumumba at a village called Mweka about twenty miles from Port Francqui, and about four hundred miles from Léopoldville. Major Pongo had earlier asked the ONUC forces to put a helicopter at his disposal "to enable him to look for Mr. Lumumba." The United Nations representatives told him that they could not place any United Nations transport at his disposal, and that the search was entirely his own responsibility.

The commission was unable to hear any eyewitnesses in regard to the actual circumstances of the arrest. Some relevant facts, however, emerged from information given by ONUC headquarters in Léopoldville. On November 30 or December 1, Mr. Lumumba made a speech before a gathering at Mweka, and it was then that the soldiers of the Congolese Army who were pursuing him learned of his whereabouts and arrested him. Those soldiers then took him to Port Francqui, from which he was sent to Léopoldville.

According to ONUC troops stationed at Ndjili airport at Léopoldville, Mr. Lumumba landed there at 5:15 P.M. on December 2, under close guard. The prisoner was then placed on a lorry and taken the same day to an unknown destination.

To my knowledge, there was no rational explanation why ONUC troops failed to intervene. If they had attempted to do something, then I cannot trace any official record to that effect. Perhaps in strict legal terms, intervention would have meant an interference in the domestic affairs of the Congo, but I felt then, and

I still feel now, that in this particular case, protection of Patrice Lumumba by the United Nations might have been justified, since it would have had the effect of preserving the status quo ante.

The following morning, December 3, he was removed under a very heavy escort of armored cars and heavily armed Congolese soldiers to Thysville. His departure was witnessed by members of the international press, who reported that Mr. Lumumba walked to the truck with considerable difficulty. He was in a disheveled condition, and his face showed signs of recent blows. Again, I see no official records stating what ONUC attempted to do to save the life of Mr. Lumumba.

United Nations troops in Thysville, however, reported on the same day that Mr. Lumumba was under detention in Camp Hardy. He was said to have been suffering from serious injuries received before his arrival. His head had been shaven, his hands remained tied, and he was kept in a cell under conditions reported to be inhumane with respect to health and hygiene.

The ONUC authorities in Léopoldville made representations to President Kasavubu and Colonel Mobutu in order that the prisoner should be treated decently. Secretary General Dag Hammarskjöld also made representations in letters addressed on December 3 and 5 to President Kasavubu, expressing the grave concern of the international community as well as his own, regarding the arrest of Mr. Lumumba.

President Kasavubu, in the course of his reply to the Secretary General, dated December 7, 1960, said that since September, Mr. Lumumba had been under a warrant of arrest for a number of reasons, "the validity of which has been amply demonstrated." He concluded with these words: "Please regard this question, as I and the entire country do, as a domestic matter."

After the approaches described above, the United Nations representatives in the Congo "received assurances that no harm would be done to Mr. Lumumba," according to the information provided to the commission by General Rikhye. He added: "I personally met Colonel Mobutu and he informed me that Mr. Lumumba would have been killed by the Congolese soldiers, and that it was only through his (Colonel Mobutu's) intervention that he was not killed."

Then, on January 17, 1961, dramatic developments took place. On that day, Mr. Lumumba and his two companions—Mr. Okito and Mr. Mpolo—left the garrison at Thysville. The commission was unable to obtain precise information regarding the circumstances in which the prisoners left the garrison.

According to one witness, a representative of the Congolese *Sûreté* (security police) arrived at Thysville military camp on January 17 and informed Mr. Lumumba and his two companions that there had been a coup d'état at Léopoldville, that President Kasavubu, Colonel Mobutu, Mr. Bomboko, and Mr. Ileo, Prime Minister designate, were in prison, and that Mr. Lumumba was needed at Léopoldville to form a new government. Mr. Lumumba, who was convinced that he was going to emerge victorious from the crisis, apparently felt that his informant's intentions were sincere, and agreed to leave the garrison. According to the same source, Mr. Lumumba seemed to have been taken to Lukala airport, a few miles from Thysville, where he was put on a small aircraft (belonging to the Belgian company Air-brousse) with two companions, as well as the representative of the Congolese *Sûreté*. The aircraft then headed for Moanda, a small place on the shores of the Atlantic, where it landed a few minutes later. From there the four passengers were transferred to a DC-4 belonging to the Air Congo company and piloted by a Belgian named Bauwens. It appeared that the prisoners were beaten up while in this plane. According to a witness, all three were tied to one another and beaten up during the whole flight from Moanda to Elisabethville.

According to Mr. I. E. Berendson, ONUC representative at Elisabethville at the time, Mr. Tshombe also told him that he had personally seen Mr. Lumumba and his companions on the previous evening (January 17). Tshombe said that, as a result of the beating and ill-treatment the three men had received on the plane, they were "in a sad state," and that Mr. Lumumba, whose face was puffed up, had appealed to him, somewhat piteously, for his protection. Mr. Berendson added that he had told Mr. Tshombe that in his opinion it would be very much in the interest of the Katanga authorities, if they wished to avoid serious repercussions, to return Mr. Lumumba and his companions to Léopoldville, and in the meantime to take every precaution to see that the prisoners were not ill-treated in Katanga. He also asked Mr. Tshombe to request the International Committee of the Red Cross to visit the prisoners to make sure that they were being well-treated. Mr. Tshombe had agreed to consider this suggestion. No action was taken, however.

Another witness stated that Mr. Tshombe, Mr. Munongo, the interior minister, and some other ministers of the provincial government of Katanga were present at the time of the murder. He could not state the exact date of the event, although he supposed it to have occurred on the day the prisoners arrived at Elisabethville.

These versions are completely different from the official version of the Katangese authorities, who maintained that repeated requests had been made by the central government to Mr. Tshombe to accept Mr. Lumumba. Mr. Tshombe had consistently refused to accept him. One more request was made to Mr. Tshombe, and while he was considering the matter, he received the news that a special plane was about to land in Elisabethville with the prisoners on board. Only then was he aware of the arrival of Mr. Lumumba and his two colleagues at the airport.

In this connection, the commission noted that on January 19, the minister of information of Katanga issued the following communiqué: "At the request of President Kasavubu and with the consent of the Katanga Government, the traitor Patrice Lumumba had been transferred to Katanga as the prison at Thysville no longer offers sufficient guarantee."

The commission also noted that after the arrival of Mr. Lumumba and his associates in Elisabethville, the International Committee of the Red Cross requested that their representative be allowed to interview Mr. Lumumba. This request was refused. It was only some three weeks later, when the United Nations Conciliation Commission became insistent in its desire to interview Mr. Lumumba, that the Katanga authorities suddenly announced the escape of the prisoners, and that they had been killed by certain tribesmen on February 12.

The commission observed: "The conduct of Mr. Tshombe and Mr. Munongo was such that the Commission is of the opinion that they were not candid but that on the contrary they had definitely tried to put everybody on a false scent."

Then the commission came to some conclusions, the relevant parts of which are reproduced below:

> The weight of evidence is against the official version of the Government of the Katanga Province that Mr. Lumumba, Mr. Okito and Mr. Mpolo were killed by certain tribesmen on 12 February 1961. On the contrary, the Commission accepts as substantially true the evidence indicating that the prisoners were killed on 17 January 1961 after their arrival in a villa not far from Elisabethville and in all probability in the presence of high officials of the Government of Katanga Province, namely, Mr. Tshombe, Mr. Munongo and Mr. Kibwe, and that the escape story was staged.
>
> A great deal of suspicion is cast on a certain Colonel Huyghe, a Belgian mercenary, as being the actual perpetrator of Mr. Lumumba's murder which was committed in accordance with a prearranged plan and that a certain Captain Gat, also a Belgian mercenary, was at all times an accessary to the crime. Regarding Mr. Okito and Mr. Mpolo, the evidence is not clear as to who actually murdered them, but the indications are that they were murdered about the same time as Mr. Lumumba. The Commission wishes to put on record its views that President Kasa-Vubu and his aides, on the one hand, and the Provincial Government of Katanga headed by Mr. Tshombe on the other, should not escape responsibility for the death of Mr. Lumumba, Mr. Okito and Mr. Mpolo.

As I have observed in the preceding pages, the United Nations contributed, perhaps inadvertently, to the tragic end of Lumumba. First, the denial to him of radio facilities on September 6, 1960, by the Secretary General's special representative generated a chain of events leading to his arrest and assassination. Second, the inexplicable indifference, or lack of initiative, on the part of ONUC, when Lumumba was observed under arrest on December 2, 1960, and when he was taken on a lorry from Ndjili airport to an unknown destination, made his tragic end inevitable.

Patrice Lumumba was a very enigmatic man. He was no doubt a passionate patriot who in his lifetime—and even after his death—generated strong emotion: idolatry or condemnation. Those who had closely followed his life and work were amazed when his book *Congo My Country,* written in 1956–57, was published posthumously in 1962. It was a moderate and sober declaration of faith, most unlike his restless, impetuous, and even foolhardy life.

Colin Lagum of the London *Observer,* a knowledgeable commentator on African matters, wrote in his brilliant foreword to the English edition of the book: "Not only did he quarrel with every United Nations representative in turn, but he ignored his own friends. . . . When he (Lumumba) was excited, his mind seemed to retreat behind an impenetrable glass wall; nothing got through him at all. It was unnerving. Incessantly he would repeat his own arguments over and over again. He saw enemies everywhere. In the end they destroyed him."

After Lumumba's assassination, both Hammarskjöld and Dayal came under increasing attack, not only from the Soviet Union, but also from many nonaligned countries. When the Security Council met on February 13 and Hammarskjöld confirmed the news of Lumumba's death, Ambassador Zorin charged Hammarskjöld with direct responsibility, and put out a statement saying that the Soviet government would have no further relations with Hammarskjöld. Two days later, on February 15, while Hammarskjöld was attending a session of the Security Council, a violent riot broke out in the public gallery of the Council chamber. In the ensuing melee, twenty UN guards were injured by various weapons wielded by hysterical rioters, who were roused to fury at the news of Lumumba's death. The main target of the demonstrators was apparently Hammarskjöld, and he had to be led out of the room while the rioters shouted "Get Hammarskjöld! Get Hammarskjöld!" They also shouted at Adlai Stevenson, who was speaking at the time.

Meanwhile, in Léopoldville, Dayal came under increasing attack for different reasons and from different quarters. He was accused of being procommunist and anti-Western. He had already alienated Kasavubu and Mobutu, who now asked for his removal. Thus Dayal's continued stay in Léopoldville became increasingly untenable. At his request, Hammarskjöld asked him to come to New York, and he arrived at United Nations headquarters on March 10, 1961. The Secretary General appointed Mekki Abbas (of the Sudan), executive secretary of the Economic Commission for Africa, as acting special representative in Léopoldville.

On May 25, Dayal was relieved of his duties at his own request, and Sture C. Linner (of Sweden), formerly chief of United Nations civilian operations in the Congo, was appointed officer-in-charge of the UN force in the Congo (ONUC).

Meanwhile, the attention of the United Nations had been focused on national reconciliation. On November 5, 1960, the Advisory Committee on the Congo in consultation with the Secretary General, had established a conciliation commission for the Congo consisting of the representatives of fifteen countries. The commission, which was to study the situation and attempt to help the Congolese toward a solution to the crisis, had decided to meet at Léopoldville on November 6, but had to postpone its departure because of the reluctance of President Kasavubu to admit it into the Congo. At the same time, Guinea, Indonesia, Mali, and the United Arab Republic decided to withdraw from the commission, because of their disagreement with the policies of the United Nations and Secretary General Hammarskjöld over the capture of Lumumba. Thus the number of members of the commission was reduced from fifteen to eleven.

The conciliation commission arrived in the Congo on January 3, 1961, and remained there until February 20, 1961, but did not receive the co-operation of the Congolese government under President Kasavubu. It was while the commission was still in Léopoldville that Prime Minister Lumumba was arrested and assassinated. Submitting its report to the General Assembly on March 21, 1961, the commission suggested, among other things, a summit conference of Congolese leaders in a neutral place, if necessary outside the Republic. The object of such a meeting would be to work out changes in the *Loi Fondamentale,* with a view to submitting amendments to a reconvened parliament.

The General Assembly considered the report of the commission and adopted a number of resolutions, in one of which a second conciliation commission, this time of six members (Argentina, Austria, Burma, Pakistan, Senegal, and Tunisia), was established to assist the Congolese leaders in achieving reconciliation and ending the political crisis. The commission met on August 28, 1961, under my chairmanship, and immediately after that meeting, I addressed a letter to Prime Minister Adoula informing him that the commission was at the disposal of his government "for the rendering of any assistance that the Government might consider helpful for the achievement of full national unity in the Congo."[7]

Then I proceeded to Belgrade to attend the conference of nonaligned governments, in which the Congo was represented by Prime Minister Adoula and deputy prime minister Gizenga, both of whom addressed the conference on September 5.

These two speeches were of particular interest to me since both of them touched on the United Nations and its Secretary General. While Mr. Adoula supported the actions the Secretary General in the Congo, Mr. Gizenga criticized the United Nations in the following words: "I shall not dwell upon the illegal acts that were performed on all sides, with the blessing of the United Nations. I deliberately refrain from doing so, firstly, because I have too much respect for international institutions, even when those who represent them betray their mission, and secondly, because the United Nations and the Governments represented in it are so imbued with a spirit of justice and peace that they have enabled right and truth to triumph." He drew a loud applause when he described the late Patrice Lumumba as "a true hero, a victim of the injustice of the two greatest plots that colonialism had ever hatched against one of its former subjects."

After these speeches, President Sukarno of Indonesia called on the delegates to pay tribute to the late Congolese Premier Patrice Lumumba with a minute's silence.

The two discordant speeches of Prime Minister Adoula and Mr. Gizenga were the subject of private comment, not only by the delegates attending the conference, but also by the international press corps that covered it. The late Dorothy Woodman (wife of Kingsley Martin, former editor of *The New Statesman* and *The Nation*) told me jokingly at a reception that evening that the two speeches must have been drafted by NATO and the Warsaw Pact countries, respectively.

The tragic death of Mr. Lumumba was very much on the minds of the delegates, and in the final declaration, a reference

---

[7] United Nations Document, August 28, 1961.

was made to the Congo in the following terms: "The participating countries demand that the tragic events in the Congo must not be repeated and they feel that it is the duty of the world community to continue to do everything in its power in order to erase the consequences and to prevent any further foreign intervention in this young African state, and to enable the Congo to embark freely upon the road of its independent development based on respect for its sovereignty, unity and its territorial integrity."

THE DEATH OF DAG HAMMARSKJÖLD

Although specific information is lacking about the actual murder of Patrice Lumumba, information is not lacking on the circumstances leading to his death; the evidence on the names of those who were likely to have been present at the murder scene are pretty well established. In the case of Dag Hammarskjöld, this does not obtain. For several months—even years—after his death, many speculations and assumptions were made about the tragic end of this most remarkable man. I have read scores of articles and half a dozen books that offer various theories of the events surrounding his death. They range from Dag Hammarskjöld's "suicidal psychosis" to a belief that Tshombe's Fouga Magister jets were responsible for his demise in the plane crash. Of course, by now the international community has come to accept the conclusions of the United Nations Investigating Commission formed under the General Assembly resolution adopted on September 27, 1961, two days before the Secretary General's burial at Uppsala in Sweden.

Under the terms of that resolution, the commission was "to conduct an investigation into all the conditions and circumstances" surrounding this tragedy. On December 8, 1961, a little over a month after my appointment as Acting Secretary General, the Assembly appointed the following persons as members of the Commission:

Mr. Justice Samuel Bankole Jones (Sierra Leone)
Mr. Raul Quijano (Argentina)
Mr. Justice Emil Sandstrom (Sweden)

Mr. Rishikesh Shaha (Nepal)
Mr. Nikola Srzentic (Yugoslavia)

Mr. Hammarskjöld left New York by air on September 12, 1961, and arrived in Léopoldville on September 13 to discuss with the central government the rapidly deteriorating situation in the country. At that time, ONUC was vigorously trying to give effect to the Security Council resolution of February 21, 1961, to take measures "for the immediate withdrawal and evacuation from the Congo of all Belgian and other foreign military and para-military personnel and political advisers not under the United Nations command, and mercenaries." Because of the total lack of co-operation of the provincial authorities of Katanga under Mr. Tshombe, ONUC was compelled to set a time limit for the surrender, for the purposes of evacuation, of all mercenaries in the service of the provincial authorities of Katanga.

On the expiration of the time limit, over a hundred mercenaries were still reported to be in Katanga, and on September 13, ONUC took precautionary measures to facilitate the task of apprehending and evacuating these men. These measures were met by force, and widespread fighting broke out at Elisabethville and in other Katangese cities. Hostilities were not limited to ground forces. Whereas the United Nations had no armed aircraft, the Katangese authorities put into action a Fouga Magister jet carrying two machine guns and a small bombload.

In the meantime, several contacts with Katangese officials were arranged for the purpose of bringing about an immediate cease-fire, but no result had been achieved until September 15, two days after Mr. Hammarskjöld's arrival in Léopoldville. On that day, the United Nations representative at Elisabethville received, through the British consul, a message informing the United Nations that Mr. Tshombe wished to meet the Secretary General at Bancroft in Northern Rhodesia on September 17. The Secretary General sent a reply expressing his willingness to meet Mr. Tshombe. He specified, however, that "the proposed meeting obviously requires that orders should be given beforehand for an immediate and effective cease-fire." He also suggested that as there were no adequate landing facilities for a large aircraft at Bancroft, the projected meeting should take place at Ndola, Northern Rhodesia.

On the morning of September 17, the British consul at Elisabethville transmitted a message to the United Nations from Mr. Tshombe stating that he agreed to "the principle of an immediate cease-fire," and was prepared to meet the Secretary General at Ndola.

After an exchange of further communications regarding the terms of the cease-fire, Mr. Hammarskjöld decided to proceed to Ndola, and took off from Léopoldville with fifteen persons at 1555 GMT in the plane of the United Nations force commander, a DC-6B. Although it was considered dangerous to fly over the Congo after dark, Hammarskjöld presumably took the risk to avoid any chance that they might be a target for Tshombe's jets. The United Nations had little faith in Tshombe. At 2210 GMT, after almost seven hours' flight, the plane radioed, "overhead Ndola," and was seen flying over the airport. A few minutes later it disappeared from sight, and all efforts to re-establish radio contact failed. On the next day, September 18, at 1310 GMT, the wreckage of the aircraft was sighted from the air nine and a half miles west of Ndola. When the Rhodesian police arrived at the site of the crash, they found only one survivor, Sergeant Harold Julian, who was in so serious a condition that he died a few days later.

Under the terms of the General Assembly resolution, the investigation, as I have said, was expected to consider all the circumstances surrounding the tragedy, and especially:

(a) Why the flight had to be undertaken at night without escort;
(b) Why its arrival at Ndola was unduly delayed;
(c) Whether the aircraft, after having established contact with the tower at Ndola, lost that contact, and whether the fact of its having crashed did not become known until several hours afterwards, and if so, why;
(d) Whether the aircraft, after the damage it was reported to have suffered earlier from aircraft hostile to the United Nations, was in a proper condition for use.

It may be noted that immediately after the crash, a board of investigation was set up by the Federal Government of Rhodesia and Nyasaland, the British colony in which the accident occurred. In accordance with the Convention on International Civil Aviation, observers from Sweden (the state of registry of the plane) were invited by the board to attend. Officials of the International Civil Aviation Organization and the International Federation of Airline Pilots Associations fully participated in the Rhodesian investigation. At the invitation of the Rhodesian commission, I assigned a counsel to represent the interests of the United Nations at its hearings. The United Nations commission, however, decided that the two different investigations should be kept separate. The UN commission also received the full co-operation of the International Civil Aviation Organization, which provided it with aeronautical and air law advisers.

The United Nations commission held several sessions, from December 15, 1961, to March 8, 1962, in New York, Léopoldville, Salisbury, Ndola, and Geneva. But since there were no survivors, and since the greater part of the aircraft was destroyed by fire, difficulties were encountered in determining the cause of the crash. Various theories had been advanced, with or without supporting evidence. The UN commission found that some were based purely on rumor. It nevertheless examined all those theories and rumors in its effort to obtain the true facts, wherever possible. Possible causes of the crash were considered under four main headings:

(1) Sabotage or internal interference;
(2) Attack or external interference;
(3) Material failure; and
(4) Human failure.

After examining all possible causes of the crash with expert technical assistance, the commission came to the conclusion that the plane crashed during what must have been its approach, with the intention of landing, to the Ndola airfield. In reply to the question asked by the General Assembly as to why the arrival of the aircraft at Ndola airport was unduly delayed, the UN commission observed that the plane took a less direct route, requiring an additional hour or two of flight. (There was no explanation why a less direct route was taken.) In fact, it said, the aircraft arrived over the airfield some minutes before its latest estimated time of arrival. The commission also observed that the crash occurred approximately five minutes after the last radio communication between the Ndola tower and the plane. It found no evidence that in those last five minutes, the tower or the aircraft attempted to communicate with each other, or were prevented from doing so by radio failure.

After examining all evidence as to why no air search for the plane was undertaken by the Royal Rhodesian Air Force until 10:00 A.M. (local time) on September 18, the UN commission placed the blame on the Rhodesian Federal Department of Civil Aviation for the delay in the initiation of an air search. The commission concluded:

> Although the aircraft crashed nine and a half miles from an airfield on which eighteen military aircraft capable of carrying out an air search were stationed, the wreckage was located . . . only fifteen hours after the crash, and more than nine hours after first light on September 18, 1961. The Commission . . . believes that . . . the delay in commencing search and rescue operations was increased by shortcomings in liaison and co-operation between the aviation officials concerned, by lack of initiative and diligence on their part, and by delay in applying the prescribed procedures. Undue weight appeared to be attached to the groundless impression that the Secretary-General had changed his mind after flying over Ndola and decided to land at another airport without informing the Ndola tower. Had . . . diligence been shown, it is possible that the crash could have been discovered at an earlier hour, and Sergeant Julian's chances of survival materially improved. Had he survived, not only would one life have been saved, but also a possible source of direct knowledge of the conditions and circumstances surrounding the tragedy.

It was apparent that the UN commission was unable to give specific answers to the four questions it itself raised.

MY FIRST EXPERIENCES AS ACTING SECRETARY GENERAL

Eight days after my appointment as Acting Secretary General, that is on November 11, 1961, a very grave incident occurred at

Kindu, in Kivu province. On that day, two United Nations aircraft arrived at Kindu with armored cars for the United Nations contingent. Congolese troops attacked and looted the United Nations mess and beat and arrested the thirteen Italian crew members of the UN planes. When their demand for the surrender of the armored cars was refused, the Congolese troops surrounded the airport near which the camp of the ONUC battalion was situated.

United Nations officials contacted the Congolese commander, Colonel Pakassa, but he said that he had little control over his troops. A senior staff officer of General Lundula (commander of Kivu province) arrived on November 13, but Colonel Pakassa refused to acknowledge his authority. General Lundula himself arrived on the next day, and issued orders to Colonel Pakassa to pacify his troops, return the Italian crewmen and the UN property, withdraw the troops from the airport, and take action against the culprits. The UN property was returned, and the Congolese troops withdrew from the airport on November 15, but Colonel Pakassa stated that he had no information on the Italian crew members, who were said to have escaped.

Later in the day, however, United Nations representatives secured information that the thirteen Italian crew members had been brutally murdered by Congolese soldiers on the day of their capture. Sture Linner, the officer-in-charge of ONUC in Léopoldville, acting on my instruction, dispatched a letter to the central government demanding the immediate arrest of Colonel Pakassa and the punishment of those guilty of the crime; he also proposed the establishment of a joint investigating committee. This was agreed to by Prime Minister Adoula. But the committee's investigation did not result in the apprehension and punishment of the actual culprits. Colonel Pakassa was apprehended and, after being questioned by the committee, was handed over to the central government, at its request, for possible prosecution. He was brought to trial and given a long prison sentence, and nothing more was heard of him.

It was my first grim experience of the Congo, the utter lack of discipline of its national army, the widespread hatred of white men in uniform (one theory being that the soldiers mistook the Italian crew members for white mercenaries in the pay of

Tshombe), and the helplessness of the central government in the face of countrywide disorders.

Ten days after my appointment as Acting Secretary General, that is, on November 13, 1961, the Security Council was convened on the initiative of Ethiopia, Nigeria, and the Sudan. At the meetings of the Council, the Soviet representative stressed the need for decisive measures "to end foreign colonial intervention" in the Congo. Mr. Zorin contended that the real situation was that the colonialists were fighting stubbornly to keep the wealth of Katanga in the hands of foreign monopolies. Ceylon, Liberia, and the United Arab Republic tabled a draft resolution with the specific objective of liquidating foreign interference in Katanga. In the latter part of November, the Security Council was convened once again. By its resolution of November 24, 1961, the Council opposed secessionist activities in Katanga and, *for the first time,* authorized the Secretary General to use force to complete the removal of foreign mercenaries.

The day after the adoption of the November 4 resolution, Mr. Tshombe addressed a large gathering in a stadium just outside Elisabethville. "Under the terms of the resolution just adopted," he said, "U Thant will launch a war on our territory. . . . Tomorrow or the day after tomorrow, there will be a trial of strength. When the time comes, let Katanga fighters arise in every street, on every path, on every highway, in every village. You cannot all have automatic weapons or rifles. But we still have our poisoned arrows, our spears, our axes for cutting down trees, our picks for digging ditches, our hearts to beat with courage. Not a road must remain passable, *not one United Nations mercenary must feel safe* in any place whatever. . . . Katanga, standing between foreign domination through the United Nations and nothing, is ready to choose, with pride, nothing."[8]

This flamboyant speech was broadcast and rebroadcast over Katanga radio with inevitable results. On the evening of November 28, two high UN officials—George Ivan Smith and Brian Urquhart—were dragged from a dinner party by some members

---

[8] Cable report to the Secretary General from his special representative, November 25, 1961.

of the *Gendarmerie* who had just listened to Tshombe's oratory. Both men were beaten with rifle butts and had ribs broken. George was rescued from the truck that was carrying him away. Brian was taken to the *Gendarmerie* camp and held for several hours. He was released only at the personal intervention of Tshombe, who evidently felt that his inflammatory speech had caused such consequences. An Indian major who searched for Brian disappeared and was never heard of again; his driver was found murdered close to Tshombe's house. On the following day, several members of the United Nations force were abducted, and others were killed or wounded. Roadblocks were also established by the *Gendarmerie,* impeding ONUC's freedom of movement and endangering its lifelines. These activities against the United Nations and its representatives culminated in renewed military conflict between UN and Katangese forces from December 2 to December 19.

It subsequently became known from the reports of Sture Linner, my special representative, that this was part of a deliberate plan to cut off the UN troops in Elisabethville and either force them to surrender or otherwise destroy them. For one week, UN officials sought to settle the crisis by peaceful negotiations. It became evident that, in the face of the bad faith displayed by the Katangese authorities, no negotiations were possible. While pretending to negotiate, these authorities were preparing for more assaults. UN officials seized a secret plan, the purpose of which was the destruction of ONUC. The UN forces therefore had to take firm action to regain and assure its freedom of movement and to restore law and order.

THE UN FORCE IN ACTION

When fighting broke out on December 2, ONUC had few troops in Elisabethville. Until December 14, ONUC forces endeavored to hold their positions and to maintain communications between them, while reinforcements were hurriedly flown in from other parts of the Congo. On December 15, having received enough reinforcements, ONUC troops moved to seize control of those positions in Elisabethville necessary to ensure their freedom of movement. In so doing, they worked their way around the perimeter of the city, in order to keep destruction and civilian casualties to a strict minimum. This objective was achieved within three days.

During the fighting, ONUC troops limited their attacks strictly to military objectives, and so did the ONUC aircraft that were sent into action only when absolutely necessary. Strict orders were given to ONUC troops to safeguard to all extent possible the lives and properties of the civilian population. Throughout the operation, they exercised a remarkable measure of self-restraint, which was all the more noteworthy in view of the conduct of the non-Congolese civilians, which made their task extremely arduous. A flagrant misuse of important civilian installations was the firing directed against United Nations troops from the plants of the *Union Minière du Haut-Katanga,* where many weapons were subsequently found. Vehicles with Red Cross markings were frequently used as cover by mercenaries and their civilian volunteer allies.

From the outset of hostilities, United Nations military and civilian officers did their best, in co-operation with the Red Cross, to relieve the distress caused to innocent civilians. Persons caught in areas where firing had been initiated by the *Gendarmerie* were escorted to safety, at the risk of the lives of ONUC personnel; food supplies were provided where needed; special arrangements for the evacuation of women and children were made by ONUC. Notwithstanding the shortage of troops, ONUC employed a whole battalion to guard the Baluba refugee camp, where more than 40,000 anti-Tshombe Balubas lived under United Nations protection. ONUC troops, on the one hand, prevented the Balubas from raiding the city and, on the other, protected them from the *gendarmes* who launched several attacks on the camp.

On December 19, 1961, having ensured the positions necessary for its security, ONUC ordered its troops to hold fire unless fired upon. The same day, Mr. Tshombe left Elisabethville to confer with Prime Minister Cyrille Adoula in Kitona, the United Nations military base in Léopoldville province. After an agreement was signed between Adoula and Tshombe, major fighting between ONUC and Katanga forces ceased. ONUC immediately turned its efforts to the re-establishment of normal conditions in Elisabethville. It co-operated closely with the local police to stop looting, to rid private houses of squatters, and, in general, to restore and maintain law and order.

The Kitona meeting was arranged with the assistance of the ONUC and the United States Ambassador in the Congo, Edmund Gullion, following a request made by Mr. Tshombe on December 14, 1961, when the fighting in Elisabethville was in full swing. After a day-long meeting with Prime Minister Adoula on December 20, Mr. Tshombe signed (early in the morning of December 21) an eight-point declaration. In this declaration, he accepted the application of the *Loi Fondamentale* recognizing the authority of the central government in Léopoldville, and agreed to a number of steps aiming at ending the secession of Katanga. He also pledged himself to ensure respect for the resolutions of the Security Council and General Assembly and to facilitate their implementation.

After the Kitona talks, ONUC made all possible efforts, through persuasion and the exercise of good offices, to ensure that the provisions of the Kitona declaration would be fully carried out, as an indispensable step toward the solution of the Katanga problem by peaceful means. Indeed, when in accordance with the Kitona agreement, Mr. Tshombe sent representatives to Léopoldville to participate in negotiations, ONUC insured their safety during their journey to and from the capital. But the efforts of ONUC were greatly hampered by the changing attitude of Mr. Tshombe, who constantly shifted from lukewarm co-operation to calculated opposition and vice versa.

For instance, Mr. Tshombe stated that he had no authority to decide on the future of Katanga, and summoned the Provincial Assembly to meet in Elisabethville for the purpose of discussing the Kitona declaration. At the Assembly, Mr. Tshombe made statements strongly criticizing the central government and ONUC. On February 15, 1962, however, the Assembly decided to accept the Kitona declaration as a basis for discussion with the central government.

Following this action, Prime Minister Adoula invited Mr. Tshombe to meet with him in Léopoldville to discuss the procedure for implementing the provisions of the declaration. Since Mr. Tshombe was reluctant to go to Léopoldville, ONUC exerted its best effort to persuade him to accept Mr. Adoula's invitation and gave him a full guarantee of his personal safety throughout his journey. He did eventually arrive in Léopoldville (on March 15) to negotiate a settlement of outstanding problems. The Provincial Assembly of Katanga had accepted the Kitona declaration, although conditionally, so that the meeting between Prime Minister Adoula and Mr. Tshombe centered on the procedure for carrying out its provisions and ending the secession of Katanga.

But the secession was not ended. During my official visits to European countries in the summer of 1962, I got reports, in early July, that Mr. Tshombe and his colleagues were insisting on celebrating their so-called "independence" on July 11, over United Nations opposition.

It was in Finland, where I arrived on the night of July 17, that I received the most disturbing news from the Congo. The messages were to the effect that Mr. Tshombe had changed his tactics. On that day, a planned and viciously conceived assault by thousands of Katangese women and children was made on Indian troops at a roadblock in Elisabethville. Those troops—cursed, abused, and spat upon by the Tshombe-organized women and children—displayed a most remarkable restraint and discipline under extreme provocation, and never fired on the mob. I also received reports from Robert Gardiner, United Nations representative in the Congo, that Mr. Tshombe had informed him that he would from then on employ civilian demonstrations, especially of women and children, instead of troops, to provoke the United Nations force, in cynical contempt for the safety and well-being of his own people. This change of tactics posed new problems for the force and put a very great strain on the troops.

At my press conference in Helsinki on July 20, in answer to a question about Mr. Tshombe and his secessionist movement, I characterized him and his colleagues as "a bunch of clowns" who were not to be taken seriously in their negotiations either with the central government or with the United Nations. This description prompted many reactions—some critical and others laudatory, depending on one's attitude toward the United Nations operation in the Congo. Even my senior colleagues at the UN Secretariat wondered whether I actually said it. When I arrived back in New York on the same day, the first question Dr. Bunche put to me at the airport was whether I actually used that expression. He was visibly surprised when I told him that I did. Perhaps he thought such undiplomatic language uncharacteristic of me. Perhaps it was.

THE FINAL PHASE

During the months after the Kitona declaration, every possible effort was made by the United Nations to give effect to the agreement between Mr. Tshombe and Mr. Adoula and to resolve all difficulties between the central government and the province of Kitanga by discussion and negotiation. These negotiations included an extended exchange between the two leaders over my Plan of National Reconciliation, generally known as U Thant's Plan, which was presented to Prime Minister Adoula on August 20 and to the Katangese authorities on August 24.

Elements of the plan included the elaboration of a federal constitution and the reconstitution of a central government representing all political and provincial groups; a division of revenue between the central and provincial governments and the unification of currency; the integration of the *Gendarmerie* and all military units into a national army; the withdrawal of all missions not serving under the central government; and the proclamation of a general amnesty.

Prime Minister Adoula accepted the plan on August 23, and Mr. Tshombe wrote me on September 3 that he received it "with enthusiasm" and "adhered to [it] wholeheartedly."

Later on, however, Mr. Tshombe hedged on several of the main provisions of the plan. I therefore proposed various measures to bring economic pressures on Katanga—by preventing exports of its copper and cobalt, and ensuring that payments of revenue to Katanga would be withheld. These measures received overwhelming support at the United Nations, but before they could be acted upon, the final stage of the Katanga chapter began.

It took the form of a military showdown provoked by Katanga's *Gendarmerie* and mercenaries.

Late in December 1962, United Nations troops in Elisabethville and other towns in Katanga were fired upon for four consecutive days. On December 24, the Katangese *Gendarmerie* shot down a United Nations helicopter, killing an Indian lieutenant serving with ONUC. There was also a heavy exchange of gunfire near a *Union Minière* installation in Elisabethville. On December 27, the *Gendarmerie* launched a well-planned attack on ONUC positions in three parts of the city.

At last—on the joint recommendation of the United Nations representative in the Congo, Mr. Robert Gardiner, of the United Nations force commander in Katanga, General Prem Chand of India, and of the Secretary General's military adviser, General Rikhye, and with the full endorsement of Dr. Ralph Bunche, undersecretary for special political affairs, who was my principal adviser on the Congo—I authorized the ONUC military actions that began on December 28. The objective of the operation was to remove the *Gendarmerie* and the mercenaries from the Elisabethville area and to establish complete freedom of movement in the whole of Katanga.

Tshombe threatened "total destruction" of all *Union Minière* installations if ONUC launched an offensive. Because of this threat, the British and Belgian representatives at the UN were extremely apprehensive about the operation and, on instructions from their governments, asked me not to go ahead with it. They told me that their governments had information that if ONUC attempted to cross the Lufira River (Jadotville is on its west bank), the force would meet with heavy resistance and that all installations at Jadotville and Kolwezi would be destroyed by the mercenaries. I immediately sent cables to Robert Gardiner, transmitting to him the information received from the two governments, and asking for his latest assessment. Then, on December 30, the London *Observer* carried a front page story: "BRITAIN HITS AT U THANT ON KATANGA." The article reported that the British government called for an immediate cease-fire and wished to "impress upon U Thant the futility of trying to impose a political settlement on the Congo by force."

The situation was indeed grim: I had already authorized the third and final round (which was code-named Operation Grand Slam) to gain complete freedom of movement for ONUC all over Katanga. Ralph Bunche felt that the risk of crossing the Lufira River and entering Jadotville was too great to take. The town had a huge cobalt processing plant of the *Union Minière*. Once ONUC crossed the Lufira River and attempted to enter Jadotville, Bunche feared—and I shared his fear—that the installations would be blown up by Tshombe's men.

On the night of December 30, I again cabled Robert Gardiner informing him of the British and Belgian apprehensions, and that I shared their fear. I therefore wanted him to caution ONUC *not* to cross the Lufira River until UN headquarters had firm evidence that installations would not be blown up.

On January 3, I received a report from Gardiner that the Lufira River had been crossed, that ONUC had entered Jadotville at 12:00 noon on that day, and that the force had been greeted by the cheers of the population. The mayor of the town and the general manager of the *Union Minière* installations there received General Prem Chand, who discussed with them ways and means of restoring normal services and economic activity. Tshombe was reported to have fled to Rhodesia!

The crossing of the Lufira River, and the entry of ONUC into Jadotville without opposition (and without the scorched-earth policy Tshombe had threatened) came to UN headquarters as a most pleasant surprise. I immediately sent Ralph Bunche to the Congo to get the facts, and he reported to me that, finding less resistance and fewer mines along the road than had been expected in the original planning, ONUC, under the brilliant command of Brigadier Reginald Noronha, found no difficulty in reaching the Lufira River, which was considered to be the major obstacle between them and the town of Jadotville. The two bridges over the river, one vehicular and one railroad, had already been destroyed. The UN troops, however, enjoyed two strokes of good fortune. Although the railroad bridge was completely down, one of its twisted steel girders was left in such a position that foot soldiers were able to scramble across it to the west bank of the river, where they established a firm bridgehead. A scouting party, in addition, found in the river a small wooden raft on floats, on which jeeps and mortars were taken across. From the bridgehead on the west bank of the river, it was but a short distance to Jadotville itself.

When the ONUC troops entered Jadotville on January 3, the mercenaries had fled, without pausing to do more than a fraction of the destruction they had threatened. On the same day, officials of the central Congolese government began arriving in Elisabethville.

In retrospect, it is clear that the elements of surprise and speed, together with the bravery and skill of the officers and men, accounted for the remarkable success of the operation at a low cost in ONUC casualties. From a captured mercenary it was learned that the advance caught both mercenaries and *Gendarmerie* off guard, for they had not expected to encounter ONUC troops on that road until two days later. A delay in the move, therefore, might well have been far more costly in United Nations lives.

When Ralph Bunche came back to New York, he brought with him letters of apology for an initial breakdown of communications—replies to my cables had been inordinately delayed —individually from Robert Gardiner, General Kebede Gebre, and General Prem Chand. I felt that it was I, not they, who should have apologized for my miscalculation and apprehension based on scare reports from London and Brussels.

There was, perhaps, another factor. As a Buddhist, I abhor all forms of violence; the feeling is embedded in my inner self. Since that memorable Security Council meeting of November 24, 1961, authorizing me to use a requisite measure of force in the Congo to evict foreign mercenaries, my conscience had been pricking me. Any news of violent death, whether of a Congolese, a United Nations soldier, or a foreign mercenary, saddened me deeply. Every morning I prayed for the sparing of lives. In the course of my meditations, I practiced *metta* (good will) and *karuna* (compassion) to all in the Congo, without distinction as to race, religion, or color. I realized, however, that the moral principles of my religion had to be adjusted to the practical responsibilities of my office. I had to view the United Nations operation in the Congo as a battle for peace, not as a war; to me, war—all war—is folly and insanity. I regarded the UN soldiers as soldiers of peace. In the final phase of the UN operation in the Congo, I thought of one of Lord Buddha's maxims:

> He who guides others by a procedure that is non-violent and equitable, he is said to be a guardian of the law, wise and righteous.[9]

I had all along prayed that the UN objectives in Katanga might be fulfilled without fighting; I had wished that the ONUC entry into Jadotville and Kolwezi could be a peaceful one. No doubt these thoughts and prayers weighed on my mind when London and Brussels impressed upon me the futility of using force.

The Jadotville operation was the first experience, under combat conditions in the field, of an armed force composed strictly of international units and strictly under United Nations command. Operation Grand Slam, launched on December 28, also represented a harmonious co-ordination of the various units. Under the command of General Prem Chand, troops from India, Ethiopia, Tunisia, Ireland, Sweden, and Ghana operated as a single unit. From December 28 to January 4 inclusive, seven United Nations fighter aircraft and one reconnaissance plane were hit by ground fire during the operations, but none of the pilots was injured. Of the Katangese air force of ten combat aircraft present in Katanga when ONUC operations began, all but one was destroyed. All vital air installations at Katangese air bases were demolished by United Nations fighters. ONUC forces sustained total casualties of nine dead and seventy-two wounded. There were no reliable estimates of *Gendarmerie* casualties.

On January 14, 1963, I received, through Belgian government channels, a message from Moise Tshombe and his ministers, who were meeting at Kolwezi. In it, they announced their readiness to end the secession of Katanga, to grant United Nations troops complete freedom of movement, and to arrange for the implementation of a plan of national reconstruction. They asked that the central government immediately put into effect the amnesty called for in the plan in order to guarantee the freedom and safety of the Katangese government and of all who worked under its au-

---

[9] *The Dhammapada,* translated by S. Radhakrishnan (London: Oxford University Press, 1962), p. 140.

thority. I welcomed Mr. Tshombe's message and informed him, on January 15, that the United Nations would do its utmost to assist in the fulfillment of the promise implicit in his statement. On January 15 and 16, President Kasavubu and Prime Minister Adoula separately confirmed that the amnesty proclamation of November 26, 1962, remained valid. On January 17, Mr. Tshombe met with UN representatives at ONUC headquarters in Elisabethville and signed a document in which he undertook to facilitate the peaceful entry of ONUC into Kolwezi. By January 21, the UN force had under control all important centers hitherto held by the Katangese, and in them quickly restored law and order. The Katangese *Gendarmerie* as an organized force had ceased to exist.

In February 1963, I reported to the Security Council, presenting an account of the extent to which the mandates given to ONUC by the Security Council resolutions had been fulfilled, and of aspects of those mandates that remained to be implemented.

With regard to the maintenance of territorial integrity and political independence, I said that it might be reasonably concluded that the secession of Katanga was now at an end. Regarding assistance in the restoration and maintenance of law and order, I stated that law and order appeared to have been firmly restored in the main centers of Katanga, and that it was expected that the ONUC presence would have the same effect in rural areas. But the need for UN assistance in maintaining law and order would remain for some time to come, probably for about a year, although with substantial reduction from present strength.

As for the mandate to prevent the occurrence of civil war in the Congo, I noted that it might be regarded as fulfilled to a major degree, although an alert and effective watch over the situation would be indispensable for some time.

As to technical assistance, I reported that I had opened consultations with the government of the Congo on the question of channeling future aid to the Congo. While there would be a continuation of multilateral or United Nations aid, there arose the question of the extent to which an increase in bilateral aid might be envisaged, without exposing the Congo to the danger of competition among states.

On September 17, 1963, I submitted to the Security Council

a report devoted to the question of United Nations military disengagement in the Congo. I proposed a phasing-out schedule for the complete withdrawal of the force by the end of 1963, noting that an extension of the force would require the appropriation of new funds. Cogent reasons existed in support of prolonging the stay of the force, but other impressive reasons, and especially the Organization's financial plight, tended to justify its withdrawal. There could be no doubt that the presence of a United Nations force in the Congo would continue to be helpful through the first half of 1964, or for a longer period. But the Congo's internal situation no longer posed a serious threat to international peace, and the time must come soon when the government of the Congo would have to assume the responsibility for security and for law and order in the country. Once the United Nations force was withdrawn, certain countries might be willing to make some of their military units available to the Congo under bilateral agreements, as indicated by the Congolese government itself. I observed that such agreements would at that time no longer be inconsistent with the position of the Security Council.

Acting upon the Congolese government's request for reduced but continued military assistance up to June 30, 1964, the General Assembly decided on October 18, 1963, to continue the ad hoc account for the UN operation in the Congo until June 30, 1964, and authorized the necessary expenditure to that effect. The force, whose total strength had been brought down from 18,000 to 5,871 officers and other ranks by the end of 1963, was further gradually reduced during the first half of 1964. On June 30, 1964, the withdrawal of the United Nations force was completed.

But the insistence of the Congolese government on the selection of certain specific countries to train its national army, and the vehement objection to that selection, within the framework of the United Nations, by most African countries, caused an open rift between the Congo and the United Nations. The Congolese government had applied to Canada, Italy, Belgium, Norway, Israel, and the United States for assistance in modernizing its army. African and Asian representatives on the Congo Advisory Committee, however, strongly objected to this selection of countries, as did the Soviet Union, on the ground that NATO powers and Israel would be in virtual control of the Congo army. On May 12, 1963, Mr. Adoula informed me that the objections of the UN were inadequate and that his government had decided to proceed immediately with the reorganization of the national army as planned. The resentment of the Congolese government against the United Nations was clearly evident when, on June 30, 1964, not a single Congolese official turned up at Léopoldville airport to bid official farewell to the last contingent of the United Nations force. It was an ironic end to the massive involvement of the United Nations in the Congolese crisis for four years.

Certain important observations should be made in connection with the experience of the United Nations force:

(a) The creation of the force in July 1960 proved the ability of the United Nations to meet grave emergency situations and to set up the largest peace-keeping operation in its history within an incredibly short time.

(b) Despite its limited authority and resources, the United Nations offered the only possible hope of keeping the peace and facilitating the finding of a solution.

(c) Four years were gained in which the government and people of the Congo had the opportunity to come to grips with their vast problems and during which the Congolese public administrators, doctors, professional people, and technicians could begin their training and acquire experience. (The cost to the UN was as follows: Total ONUC casualties included 126 killed in action and 75 in accidents. Expenditures incurred totaled more than $400 million.)

(d) On the whole, the record of the United Nations force in the Congo was characterized by discipline and restraint.

(e) The force presented certain weaknesses common to all United Nations peace-keeping forces, since the national contingents composing it were never fully merged, used their own arms, and had their own commanding officers. The authority of the commander of the force did not extend to the discipline of its members, that being left to the commanders of each national contingent.

(f) Relations with the Congolese government were generally good and weathered the relatively few major crises, although the last days of the UN military presence were marred by the sulky mood of the Congolese government.

Following the withdrawal of the UN force, the situation in the Congo rapidly deteriorated. Even before the withdrawal, a number of opposition leaders went underground and some of them set up at Brazzaville a national liberation committee with the avowed purpose of overthrowing the Adoula government by violent means. At the same time, disturbances broke out in several parts of the country. On May 31, exactly a month before the date of withdrawal, Prime Minister Adoula asked ONUC to send a detachment of UN troops to the Bukavu area to assist the government in the maintenance of law and order. I immediately authorized the operation, even at that late date, to respond to the government's request, but on June 6, the Prime Minister withdrew his request and asked instead that ONUC should place at the government's disposal some of their surplus military material. After consultation with the Congo Advisory Committee, I authorized ONUC to comply with that request.

Of all the Congolese leaders, Cyrille Adoula was, in my experience, the most decent, the most moderate, and the most highly regarded by his African colleagues. Although he was colorless and lacking in charisma—unlike Patrice Lumumba—he proved himself an able negotiator and a refined diplomat, always modest and persuasive. He was surely imbued with a pan-African outlook and was a firm supporter of genuine nonalignment, although in his last year as Prime Minister, stronger elements around him made his government lean heavily toward the West, for pragmatic economic reasons.

Immediately after the withdrawal of ONUC, the Adoula government was faced with two rival opposition forces: one led by leftist Pierre Mulele, and the other led by rightist Moise Tshombe himself. In that highly confused situation, on July 9, Cyrille Adoula resigned, and to the shock and anger of most African countries, Moise Tshombe became Prime Minister, to head a transitional government with the main task of preparing the forthcoming elections. On assuming his new post, Mr. Tshombe made an attempt to rally the opposition behind him, but his attempt failed. Shortly thereafter, insurgent forces extended their control

over vast regions in the eastern part of the country, including
Stanleyville, where they established a dissident government under
Christopher Gbenye. With increased military assistance from outside (Belgium), and having recruited foreign mercenaries again to
bolster the army, Mr. Tshombe attempted to regain the lost territory. By September 1964, there was widespread internal conflict
and fighting, and chaos returned to the Congo.

In November 1964, news reached the United Nations that
nearly a thousand persons of eighteen different nationalities had
been arrested and held as hostages by the rebel authorities in the
Stanleyville area (now in revolt against Prime Minister Moise
Tshombe), and that their lives were in imminent danger.

On November 24, the representatives of Belgium and the
United States notified the Security Council that in view of the failure of the rebel authorities to respond to appeals for the release of
the hostages, and of their refusal to guarantee the safety of the civilians at Stanleyville, the Belgian and the United States governments had found it necessary to undertake a rescue operation, and
that Belgian para-commandos carried by United States aircraft
had been parachuted, a few hours earlier, into the Stanleyville
area. The Council was informed by Prime Minister Moise
Tshombe that his government had authorized the rescue operation, and by the United Kingdom that, in view of the humanitarian objective of the operation, it had granted to the Belgian and
United States governments, at their request, the use of airport facilities on Ascension Island, off the west coast of Africa.

It seemed that the history of the Congo in 1960 would repeat
itself at the end of 1964. The country was once again plunged into
a nightmare of violence and lawlessness. The only difference between the two periods was that four years earlier Mr. Tshombe
was the rebel; in the second half of 1964, he was the Prime
Minister.

On December 1, 1964, twenty-two UN member states requested the Security Council to consider the situation urgently, as
did Mr. Tshombe on December 9. The member states considered
that those operations constituted an intervention in African
affairs, while Mr. Tshombe complained about the various states
that were aiding the rebel movement in the Congo.

The Council held seventeen meetings to consider these two

complaints between December 9 and 30, 1964. The bitter debates in the Council centered on various complaints made by various governments on the chaotic situation in the Stanleyville area. Belgium complained that innocent civilians had been beaten, ill-treated, and, in certain cases, murdered. The United States, the United Kingdom, and Italy associated themselves with the government of Belgium, and said that rescue operations were conducted purely for humanitarian reasons.

The Soviet Union told the Security Council that it considered the landing of Belgian parachutists at Stanleyville to be a flagrant act of armed interference by Belgium, the United States, and the United Kingdom in the internal affairs of the Congo. The Soviet government called for the immediate cessation of the military intervention and the withdrawal of all Belgian troops and foreign mercenaries from the Congo.

At the Council meeting on December 9, 1964, the Foreign Minister of the Congo (Brazzaville) set the tone of the meeting by stating that "the problem before the Council was surely the latest aggression committed by the Americans, the Belgians and the British against the black populations."[10] From then on, the Security Council debates developed into a racial wrangle between the black Africans and the white Europeans, the latter being joined by the Americans. By and large, the African position was that the ultimate solution of the Congolese political problem must be left in the hands of the Congolese people, who had already sought the assistance of the OAU in this regard. In the view of the African governments, the Security Council was dealing solely and specifically with "military aggression and intervention in the heart of Africa." Many African representatives said that "the American-Belgian-British intervention" was carried out deliberately, in order to hinder the action of the OAU, and thus "deal a blow to that Organization."

Paul Henri Spaak, Foreign Minister of Belgium, said that the Stanleyville operation was in no way a military operation, nor an effort to aid the Congolese national army against the rebels or hold any territory, but "a question of saving the endangered lives

---

[10] *United Nations Security Council Official Records, No. 1170*, December 9, 1964.

of some 1,500 to 2,000 persons." To the charge that it had been a racist operation, Mr. Spaak replied that among those evacuated from Stanleyville, there were at least four hundred Indians and Pakistanis, and more than two hundred Congolese, loyal to Tshombe.

The Algerian representative pointed out that since its independence, the history of the Congo had been marked by many armed interventions; in this one, he said, the United States was using the United Nations as a "Trojan horse." He insisted that to call Tshombe's government a legal government was an insult to Africa; instead, "it was an imposed government set up to serve the colonialists."

After one of the most acrimonious debates ever conducted in the halls of the United Nations, the Security Council, in a resolution adopted on December 30, requested all states to refrain or desist from intervening in the domestic affairs of the Congo. It also appealed for a cease-fire in the Congo.

THE LAST DAYS OF TSHOMBE

Mr. Tshombe's term of office, which lasted about fifteen months, was marked not only by widespread unrest in the country, but also by hostility on the part of the Organization of African Unity. It will be recalled that when he was leading the secessionist movement of Katanga, not a single African state recognized the independence of Katanga. When he became Prime Minister of the Congo, the whole of black Africa was shocked and distressed. The real test came in July 1964, barely a week after his assumption of power, when the heads of African states made preparations for their second annual summit meeting at Cairo. Many African leaders announced that they would not sit at the conference table with Tshombe. To soothe African tempers, Tshombe announced that his government had released Antoine Gizenga, who had been held on an island in the mouth of the Congo River for the past two and a half years. This move did not change the mind of the Africans, and so on July 15, one day before the African summit conference, Tshombe announced that the Congo would boycott the conference.

In the domestic scene also, Tshombe was faced with increasing difficulties. Particularly after the Stanleyville rescue operations conducted by Belgium, with the assistance of the United States and the United Kingdom, Tshombe was increasingly identified with "the imperialists" against the interest of black Africa. The late Patrice Lumumba emerged as a national hero and martyr, and many members of Parliament began to accuse Tshombe of having taken part in the assassination of the former Prime Minister. In the fall of 1965, the Congolese Parliament deprived him of his parliamentary seat. Sensing danger to his life, he fled the country and sought political asylum in several European countries. All those countries closed their doors to him, but finally Spain was persuaded to give him asylum. A military court in the Congo indicted him for treason and sentenced him to death in absentia.

Some newspaper correspondents who interviewed him in Madrid reported that he bore no ill will toward the United Nations. According to a correspondent, he repented his defiance of the international community—at tremendous cost to the United Nations, both in human and financial terms.

Suddenly, on July 1, 1967, newspapers carried banner headlines about Mr. Tshombe. On the previous day, his private airplane, flying from Ibiza in the Balearic Islands to Majorca, was hijacked by the Frenchman Francis Bodenan, as I mentioned at the beginning of the chapter, and taken to Algiers. The Algerian government, which had consistently regarded Tshombe as a traitor, did not allow him to return to Spain. While he was in detention, the government of the Congo under General Mobutu repeatedly tried to persuade the government of Algeria to extradite Tshombe, ostensibly to give effect to the death sentence passed against him in absentia. For understandable reasons, Algeria refused to comply with the Congolese request. On June 30, 1969, Tshombe died in confinement. The Algerian government, eager to avoid any suspicion of foul play, invited eleven surgeons to perform an autopsy. They all agreed that the cause of death was heart failure.

CHAPTER VIII

THE CUBAN MISSILE CRISIS

October 1962 was a month of crisis situations and dramatic developments. Day after day, news of the lingering Berlin crisis, the Sino-Indian war, and the war in Laos attracted the attention of delegates at the United Nations, although none of those crises had been brought before any deliberative organ of the World Organization by any member state. Newspaper editorials and commentaries throughout the world were sharply divided over the question of Chairman Khrushchev's intention regarding access routes to Berlin. While some were skeptical about an imminent crisis over Berlin, others were convinced that the Soviet leader meant what he said regarding the closure of access routes to the divided city. Based on my talks with Khrushchev near Yalta seven weeks earlier, I did not believe that he wanted a showdown with the West. At that time, he was quite relaxed about Berlin, and he told me that he did not want to damage the developing East-West détente. The main cause of alarm appeared to have been the reports from Moscow that Mr. Khrushchev had been telling recent foreign visitors that the West would never fight for Berlin.

When Soviet Foreign Minister Andrei Gromyko saw President Kennedy at the White House on October 18, the main topic of discussion was Berlin. There was no indication at that time that the question of Cuba was seriously discussed, although it was revealed two days later that President Kennedy was in possession of facts concerning the presence of Soviet missiles in Cuba.

Ambassador Stevenson told me later that President Kennedy had decided that, if necessary, the United States would fight alone to hold the Western position in Berlin. Many Western diplomats, however, believed that Chairman Khrushchev was more interested in negotiations than an actual showdown.

On Saturday, October 20, Brigadier General Indar Jit Rikhye, my military adviser, told me that Washington had "definite proof" of the presence of Soviet missiles in Cuba. On the same day, Philip Dean, the United Nations representative in Washington, reported to me on the phone that according to information available to him, President Kennedy believed that the evidence was irrefutable. Not only were some missiles there already, but the sites for others, with Washington within their range, were being installed.

On Monday morning, General Rikhye informed me that President Kennedy was reported to be preparing a very important statement on the crisis, and he advised me that I should send for Ambassador Stevenson and discuss the matter. At my request, Mr. Stevenson came to my office at 4:30 P.M. Before then, a White House announcement on the radio had already confirmed Rikhye's information. Mr. Stevenson told me that the President's statement would be on Cuba, and that it was going to be a very tough one. He did not have the text of the statement, which was being "revised over and over again," but he promised to make one available to me as soon as he received it. Earlier in the day, during the debate on the perennial question of the representation of China in the United Nations, Mr. Stevenson did not mention Cuba at all in his statement.

That evening, I attended that Ghana reception at the delegates' dining room. After staying there for a few minutes, I returned to the thirty-eighth floor and watched President Kennedy on television.

In my memory, it was the grimmest and gravest speech ever made by a head of state. The President told the American people that the Soviet Union, contrary to promises, was building offensive missile and bomber bases in Cuba. He said that the bases could operate missiles carrying nuclear warheads up to a range of two thousand miles. Then he announced that, with effect from that night, he had imposed a naval and air "quarantine" on the shipment of offensive military equipment to Cuba.

Thus, a most critical moment—perhaps *the* most critical moment since the end of World War II—had arrived. The President's militant thrust at the Soviet Union as the party responsible for the crisis, and his unconcealed commitment to act alone against the missile threat to his country, came as a thunderbolt. He said that his country would not stop short of military action to end what he called a "clandestine, reckless, and provocative threat to world peace." He also said that the United States was asking for an emergency meeting of the United Nations Security Council to consider a resolution "for the dismantling and withdrawal of all offensive weapons in Cuba." He called on Chairman Khrushchev to withdraw the missiles from Cuba and thus "move the world back from the abyss of destruction."

I could scarcely believe my eyes and ears. If the United States were at war with the Soviet Union, such a violent public accusation could be understandable. Even if the President's revelations were correct, would it not be wiser, I thought, to ask Chairman Khrushchev privately to do what he was publicly asked to do? Was it the President's intention to corner the Chairman? Would the Chairman, with his back to the wall, hold up his hands and give in?

If the allegation of the *secret* installation of missiles and bomber bases in Cuba were true, then the Chairman must have been out of his mind. Everybody knew that U.S. reconnaissance planes were flying all over the world—Russia, Eastern Europe, China, and certainly Cuba. Why was Khrushchev building such bases in Cuba—bases that were fully exposed to the supersharp camera lenses of American U-2s? Did he build them just to demonstrate to the Americans that the Soviet Union had the same right as the United States in building offensive missiles and bomber bases in any country that wanted them?

And was the United States, the most powerful country in the world, prepared to plunge the world into a nuclear holocaust? Never before had the lives of so many millions around the world been at the mercy of two men who had the power to make the ultimate decision. I was more deeply troubled than I had ever been in my life.

The stern demeanor of the young President and the sharp tone of his address reminded me of what I had said at the sixth national conference of the United States national commission for UNESCO at San Francisco on November 8, 1957: "The vitality of the American people is reflected in the extraordinary pace of your everyday life, the vehemence of your reactions and your feeling and the fantastic growth of your economic enterprises. This vitality, this vigor, and this exuberance of your national character have been in the past both an asset and a liability." I wondered whether the President's vigor and vitality—and the vehemence of his reaction—were reassuring or frightening.

At about 10:00 P.M., I received from Ambassador Stevenson an official request for an emergency meeting of the Security Council. On the next morning, I received a similar request from Ambassador Zorin of the Soviet Union, who happened to be president of the Council for that month under the system of rotation. The Soviet Union's request was for "immediate examination of the question of violation of the Charter of the United Nations and the threat to the peace on the part of the United States." It charged that the United States was taking a step towards the unleashing of a thermonuclear war and was violating international law and the United Nations Charter by arrogating to itself the right to attack foreign vessels on the high seas. It emphasized that Soviet assistance to Cuba was exclusively designed to improve Cuba's defensive capacity, made necessary by continuous acts of provocation on the part of the United States. The Soviet Union also submitted a draft resolution under which the Security Council would condemn the action of the United States for violating the UN Charter and increasing the threat of war; the resolution would also insist that the United States revoke its decision to inspect ships bound for Cuba, and request the United States to cease any interference whatsoever in the internal affairs of Cuba.

On the same day, Cuba requested an emergency meeting of the Security Council to consider "the act of war unilaterally committed by the United States" in ordering the naval blockade of

Cuba. It charged that the U.S. action was in disregard of international organizations, particularly of the United Nations, and was creating an imminent danger of war. The request was dated October 22.

The Security Council met on Tuesday, October 23. Before and after the meeting, several delegates met in closed informal sessions to discuss the crisis, and their spokesmen were in touch with me to devise ways and means of averting the impending catastrophe. Before I deal with the substantive discussions at the historic Security Council meetings and their outcome, it will be relevant to outline the circumstances leading to the crisis.

PRELUDE

The Cuban missile crisis of 1962 brought the world to the edge of a nuclear holocaust. Never in the history of the United Nations did it face a moment of graver responsibility and grimmer challenge.

Although the crisis lasted only thirteen days—from October 15 to 28—relations between the United States and Cuba had been deteriorating steadily since the establishment of the Revolutionary Government in Havana on January 1, 1959. The impact of the tension that existed between the two countries was felt in the United Nations from that time.

In October 1959, the United States placed an embargo on exports to Cuba. Cuba then charged that the United States was planning to launch an armed attack against the island. These charges reached the United Nations on July 11, 1960, when the Cuban government requested the Security Council to discuss the whole problem of United States-Cuba relations.

When the Security Council met (on July 18) to consider the complaint, Cuba alleged that a grave situation endangering international peace had arisen as a result of repeated threats, reprisals, and aggressive designs against Cuba. The United States denied the charges and accused Cuba of carrying out a violent anti-American propaganda campaign. The matter was already under consideration by the Organization of American States (OAS) which, in the U.S. view, was the proper forum for its discussion. The Council adjourned its consideration of the question pending a report from the OAS.

Later, the OAS transmitted to the Security Council documents in which it condemned intervention, or the threat of intervention, from an "extra-continental" power (clearly meaning the Soviet Union) in the affairs of the American republics.

On September 26, 1960, Prime Minister Fidel Castro charged the United States with subversion and aggression in the United Nations General Assembly. In a letter dated October 12 and addressed to the Secretary General, the United States replied that it had, over a long period, sought the friendship of the Cuban government and had recognized Cuba's right to exercise its national sovereignty. But the United States charged that the Cuban government sought to intervene in the internal affairs of other Latin-American states and to undermine the inter-American system by drifting toward communism. Premier Khrushchev, speaking on Cuba before the General Assembly on September 23, asked the United Nations to take action to stem the overhanging threat of interference from the United States.

On December 31, 1960, Cuba asked for an immediate meeting of the Security Council to consider what it said was the intention of the United States to commit direct military aggression against Cuba. The Cuban government claimed that it had in its possession evidence of a plan for U.S. armed aggression against Cuba, and that in its preparation, the United States was exerting pressure to bring about the diplomatic isolation of Cuba from Latin America. The United States severed diplomatic relations with Cuba on January 2, 1961.

During the winter and spring of 1961, Cuba made repeated charges that the United States was planning to invade Cuba or intervene in its domestic affairs. These events culminated in the Bay of Pigs invasion on April 17 by (as Cuba announced) "a mercenary force from Guatemala and Florida, organized, financed, and armed by the United States"—a charge subsequently denied by the United States.

At the end of January 1962, the OAS transmitted to the UN its "Final Act" of a meeting held that month at Punta del Este,

Uruguay. The act declared, among other things, that the Cuban government, having officially identified itself as Marxist-Leninist, was incompatible with the inter-American system, and, as such, should be excluded from participating in the system. Cuba then charged that the declaration had been inspired by the United States as a prelude to invasion; it further charged that the declaration was in violation of the UN Charter and requested the Security Council to consider the matter.

When in February the Council failed to include the Cuban request on its agenda, Cuba asked that the Council request the International Court of Justice to give an advisory opinion on certain legal questions relating to the resolutions adopted by the OAS at Punta del Este. Among the legal questions Cuba wanted the Court to consider were: Did the OAS have the right to take enforcement action against a member state without the authorization of the Security Council? And could the OAS expel a member state "particularly because of its social system"? But the Security Council on March 23 rejected the Cuban draft requesting an advisory opinion.

The central issue was whether a regional organization, such as the OAS, could take enforcement action against one of its members without the authorization of the Security Council. The Council's rejection of Cuba's request thus upheld, in effect, the right of any regional organization—whether the OAS or the Warsaw Pact—to act against a member without the sanction of the Council. No doubt this decision contributed to the freedom of action of regional organizations in the Dominican Republic in 1955 and in Czechoslovakia in 1968.

The rejection was a tragedy. Cuba was justified in proposing, as a preliminary step, that a request be addressed to the International Court of Justice for an advisory opinion on legal questions, in order to help the Security Council to take just and legal decisions. In doing so, Cuba was acting in strict conformity with Article 96 of the Charter, which provides that: "The General Assembly or the Security Council may request the International Court of Justice to give an advisory opinion on any legal question." At the same time, the Statute of the International Court of Justice provides that the Court may give an advisory opinion on any legal question at the request of anybody authorized by the Charter of the United Nations.

These, then, were some of the developments that formed the prelude to the coming storm. It is clear that total incompatibility between the two systems had developed within a span of three years. Diplomatic relations between Cuba and the United States had been broken off; Cuba had become more and more isolated in the Western Hemisphere; and the deliberations on the question both at the United Nations and at the OAS proved to be ineffective and unproductive. After the rebuff of the Cuban attempt to seek an advisory opinion from the International Court of Justice, the situation in the Caribbean became critical indeed.

THE CONFRONTATION

The crisis that started about the middle of October 1962, when the deployment of Soviet missiles in Cuba was "confirmed" by the United States, was not brought before the United Nations until October 22. The Security Council met urgently on October 23.

Before discussing the debates that took place at this and subsequent meetings, I must describe my own activities behind the scenes, for I had already decided that I must take certain initiatives to avert the coming nuclear showdown.

According to the information available to General Rikhye, there were about thirty missiles in Cuba, half of which were capable of striking almost any part of the United States. He did not believe that they were yet operational, however, nor that they could be activated without further supplies from the Soviet Union. In this connection, it should be noted that in the ensuing days, it was often pointed out that the United States had missiles in Turkey, right next door to the Soviet Union. After Rikhye left my office, I started to draft appeals I had decided to make to President Kennedy and Chairman Khrushchev, as well as a short statement to be made in the Security Council scheduled to be resumed the next day. I left the office just before midnight.

On the morning of October 24, I was informed that a great many member states—actually forty-five in number—wanted me to intervene in the titanic conflict, in order to avert the coming catastrophe. I told the diplomats who brought us this information that I planned to intervene in the Security Council meeting that evening.

Ironically, it was United Nations Day, and the customary evening concert had to go on as originally scheduled. The Security Council was called to order after the concert, during the intermission of which, incidentally, I gave a brief address.[1]

While the concert was still on, identical messages from me were on their way to President Kennedy and Chairman Khrushchev. (These messages are described in detail in the next section.)

In the course of the dramatic debate that took place on the night of October 24, the United States asserted that the transformation of Cuba into a base for offensive weapons of sudden mass destruction constituted a threat to the peace of the Western Hemisphere and of the world, and had led to the United States quarantine of Cuba. The foremost objection of the United States to the Cuban regime was that it had given the Soviet Union a bridgehead and staging area in the Western Hemisphere. It was stressed that a grave issue confronted the Security Council and that the Council's action might determine the future of civilization.

Cuba rejected these charges, replying that it had been forced to arm in order to defend itself against U.S. aggression. The United States, it said, had made a unilateral act of war by sending its planes and ships toward Cuba and had presented the Security Council with a fait accompli. The Cuban government would not, moreover, accept United Nations observers in matters within its domestic jurisdiction; the observers, in its view, should be sent to the U.S. bases from which Cuba was being harassed. It called for the immediate withdrawal of the U.S. forces from the Cuban coast and for the cessation of the blockade.

The Soviet Union declared that the naval blockade of Cuba and all the military measures that had been put into effect by the United States were in flagrant violation of the UN Charter

_____

[1] *United Nations Press Release SG/1352*, October 24, 1962.

and of the principles of international law, and constituted a step toward the unleashing of thermonuclear war. The Soviet government, it continued, had officially declared that it had not sent, and was not sending, any offensive weapons to Cuba, and that Soviet military aid was intended solely for defensive purposes, the nature of which only Cuba was entitled to determine.

Views were expressed by other Council members on the seriousness of the situation. Venezuela said that it voiced the gravest concern of all Latin-American countries over the threat to their security created by the installation of rocket bases and nuclear missiles in Cuba. The representative of Chile made a similar observation.

MY APPEAL

At that stage, I made my appeal. After observing that the United Nations was facing a moment of grave responsibility, and that the very fate of mankind was at stake, I called for urgent negotiations between the parties directly involved. Then I informed the Security Council that, at the request of a large number of member states, I had sent identical messages to President Kennedy and Chairman Khrushchev. The messages addressed an urgent appeal to both sides for a moratorium of two to three weeks involving, on the one hand, the voluntary suspension of all arms shipments to Cuba, and on the other, the voluntary suspension of quarantine measures, especially the searching of ships bound for Cuba. I also offered to make myself available to all the parties concerned for whatever services I might be able to perform. (The texts of my messages to President Kennedy and Chairman Khrushchev are reproduced, with their replies, in Appendixes A–E, Part III.)

At the same meeting, I appealed to the President and the Prime Minister of the Revolutionary Government of Cuba to suspend the construction and development of major military facilities and installations in Cuba during the period of negotiation.

I concluded my statement with the expression of hope that "at this moment, not only in the Council Chamber but in the world outside, good sense and understanding will be placed above the anger of the moment or the pride of nations. The path of negotiation and compromise is the only course by which the peace of the world can be secured at this critical moment."[2]

When the meeting was adjourned and most of the members had left the Chamber, Ambassador Zorin (of the U.S.S.R.), who was seated on my left on the president's chair, turned to me and said that I should not have made such a statement. What I should have done, he said, was to criticize the United States, as the representatives of Ghana and United Arab Republic had done. I told him that I was no longer the representative of my country, but the Acting Secretary General of the United Nations, and that my conscience was very clear about the propriety and correctness of my action. He showed signs of continuing the dialogue, but the hour was late, and I asked him to see me the next day at 2:45 P.M. to continue the discussion for a few minutes, since I had to perform the flag-raising ceremony for the newest member of the United Nations—Uganda—at three o'clock.

He came to my office at the appointed time, accompanied by the Soviet deputy permanent representative, Ambassador Platon Morozov, and an interpreter. The main point of his argument was that, as Acting Secretary General, I should have condemned all violations of the United Nations Charter. He did not understand why I did not condemn the unilateral action by the United States of quarantining a sovereign member state, without a war situation prevailing. I repeated my stand taken on the previous day—that in my position, the appeal I had made was the only helpful means of preventing a confrontation between the two nuclear giants.

Since he went on insisting that my statement was "a bad one," I had to cut the conversation short. I told him firmly that if he really felt that way, he had better condemn me openly in the Security Council meeting scheduled late in the evening. He was visibly taken aback by that suggestion. It was now three minutes to 3:00 P.M., and I had to go downstairs to perform the flag-raising ceremony. We broke off our conversation and left my office together.

---

[2] *United Nations Security Council Official Records, No. 1024,* October 24, 1962.

After the very brief ceremony, I went straight to the General Assembly hall to attend a plenary session. At 3:30 P.M., while I was still on the podium, I got a note from my secretary saying that Ambassador Morozov wanted to see me urgently and was already waiting behind the podium. I immediately left my seat and took him to my office adjoining the General Assembly hall. His first question was whether I had received any communication from Chairman Khrushchev. When I replied in the negative, he took a small piece of paper from his pocket and said that the Soviet mission had just received a copy of Mr. Khrushchev's reply to my message. It was in Russian, and he translated it for me. The message was:

> Dear U Thant,
> I have received your message and have carefully stud-
> ied the proposal it contains. I welcome your initiative. I
> understand your concern over the situation which has
> arisen in the Caribbean, for the Soviet Government too
> regards it as highly dangerous and as requiring immedi-
> ate intervention by the United Nations. I wish to inform
> you that I agree to your proposal, which is in the interest
> of peace.
>
> With respect,
> (signed) N. Khrushchev.[3]

I then understood why Ambassador Zorin personally did not come to inform me of the message. He would have been very embarrassed to convey it, in view of what he had said to me on the thirty-eighth floor only a few minutes earlier. When Ambassador Morozov left me, I wondered why Ambassador Zorin was so vehement in criticizing my appeal, obviously without any instruction from Moscow. On my way to the Security Council chamber, I told Omar Loutfi, undersecretary for special political affairs, about the strange outburst of Ambassador Zorin only sixty minutes before. His only explanation was that perhaps Mr. Zorin had anticipated

---

[3] *United Nations Security Council Official Records, No. 1025,* October 25, 1962.

a stern rebuff by Mr. Khrushchev to my appeal, since in his (Zorin's) view, there were no Soviet nuclear missiles in Cuba. Mr. Loutfi's assumption proved to be true; as it turned out later, Mr. Zorin had been completely in the dark about the presence of Soviet missiles in Cuba.

I received the original reply from Chairman Khrushchev only at 5:00 P.M., while I was attending the Security Council meeting. Ambassador Zorin, who was seated at my left, did not once turn toward me. I knew that he was terribly embarrassed.

During the Security Council meeting, Ambassador Stevenson handed to me the reply to my appeal from President Kennedy. It was warm but less positive. The text of the message is reproduced below:

> I deeply appreciate the spirit which prompted your message of yesterday.
>
> As we made clear in the Security Council, the existing threat was created by the secret introduction of offensive weapons into Cuba, and the answer lies in the removal of such weapons.
>
> In your message and your statement to the Security Council, you have made certain suggestions and have invited preliminary talks to determine whether satisfactory arrangements can be assured.
>
> Ambassador Stevenson is ready to discuss promptly these arrangements with you.
>
> I can assure you of our desire to reach a satisfactory and peaceful solution of this matter.[4]

On the basis of these two replies, I immediately sent the following identical messages to Chairman Khrushchev and President Kennedy:

> I am most grateful to Your Excellency for your encouraging reply to my appeal of yesterday. I hope to begin discussions with Ambassador Zorin (Ambassador Stevenson) tomorrow, and I trust that the outcome of these discussions will be satisfactory to all concerned, and will advance the cause of peace.[5]

After the Council meeting of October 25, I sent my third messages to the two heads of government. (The full texts of these

---

4 Ibid.
5 United Nations Files.

messages and the replies I received are also included in Appendixes A–E, Part III.) In brief, the messages expressed my grave concern that Soviet ships already on their way to Cuba might challenge the quarantine imposed by the United States and produce a confrontation at sea between Soviet and U.S. vessels, thus destroying any possibility of the discussions I had suggested. I accordingly asked Chairman Khrushchev to instruct any Soviet ships already steaming toward Cuba to stay away from the interception area for a limited time only. And I asked President Kennedy to instruct U.S. vessels in the Caribbean to do everything possible to avoid direct confrontation with Soviet ships. To each I said that if I could have assurances of co-operation in avoiding all risk of an untoward incident, I would inform the other side of such assurances, thus gaining a breathing spell.

President Kennedy immediately accepted my proposal, contingent upon acceptance by the Soviet government; he pointed out, however, that the matter was now one of great urgency, since Soviet ships were still proceeding toward the interception area and work on the missile systems was continuing.

Chairman Khrushchev also accepted the moratorium. He informed me that he had ordered Soviet vessels bound for Cuba to stay out of the interception area, but stressed that since he could not keep ships "immobilized on the high seas," his order had to be "purely temporary."

On October 26, I sent a message to Prime Minister Fidel Castro informing him of the encouraging responses I had received to my appeals and asking that construction of major military installations in Cuba, and especially those designed to launch medium- and intermediate-range ballistic missiles, be suspended during the period of negotiations that were now underway. I reminded Mr. Castro of President Dorticós' statement to the General Assembly on October 8, in which he said that if Cuba had proof that the United States would not carry out aggression against it, their weapons would be unnecessary. The text of this message is reproduced in Appendix F, Part III.

(The significance of President Dorticós' statement made in the General Assembly on October 8 cannot be overemphasized. In effect, he had pledged to remove the weapons that the United

States regarded as offensive, if the latter were to "give proof" that it would not carry out aggression against Cuba. The United States should have taken advantage of that solemn statement and promptly declared that it would not carry out aggression against Cuba. In my opinion, that statement made President Kennedy's ultimatum unnecessary, and it only brought the world to the brink of a nuclear war.)

Prime Minister Castro's reply to my appeal (reproduced in Appendix G, Part III) was courteous and forceful—but far from encouraging. Although he said that Cuba was prepared to do everything in its power to resolve the crisis, he stressed that Cuba "flatly rejects" both the violation of its sovereignty involved in the blockade and "the presumption of the United States to determine what actions we are entitled to take within our country," including the kind of arms Cuba should consider appropriate for its defense, and the relations it was to have with the U.S.S.R. Cuba, he said, would accept the compromises I had proposed provided that the U.S. government "desist from . . . aggressive actions," including the naval blockade. An important part of the message, however, was an invitation the Prime Minister extended to me to visit Cuba with a view to direct discussion.

My judgment was that Cuba was fully within its rights to ask for and receive the missiles and bombers from a Big Power, in the same way that Turkey, Pakistan, Thailand, and Japan (Okinawa), on the perimeters of communist countries, were fully within their rights to act similarly. The only difference was that while the latter NATO, CENTO, and SEATO participants received the missiles and bombers openly from the United States, Cuba received them secretly from the Soviet Union.

During this period, I held private and separate consultations with the representatives of the United States, Cuba, and the Soviet Union with a view to beginning negotiations.

Meanwhile, my office was deluged with cables and letters, not only from heads of state and heads of government, but also from organizations and private individuals. Reactions among heads of state varied. While some criticized the United States for its "illegal and chauvinistic action," others were critical of the Soviet Union for "its dangerous nuclear gamble." Still others did not put the blame on either side, but simply expressed the hope that the United Nations could resolve the crisis. To cite a few examples, President Keita of Mali proposed the "eviction from . . . the U.S. of the Cuban refugees who are preparing . . . the invasion of Cuba." The Swedish government protested the U.S. naval blockade and in fact successfully tested it on October 26 by sending a ship, reportedly with a cargo from the U.S.S.R., through the interception zone to Havana. The Prime Ministers of India and Yugoslavia, together with Emperor Haile Selassie of Ethiopia, welcomed the initiative I had taken to ease the crisis. The individuals who cabled me included such men of international stature as Earl Bertrand Russell and Dr. Linus Pauling.

Linus Pauling's cable was curt and forceful: "I strongly urge that you strive to prevent the great immorality and illegality of an armed invasion of Cuba by the overwhelmingly powerful United States."[6]

Throughout October, Bertrand Russell sent an extraordinary series of equally forceful messages to President Kennedy, Chairman Khrushchev, and myself, as well as to other heads of government and various newspapers. On October 18, he sent me a letter expressing his grave concern at the seriousness of the international situation; in it he also asked me if he could address the General Assembly of the United Nations. Bertrand Russell was no doubt among the greatest thinkers of our time, and in addition one of the most courageous and passionate activists for peace. Like many wise and courageous men, however, he was innocent of United Nations procedures and practices. In my reply to him (reproduced in Appendix H, Part III), I had to say that unfortunately, under the rules, only delegations of member governments and heads of state can participate in Assembly debates.

A day before I sent that reply, I received from him a cable dated October 23: "I appeal to you for swift condemnation of tragic United States action. I am willing to do as I suggested in recent letter if you approve me. Earnest good wishes."[7] On the same day, I sent him the following cable: "Thank you for your telegram

---

[6] Ibid.

[7] This and following telegrams from *Unarmed Victory* (London: Allen Unwin, 1963), pp. 31, 32, 38, 45.

of 23 October. As you are aware, matter is already before Security Council."

On October 23, Russell sent telegrams both to President Kennedy and Chairman Khrushchev.

To President Kennedy: "Your action desperate. Threat to
human survival. No conceivable justification. Civilized man condemns it. We will not have mass murder. Ultimatums mean war. I
do not speak for power but plead for civilized man. End this
madness."

To Chairman Khrushchev: "I appeal to you not to be provoked by the unjustifiable action of the United States in Cuba.
The world will support caution. Urge condemnation to be sought
through United Nations. Precipitous action could mean annihilation for mankind."

He also sent a telegram to Prime Minister Macmillan on the
same day: "Urge you to prevent American madness from bringing
on nuclear war. Speak out while time permits."

To Hugh Gaitskell, leader of the Labour Party: "Urge opposition to join our mass protests against imminent disaster threatened by American madness over Cuba. This is the moment to
act."

On October 24, Khrushchev sent Russell a long and friendly
cable expressing his sincere "gratitude for the concern you have
displayed in connection with the aggressive actions of the United
States in pushing the world to the brink of war." He then added,
"The question of war and peace is so vital that we should consider
a top-level meeting in order to discuss all the problems which
have arisen, to do everything to remove the danger of unleashing
a thermonuclear war."

The same evening, Russell sent Khrushchev another telegram: "Thank you for your heartening reply. I congratulate you
on your courageous stand for sanity. I hope you will hold back
ships in Cuban waters long enough to secure American agreement
to your proposal. Whole world will bless you if you succeed in
averting war."

At the same time, he telegraphed to President Kennedy: "I
urge you most strongly to make a conciliatory reply to Khrushchev's vital overture and avoid clash with Russian ships long

enough to make meeting and negotiations possible. . . . I appeal to you to meet Khrushchev."

Meanwhile, Russell kept on sending telegrams and letters to heads of government and newspapers. On October 26, he received a reply from President Kennedy: "I am in receipt of your telegram. We are currently discussing the matter in the United Nations. While your messages are critical of the United States, they make no mention of your concern for the introduction of secret Soviet missiles into Cuba. I think your attention might well be directed to the burglars rather than to those who have caught the burglars."

In his *Unarmed Victory,* by way of comment on Kennedy's reply, Bertrand Russell wrote the following:

> It is true that I had not expressed concern for the introduction of secret Soviet missiles into Cuba. I could understand the hysteria that swept over the U.S. upon hearing of them, for the U.S. has heretofore had no powerful enemies upon its borders. But the presence of these missiles, even if they had really been secret and even had they been long-range, did not materially change the situation. Russia already possessed the power to blot out the U.S. if she wished to do so by long-range missiles based in Russia and missiles based upon submarines—a fact which the U.S. under other circumstances is fond of mentioning—just as the U.S. possesses the power to blot out most of Russia. The point of the Cuban affair was to avoid war whatever the provocation, and thereby to avoid the destruction of both the U.S. and Russia as well as the rest of the world. As to President Kennedy's remark about burglars: it is singularly *mal à propos.* Nobody could accuse the Cubans of being burglars, since they had not left their own island. As for the Russians, they came at the invitation of the Cubans and were no more burglars than are the American forces in Britain and Western Europe. But in view of the repeated American threats of invasion of Cuba, the Americans were at least contemplating "burglary."[8]

I am writing at some length on Bertrand Russell's activities regarding the crisis because I felt at that time, and still feel, that Khrushchev's positive reply to my first appeal of October 24 was,

---

[8] Ibid., p. 31.

at least in part, due to Earl Russell's repeated pleadings to him, and to his congratulating him on his "courageous stand for sanity." It will be recalled that in his message to President Kennedy, dated October 26, Mr. Khrushchev had the following reference to Earl Russell:

> We welcome all forces which stand on positions of peace. Consequently, I expressed gratitude to Mr. Bertrand Russell, too, who manifests alarm and concern for the fate of the world, and I readily responded to the appeal of the Acting Secretary-General of the U.N., U Thant.[9]

In one of my later meetings with Khrushchev, he spoke of Bertrand Russell with genuine feelings of respect and admiration, although he did not mention any specific case or action.

On October 23, a resolution adopted by the OAS on the same date was transmitted to me in accordance with Article 54 of the UN Charter. In effect, it called for the immediate dismantling and withdrawal from Cuba of all missiles and other weapons with any offensive capability. It further recommended that the member states of the OAS take all measures, including the use of armed force, to ensure the dismantling of the missiles and to prevent Cuba from obtaining additional weapons from the Sino-Soviet bloc. The resolution also recommended that the UN Security Council dispatch observers to Cuba.

Some historians have suggested that President Kennedy urgently sought such OAS action as the legal basis for any later military steps he might feel he had to take.

(Many constitutional experts and jurists have dealt with the delicate and complex question of the jurisdiction of regional organizations vis-à-vis that of the United Nations. The Charter of the United Nations, of course, attempts to define the nature of actions that regional organizations or agencies may take, and Article 52 clearly states that such action may be taken "provided that such arrangements or agencies and their activities are consistent with the Purposes and Principles of the United Nations." In this particular case, President Kennedy sought OAS action, for he knew such action would be in line with his own wish. The United

---

[9] United Nations Files.

States' resort to OAS action in the Cuban missile crisis of 1962, and in the Dominican Republic crisis of 1965, are comparable to the Soviet Union's invocation of the Warsaw Pact in its action in Hungary in 1956, and in Czechoslovakia in 1969. The failure of the Security Council, in March 1962, to request the International Court of Justice for an advisory opinion on the question of "enforcement action" was therefore most regrettable. By this *nonaction*, the Security Council implicitly endorses "Monroe Doctrines" everywhere on earth.)

It will be recalled that Prime Minister Castro, in his reply to my appeal of October 26, invited me to Cuba for discussions. In accepting his invitation on October 28, I expressed the hope that a solution would be reached whereby the principle of respect for the sovereignty of Cuba would be assured. It would also be possible, I added, to take measures that would reassure other countries that had felt themselves threatened by recent developments in Cuba.

Meanwhile, on October 27, I had received heartening news: a *note verbale* from the representative of the United States transmitting a copy of a letter from President Kennedy to Chairman Khrushchev indicating that according to the proposals, which were generally acceptable to the United States government, the Soviet Union would agree to remove the weapons systems from Cuba under appropriate United Nations observation and supervision, and also undertake, with suitable safeguards, to halt the further introduction of such weapons systems into Cuba. The United States, on its part, would agree, upon the establishment of adequate arrangements (through the United Nations) ensuring the carrying out and continuation of these commitments, to remove promptly the quarantine measures and also to give assurance against invasion of Cuba.

In a letter of October 28 addressed to me, Prime Minister Castro referred to President Kennedy's letter to Chairman Khrushchev, which said in effect that the United States would, after the arrangements noted above had been made, remove the blockade and give guarantees against invasion. He also referred to the decision announced by Chairman Khrushchev to withdraw strategic defense weapons facilities from Cuban territory. Prime Minister Castro said that the guarantees mentioned by President

Kennedy would be ineffective unless, in addition to the removal of the blockade, the following essential measures were adopted: (1) the cessation of the economic blockade and of all the measures of commercial and economic pressure being carried out by the United States against Cuba; (2) the cessation of all subversive activities, including the dropping and landing of weapons by air and sea, the invasion by mercenaries, and the infiltration of spies and saboteurs; (3) the cessation of piratical attacks carried out from the United States and Puerto Rico; (4) the cessation of violations of Cuban airspace and territorial waters by United States aircraft and warships; (5) withdrawal by the United States from its military base at Guantanamo.[10]

The *note verbale,* incidentally, was brought to me by Ambassador Stevenson and Mr. John McCloy, who was assisting him in the negotiations with the Russians. When Mr. Stevenson was alone with me, I asked him what he thought of a newspaper description of Mr. McCloy as a "hard old frontiersman." He laughed and said that Mr. McCloy "perhaps knows more about the Russians than I do."

I had known Mr. McCloy for a good number of years. He used to invite me to speak before the members of the Council on Foreign Relations, and at least on two occasions, he presided over those off-the-record and off-the-cuff affairs. At those closed-door meetings, I tried to be as frank and as candid as possible in my assessment of the international scene, whether it related to East-West relations or to the war in Vietnam. Whenever I stressed the need for peaceful coexistence or tolerance, Mr. McCloy was visibly ill at ease. On one occasion, while I was recounting my personal efforts to bring about a meeting of the representatives of Washington and Hanoi, he interrupted me briefly and cautioned the audience that my statement was off the record.

Although reputed to be a hard-liner with respect to the communist world, Mr. McCloy is an honest man with the courage of his convictions, a pleasant conversationalist, and a highly intelligent and knowledgeable observer of United Nations affairs. I

[10] Ibid.

do not know what Mr. Stevenson thought of him; he did not wish
to characterize Mr. McCloy in any way.

At the same meeting, Mr. Stevenson confided to me that
President Kennedy had asked Dean Acheson to join his group of
advisers. Mr. Acheson had fallen out with President Kennedy
when the United States opened talks with the Russians over Berlin
a year earlier. At that time, Mr. Acheson had said with bitterness
that President Kennedy did not understand the Russians. It will be
recalled that Mr. Acheson, in his autobiography, *Present at the
Creation,* observed that President Kennedy was "out of his depth"
in the Cuban crisis.

In my view, Dean Acheson was one of the most overrated
diplomats of his time. No doubt he was a man of great personal
charm and dignity. He used to see me in Geneva, in 1967, in connection with the situation in Cyprus. His only concern then was
the possible disruption of the southeastern flank of NATO, if the
situation in Cyprus were to get out of hand. Never once during
our meetings did he mention the role of the United Nations on
that troubled island. As far as he was concerned, the government
of Cyprus did not exist. His one objective was the cementing of
ties between Greece and Turkey—both members of NATO. Like
Foster Dulles, he thought it was immoral to be neutral or
nonaligned.

On October 28, the Soviet government directed Mr. V. V.
Kuznetsov, first deputy foreign minister of the Soviet Union, to
proceed to New York to co-operate with me in my efforts aimed
at the elimination of this dangerous situation. I was delighted at
the news. Mr. Kuznetsov, unlike Mr. Zorin, is a modest, persuasive, and charming man, and highly esteemed in United Nations
circles. I felt very much at ease with him, as I did with Mr.
Stevenson. The fact that Chairman Khrushchev sent Mr. Kuznetsov to "co-operate" with me indicated the recognition in Moscow
that my relations with Mr. Zorin had been deteriorating. There
came a stage in which I could no longer communicate with him.
He was not only a hard-liner (which I did not mind), but he
foolishly regarded me as an American stooge (which I did mind).

President Kennedy's sending Mr. McCloy to "help" Mr.

Stevenson was prompted by different reasons. The President (or someone in Washington) felt that Mr. Stevenson was too soft on the Cuban issue before the Security Council. There were even unconfirmed rumors at the time that Stevenson was privately advocating an exchange of Soviet missiles in Cuba for the American missiles in Turkey. In fact, he performed a most distinguished job at the Security Council as well as in the corridors of the UN. I cannot think of any other American diplomat who could have performed half as effectively as Stevenson during the Cuban missile crisis.

Chairman Khrushchev, in sending me his letter about Mr. Kuznetsov, also attached a copy of the letter he had sent to President Kennedy on the same day. In that letter he had said:

> I regard with respect and trust the statement you made in your message of October 27, 1962, that there would be no attack, no invasion of Cuba, not only on the part of the United States, but also on the part of other nations of the Western Hemisphere, as you said in your same message. Then the motives which induced us to render assistance of such kind to Cuba disappear.

He added that instructions had been given to Soviet officers "to take appropriate measures to discontinue construction of the aforementioned facilities, to dismantle them, and to return them to the Soviet Union. As I had informed you in the letter of October 27, we are prepared to reach agreement to enable UN representatives to verify the dismantling of these means [sic]. Thus in view of the assurances you have given and our instructions on dismantling, there is every condition for eliminating the present conflict."[11]

On October 28, I sent a message to Chairman Khrushchev and expressed my gratitude to him for having sent me a copy of his message. I said that I had noted the constructive proposals he had made in order to remove tension in the Caribbean area, and was particularly gratified that the Soviet Union had agreed to stop the building of missile bases, to dismantle them, and to return the missiles to the Soviet Union, and that he was ready to come to an agreement whereby representatives of the United Nations might

---

11 Ibid.

verify the dismantling of those bases. I added that I would discuss with Mr. Kuznetsov, as well as with Prime Minister Castro, the modalities of verification by United Nations observers to which he had so readily agreed.[12]

On the same day, President Kennedy replied to Chairman Khrushchev's message of that date by saying that he welcomed it and considered it an important contribution to peace. He also said that he regarded the efforts of the Acting Secretary General of the United Nations as having greatly facilitated their tasks. The President considered his letter of October 27 to Chairman Khrushchev and the latter's reply of October 28 as firm undertakings, which should promptly be carried out, on the part of both governments. He hoped that the necessary measures could at once be taken through the UN, so that the United States in turn would be able to remove the quarantine measures.[13]

Thus, the crisis had been solved. Both Khrushchev and Kennedy were now in a position to extricate themselves from the brink. The question of inspection, demanded by the United States and agreed to by the Soviet Union, remained to be pursued, however. Ironically, to everybody's surprise, Castro was not consulted when Khrushchev gave the green light for inspection. Since the Security Council had left the matter to me, I had no alternative but to attempt to explore the possibility of establishing a "UN presence" in Cuba.

MY TRIP TO HAVANA

During the few days between my acceptance of Premier Castro's invitation to visit Cuba and my flight to Havana, there were important developments that had considerable bearing on my trip. Although Chairman Khrushchev and President Kennedy had ostensibly come to an agreement, actually they had moved to the very edge of the brink.

On the evening of Saturday, October 27—while the Kennedy-Khrushchev messages for a moratorium on the high seas

---

[12] Ibid.
[13] Ibid.

were being exchanged—Moscow radio announced a dramatic proposal for an exchange of missile bases on Cuba and in Turkey. Chairman Khrushchev was reported to be ready to remove nuclear weapons from Cuba if the United States withdrew its missiles from Turkey; the withdrawal from both countries was to be controlled by the UN Security Council.

As Robert Kennedy pointed out in his book *Thirteen Days,* there was now doubt in Washington as to whether Saturday's tougher message superseded the secret conciliatory messages of Friday, or whether there had been some sort of mixup inside the Kremlin that had caused the tougher statement to be issued, even though Khrushchev had decided on a more conciliatory approach. There was even speculation that Khrushchev had changed his mind and was now pursuing a tougher line, or that the Presidium had overruled the softer approach of Friday. But it became clear on Sunday that Khrushchev was still following a conciliatory line, when Radio Moscow reported that the Soviet Union would remove the missiles now that the United States had agreed to guarantee Cuba's safety and end the blockade.

In any case, the offer to exchange missile bases raised some important questions about what Mr. Khrushchev's intentions in Cuba had been during those past few weeks. Had it been his intention all along to effect such an exchange? It seemed unlikely that he thought the U.S. bases in Turkey worth such a crisis. Or had he been taken by surprise by the vigor and obvious determination of President Kennedy's reactions, so that he then had to try to find a way to get himself out of a dangerous situation? These questions remained unanswered.

On the same evening, at about 7:00 P.M. General Rikhye told me that the news from Washington was grim. He feared that the possibility of a United States air strike at the missile sites and IL-28 Soviet bombers in Cuba could not be ruled out. According to his information, Khrushchev's latest reply to Kennedy was interpreted in Washington as less conciliatory than the one received a day earlier. Only an hour before, at 6:00 P.M., Zorin refused to accept from me a letter sent to me earlier by Stevenson for transmission to him. The letter (reproduced in Appendix I, Part III) defined an "interception area" of five hundred nautical miles around Cuba.

I left the office at 11:00 P.M. Exactly at midnight, Rikhye phoned. He said that United States bomber squadrons were reported to be on the alert, and that anything could happen within twenty-four hours.

At that time, the United States had not received Khrushchev's acceptance of Kennedy's understanding of the Chairman's proposals, and the United States was preparing to tighten the screws.

I immediately phoned Stevenson at the Waldorf Towers, but his phone was busy for quite some time. When I got him at last, he sounded tired. He said that he had no information about the U.S. air squadrons being on the alert, but added that the situation was "touch and go." I asked him if he could see me on Sunday morning. With his customary wit and aplomb he said: "Secretary General, it is already Sunday morning. Can I see you now?" I lived in the Riverdale section of the Bronx, and it would take him a good thirty minutes to drive to my residence. I told him that both of us needed some rest, and suggested 9:30 or 10:00 A.M. He was in my office at ten and said that there was no confirmation from Washington of the information I received the previous midnight.

He looked very weary, almost distraught. I got the impression that he resented being left out of inner-circle discussions. He was completely unaware of Khrushchev's proposed exchange of United States missiles from Turkey and Soviet missiles from Cuba. The Moscow radio announcement of that proposed deal got banner headlines in the Sunday papers.

Then we discussed matters relating to my visit to Havana. I asked Mr. Stevenson to convey my request to Washington that the naval quarantine be lifted, irrespective of any other consideration, for the time I would need to appeal to Cuba, and at least during my presence in Havana. On the morning of Monday, October 29, after the Kennedy-Khrushchev agreement had become known, Washington announced that the quarantine would be lifted for forty-eight hours with effect from Tuesday, October 30.

On the same day, October 29, Mr. Zorin brought with him Mr. Kuznetsov, who had arrived in New York only the previous night. Mr. Kuznetsov told me that, while Moscow would not object to the United Nations being asked to send an observation team to certify the dismantling of the missile launching pads in Cuba, his government would prefer verification of the removal of the missiles by the International Red Cross. Both Kuznetsov and Zorin agreed with me that such UN involvement would need the consent of the Cuban government.

I then had the UN office in Geneva contact the International Committee of the Red Cross (ICRC), and that same afternoon received the reply that ICRC would undertake the assignment, but only, of course, with the consent of the Cuban government. On Monday, I told Mr. Stevenson of the possible involvement of ICRC. He said he thought his government would go along with it. I gave the same information to Ambassador Mario García Incháustegui of Cuba, and he said he would immediately report to Havana. Mr. Stevenson, incidentally, asked me to use my good offices to get the release, if he were still alive, of a Major Rudolf Anderson, the pilot of a U-2 plane that had been shot down over Cuba.

What was more significant and more relevant to my projected visit to Havana was Premier Castro's broadcast statement on October 28. It in effect declared that while President Kennedy's "no-invasion guarantee" might have been sufficient to satisfy Premier Khrushchev, it was not acceptable to him. It was also significant that the Cuban press and radio did not mention Premier Khrushchev's proposal of October 27 for a deal involving the Cuban and Turkish missile bases. The Cubans were not told what the Kennedy-Khrushchev exchanges had been, nor that Moscow had advised Washington that orders had been issued to halt the construction of the bases.

On Sunday morning (October 28), after Ambassador Stevenson left my office, I watched from the thirty-eighth floor window a massive peace demonstration of about ten thousand people, gathered in front of the United Nations. Up to that time, it was perhaps the largest demonstration ever staged near the World Organization. I could see hundreds of signs and banners, and almost everybody was shouting slogans, which were not, of course, audible from my office. Later, I found out that the demonstrators carried signs reading: "We oppose all bases and all blockades," "Negotiations—not war," and so on.

Against that background and in that atmosphere, I left for Havana on the morning of Tuesday, October 30, on a Varig Airlines plane chartered by the United Nations. I was accompanied by Mr. Omar Loutfi, undersecretary for special political affairs, Dr. Hernane Tavares de Sá, undersecretary for public information, Brigadier General I. J. Rikhye, my military adviser, and a party of fifteen others, including my personal staff, secretaries, security guards, interpreters, and telecommunications personnel. In the hope that Premier Castro might agree to permit a small group of observers to be stationed in Cuba, I took with me telex machines and some radio transmission and receiving equipment.

We arrived in Havana at 1:15 P.M., and were met at the airport by Mr. Raúl Roa, Foreign Minister of Cuba, Mr. Pelegrin Torras, deputy foreign minister, and a large party of visiting foreign dignitaries, including General Albino Silva, special envoy of the President of Brazil to Cuba. After greeting the diplomats at the airport, we were driven straight to the government guest houses. The guest houses are three elegant mansions, situated in the fashionable diplomatic quarter of Havana. All the rooms were tastefully furnished, the motif being essentially Spanish. One is reminded of the iron-grated villas in affluent sections of Panama City, or the Mediterranean mansions in the fashionable suburbs of San Francisco.

Before we left the guest houses for the presidential palace, I discussed with Omar Loutfi the procedures of the projected meetings. I felt that the first day's meeting should be formal and in essence exploratory, and that the meeting on the second day should be more frank, based on the outcome of the first meeting. If necessary, I would like to attend the second meeting alone, accompanied only by my interpreter. He agreed.

The drive from the guest houses to the palace was along the deserted but scenic road skirting the seashore. We could clearly see a United States destroyer patrolling just outside Cuban territorial waters (three miles). The cars passed through two sandbagged antiaircraft emplacements, each manned by two or three militiamen.

Foreign Minister Raúl Roa and a few aides were waiting at the entrance to the presidential palace, where we arrived at about 3:00 P.M. Participating in the talks at the first meeting were, on the Cuban side, President Osvaldo Dorticós, Prime Minister Fidel Castro, Foreign Minister Roa, and Ambassador Mario García Incháustegui. On my side were Mr. Omar Loutfi, Dr. Hernane Tavares de Sá, and Brigadier General Rikhye.

The conference room was sparsely furnished, with a long table and a set of Mediterranean-style chairs, and almost nothing else. While President Dorticós, in dark business suit, was all smiles, Premier Castro looked grim. He wore khaki military fatigues and had a large pistol dangling from his belt. In the course of over two hours' talk, he smiled only two or three times. Miguel Marín of Spain, who was in my party, acted as interpreter when I spoke to Spanish-speaking diplomats. The talks were conducted in a businesslike manner.

I opened the discussion by explaining the nature of the mandate the United Nations had given me in Cuba and outlining the UN position on a number of issues. I said that the overwhelming opinion at the United Nations, particularly that of forty-five nonaligned nations, was behind me in my quest for peace, not only in the Caribbean, but throughout the world. To achieve this objective, a spirit of accommodation was necessary on the part of those directly concerned in the conflict. It seemed to me, I said, that the problem had two aspects: immediate and long-term. I had a mandate to deal only with the immediate aspects of the problem. Mr. Khrushchev had already instructed his officers to take the necessary measures to stop the building of missile bases, to dismantle them, and to return the missiles to the Soviet Union. He had also informed me that he was ready to come to an agreement that representatives of the United Nations might verify the dismantling of the bases. On this question, I continued, I was fully conscious of the fact that the United Nations could undertake that task only with the consent of the Cuban government. I appealed to the President and the Premier to give their consent. Mr. Kennedy had assured me that if such an action were taken by the United Nations, as agreed to by Mr. Khrushchev, the United States would avoid direct confrontation with the Soviet ships and the blockade would be lifted. I also explained the possibility of Red Cross (ICRC) involvement in verifying the withdrawal of Soviet missiles from Cuba. I said that I shared Mr. Castro's feeling, expressed in his communications to me, that unreserved respect for the sovereignty of Cuba was an essential prerequisite to any solution of the problem. Finally, I told the Cuban officials that I brought with me a few aides and hoped to leave some of them behind to continue our common effort towards the peaceful solution of the problem.

The Premier asked me whether the demand of the United States for the dismantling of the launching pads in Cuba was based on right or on a position of might. I answered that it was not based on right, but based on apprehension. He replied that he saw no reason for this request, since Cuba had always acted in strict conformity with international law and committed no aggression against any country. On the other hand, he continued, the United States had frequently violated international law (Cuban airspace) and was instrumental in aggression against Cuba (the Bay of Pigs). He went on to say that the United States always attempted to justify its aggressive acts by getting the agreement of the Organization of American States. As far as Cuba was concerned, he said, the OAS had no value, the more so as Cuba had been expelled from that organization. He stressed that Cuba would accept anything within the limits of international law that would imply no "maiming" of its sovereign rights; it would not accept anything imposed by force. Mr. Castro stressed that the demand for inspection was intended to humiliate the Cuban state and Cuban people, and his government would never accept it. Cuba had to take measures to defend its security against a systematic policy of hostility and aggression.

I stressed the interim character of the solution I was seeking, since I had no mandate to discuss long-term solutions. The immediate crisis must be brought to an end on the basis of the agreement reached between two of the three parties involved. I reiterated my position that no United Nations action could be undertaken on Cuban soil without the consent of its government, as in the cases of Laos, Egypt, and Lebanon, in which situations had also developed that greatly endangered world peace, and in which the UN presence was established only with the consent of their respective governments.

The Premier, after expressing his government's great esteem for me personally and for my "noble mission," spoke at length on the legitimate rights of all peoples to defend themselves against aggression. He said that Cuba fully knew the ways of aggressors, and especially the intentions of the United States regarding his country. He could not understand how immediate solutions could be separated from long-term solutions. Cuba's interest was not to buy peace *now* at any price, but to have it secured forever. He did not want to pay a price daily for short-lived peace.

I told him that I understood his feelings, but said that what was necessary at the moment was to avert a terrible catastrophe. President Dorticós, at that stage, joined Premier Castro in praising my "noble mission." He said, however, that the important point was to determine the causes and motivations of aggression. He believed that the danger of war was created by the aggressive intentions of the United States, and not by the presence of arms in Cuba or elsewhere. "Why," he asked, "is inspection needed to guarantee peace?" A UN presence in Cuba for a few weeks could not guarantee it. The danger of aggression would reappear so long as the United States had aggressive intentions against Cuba. The Five-Point Formula proposed by Premier Castro on October 28 would solve both short- and long-term problems, and that formula alone would constitute a basis for peace.

I thanked the President, and reiterated that my mandate did not include the discussion of the Five-Point Formula. The purpose of my visit was to avert the impending catastrophe.

Premier Castro repeated his assertion that the U.S. insistence on inspection was simply meant to humiliate Cuba. The Cuban government had raised no obstacles to the withdrawal of strategic weapons, and the United States knew full well that the Soviet Union was sincere in its pledge to withdraw them. Then why the inspection? The only purpose was to humiliate his country. He added, "We will never accept humiliating conditions imposed on us. Before the aggressors succeed, they will have to annihilate all of us first."

I referred again to the public pledge given by the United

States that it would not commit any aggression, once the missile bases had been dismantled and removed from Cuba. Of course, I added, if the government of Cuba could not permit the presence of the United Nations team on its soil, all I could do was to report back to the Security Council.

Premier Castro summed up his government's position: It was opposed to a United Nations presence in Cuba for any purpose; the Soviet pledge to withdraw its "strategic arms" should be accepted as binding; Cuba was opposed to Red Cross inspection in Cuban ports; if the Soviet Union permitted the Red Cross to inspect its vessels on the high seas, then that was "their business." Then he made the final point: stress had been laid on the U.S. pledge not to invade Cuba. What right had the United States to invade Cuba? To do so would be a crime. And why did the United Nations attach such great importance to the U.S. pledge, while at the same time it did not attach equal importance to a public pledge given by the Soviet Union to dismantle the strategic arms and withdraw them? There were two pledges. Why was it that additional guarantees were required to give effect to one pledge and not to the other?

Since the position of the Cuban government was firm and categorical, I decided to interrupt the proceedings, and proposed that another meeting should take place at ten the next morning, when I would be accompanied only by my interpreter. Premier Castro agreed. The meeting was adjourned, and we left for our guest houses.

At the guest house, my secretary told me that the Soviet ambassador wanted to see me briefly before dinner. He turned up at 7:45 P.M., and I saw him alone. He looked very young for an ambassador and was extremely polite—or was he nervous? The purpose of his visit was just "to pay his respects" to me, and to thank me for my efforts for a peaceful settlement of the crisis. In reply to my question, he said that he had received instructions from his government to dismantle the missiles and launching pads. At that point, he asked if he could bring in the general in charge of the missiles; the general was apparently waiting in a den between the living room and the room in which I received the ambassador.

At that moment, I asked Rikhye to join us, and he came in

with the Soviet general. The general must have been about forty, with a boyish look and manners—the last man one would have thought to be in charge of missiles. I asked him when the process of dismantling would start. To the surprise of both Rikhye and myself, he said that the dismantling of the missiles and their installations was already in progress, and that this process would be completed on Friday, November 2. He had no information about when they would be crated and returned to the Soviet Union, but hoped that in a few days he would receive word from Moscow, and then "all the missiles and their installations" would be loaded and returned.

It was obvious that both the ambassador and the general had been instructed by Moscow to see me and reassure me of what Khrushchev had assured Kennedy. I thanked them for the visit and information, and after they left, Rikhye told me that our visit to Havana was extremely worthwhile—for this information alone, from a completely unexpected but authentic source, if for nothing else.

Although the foreign diplomats in Cuba were convinced that the missiles would be dismantled and withdrawn, nobody seemed to be aware at that time that the process of dismantling had already started.

After dinner, I jotted down my notes for the day and went to bed at about midnight.

I got up at six-thirty the next morning (October 31), and tried to meditate, as usual. I sat up in bed and closed my eyes, but my mind wandered. Scenes of the United States destroyer off the Cuban coast, the Cuban antiaircraft emplacements, an unsmiling Castro, a nervous Soviet ambassador and a youthful missile general flitted across my mind's eye. It was difficult to shut off my senses, even for a brief moment, and feel inner peace. Perhaps loss of sleep was the reason. Or was I very worried? In any case, I managed to practice *metta* (good will) and *karuna* (compassion) to all.

Exactly at 10:00 A.M., I attended the scheduled meeting accompanied by Mr. Marín, my interpreter. As on the previous day, the President, the Premier, the Foreign Minister, and the ambassador were present. Since we had agreed to release the full text of the proceedings of our first meeting, but not those of the second, this meeting was far more frank than the previous one.

Regarding Chairman Khrushchev's pledge to dismantle the missile launching pads and withdraw them, Premier Castro said in effect that Mr. Khrushchev could not legitimately make such a pledge without consulting the Cuban government. He stressed that such a pledge or assurance could be given only by the Cuban government, and "by nobody else," and told me that he had already informed the Soviet government of his position. (On this question, there is no doubt about the correctness of Castro's position. Since it was his government that had requested and received the missiles from Khrushchev, Cuba should have been consulted before Khrushchev gave the pledge to Kennedy.)

He also told me that he was going on the air that night to give a comprehensive account of his government's position on the crisis. In his speech, he was going to tell Chairman Khrushchev, among other things, that he had no right to invite United Nations inspectors on Cuban soil.

I told the Premier that an inflammatory broadcast would certainly worsen the already critical situation, and I requested him not to go ahead with it. Since he had already announced it on the radio the previous night, he said he had to go ahead with it. But at my further request, he agreed to delete the inflammatory portions of his speech, and promised that it would be a "mild one."

He then elaborated on his Five-Point Formula, which alone, he said, could lead to a lasting solution. I explained to him that only the Security Council could deal with that formula, and that the chances of its adoption were almost nil because of Big-Power attitudes to the problem. He did not make any comment.

At that point, I asked him if it would be agreeable to his government if I were to leave behind one or two of my aides in Havana to continue to have a direct link between the government of Cuba and the Secretary General, since developments were moving very fast, and constant contact between the two would be essential. He said that he regretted that such an arrangement was impossible: the Cuban people would conclude that the Secretary General had left behind some people with a view to inspecting the dismantling of missile installations, as had been repeatedly broadcast from the United States radio and television for the past three days. The acceptance of such an arrangement would be interpreted by the Cuban people as humiliating to Cuba. He made one very important, and totally unexpected, proposal, however. His government would accept United Nations inspection on Cuban soil, if similar inspection could be made in "the invasion camps across the seas, including Florida." He said that everybody knew where the Bay of Pigs invasion was launched from, who trained the invaders, and where the training took place.

He then said that the United States would never agree to such an arrangement, since it would reveal "their criminal plots." He said the Cuban government would therefore send a mission to the United Nations, led by the Foreign Minister, for high-level negotiations in New York. He added that the Foreign Minister and his colleagues in New York would be better contacts with the Secretary General than his representatives in Havana.

Then I brought up the question of Major Anderson, the U.S. pilot whose plane was reported to have been shot down over Cuba. I requested the Premier to return him to the United States, on humanitarian grounds, if he were still alive. Mr. Castro replied that the pilot was not alive, and if the United States desired, his body could be sent back under the auspices of the Secretary General. He explained that the U-2 had been brought down by Cuban antiaircraft guns, manned only by Cubans, and that the airman fell with the plane and died instantly. He went on to say that he could not accept the legalization of foreign intrusion of Cuban airspace. The Cuban people would destroy any plane that intruded at any time. This continued infringement of Cuban airspace by the United States was one of the major problems confronting not only Cuba, but the whole world. The casket containing the body of the pilot was returned to the United States, under the escort of General Rikhye, on November 4.

Before I left the presidential palace in Havana on October 31, Premier Castro told me that he had just received news from the wire services that the United States would not give up their intention of launching another aggressive attack. He wanted me to carry back one impression above all—that the Cuban people were determined to protect their national sovereignty by every means at their disposal.

When we all rose, Mr. Castro asked me if I would mind posing for photos, and I said I would not. He gave one of his rare smiles and said that this photo would be historic if the Cuban problem were solved, and would mean nothing if not.

After lunch at the guest house, we all returned to New York in the same Varig plane that had brought us to Cuba the previous day. Almost the entire press corps in New York seemed to be at Idlewild airport. I made a brief statement and answered a few questions. In my statement, I said that there was agreement that the United Nations should continue to participate in the peaceful settlement of the problem, and that the dismantling of the missiles and their installations was already in progress and should be completed by Friday. Thereafter, there would follow their shipment and return to the Soviet Union, arrangements for which are understood to be in hand.

Before I drove to my office, I asked an information officer who was a member of my party to monitor Premier Castro's speech scheduled to be broadcast that night. He reported to me on the next day, November 1, that it was one of the most moderate speeches ever made by Premier Castro. In the broadcast, which began at 8:44 P.M., the Prime Minister read the full verbatim of the first meeting, as recorded by the Cuban side, stressing the Cuban government's firm rejection of any United Nations inspection of installations in Cuba, and that the U.S. insistence on inspection was intended to humiliate Cuba. From time to time, he interrupted the recital of the proceedings of the first meeting with his own comments, and at one point, he described me as "sincere and impartial, desirous to find a solution to these problems." He then added: "U Thant respects the rights of our country."

As agreed, Mr. Castro did not disclose the substance of our discussion on the second day, except to say that "certain discrepancies had arisen between Cuba and the Soviet government." He said that he did not want to give Cuba's enemies an opportunity to "cash in" on these differences. "There will be no split," he said, "between the Soviet government and Cuba." In his concluding remarks, he said that the strategic weapons sent by the Soviet Union to strengthen the Cuban defense did not belong to Cuba, and that this was why Cuba had not opposed the withdrawal of the weapons.

THE SETTLEMENT OF THE CRISIS

Among those who saw me on Thursday, November 1, was Anastas Mikoyan, first deputy prime minister of the Soviet Union, who was on his way to Havana. It was obvious that Moscow had to convince Havana of the "rightness" of Mr. Khrushchev's decision to withdraw the missiles from Cuba. Perhaps massive additional aid, in the form of civilian supplies and even further deliveries of non-nuclear military equipment, would be offered.

Tensions began to ease during Mr. Mikoyan's visit to Cuba, when neither the Russians nor the Cubans put up any opposition to the low-flying reconnaissance planes that the United States was keeping on nonstop operations over Cuban sites. Their flights were meant primarily to provide maximum information on the final stages of the dismantling processes. At this time, I had almost daily discussions with a member of the Red Cross Committee on the modalities of verification of dismantled Soviet missiles on the high seas.

On November 13, Mr. Kuznetsov gave me a copy of a draft protocol outlining an agreement reached, with my participation, by the governments of the U.S.S.R., the United States, and Cuba.

There were fourteen articles in the draft protocol, and although all the articles were not acceptable to Cuba, it became clear that the United States would not insist on actual United Nations inspection of the dismantling of the launching pads on Cuban territory. Nor would it insist on Red Cross verification of missiles withdrawn from Cuba on the high seas. In view of the complications, the United States had decided to rely on its own observation flights, which were tacitly permitted by Cuba.

Meanwhile, Foreign Minister Chen Yi of the People's Republic of China sent a note to the Cuban chargé d'affaires in Peking: "Cuba's destiny is in the hands of the Cuban people and not in the hands of any other country." A high Chinese official was reported to have told a visiting dignitary that Cuba was "Khrushchev's Munich."

On November 20, 1962, President Kennedy made this announcement:

> I have today been informed by Chairman Khrushchev that all of the IL-28 bombers now in Cuba will be withdrawn in thirty days. He also agreed that these planes can be observed and counted as they leave. Inasmuch as this goes a long way toward reducing the danger which faced this Hemisphere four weeks ago, I have this afternoon instructed the Secretary of Defense to lift our naval quarantine.[14]

Thus, the crisis in the Caribbean ended in a compromise.

The settlement was an eloquent illustration of the usefulness of the United Nations to member states as a place for peaceful settlement of international conflicts. It is clear that direct, and almost daily, communication between President Kennedy and Chairman Khrushchev was mainly responsible for bringing to an end a most frightening confrontation between the two nuclear giants.

Although neither Kennedy nor Khrushchev distinguished himself in allowing the crisis to develop, both of them showed a sense of responsibility and statesmanship, once the situation almost got out of hand. This spirit of give-and-take must be regarded as a decisive factor in averting what appeared to be an inevitable confrontation between the two nuclear powers. It was revealed much later that on Friday, October 26, a secret meeting between John Scali, then diplomatic correspondent of the American Broadcasting Company (now the U.S. permanent representative to the United Nations), and Alexander Fomin, a Soviet embassy counselor in Washington, sparked off a series of events that culminated in the agreement between the United States and the Soviet Union. Cuba, no doubt, was left in the cold, dissatisfied and disgruntled. But war—perhaps nuclear war—was averted.

The United Nations played an important role at the peak of the crisis. All three parties directly involved knew from the beginning that they could not ignore the World Organization; they

---

14 Ibid.

turned to the United Nations, either because they needed help or
because they needed to prevent the world forum from being
monopolized. As subsequent developments show, the debates in
the Security Council had tremendous impact in turning the general
opinion of a large number of member governments in favor of
finding an alternative to war; the acceptance by the Soviet Union
and the United States of my suggestions helped avert an armed
clash at sea, and the fact that both the Soviet Union and the
United States agreed to the inspection role of the United Nations
is evidence of a potential of considerable importance for the Organization in the future.

Although the immediate danger was averted, a long-term enduring peace in the Caribbean needed to be sought. There was
logic in Castro's demand. He would accept United Nations inspection on Cuban soil on only one condition: similar inspections
should take place in the invasion camps across the seas, including
Florida. With this in view, I presented a working paper—marked
"strictly confidential"—to Stevenson on Monday, November 12,
for his government's consideration. In it, I proposed establishing a
UN observation group consisting of eminent personalities from
nonaligned countries, the primary task of which would be to verify, on the ground, the dismantling and return to the U.S.S.R. of
the missile systems in Cuba. The group would also investigate
complaints of offensive preparations, in any part of the Caribbean
or Central America, for launching an invasion against any country. The full text of the paper is reproduced in Appendix J, Part
III.

A week later, on Tuesday, November 20, at a luncheon I
gave to both United States and Soviet Union delegates (attended
among others by McCloy, Stevenson, and Kuznetsov), Stevenson
took me aside and informed me that my idea of a United Nations
observation group was not acceptable to his government. He also
slipped into my hands a paper marked "confidential." This turned
out to be a U.S. draft declaration outlining the settlement between
Kennedy and Khrushchev that had already taken place. The declaration noted that although the proposed inspection by UN observers had not come about, a "minimum inspection procedure
was . . . arranged with the U.S.S.R." under which U.S. vessels

carried out the number of missiles that had been taken in, and that the U.S.S.R. had agreed to similar form of verification of the withdrawal of bomber aircraft. As to Cuba, the paper noted further that since Cuba had refused inspection by the UN, the United States would "employ . . . other means of observation." The full text of the confidential paper is reproduced in Appendix K, Part III.

Since the declaration made no reference to my confidential proposal regarding United Nations observers, it was obvious that the United States would not accept any United Nations involvement on its territory or on the territories of its allies. After repeated consultations with Ralph Bunche, who was fully behind my confidential proposal of November 12, I saw no point in pursuing the matter any further. Thus, the long-term problem in the Caribbean still remains. But by the end of the year, the situation in the Caribbean had reached a point at which it ceased to give rise to anxiety. Indeed, after the crisis there was an easing of tension around the world, and a détente between the United States and the Soviet Union seemed to emerge.

The dawn of the détente was apparent from the joint letter I received on January 7, 1963, signed by Ambassador Adlai E. Stevenson and Vasili V. Kuznetsov, first deputy minister of foreign affairs of the U.S.S.R. The text of the letter is reproduced below:

> On behalf of the Governments of the United States of America and the Soviet Union, we desire to express to you our appreciation for your efforts in assisting our Governments to avert the serious threat to the peace which recently arose in the Caribbean area.
>
> While it has not been possible for our Governments to resolve all the problems that have arisen in connection with this affair, they believe that, in view of the degree of understanding reached between them on the settlement of the crisis and the extent of progress in the implementation of this understanding, it is not necessary for this item to occupy further the attention of the Security Council at this time.
>
> The Governments of the United States of America and of the Soviet Union express the hope that the actions taken to avert the

threat of war in connection with this crisis will lead toward the adjustment of other differences between them and the general easing of tensions that could cause a further threat of war.[15]

On January 9, 1963, I sent to them identical letters in which I noted the heartening information they had sent me and said that their letter would be issued as a Security Council document. My letter concluded:

> I share the hope expressed by your Governments that "the actions taken to avert the threat of war in connection with this crisis will lead toward the adjustment of other differences between them and the general easing of tensions that could cause a further threat of war." I am also confident that all Governments concerned will refrain from any action which might aggravate the situation in the Caribbean in any way.
>
> I also take this opportunity to thank you and your Governments for the appreciation expressed in the letter in regard to such assistance as I may have been able to render.[16]

---

[15] Ibid.
[16] Ibid.

PART IV

THE
MIDDLE
EAST

CHAPTER IX

A PERSONAL NOTE

My first contact with Israel was through its first minister to
Burma, David Hacohen, who later became a member of Israel's
Knesset (Parliament) and chairman of its Foreign Relations
Committee. As head of Prime Minister U Nu's office, I had constant contact with Mr. Hacohen, and I came to like him for his
humanity, unconventional manners, and the free and frank views
he expressed with a total lack of diplomatic subtlety. He was the
Prime Minister's favorite "diplomatic friend," and it was mainly at
his persuasion that U Nu decided to pay an official visit to Israel
in May 1955.

As was the case with previous visits by the Prime Minister to
foreign countries, I was to accompany him; I therefore had to
study the relevant literature on Israel—its background, government, domestic and foreign policies, and economic and social
structure. For many years, we Burmese had read with anguish of
the brutal persecution of the Jews during the Hitler years. We
recalled our own life of terror, death, and destruction during
World War II. Of course, the two situations do not bear com-
parison: the suffering of the Jews in Europe before and during
the war was unprecedented in human history, while the suffering
of the Burmese was confined to indiscriminate arrests, mysterious

disappearances of suspected "Anglo-American sympathizers," and, of course, the extensive devastation of our country.

Apart from that inherent sympathy for the Jews among the Burmese leadership, one other factor tended to strengthen the friendship between Burma and Israel. The leaders of both countries played a prominent part in the first Asian Socialist Conference held in Rangoon in 1951, and both pledged the building of socialist societies through democratic parliamentary processes.

In the course of my pretrip studies of Israel, I took account of another factor: the plight of the Palestinian refugees. U Nu told me that since his projected trip was to be purely a good will visit, he did not wish to raise any matter not germane to Burma-Israel relations. His sole intention was to improve relations between the two countries, and he was averse to taking up any matter relating to Israel and her neighbors.

This was the background to U Nu's first visit to the West (starting with Israel), and for Israel it was the first official visit by a Prime Minister of a foreign country since its creation by the United Nations. The reception accorded to him was extraordinary. For nine days, from the moment we set foot upon Israeli territory at Lod airport on the evening of May 29, 1955, the whole country was in a festive mood. The entire population, from the political leaders to the humblest settlers, extended to U Nu the warmest welcome I had ever experienced.

David Hacohen had left for Israel ahead of us to put the finishing touches to the program, and he accompanied U Nu's party throughout the tour. We flew from Nicosia to Israel in a special El Al Constellation, provided for us by Prime Minister Moshe Sharett. For the fifty-minute flight, the Israeli authorities especially selected an air hostess who, we were informed, had been a winner in an international beauty competition held in South Africa!

From Nicosia onwards, besides David Hacohen, three Israeli officers were attached to our party: Colonel Shaul Ramati, who was later the Israeli consul general in Chicago, Arthur Laurie, a specialist on Asian and Far Eastern affairs, and Michael Elizur of the Information Department. An interpreter for Mrs. Nu was found in Mrs. Sima Stosvic, a citizen of Haifa who had been born and brought up in Mandalay, and who spoke perfect Burmese.

U Nu and members of our party had opportunities of speaking to the settlers in the hills of Galilee and in the valleys of Jordan and Yezree, which were thriving agricultural centers. We saw Israel's bold and imaginative plans for the conquest of the desert. We visited collective and co-operative settlements, both of which were unique social experiments. We visited several industrial enterprises, and in Rehovah we witnessed the efforts of scientists to develop modern technology. Extensive talks were held between U Nu and President Yitshak Ben-Zvi, Prime Minister Moshe Sharett, David Ben-Gurion, Golda Meir (then Labor Minister), Joseph Sapir (then Minister of Transport and Communication), and other leaders.

U Nu was so impressed with what he saw and experienced in Israel that on his return to Burma he seldom failed to cite Israel as a model for any emerging nation. What impressed him most was Israel's conquest of the desert. In his farewell toast at the state banquet in Jerusalem, he said: "Such accomplishments as the conquest of the desert are in fact much more significant and of more lasting effect than military conquests, which are only capable of destroying human lives, property, and all that humanity stands for. Conquests that you are after serve humanity more effectively than other types of conquests, and that is, therefore, all the more reason that they are greater than all other conquests."

Two things struck me at that time and are still fresh in my mind: the first was the genuine warmth of the welcome we were accorded; the second was the vigor, inventiveness, and determination of the people. The Israelis are undoubtedly a very innovative nation.

I might add that when I got back to Burma, I recorded these impressions in a booklet I wrote about our trip. Other members of the party also recorded their own impressions. The Israeli authorities later translated our comments into English and published them as an official government pamphlet entitled *Israel Through Burmese Eyes.*

In view of the subsequent attacks made upon me by certain

Israeli spokesmen and particularly by the pro-Israel press across
the world, I should like to make it plain not that only have I been
a firm friend of Israel throughout the growth and vicissitudes of
that struggling country, but also that its leading and most representative spokesmen have constantly acknowledged the depth of
my personal concern for their national aspirations and well-being
and have accorded me the privilege of their friendship over these
difficult years. The instances that follow are only a few of the tan-
gible expressions of this close relationship.

When I was posted to the United Nations as Burma's permanent representative, my contacts with the Israeli permanent representative (later Foreign Minister), Abba Eban, were most cordial.
To my knowledge, I was the only permanent representative invited to speak before audiences at the commemorative ceremonies
of Israel's Tenth Independence Anniversary in 1958. These gath-
erings spread from Springfield, Massachusetts, to Miami Beach,
Florida. I was also invited to address fundraising meetings of the
United Jewish Appeal.

My remarks at one of these meetings are typical of my beliefs. At the Jewish Community Center of Springfield, Massachusetts (on May 28, 1958), I said:

> As a citizen of a country which has consistently maintained the
> friendliest of relations with Israel, I wish to venture on an analysis
> of common factors between our two countries. Despite all dispari-
> ties of history, geography, and climate, Israel and Burma are en-
> deavoring to revive their respective ancient cultures against the
> background of modern civilization. . . . Both Israel and Burma
> have one aim in common: the creation of a society of free and
> equal peoples, with equal opportunities for all, a society based on
> certain values of human and social life.

At the farewell dinner given for Abba Eban at the United
Nations on May 11, 1959, I was the only permanent repre-
sentative from the Third World invited to speak. Mrs. Eleanor
Roosevelt, who was seated at the head table with me (along with
Senator Jacob Javits, Governor Thomas Dewey, and Dr. Henry
Steele Commager) told me that it was very difficult to get other
ambassadors to speak, in view of Arab hostility toward Israel. I
spoke with genuine feeling for the departing diplomat.

In May 1967, however, the mood and attitude of Israel and its people toward me changed overnight and became, besides, extremely critical of the United Nations. The ostensible reason was my decision to withdraw the United Nations Emergency Force (UNEF) from Sinai and the Gaza Strip at the request of the Egyptian government. This decision has been so widely publicized —and became, in fact, so much a cause célèbre for critics of the United Nations, who vented their dismay and frustration on me— that I propose, first, to examine the facts of the situation that confronted me at the time and, second, to delineate, step by step, the action that took in consequence of those facts.

My sole purpose is to present the picture from only one vantage point: that of the United Nations, which has been deeply involved in the problem of the Middle East from the partition of Palestine to the present. I will present only the essential facts, based on the records of the principal deliberative organs of the World Organization, without any attempt at passing judgment on the course of events prior to my action of May 1967.

CHAPTER X

THE ARAB-ISRAELI WAR OF 1948 AND ITS AFTERMATH

Palestine, the narrow strip of land lying on the eastern shores of the Mediterranean, bounded on the east by Transjordan (now Jordan), on the north and northeast by Lebanon and Syria, and on the south by Egypt, was part of the Turkish Empire before the First World War. After that, Palestine was placed under a League of Nations mandate with the United Kingdom as the mandatory power. Hostility between the Jews and Arabs had been growing ever since the establishment of the British mandate. After the Second World War, those hostilities exploded into widespread violence, which led the government of the United Kingdom to decide to relinquish the mandate and bring the question of Palestine before the United Nations.

On April 2, 1947, the United Kingdom requested Secretary General Trygve Lie to place the question of Palestine before the General Assembly at its next regular session, and to summon a special session of the Assembly to study the problem. The first special session, held between April 28 and May 15, 1947, established a special committee on Palestine (UNSCOP) composed of representatives of eleven member states: Australia, Canada, Czechoslovakia, Guatemala, India, Iran, the Netherlands, Peru, Sweden, Uruguay, and Yugoslavia.

After a visit of inspection in the Middle East, the committee submitted a report to the General Assembly that contained twelve general recommendations, comprising a majority plan and a minority plan. The main recommendations were that the mandate for Palestine should be terminated as soon as possible and that there should be a short transitional period preceding Palestine's independence, during which the authority administrating Palestine should be responsible to the United Nations.

The majority plan was subscribed to by seven members of the special committee: Canada, Czechoslovakia, Guatemala, the Netherlands, Sweden, Peru, and Uruguay. It provided for the partition of Palestine into an Arab state and a Jewish state, bound together by an economic union. The city of Jerusalem, including Bethlehem, was to be placed under international trusteeship, with the United Nations as the administering authority. The minority plan, supported by three members (India, Iran, and Yugoslavia), provided for a federal state with Jerusalem as the federal capital. One member (Australia) abstained.

On November 29, 1947, the General Assembly adopted the majority plan; its resolution was accepted by the Jewish Agency for Palestine, but not by the Arab Higher Committee.

The partition plan contained in the Assembly resolution provided that the British mandate over Palestine should terminate and that British armed forces be withdrawn as soon as possible, in any case not later than August 1, 1948. (The United Kingdom later announced its intention to terminate the mandate on May 15, 1948.) The independent Arab and Jewish states and the international regime for Jerusalem were to come into existence two months after the departure of the British armed forces. Boundaries were established for the two states and for Jerusalem. A joint economic board was to be established, to consist of three representatives of each of the states and three members appointed by the United Nations Economic and Social Council. The United Nations Trusteeship Council was asked to draw up a detailed Statute for Jerusalem. The Assembly also established the United Nations Commission on Palestine, consisting of five members (Bolivia, Czechoslovakia, Denmark, Panama, and the Philippines), to implement the recommendations.

The Security Council, under the resolution, was requested to take the measures necessary to implement the plan and consider whether the situation in Palestine constituted a threat to the peace. If it decided that such a threat existed, the Council was to supplement the authorization of the General Assembly—in order to maintain international peace and security—by taking measures to empower the UN Palestine commission to exercise in Palestine the functions that were assigned to it. The Security Council was supposed to determine, as a threat to the peace, any breach of the peace or act of aggression, or any attempt to alter by force the settlement envisaged by the resolution.

Following the adoption of the partition resolution on November 29, immediate widespread disturbances, initiated by angry Palestinian Arabs who protested the partition, broke out in Palestine on an even larger scale than before. On December 9, the Security Council was apprised of the question of Palestine. The Palestine commission, in reports to the Council in December 1947 and January 1948, described a steadily worsening situation and stated that when the time came for it to take over the responsibility for administering Palestine, it would not be able to maintain law and order and implement the Assembly's resolution unless military forces in adequate strength were made available to it.

The Security Council did not take any action. Not until March 5, 1948, did it call on its permanent members to make recommendations on the guidance and instructions to be given to the commission. As a result, they recommended that the Council should make it clear to the parties concerned that it was determined not to permit a threat to international peace in Palestine.

An April 1, 1948, the Council called for a truce between "Arab and Jewish armed groups in Palestine," and also for the convening of another special session of the General Assembly. On April 17, the Council called for specific measures to be taken toward the implementation of the truce, and on April 23, established a truce commission for Palestine composed of the representatives of three states having career consuls in Jerusalem (Belgium, France, and the United States) to assist the Council in supervising the implementation of its April 17 resolution.

Meanwhile, the second special session of the General Assembly was convened on April 16. There being no prospect of implementing the partition plan because of Arab opposition, the Assembly, on May 14, decided to ask a committee composed of representatives of China, France, the Union of Soviet Socialist Republics, the United Kingdom, and the United States to choose a United Nations mediator for Palestine. It also decided to relieve the Palestine commission of its responsibilities. On May 20, 1948, Count Folke Bernadotte of Sweden was chosen UN mediator.

But on May 15, the United Kingdom relinquished its mandate over Palestine, and a Jewish state was immediately proclaimed, within the boundaries of the partition plan, under the name of Israel. The following day, several Arab states (Egypt, Jordan, Lebanon, Syria, and Iraq) attacked Israel.

The Security Council, on May 22 and 29, called on all governments and authorities to issue cease-fire orders and to abstain from any hostile military action in Palestine for four weeks. The mediator, in concert with the truce commission, was instructed to supervise the observance of the resolutions. Sufficient military observers were to be provided. The Security Council decided that if its resolutions were not accepted or were subsequently violated, the Council would reconsider the situation under Chapter VII of Charter, which provides for mandatory enforcement action. Both parties accepted the resolutions, and the unconditional truce became effective on June 11. Both sides appeared to accept the partition plan.

Early in July, the Security Council urgently appealed to the parties to accept a prolongation of the truce for a period to be decided upon in consultation with the mediator. The provisional government of Israel agreed to extend the truce, but the Arab states refused, and hostilities broke out anew. On July 15, 1948, the Security Council determined this to be a threat to the peace and ordered the governments and authorities concerned to desist from further military action and to issue cease-fire orders. Failure to comply would be construed as a breach of the peace requiring immediate enforcement action under the Charter. Observance of the truce, which was to remain in force until a peaceful settlement in Palestine was reached, was to be supervised by the mediator. The second truce became effective throughout Palestine on July 18, 1948.

On September 17, 1948, the mediator, Count Bernadotte, and the chief of the French observers, Colonel André Serot, were shot and killed by Jewish terrorists in the Israeli sector of Jerusalem. The functions of the mediator were taken over by Dr. Ralph Bunche, personal representative of the Secretary General in Palestine, who was confirmed as acting mediator by the Security Council.

In October, large-scale fighting broke out between Israelis and Egyptians in the Negev. The Security Council, on October 19, adopted a resolution calling for an immediate cease-fire, which was accepted on October 22 by both Israel and Egypt. On November 4, in another resolution, the Council called upon the governments of Israel and Egypt to withdraw their forces to positions held on October 14, and establish, through the United Nations, permanent truce lines.

On November 16, the Council decided that in order to facilitate the transition from the present truce to permanent peace, a general armistice should be established in all sectors of Palestine. It called on the parties directly involved in the conflict to seek, by negotiating either directly or through the acting mediator, an agreement that would include the delineation of permanent armistice demarcation lines.

Fighting flared up again in the Negev in December, and the Council (on December 29) once again called on the governments concerned to order an immediate cease-fire, to implement the resolution of November 4, and to facilitate supervision of the truce by United Nations observers. A cease-fire was arranged, effective January 7, 1949.

After intensive negotiations (conducted with the assistance of Ralph Bunche), Egypt and Israel signed a general armistice agreement at Rhodes on February 24, 1949. This was followed by general armistice agreements between Lebanon and Israel, Jordan and Israel, and Syria and Israel. For his outstanding contribution to the success of the negotiations, Ralph Bunche was awarded the Nobel Peace Prize in 1950.

Meanwhile, the General Assembly (on December 11, 1948) adopted a resolution that, among other things, provided for the establishment of a Conciliation Commission for Palestine composed of three members (France, Turkey, and the United States) to assume the functions given to the mediator and to seek a final settlement of all questions.

The armistice agreements between Israel and the various Arab states differed in certain particulars, but each agreement recognized the principle that none of its provisions should in any way prejudice the rights, claims, and positions of any party in the ultimate peaceful settlement of the Palestine question.

The agreements established armistice demarcation lines, the basic purpose of which was "to delineate the line beyond which the armed forces of the respective parties shall not move." In certain areas behind the demarcation lines—the so-called defensive areas—the military forces of the parties were to be confined to the defensive forces defined in the agreements. Certain other areas lying between the lines, expressly provided for in the Israel-Egypt and the Israel-Syria agreements, were to be demilitarized zones.

The armistice agreements also instituted four Mixed Armistice Commissions (MAC) to supervise their implementation. The commissions each consisted of an equal number of members designated by each party, and were under the chairmanship of the chief of staff of the United Nations Truce Supervision Organization (UNTSO), or a senior officer from the observer personnel of UNTSO designated by him. Thus the four Mixed Armistice Commissions were to operate within the UNTSO framework. UNTSO was to carry on with observer tasks similar to those entrusted to it under the truce of 1948. The main tasks of the Mixed Armistice Commissions were: to prevent any resumption of hostilities; to arrange for the exchange of prisoners of war; to establish permanent armistice demarcation lines in accordance with the principles laid down in the agreements; and to carry out specific provisions made in those agreements with a view to facilitating the transition to a permanent peace in Palestine.

The observers from UNTSO were to remain under the command of the chief of staff. The agreements also provided procedures for taking action on complaints from either side. Decisions were to be unanimous as far as possible; otherwise, by majority vote.

The Security Council subsequently relieved the acting mediator of his responsibilities and gave the UNTSO chief of staff the continuing duty to report to the Council on the observance of the cease-fire. The truces of May 29 and July 15 were now superseded by the armistice agreements.

Certain factors played an important role in the ultimate failure of the armistice system. The main function of UNTSO was merely to observe violations of armistice lines. The functions of MAC were confined to the consideration of violations of armistice agreements that had already taken place. Under this limited mandate, UNTSO and MAC could not take steps to strengthen the armistice. And from the beginning of the armistice, many border incidents broke out because the boundary was artificially drawn; villages, for instance, were separated from their agricultural fields. As a result, there were serious breaches of the armistice that led to massive retaliations.

There is a close relationship between the effectiveness of truce supervision and hope for an ultimate peace. Since the Palestine Conciliation Commission failed in its efforts to promote a final settlement, truce supervision was indefinitely prolonged. When an armistice lasts too long without turning into peace, violence is bound to increase, and ultimately the armistice system erodes.

In reviewing the results of truce supervision during this period, the importance of the unsolved problem of the Palestinian refugees cannot be overemphasized. The Arab states consistently declined to discuss a peace settlement until the refugee problem was solved. This problem has been a major cause of the failure to convert the armistice into a peace settlement.

Some 30,000 Palestinian Arabs were estimated to have left the area in the first few months after the adoption of the partition resolution. When the armistice agreements were signed, the number of Arab refugees in neighboring Arab countries was generally estimated to have been between 800,000 and 900,000.

In dealing with the Arab refugee problem, the measures taken by the General Assembly were concerned, on the one hand, with the ultimate solution of the question and the principles on which such a solution should be based, and on the other, with the provision of emergency relief.

On December 11, 1948, the Assembly adopted a resolution laying down the principles for settlement. Following is the relevant paragraph of the resolution:

[The Assembly] Resolves that the refugees wishing to return to their homes and live at peace with their neighbours should be permitted to do so at the earliest practicable date, and that compensation should be paid for the property of those choosing not to return and for loss of or damage to property which, under the principle of international law or in equity, should be made good by the Governments or authorities responsible.

It was in the same resolution, as we have seen, that the Assembly established the Palestine Conciliation Commission. In connection with the refugees, the Assembly instructed the commission "to facilitate the repatriation, resettlement and economic and social rehabilitation of the refugees and the payment of compensation. . . ." In its various reports, the commission stressed the seriousness of the refugee question, but acknowledged (in November 1951) that it had been unsuccessful in its endeavor to persuade both the Israelis and the Arabs to discuss the proposals in a fair and realistic spirit.

The Arab states insisted on the priority of a solution to the refugee question on the basis of the right of the Palestinian Arabs to repatriation, as recognized in the Assembly resolution. Israel maintained that the question could only be dealt with as part of a general peace settlement. While not ruling out the possibility of repatriation on a limited scale, Israel asserted that the majority of the refugees should be resettled in the Arab states rather than return to Israel where, it was stated, they represent a threat to Israel's security.

In taking emergency relief measures to prevent the refugees from starving, the General Assembly, on December 1, 1948, established the United Nations Relief for Palestine Refugees (UNRPR), and received voluntary contributions of $35 million from thirty-two governments. On December 8, 1949, the Assembly established the United Nations Relief and Works Agency for Palestinian Refugees in the Near East (UNRWA) to carry out relief and works projects in collaboration with local governments. An advisory commission was created to advise and assist the director of the agency, who was to be appointed by the Secretary General in consulation with the commission. On May 1, 1950, the assets and liabilities of UNRPR were transferred to UNRWA, which officially assumed responsibility and established its headquarters in Beirut, Lebanon. The mandate of UNRWA was extended successively by the General Assembly, the last extension being for three years and ending June 30, 1975. Total expenditure by UNRWA from May 1, 1950, to the end of 1971, was approximately $811,000,000.

The basic difficulties that faced the agency in fulfilling its task have been summed up each year by the commissioner general of the agency in his reports to the General Assembly. In his report to the twenty-seventh session of the Assembly in 1972, for instance, the commissioner general stated that "during the three-year period of the extension of its mandate which ended on June 30, 1972, the Agency was beset by operating difficulties that were a consequence of the events of 1967, and the political environment fostered by perpetuation of the *status quo* post-June 1967. The Palestine refugees were in ferment: there were sporadic violence and security problems; at its height in 1969–70, the political tension exacerbated staff and student problems."

CHAPTER XI

THE ARAB-ISRAELI WAR OF 1956 AND ITS AFTERMATH

During the period between 1949 and 1956, the armistice system in the Middle East broke down. The refusal of both sides to accept the rulings of MAC inevitably led to direct clashes with each other and to breaches of the agreements. Arab border raids—a significant factor in the breakdown of the system—were usually followed by Israeli retaliations.

Meanwhile, the power struggle in the Middle East intensified. The Baghdad Pact (Britain, Turkey, Iraq, Iran, and Pakistan), under the auspices of the United States, was formed in 1955. The French were supplying Mystère fighter aircraft to Israel, and Egypt obtained Russian weapons through Czechoslovakia. On July 19, 1956, the United States announced her decision not to proceed with the financing of the Aswan Dam project in Egypt.

On July 26, 1956, Egypt proclaimed the nationalization of the Suez Canal and placed the management of the Canal in the hands of the Egyptian operating authority. It also declared that Canal dues would be used to finance the Aswan Dam. The decree provided for compensation to the stockholders in the Canal Company on the basis of the market value of the shares.

The Security Council discussed the question of the Canal at several meetings held between September 26 and October 13, and on the latter date unanimously adopted a resolution by which it was agreed that any settlement of the Suez question should meet several requirements. The resolution required that there should be free and open transit through the Canal without discrimination, but that the sovereignty of Egypt should be respected; that the operation of the Canal should be insulated from the politics of any country; and that the manner of fixing tolls and charges should be decided by agreement between Egypt and the users. A fair proportion of the dues was to be allotted to the development of the Canal. In case of disputes, unsolved problems between the Suez Canal Company and the Egyptian government were to be settled by arbitration, with suitable terms of reference and suitable provisions for the payment of sums found to be due.

But war had already broken out. On October 29, 1956, the United States informed the Security Council that armed forces of Israel had penetrated deeply into Egyptian territory, in violation of the armistice agreement between Israel and Egypt, and requested an immediate meeting of the Security Council.

On October 30, the United Kingdom and France sent a joint ultimatum to Egypt and Israel calling upon both sides to stop all fighting and withdraw to a distance of ten miles from the Canal, and further requested Egypt to allow Anglo-French forces to be stationed temporarily on the Canal at Port Said, Ismailia, and Suez. "By previous arrangement the ultimatum was accepted at once by Israel, but its anticipated rejection by Egypt opened the way for the Anglo-French invasion."[1] The British and French air offensive against Egypt began at dusk on October 31, and on the same day, the United Kingdom and France vetoed a Security Council resolution calling on Israel to withdraw its forces from Egypt. Thereupon, the Security Council, under the "Uniting for Peace" resolution, called an emergency special session of the General Assembly to deal with the situation.

The first emergency special session of the Assembly convened on November 1, and on November 2 adopted a resolution by which it urged that all parties involved in hostilities in the area agree to an immediate cease-fire and withdraw all forces behind

---

[1] Brian Urquhart, *Hammarskjöld* (New York: Alfred A. Knopf, 1972), p. 173.

the armistice lines. It also urged that, when the cease-fire became effective, steps be taken to reopen the Suez Canal and restore freedom of naviation.

On November 4, the General Assembly requested the Secretary General, as a matter of priority, to submit to it within forty-eight hours a plan for setting up, with the consent of the nations concerned, an emergency international force to secure and supervise the cessation of hostilities. The Secretary General was also authorized, with the assistance of the chief of staff and members of UNTSO, to arrange with the parties concerned for the implementation of the cease-fire and to obtain compliance with the order for withdrawal of all forces behind the armistice lines. A cease-fire was achieved soon after the adoption of the resolution of November 4. The following day, the Assembly adopted a resolution establishing a United Nations Command for an Emergency International Force (UNEF) to secure and supervise the cessation of hostilities. Major General E. L. M. Burns, chief of staff of UNTSO, was appointed chief of the new command. Secretary General Dag Hammarskjöld submitted two reports to the Assembly on the functions of UNEF. His analysis indicated that UNEF should be of a temporary nature, the length of its assignment being determined by the needs arising out of the present conflict; he added that the stationing and operation of UNEF would be limited to the extent that consent of the governments of the countries concerned was required under generally recognized international law. The Secretary General stated that the UNEF would enter Egyptian territory, with the consent of the Egyptian government, in order to help maintain quiet during and after the withdrawal of non-Egyptian troops, and to secure compliance with the other terms established in the resolution of November 2.

At the beginning, the task of UNEF was defined in very general terms as being "to secure and supervise the cessation of hostilities." Its purpose in reality was to replace the withdrawn forces of Israel, France, and the United Kingdom. On February 2, 1957, the General Assembly, however, broadened the function of UNEF by calling upon Egypt and Israel to observe scrupulously the provisions of the general armistice agreement between them. It also provided that after full withdrawal of Israeli forces from the

Sharm-el-Sheikh and Gaza areas, this scrupulous maintenance of the armistice agreement required placing UNEF on the Egypt-Israel armistice demarcation line. In pursuance of the resolution, *UNEF would be stationed on both sides of the line.* In fact, however, Israel exercised its sovereign right to refuse the stationing of UNEF on its side, and the force throughout its existence was stationed only on the Egyptian side of the line, with consequences we will see later.

The first UNEF forces were airlifted to Egypt on November 15. By March 8, 1957, all Israeli, French, and British troops had been withdrawn.

With the deployment of UNEF along the international frontier in Sinai and the armistice demarcation line in the Gaza Strip, tension between Israel and Egypt was somewhat reduced during the next few years. Infiltration across the line from either side was almost ended, and military clashes between the armed forces of Israel and Egypt practically ceased.

In the early 1960s, however, a new factor greatly increased tension in the area. The Palestinian Arabs formed their own independent guerrilla organizations to harass Israel, which had consistently refused to comply with the recommendations of the General Assembly regarding the Palestinian refugees. These organizations —especially the one called *El-Fatah* (conquest)—enjoyed popular appeal in the Arab world, and their activities prompted Israel to retaliate with regular forces against the Arab states in which the commando attacks were organized.

In the later part of 1966 and the early part of 1967, the situation in the Middle East became increasingly ominous. The renewed violence along the Syrian and Jordanian frontiers contained the seeds of serious danger. There were frequent complaints to the Security Council by Israel of "armed incursions into Israeli territory of the Arab terrorist and sabotage group known as *El-Fatah*," and Jordanian denials of government complicity in such attacks.

Meanwhile, King Hussein of Jordan had more problems with the Arab refugees in his country than with Israel. Palestinian Arabs in Jordan considered the King to be more conciliatory to Israel than they would have liked. From time to time, violent demonstrations were staged by the refugees against Hussein's government, and they got full encouragement from the Palestine Liberation Organization radio station in Cairo. Palestinian Arabs, most of whom had come to Jordan from what is now Israel, bitterly hate the Israelis, whom they call usurpers. From time to time, without the knowledge of the Jordanian government, they crossed the Jordanian border and committed terrorist attacks and sabotage inside Israel. These attacks became more frequent in late 1965 and 1966. In November 1966, there were dozens of attacks, including the dynamiting of an apartment house in Jerusalem itself (the part held by Israel) and the derailment of a freight train near the city.

On November 13, in broad daylight, Israel launched a massive reprisal raid on the Jordanian town of As Samu, about nineteen miles northeast of Beersheeba. According to reports I received from the United Nations military observers, at least seventeen tanks and eighty armored half-track personnel carriers had taken part in the raid. At least a hundred twenty-five houses, a clinic, and a school were totally destroyed, as well as three military jeeps, seventeen military trucks and a civilian bus. In the village of Jimba, about five miles southeast of As Samu, fifteen stone huts were totally destroyed and seven others damaged; eighteen Arabs were killed.

The Security Council met immediately, and on November 16, all four major powers—the United States, the Soviet Union, the United Kingdom, and France—vigorously condemned Israel for her massive raid. Ambassador Goldberg, president of the Council for that month, speaking on behalf of the United States, said that the government of Israel

> . . . carried out a raid into Jordan the nature of which and whose consequences in human lives and in destruction far surpass the cumulative total of the various acts of terrorism conducted against the frontiers of Israel.[2]

As president, he summed up the atmosphere of the Council when he said that although earlier incidents were deplorable, "this

---

[2] *United Nations Security Council Official Records, No. 1320,* November 16, 1966.

deliberate governmental decision must be judged as the conscious act of responsible leaders of a member state and therefore on an entirely different level from the earlier incidents which we continue to deplore." The ambassadors of Britain, France, and the Soviet Union made similar statements.

The Council met in continuous session, and on November 24, Nigeria and Mali introduced a draft resolution whereby the Council, among other things, would deplore the loss of life and heavy damage to property resulting from the action of the Israeli government on November 13, 1966, and would censure Israel for that large-scale military action in violation of the Charter and of the general armistice agreement between Israel and Jordan. The resolution emphasized to Israel that actions of military reprisal could not be tolerated, and that if they were repeated, the Council would have to consider further and more effective steps, as envisaged in the Charter, to ensure against the repetition of such acts. Finally, it requested the Secretary General to keep the situation under review and report to the Council as appropriate.

The draft resolution was adopted on November 25; there were fourteen votes in favor, none against, and one abstention (New Zealand). It was one of the rare occasions in which the United States joined other members not only in censuring Israel, but also in giving notice to Israel not to repeat such acts.

On November 27, Premier Levi Eshkol of Israel made a statement in Jerusalem criticizing the "one-sided decision of the Security Council." He pledged that his country would continue to defend itself against Arab terrorism.

Syria, meanwhile, had its own *El-Fatah,* whose commando units began to attack in 1965, usually infiltrating through Lebanese and Jordanian territory to raid nothern Israel. The Israeli reaction was, as usual, one of massive retaliation. In May 1965, their armed forces attacked some Jordanian frontier villages that they suspected of harboring *El-Fatah* commandos. In October of that year, they struck at a Lebanese village. These massive reprisals did not seem to affect the Syrians who, of all Israel's neighbors, were the most militant.

While it is probably true that regular incursions by Israeli farmers into the demilitarized zone were part of an Israeli plan to expand its own frontiers, it is also undoubtedly true, as the Israelis claimed, that the Syrians had encouraged members of *El-Fatah* to stage frequent raids into Israeli territory. In his statement on January 18, 1967, Prime Minister Eshkol said:

> The source of the present tension does not lie in differences of opinion regarding cultivation problem rights. The Syrian aggression started before the sowing season and has continued after its completion. It has comprised acts, and taken place in areas which have no connection with problems of cultivation.

Whenever there was an *El-Fatah* raid, Israel retaliated with massive force. Although Syria had a topographical advantage on the Israeli border (it controlled all the heights), that advantage disappeared completely when the military exchange escalated to the level of air battles, in which Israel had a decided advantage. Several air battles took place after 1965, and one of the fiercest was fought on August 15, 1966. Accounts of aircraft losses differed, but it was established later that the Syrian gun positions on the Golan Heights were silenced and that the Syrians suffered a decisive defeat. Both Syria and Jordan, never on good terms, jointly complained of the Egyptian failure to do anything to help them, taunting President Nasser with sheltering behind the United Nations Emergency Force. Public opinion in the United Arab Republic reacted with a show of solidarity with their two Arab allies. Could Nasser afford to stand by indefinitely and watch Jordan and Syria suffer humiliating reversals?

Premier Eshkol warned on May 11 that Israel would not hesitate to use air power in response to continued border harassment from Syria. He spoke of the "gravity of recent incidents" and said there had been fourteen of them in the previous month. The nature of the operations, he said, suggested the work of Syrian army commandos, rather than the *El-Fatah* previously employed for infiltration and sabotage. Terrorists, he added, had recently been using mortars to shell Israeli settlements and had been penetrating deeper into Israel to carry out terrorist acts.

This heightened border activity had coincided with the approach (on May 15) of Israel's Independence Day, a holiday that usually sharpened feelings of national pride in Israel. For the Israelis it was a day of rejoicing and of military parades. For the Arabs—particularly the Palestinian exiles—it was an occasion for mourning. At that time, the main national celebration was held in each large Israeli town in turn. In 1967, it was the turn of Jerusalem. Apart from the sensitivity of the Jordanians to any ceremonies in this disputed city, Jerusalem lay within the "defensive area," as defined by the armistice agreement, in which the deployment of armed forces was rigorously limited. In 1961, in defiance of the resolution of the Security Council, Israel had ignored these limitations. In 1967, she hoped to obtain the attendance of the diplomatic corps at the parade. She did not succeed; not even the Western powers sent official representatives. Israel therefore decided to reduce the military parade to dimensions that would be in conformity with the armistice agreement. But Premier Eshkol then came under heavy domestic criticism for arranging the parade without heavy military units. Violent criticism in the Knesset and the press were largely responsible for bellicose statements by Mr. Eshkol and other Israeli leaders during the week leading up to Independence Day. Rumors of an impending blow against Syria were current throughout Israel. Whatever the origins of these rumors, they reached Cairo and other Arab capitals, where they generated the belief that Israel was about to mount a massive attack on Syria.

On May 12, the State Department in Washington announced that the United States had decided to boycott Israel's Independence Day parade to be held on May 15, in compliance with the Security Council resolution of 1947. The United Kingdom and other Western governments made similar announcements. On the same day (May 12) I said through a spokesman that "a military parade in Jerusalem at this time will intensify the already dangerous tension" in the Middle East. The spokesman, in reply to a correspondent's question, was authorized to say that General Odd Bull, chief of staff of UNTSO, had decided that officials of his organization would not attend the parade.

On May 11 and May 13, I made fervent appeals to all parties to observe the armistice agreements. In reply to questions regarding the reports emanating from Israel on "contemplated use of force by Israel against Syria," I authorized a spokesman to say that I had expressed very serious concern over such reports.

Bellicose statements by Israeli leaders, obviously meant to mollify domestic public opinion, created panic, however, in the Arab world. On May 13, the influential Cairo newspaper *Al-Ahram* wrote that the statements by Premier Eshkol meant that an attack on Syria was imminent. It continued, "If Israel now tries to set the region on fire, then it is definite that Israel herself will be completely destroyed in this fire, which will surround it on all sides, thus bringing about the end of this aggressive racist base."

In Damascus, Syrian Foreign Minister Ibrahim Makhous informed ambassadors of the states represented on the Security Council of the threat of Israeli aggression. The following day, May 14, General Mahmoud Fawzi, chief of staff of the Egyptian armed forces, flew to Damascus to examine the situation and co-ordinate plans with the Syrian government. On May 15, the Egyptian army began to converge on Cairo from military camps in the south, passing through the streets of the city for hours. On the next day, May 16, a state of emergency was proclaimed for the Egyptian armed forces.

The Syrian cry for help and the Egyptian military demonstrations set off throughout the Arab world a wave of emotion. There was hardly an Arab city in which demonstrations of some kind did not occur.

It was then that the United Nations Emergency Force— behind whose shelter Damascus and Amman had been repeatedly accusing President Nasser of hiding—was asked to withdraw by him. In the following pages I shall narrate the events leading to the withdrawal of UNEF from the Middle East and the outbreak of the Six-Day War.

CHAPTER XII

THE WITHDRAWAL
OF UNEF

At 5:30 P.M. on May 16, 1967, I received a message from the commander of UNEF, a message that would set in motion events that would change the course of history in the Middle East. General Indar Jit Rikhye notified me (at 10 P.M. local time) that he had been requested by the chief of staff of the U.A.R. armed forces to withdraw "all UN troops which install observer posts along our borders." I immediately cabled General Rikhye to await further instructions and, in the meantime, "to be firm in maintaining UNEF positions, while being as understanding and diplomatic as possible in your relations with local U.A.R. officials."

I then plunged into one of the most intensive periods of diplomatic activity in my ten years as Secretary General. After taking the series of steps outlined below, I met informally the next afternoon with the representatives of countries providing contingents to UNEF (Brazil, Canada, Denmark, India, Norway, Sweden, and Yugoslavia) to inform them of the seriousness of the situation, as it was then known to me. I told them how I intended to proceed, observing that, in my view, if a formal request for the withdrawal of UNEF were to be made by the government of the United Arab Republic, I would have to comply with it, since the force was on United Arab Republic territory only with the consent of the government and could not remain there without it. I informed the group that it was my intention to report my action to the General Assembly immediately. I also said, however, that "if there is any request from the government of the United Arab Republic for withdrawal or deployment of UNEF, the first action I propose to take is to appeal to the government to reconsider, without immediately complying with the request."

Two representatives (Brazil and Canada) expressed serious doubts about the consequences of agreeing to a peremptory request for the withdrawal of UNEF, and raised questions of possible consideration by the General Assembly of such a request and a possible appeal to the United Arab Republic not to request the withdrawal.

Two other representatives (India and Yugoslavia, who jointly contributed approximately one half of the UNEF contingent at that time) expressed the view that the United Arab Republic was entitled to request the removal of UNEF at any moment, and that that request would have to be respected regardless of what the General Assembly might have to say in the matter, since the agreement for UNEF's presence had been concluded between the then Secretary General (Dag Hammarskjöld) and the government of Egypt. A clarification of the situation from the United Arab Republic should therefore be awaited. Meanwhile, Ralph Bunche and Constantin Stavropoulos (a UN legal counsel) explained the political and legal aspects of the question. A complete description of the composition of UNEF, incidentally, appears in Appendix A, Part IV.

On May 17, I saw the permanent representative of the United Arab Republic, Ambassador Mohammed Awad El-Kony, and handed to him an aide-mémoire setting out the recent sequence of events. I also gave him a second aide-mémoire calling to the attention of his government the "good faith" accord. The great significance of this "good faith" accord will be discussed in detail later. Because of the historical importance of the first aide-mémoire, the full text is reproduced in Appendix B, Part IV. Here I will confine myself to summarizing its main points. The aide-mémoire was careful to acknowledge two undeniable facts: first, that I did not in any sense question the authority of the U.A.R. to deploy its troops as it sees fit in its territory; and second, that if it was the intention of the U.A.R. to withdraw the consent that it had given in 1956 for the stationing of UNEF in its territory, it was entitled to do so, and that I would, on receipt of a proper request, order such a withdrawal. The thrust of the aide-mémoire, however, was that the request made to General Rikhye by the chief of staff of the U.A.R. was *not* a proper request: it was not, I said, "right procedurally," and was therefore quite properly "disregarded by General Rikhye." I reminded the government of the U.A.R. that the basis of the presence of UNEF was an agreement made directly between President Nasser and Dag Hammarskjöld; any request for the withdrawal of UNEF must therefore come directly to the Secretary General from the government of the U.A.R. I had accordingly instructed General Rikhye to maintain all UNEF positions, pending further instructions.

I then asked the government of the U.A.R. to clarify its request. I pointed out that if the intention were a temporary withdrawal of UNEF from the armistice demarcation line, the request was "unacceptable" because the purpose of the force was to prevent a recurrence of fighting. I said that UNEF "cannot now be asked to stand aside in order to become a silent and helpless witness to an armed confrontation between the parties." If complete withdrawal were intended, and if that intention were properly communicated to me, I would have "no choice but to order the withdrawal of UNEF from Gaza and Sinai as expeditiously as possible."

Meanwhile, events in Gaza and Sinai were moving fast. On May 18, the commander of UNEF reported to me that Mahmoud Riad, Minister of Foreign Affairs of the United Arab Republic, had summoned the representatives of nations with troops in UNEF to the Ministry of Foreign Affairs in Cairo, and had informed them that UNEF had ended its tasks in the United Arab Republic and in the Gaza Strip and must depart from these territories forthwith. Although Mr. Riad had informed those diplomats accredited to Cairo of the "termination of UNEF," I had still not received any official request from the government at this time.

Early on May 18, the UNEF sentries proceeding to man the observation post at El-Sabha in Sinai were prevented by United Arab Republic soldiers from entering the post and from remaining in the area. The sentries were then forced to withdraw. Since they had no mandate to resist by use of force, they did not do so; they were not armed for combat duty, but carried only personal arms for self-defense. U.A.R. soldiers (also on May 18) forced Yugoslav UNEF sentries out of the observation post on the international frontier facing the El-Kuntilla camp; U.A.R. officers then visited the Yugoslav camp at Sharm-el-Sheikh and informed the commanding officer that they had come to take over the camp, as well as the UNEF observation post at Ras Nasrani, demanding a reply within fifteen minutes. The contingent commander replied that he had no instructions to hand over the positions.

On the same day, United Arab Republic forces entered the UNEF observation post on the international frontier facing El-Amr camp and forced the Yugoslav soldiers to withdraw. Later, two United Arab Republic officers visited El-Amr camp and asked the UNEF platoon to withdraw within fifteen minutes.

The UNEF Yugoslav detachment at El-Quseima camp reported that two artillery shells, apparently rounds from United Arab Republic artillery, had burst between the UNEF Yugoslav camps at El-Quseima and El-Sabha.

I met on May 18 with Ambassador Gideon Rafael, permanent representative of Israel to the United Nations, who gave his government's views on the situation, emphasizing that a UNEF withdrawal should not be achieved by a unilateral United Arab Republic request alone, and asserting Israel's right to a voice in the matter. I asked him, in the event of the United Arab Republic's official request for a UNEF withdrawal, if the government of Israel would be agreeable to permit the stationing of UNEF on the Israeli side of the line, for a limited duration, to enable me to negotiate with the government of the United Arab Republic. Ambassador Rafael replied that such a proposal was entirely unacceptable to his government.

I believed then, and I still believe now, that if only Israel had agreed to permit UNEF to be stationed on its side of the border, even for a short duration, the course of history could have been different. Diplomatic efforts to avert the pending catastrophe might have prevailed; war might have been averted.

At 12 noon (New York time) on May 18, the formal request

from the U.A.R. government for withdrawal of UNEF came directly to me. I received through the U.A.R. permanent representative, Ambassador El-Kony, the following message from Mahmoud Riad, Minister of Foreign Affairs of the United Arab Republic:

> The Government of the United Arab Republic has the honour to inform Your Excellency that it has decided to terminate the presence of the United Nations Emergency Force from the territory of the United Arab Republic and Gaza Strip.
>
> Therefore, I request that the necessary steps be taken for the withdrawal of the Force as soon as possible.

At the same time, the ambassador informed me of the strong feeling of resentment in Cairo at what was there considered to be attempts to exert pressure and make UNEF an "occupation force." In the presence of Ralph Bunche, I expressed deep misgivings about the probable disastrous consequences of the withdrawal of UNEF and informed him that I intended to appeal urgently to President Nasser to reconsider the decision before I took any action regarding the withdrawal of UNEF. Ambassador El-Kony advised me to withhold my appeal, assuring me that he would discuss with his Foreign Minister on the phone my intention to appeal. At 6:30 P.M. on the same day, he saw me again and informed me that he had talked to his Foreign Minister, who had asked him to convey to me his urgent advice that I should not make an appeal to President Nasser to reconsider the request for withdrawal of UNEF and that, if I did so, such a request would be sternly rebuffed. I then raised the question of a possible visit to Cairo and was informed that such a visit, and as soon as possible, would be welcomed by the government of the United Arab Republic.

I subsequently met with the UNEF Advisory Committee (Brazil, Canada, Ceylon, Colombia, India, Norway, and Pakistan), and the representatives of three countries (Denmark, Sweden, and Yugoslavia) that provided contingents to UNEF, to inform them of developments. At this meeting, the permanent representative of Canada expressed the view that the United Arab Republic's demand for the immediate withdrawal of UNEF was not acceptable, on the ground that the ultimate responsibility for the decision to withdraw should rest with the United Nations. The permanent representatives of Brazil and Denmark supported the Canadian view and urged further discussion with the government of the United Arab Republic, as well as with the other governments involved.

Another position, held by Pakistan and Yugoslavia, was that I had no choice but to comply with the request of the government of the U.A.R. The Yugoslav representative stated that the moment the request for the withdrawal of UNEF was officially known, his government would comply with it and withdraw its contingent. A similar position had been taken in Cairo by the government of India. No proposal was made by any permanent representative that the Advisory Committee should exercise the right vested in it by General Assembly Resolution 1001 to request the convening of the General Assembly to take up the situation arising from the U.A.R. communication. At the conclusion of the meeting, it was understood that I had no alternative other than to comply with the United Arab Republic's demand, although some representatives felt that I should clarify with that government the meaning of its request that withdrawal should take place "as soon as possible." Ralph Bunche gave a lengthy explanation of the dangerous situation the UNEF was in, and the political and constitutional aspects of the case. I informed the Advisory Committee that I intended to reply promptly to the United Arab Republic, and immediately to report to the General Assembly and to the Security Council on the action I had taken. It was for the member states to decide whether either of these organs should or could take up the matter, and to act accordingly.

As regards the Security Council, no member proposed the convening of a meeting at that time. The permanent members were divided. France and the Soviet Union believed that the request of the United Arab Republic for the withdrawal of UNEF must be complied with. The United States and the United Kingdom felt that the Secretary General should defer the decision to withdraw, in the hope that the United Arab Republic would change its mind or that some other alternative arrangement could be devised. To my knowledge, China did not express its views even privately. Among the nonpermanent members of the Security

Council for that year (Argentina, Brazil, Bulgaria, Canada, Denmark, Ethiopia, India, Japan, Mali, and Nigeria) opinion was sharply divided, and no member attempted to request a meeting. It should also be borne in mind that in 1956, the Security Council failed to agree on any draft resolution on the situation in the Middle East, and the matter had to be referred to the General Assembly. Assembly Resolution 1001 was the sole basis for the creation of UNEF.

In one of his interventions at the meeting of the Advisory Committee on May 18, Ralph Bunche stressed the fact that UNEF went into Egyptian territory, not on the order of the General Assembly, but on the basis of an agreement between the Secretary General (Dag Hammarskjöld) and President Nasser. "It involved consent," he said. And since the consent of the Egyptian government had been withdrawn, "there is not a thing in the world that UNEF troops can do about it." Ralph also brought up the question of the security of UNEF troops, warning of the possibility that the Egyptian population might turn against them if the UN force should try to remain against the will of U.A.R. authorities.

After the meeting the Advisory Committee, at approximately 7:00 P.M. (New York time) on May 18, I replied to the Minister of Foreign Affairs of the United Arab Republic. My message included the following remarks:

> As I have indicated to your Permanent Representative on May 16, the United Nations Emergency Force entered Egyptian territory with the consent of your Government and in fact can remain there only so long as that consent continues. In view of the message now received from you, therefore, your Government's request will be complied with and I am proceeding to issue instructions for the necessary arrangements to be put in train without delay for the orderly withdrawal of the Force, its vehicles and equipment, and for the disposal of all properties pertaining to it. I am, of course, also bringing this development and my actions and intentions to the attention of the UNEF Advisory Committee and to all Governments providing contingents for the Force. A full report covering this development will be submitted promptly by me to the General Assembly and the Security Council.

> Irrespective of the reasons for the action you have taken, in all

frankness, may I advise you that *I have serious misgivings about it* for, as I have said each year in my annual reports to the General Assembly on UNEF, I believe that this Force has been an important factor in maintaining relative quiet in the area of its development during the past ten years and that its withdrawal may have grave implications for peace.

It is to be noted that the decision communicated to the United Arab Republic in this letter did not signify the actual withdrawal of the force, which, in fact, was to remain in the area for four more weeks. During this orderly process of withdrawal, fifteen soldiers of peace (fourteen Indian and one Brazilian) lost their lives. UNEF suffered these casualties as a result of being involuntarily caught up in the hostilities that began on June 5. In addition to these casualties, there were sixteen wounded in the Indian contingent and one wounded in the Brazilian contingent.

Formal instructions relating to the withdrawal of UNEF were sent to the UNEF commander by me on the night of May 18, and the withdrawal from the area was completed only on June 17. I instructed that the force remain under the exclusive command of its United Nations commander and take no orders from any other source.

Also on the same evening (May 18), I submitted a special report to the General Assembly.[1] After recounting the series of events leading to my compliance with the request of the government of the United Arab Republic, I observed:

> I cannot conclude this report without expressing the deepest concern as to the possible implications of the latest developments for peace in the area. For more than ten years UNEF, acting as a buffer between the opposing forces of Israel and the United Arab Republic on the Armistice Demarcation Line in Gaza and the International Frontier in Sinai, has been the principal means of maintaining quiet in the area. Its removal inevitably restores the armed confrontation of the United Arab Republic and Israel and removes the stabilizing influence of an international force operating along the boundaries between the two nations. Much as I regret this development, I have no option but to respect and acquiesce in the request of the Government of the United Arab

---

[1] United Nations Document A/6669.

Republic. I can only express the hope that both sides will now exercise the utmost calm and restraint in this new situation, which otherwise will be fraught with danger. . . .

On May 19, I issued a report to the Security Council[2] in which I drew the attention of the Council to the dangerous situation developing in the Middle East. I described the prevailing state of affairs in the whole area as "extremely menacing." There had been a steady deterioration along the line between Israel and Syria, particularly with regard to disputes over cultivation rights in the demilitarized zone, since the first of the year. I reported that General Odd Bull, chief of staff of United Nations Truce Supervision Organization, was trying to initiate separate discussions with Israel and Syria in order to work out practical cultivation arrangements affecting disputed lands along the line.

A number of factors had served to aggravate the situation to an unusual degree, increasing tension and danger. *El-Fatah* activities, terrorism, and sabotage were major factors provoking strong reactions from the government and population of Israel. Intemperate and bellicose utterances by officials and nonofficials were unfortunately more or less routine on both sides of the line. In recent weeks, moreover, reports emanating from Israel had attributed to some high officials statements so threatening as to be particularly inflammatory. There had been in the past few days persistent reports about troop movements and concentrations, particularly on the Israeli side of the Syrian border. These had caused anxiety and, at times, excitement. The government of Israel had very recently assured me that there were no unusual Israeli troop concentrations or movements along the Syrian line, that there would be none, and that no military action would be initiated by the armed forces of Israel unless such action was first taken by the other side. Reports from UNTSO observers had confirmed the absence of troop concentrations and significant troop movements on both sides of the line.

I also reported that the request of the government of the United Arab Republic for the withdrawal of UNEF was sudden and unexpected, and that although the reasons for the request had

---

[2] United Nations Document S/7896.

not been officially stated, the U.A.R. government clearly regarded them as overriding. One thing was certain—they had nothing to do with the conduct of UNEF itself or the way in which it was carrying out its mandate; in fact, UNEF had discharged its responsibilities with remarkable effectiveness and great distinction. I pointed out that there was widespread misunderstanding about the nature of United Nations peace-keeping operations in general and UNEF in particular: it was a peace-keeping, not an enforcement, operation. "This means, of course, that the operation is based entirely on its acceptance by the governing authority of the territory on which it operates and that it is not in any sense related to Chapter VII of the Charter. It is a fact beyond dispute that neither UNEF nor any other United Nations peace-keeping operation thus far undertaken would have been permitted to enter the territory involved if there had been any suggestion that it had the right to remain there against the will of the governing authority."

After advising the Council that the withdrawal of UNEF would give rise to increased danger, not only along the armistice demarcation line but in the Strait of Tiran and in Gaza, I said:

> It is true to a considerable extent that the UNEF has allowed us for ten years to ignore some of the hard realities of the underlying conflict. The Governments concerned, and the United Nations, are now confronted with a brutally realistic and dangerous situation.
>
> The Egyptian-Israel Mixed Armistice Commission (EIMAC) . . . remains in existence, with its headquarters at Gaza, and could, as it did prior to the establishment of UNEF, provide a limited form of United Nations presence in the area, as in the case of the other Mixed Armistice Commissions which are served by UNTSO. The Government of Israel, however, has denounced EIMAC and for some years has refused to have anything to do with it. The United Nations has never accepted as valid this unilateral action of the Government of Israel. It would most certainly be helpful in the present situation if the Government of Israel were to reconsider its position and resume its participation in EIMAC.
>
> Similarly, I may repeat what I have said in the past, that it would be very helpful to the maintenance of quiet along the Israel-Syria line if the two parties would resume their participation

in ISMAC (the Israel-Syria Mixed Armistice Commission) both in the current emergency session and in the regular sessions.

I do not wish to be alarmist, but I cannot avoid the warning to the Council that in my view the current situation in the Near East is more disturbing, indeed, I may say more menacing, than at any time since the fall of 1956.

My decision to comply with President Nasser's demand for the withdrawal of UNEF from U.A.R. territory drew widespread criticism. President Johnson was "dismayed." The British press, with a few exceptions, criticized me and the United Nations for not resisting Nasser's demand: *The Spectator* of London captioned its editorial page "U Thant's War."[3] C. L. Sulzberger wrote in the New York *Times* that the Secretary General had "used his international prestige with the objectivity of a spurned lover and the dynamism of a noodle."[4] Sir Alec Douglas-Home termed my action "a dreadful mistake,"[5] while Joseph Alsop denounced the action as "poltroonery."[6] Senator Dirksen accused me of acting "like a thief in the night."[7]

I was, of course, not bereft of defenders. John A. F. Ennals, director general of the United Nations Association of Great Britain and Northern Ireland, wrote:

> Our Association has followed with admiration your handling of one of the most difficult crises the United Nations has yet faced. . . . May we assure you of our full support for all your efforts on behalf of the world community.

Father G. Dominique Pire, Nobel Peace Laureate, wrote to me on June 21:

> In the disputes between States, as in the disputes between individuals, there is always wrong on both sides. The wrong on the Arab side has been strongly emphasised, and it does exist. I do not see why the wrong on the other side is not emphasised: it is real.

---

[3] Andrew Boyd, *Fifteen Men on a Powder Keg*, (New York: Stein & Day, 1971), p. 196.
[4] Ibid.
[5] Ibid.
[6] Ibid.
[7] Ibid.

In 1969 I visited all the refugee camps in Jordan, Syria, Lebanon and Egypt, and I have fully appreciated the problem. My sympathies are with you more than ever because I feel that, on one hand, you are acting according to your conscience and that, on the other hand, this conscience must often be shaken by the dishonesty of those you are with. Life really has a certain circus element.

Morris H. Rubin, editor of *The Progressive,* also wrote to me on June 21:

> Although my own sympathies in the present conflict lie largely with Israel, I feel strongly that you have conducted yourself throughout these trying days of continual crisis with great dignity, fairness, and statesmanship. My basic support of Israel's position does not deter me from criticizing that country for refusing to accept a United Nations presence on its side of the line.

James A. Wechsler, editor of the New York *Post,* in a lengthy article entitled "Ordeal of a Peace-Maker" that appeared in the August, 1967, issue of *The Progressive,* vigorously came to my defense, as did Frank Judd, a prominent member of the British Parliament, and many others.

To return to my narrative, on the evening of May 18, when Ambassador El-Kony transmitted to me the message from his Foreign Minister that any appeal by me to his government for reconsideration would be "sternly rebuffed," I requested him to inform his government that I proposed to visit Cairo as soon as possible, preferably accompanied by Ralph Bunche, to discuss the whole situation. At noon on May 19, he saw me and said that although Ralph Bunche was held in very high esteem in his country "from President Nasser down to the man in the street," he suggested that I should go to Cairo without Ralph, because his presence in Cairo at this time, since he was an American, would be resented at least by a section of the Egyptian people. At this moment, he said, the people of the United Arab Republic felt bitter toward the United States for its all-out support for Israel and its strong criticism of the U.A.R. request for the withdrawal of UNEF.

Long after the Six-Day War, incidentally, President Nasser made a statement I can only consider to be most bizarre. In an interview with Eric Rouleau of *Le Monde,* an account of which appeared in that paper on February 18, 1970, the President said:

> I did not want to start the 1967 war and the Israeli leaders know it perfectly well. I did not intend to close off the Gulf of Aqaba to Israeli shipping. I did not ask U Thant to withdraw United Nations troops from Gaza and from Sharm-el-Sheikh—controlling the entry to the Gulf—but only from a part of a frontier extending from Rafah to Eilat. Nonetheless, the UN Secretary-General, on the advice of the American diplomat Ralph Bunche (a UN diplomat who acted as mediator at the 1948 Rhodes talks) decided to withdraw UN forces, thus forcing me to send Egyptian troops into Sharm-el-Sheikh and to impose the blockade. That is the way we fell into the trap that was set for us.

When the text of this interview was brought to the attention of Ralph and myself, both of us were shocked. As Father Pire put it, life really does have a certain circus element!

But it is significant that when the Middle East News Agency published the official text of the interview in Arabic, the Arabic version was one-third shorter than the one published by *Le Monde.* President Nasser's remarks on his request to me in May 1967, and on the role played by "the American diplomat Ralph Bunche" were not included in the Arabic text released in Cairo. When I sent this to Ralph, he returned it to me with the remark, "Thanks. Important omission!" Ambassador El-Zayyat, to whom I referred the *Le Monde* interview and the different version of the Middle East News Agency, was unable to explain his President's reference to Ralph in the first and the omission of this reference in the second. After the war, Ralph also sent a letter to the New York *Times* responding to an editorial (of June 4, 1967) by James Reston that, curiously, made the same charge Nasser had made in *Le Monde.* Reston said that Egyptians he had been talking to "even deny that they planned to get rid of the United Nations troops at the mouth of the Gulf of Aqaba. This, they say, was proposed by the Secretary-General of the United Nations on the ground that if the UN couldn't keep its troops in one part of the crisis area, it couldn't keep them in another part."

On June 11, Ralph replied (in his letter to the *Times*): "If only for the sake of historical accuracy, I wish to make the following observations: Whatever may have been said to Mr. Reston in Cairo, or by whom, I can assure you that there has not been the slightest hint of such a position here, and with good reason, for there is not a shred of truth to it. In critical times such as these, of course, it is common in official and unofficial circles alike to seek scapegoats (to a shameful degree at present in the U.S.A.) and to indulge in what may be called deception, if one wishes to be polite about it."

On May 19, I had sent a message to General Rikhye that I would leave New York on Monday, May 22, and arrive in Cairo on Tuesday, May 23. After asking General Rikhye, General Odd Bull, chief of staff of UNTSO, and Laurence Michelmore, commissioner general of UNRWA, to meet me in Cairo, I left New York on the evening of May 22. On Tuesday morning, when I arrived at Orly airport in Paris, I was greeted by Guy de Lacharriere, director of United Nations affairs at the French Foreign Office, and W. Gibson Parker, director of the United Nations Information Center in Paris. Each of them had a grim and ominous message for me. Mr. Lacharriere showed me a message (received by the French Foreign office the previous night) that President Nasser had announced the closure of the Strait of Tiran to Israeli shipping. Gibson Parker gave me a cable sent from Ralph Bunche informing me that late on Monday night he had received a cable from UNEF conveying the same news. Nasser was reported to have announced the decision in the course of his speech delivered to the U.A.R. air force's advance command.

My first reaction was to cancel my trip to Cairo, return to New York, and report to the Security Council. It was common knowledge that Israel had all along considered the blockade of the Strait of Tiran (the Gulf of Aqaba) to be a *casus belli* (act of war). Why did Nasser do it? Was it a snub to me? The French government served us breakfast at the V.I.P. Lounge at the airport, but I could not take anything. It was 3:00 A.M. New York time, and I did not want to wake up poor Ralph, who was already in declining health due to overwork and undisciplined eating habits. (Although he had a long-standing case of diabetes, I could never dissuade him from eating ice cream and cake, which he adored.) I had a brief conference with Lacharriere and Gibson Parker and told them that I believed war was inevitable. Perhaps, I told them, the four permanent members of the Security Council (the United States, the United Kingdom, France, and the Soviet Union) could collectively save the peace in the area. The four were sharply divided, however. Ramses Nasiff, a United Nations press officer who accompanied me on the trip, and who is an Egyptian, looked miserable; he wanted me to proceed to Cairo. I had only thirty minutes to decide, and I decided that I would go ahead and find out what Nasser had in mind. In any case, I would have first-hand information not only from the U.A.R. authorities but also from Rikhye, Odd Bull, and Michelmore.

At Rome, Amintore Fanfani, former Foreign Minister of Italy and (in 1964) president of the United Nations General Assembly, greeted me at the airport. He told me (and I agreed) that the situation was extremely serious. I received long extracts of President Nasser's alarming statement from the United Nations Information Office in Rome, sent to me by Ralph, and I studied them during my flight to Cairo. The Egyptian President had claimed that Israel was concentrating eleven to thirteen brigades on the Syrian border; he said that if Syria were attacked, "Egypt would enter the battle from the first minute." He also discussed "a big world-wide campaign, led by the United States, Britain and Canada" that was opposing the withdrawal of UNEF in an attempt to turn it into a force "serving neo-imperialism." In addition, he noted "another campaign . . . mounted against the Secretary General . . . because he made a faithful and honest decision and could not surrender to the pressure brought to bear upon him. . . ." The President said that had we not withdrawn UNEF, he would have regarded it as a hostile force and "forcibly disarmed it." Finally, he reported that U.A.R. forces had occupied Sharm-el-Sheikh as "an affirmation of our rights and sovereignty over the Aqaba Gulf." The full text of President Nasser's statement is reproduced in Appendix C, Part IV.

After reading this, I had no doubt in my mind that war was inevitable. Would I be able to persuade Nasser to change his decision? Could I get an assurance from him that the United Arab Republic would not be the first to strike? And would the Egyptian President agree to accept the Secretary General's special representative, who would deal with his government and the Israeli government promptly whenever a crisis situation developed? With these thoughts troubling me, I landed at Cairo International Airport at 5:00 P.M. on Tuesday, May 23. Among those who met me were Foreign Minister Mahmoud Riad, General Rikhye, General Odd Bull, and Laurence Michelmore. We drove directly to the Nile Hilton Hotel, where I stayed as the guest of the government. At 7:00 P.M., I had a comprehensive review of the whole situation with Rikhye, and he reported to me that the United Arab Republic forces had completely taken over Sharm-el-Sheikh from the thirty-one Yugoslav officers and men, and that they got only fifteen minutes' notice to evacuate. He also said that no single ship passing through the Strait of Tiran had in the past ever flown the Israeli flag, but now that Nasser had officially closed it to Israeli shipping, the latter might challenge his decision. At 8:00 P.M., I hosted a small dinner for Rikhye, Odd Bull, and Michelmore in my hotel suite, and after dinner I went over the notes brought over from New York as well as cables sent from UN headquarters.

At 9:25 A.M. on the next day, May 24, we went to the Foreign Office for a meeting with Mr. Riad. I arrived at the office a few minutes before the scheduled time of the meeting, and the first question I asked the Foreign Minister privately was the reason for the announcement of the closure of the Strait of Tiran while I was on the way to Cairo. He said that the President would explain it to me at the dinner that night. The morning meeting was attended by General Rikhye on my side, and on Mr. Riad's side, by Ambassador Ahmed Hassen Elfki, undersecretary in the Ministry of Foreign Affairs, and Ismail Fahmy, director of the International Organization Department. For the sake of accuracy, I reproduce General Rikhye's notes, which were prepared for me on my return to New York, in Appendix D, Part IV. For the reader who wishes a brief account of the exchanges that took place, they were as follows:

I opened the meeting by explaining the developments that led to my ordering the withdrawal of UNEF. Then Foreign Minister Riad gave the long-awaited explanation of the reasons for his government's request. He said that there had recently been an escalation of pressure by Israel against Jordan and Syria—attacks against Jordanian water projects, many exchanges of fire, and threats by Eban and Rabin to invade Syria and take Damascus. According to the Foreign Minister, the U.A.R. had received information of a plan of invasion by Israel against Syria. He said, however, that Israel did not intend to annex Syria, but that their plans were confined to destroying the bulk of the Syrian army and the military and economic installations in southern Syria. For these reasons, the U.A.R. moved into Sinai and closed the Gulf of Aqaba, moves that were "defensive in posture." I informed the Foreign Minister that the Israeli delegation had told me that they would fight for the Strait of Tiran.

It was at this point that I suggested a freeze on the situation in the Gulf of Aqaba, similar to the one I had arranged during the Cuban missile crisis. I suggested a moratorium of two to three weeks to give time to both sides for consultations and discussions. The Foreign Minister replied that his government could not show weakness to its people, especially the army. I said that I would nevertheless appeal to Israel not to send ships through the Gulf for a certain period and requested Mr. Riad not to take any precipitate action. I also said that I would attempt to obtain Israel's agreement to reactivate the general armistice agreement, a move for which I would seek U.S. support, and that I would recommend to the Security Council the appointment of a special UN representative to the area.

At 2:30 P.M., I attended a luncheon given in my honor by Foreign Minister Riad at the Tahrir Club, and at 8:00 P.M., I was the guest of President Nasser at his official residence. I had seen him several times before—in Rangoon, Bandung, New York, Belgrade, and Cairo—and he was a very simple, charming, polite, and somewhat shy man. He had that indefinable quality generally described as charisma. He looked, and he was, the real leader of his people.

The first time I met President Nasser was in Rangoon, in April 1955, when he was on his way to the historic Bandung Conference in Indonesia. He arrived in the same plane with Prime Minister Nehru of India. At the airport, he was met by Burma's Prime Minister U Nu, and by China's Chou En-lai, who had arrived one day earlier. It was the time of the year in Burma for the celebration of the annual water festival, perhaps the gayest of all festivals in our country.

The normal apparel to wear at a Burmese water festival is ordinary, everyday Burmese dress, which comprises a collarless shirt, a *longyi,* which is a wrap-around sarong, and a Chinese-style jacket. When U Nu asked the three leaders if they would care to take part in the festival—in which everybody had to be prepared to be thoroughly soaked with water that is thrown about by young and old, men and women—Nasser smiled, looked around, and readily agreed. Nehru was more skeptical and protested half-heartedly, but finally agreed. Chou En-lai, however, laughed and insisted that he would look terrible in any dress other than his own; he did not yield to U Nu's repeated invitations. It was the first time U Nu met Nasser, and also the first time that Nasser and Chou En-lai met. The next day, Burmese newspapers front-paged pictures of a towering Nasser flanked by Nehru and Nu, all thoroughly enjoying the festival in water-soaked Burmese dress.

(U Nu was in the habit, incidentally, of asking almost all foreign dignitaries to don Burmese dress for special occasions. I remember his asking Lord Mountbatten of Burma if he would care to attend a state dinner in formal Burmese dress, which comprises a silk turban, a Chinese-style jacket, and a long, flowing, ornate silk wrap-around, called *taung-shay paso.* Mountbatten politely declined. In any case, it would have been difficult to get a ceremonial silk skirt to fit his six-foot, six-inch frame. Among those who succumbed to U Nu's entreaties were Marshal Tito and Agha Khan.)

On May 24, before the dinner at the President's residence in Cairo, Nasser showed me some highly polished teak furniture, which he told me was presented by U Nu to his daughter on the occasion of her wedding. He was very friendly and asked me whether I was tired after my long journey. A few minutes after 8:00 P.M. after sipping orange juice, we sat down to dinner. Others in the small group were the deputy prime minister for foreign affairs, Mahmoud Fawzi, Foreign Minister Mahmoud Riad, and General Rikhye, who again took notes. Since this meeting occasioned a controversy as to whether President Nasser did or did not accept a moratorium in the Gulf of Aqaba, I again reproduce

General Rikhye's notes in full in Appendix E, Part IV, but will outline the principal exchanges of the meeting here.

I opened the conversation by asking President Nasser for his reaction to my proposal for a moratorium in the Gulf of Aqaba, and I incidentally expressed my surprise that the decision to close the Gulf seemed to have been taken while I was on my way to Cairo. Mr. Nasser said that the decision had been made some time earlier and that the timing of the announcement had been carefully considered. If it were made, he said, after my visit to Cairo, it would be widely interpreted as a snub to me; so it was decided to announce it before my arrival.

Mr. Nasser then said that he would accept a moratorium for two weeks, provided Israel also complied with my request. I said that I would try to persuade Israel not to send shipping through the Gulf for some time. The President rejected UN supervision of compliance with this agreement on the ground that armed forces security would be breached by any UN presence. He did, however, accept a UN diplomatic presence in Cairo (but not in Gaza).

Mr. Nasser said that by returning to the pre-1956 position, the U.A.R. had now achieved its goal, with one difference: that they were now in a position to defend their country. Nevertheless, he assured me that the U.A.R. would not be the first to attack. The President ended the meeting by asking General Rikhye to convey his personal thanks to all ranks of UNEF for services rendered to the U.A.R.

I arrived back at the hotel at 11:30 P.M. and immediately sent a cable to Ralph on the result of my talks with the President. Mohammed Heikal, editor-in-chief of *Al-Ahram* and confidant and adviser to President Nasser, writes in *The Cairo Documents:*

> U Thant came to Cairo with a plan that was said to have the backing of the United States. The plan was in three parts:
> 1. Israel would be asked not to send any ships through the Straits of Tiran to test the Egyptian decision to close them.
> 2. Other nations with ships passing through the Straits would be asked not to send strategic materials on them to Israel.

3. The United Arab Republic would be asked to wait before it exercised the right of inspection of ships passing through the Straits.

This plan, according to U Thant, would give everybody a breathing space. Nasser accepted.[8]

This summary, though accurate, is inadequate. Nasser's agreement to the moratorium, and to accept a United Nations representative in Cairo was very significant. According to my own notes, however, this arrangement was obviously contingent on two factors: agreement of *Israel* also to accept a moratorium of two to three weeks, and on Israel's agreement to the Security Council's appointment of a United Nations representative for the area. But Israel did not agree to either of these conditions.

I left Cairo on May 25 and reached New York the same day, just before midnight. On May 26, my first day in the office, Ralph Bunche told me that my proposal in Cairo of a moratorium of two to three weeks, which Nasser had accepted, was not acceptable to Israel. Ambassador Rafael, who like Ambassador El-Kony of the U.A.R. worked very closely with me during those hectic days, explained that he did not think that a moratorium would help ease the situation. I explained to him that the proposed moratorium was primarily meant to achieve a breathing spell, during which several measures could be taken, including the appointment of a United Nations representative to the area. I also told him that President Nasser had agreed to that proposal. He said that his government would not be agreeable to such an arrangement, since Nasser was bent on war. He also told me (in a friendly way) that if I were to make the proposal of a United Nations representative in my report to the Security Council, he regretfully would have to oppose it. He said that he saw no need for such a representative, and, added that it would be better for the Secretary General to deal with the governments through their representatives at the United Nations. After the meeting, I added the following words to my report, which had already been drafted:

---

[8] (New York: Doubleday & Company, Inc., 1973), p. 243.

If the Security Council sees fit to appeal to the parties concerned to agree to a breathing spell, and if the parties comply with that appeal, the question of the appointment of a United Nations special representative to the area can be considered. In Cairo I had suggested to President Nasser the appointment of such a representative in the Middle East to act as a go-between and moderator during this period of unusually dangerous tension. President Nasser agreed to this suggestion, but it proved to be unacceptable to Israel.

I then discussed the draft with both Ralph Bunche and Alexei Nesterenko, undersecretary for political and Security Council affairs. Neither of them favored the inclusion of this passage. Their argument was that the first requisite step was to gain a breathing spell. If that were achieved, several steps could be taken, including the appointment of a special representative. Mentioning this specific proposal would receive mixed reactions, they maintained, and the idea of a breathing spell would be killed. After a lengthy discussion, I decided to drop the passage.

But I mentioned the passage to several delegates, most of whom were surprised that I had omitted it from my report. After the Six-Day War, some correspondents brought up the question, though casually—perhaps not to offend Israel. To my knowledge, the first mention of this information in a book appeared in Maxine Rodinson's *Israel and the Arabs,* published early in 1968.[9]

> On the 23rd May (actually on 24th May) he (Nasser) received U Thant in Cairo and concluded a secret agreement with him. No new move would be taken which might increase tension; a representative of the Secretary-General would do the rounds between Cairo and Tel Aviv in an attempt to find some common ground.

I disclosed the information officially only on December 3, 1970, in the course of my speech to the news media seminar sponsored by the Stanley Foundation at United Nations headquarters.[10] In that address, I used the same wording I had proposed in my report three and a half years earlier.

I reported to the Security Council on the same day (May

[9] New York: Pantheon, p. 193.
[10] United Nations Document SG/SM/1394, December 3, 1970.

26). After recalling my previous report to the Security Council of May 19, 1967, in which I described the general situation in the Middle East as "more disturbing, indeed more menacing, than at any time since the fall of 1956," I provided the Council with a full account of my meetings with President Nasser and Mr. Riad, together with an analysis of the U.A.R. and Israeli positions on the question of passage through the Strait of Tiran, reminding the Council that Israel would regard the closing of the Strait as a *casus belli*. As to the proposed moratorium, I said:

> In my view, a peaceful outcome to the present crisis will depend upon a breathing spell, which will allow tension to subside from its present explosive level. I therefore urge all the parties concerned to exercise special restraint, forgo belligerence, avoid all other actions which could increase tension, and allow the Council to deal with the underlying causes of the present crisis and seek solutions.

Because of Israel's opposition to the proposed UN representative to the area, I did not, as I have already indicated, mention the proposal in my report, but only added:

> In my discussions with officials of the United Arab Republic and Israel, I have mentioned possible steps which could be taken by mutual consent and which would help to reduce tension. I shall of course continue to make all possible efforts to contribute to a solution of the present crisis. The problems to be faced are complex and the obstacles are formidable. I do not believe, however, that we can allow ourselves to despair.

This report also contained my first formal explanation to the Council of my withdrawal of UNEF. In view of the controversy surrounding the withdrawal, the relevant passages are worth quoting:

> My decision in this matter was based upon both legal and practical considerations. It is a practical fact that neither UNEF nor any other United Nations peace-keeping operation could function or even exist without the continued consent and co-operation of the host country. Once the consent of the host country was withdrawn and UNEF was no longer welcome, its usefulness was ended. In fact, the movement of U.A.R. forces up to the line in

Sinai, even before the request for withdrawal was received by me, had already made the effective functioning of UNEF impossible. I may say here that the request received by me on May 18 was the only request received from the Government of the United Arab Republic, since the cryptic letter to Major General Rikhye from General Fawzi on May 16 was both unclear and unacceptable. Furthermore, I had very good reason to be convinced of the earnestness and determination of the Government of the United Arab Republic in requesting the withdrawal of UNEF. It was therefore obvious to me that the position of the personnel of UNEF would soon become extremely difficult, and even dangerous, if the decision for the withdrawal of the Force was delayed, while the possibility for its effective action had already been virtually eliminated. Moreover, if the request were not promptly complied with, the Force would quickly disintegrate due to the withdrawal of individual contingents.

I pointed out the often-forgotten fact that UNEF was never permitted on the Israeli side of the line:

It may be relevant to note here that UNEF functioned exclusively on the United Arab Republic side of the line in a zone from which the armed forces of the United Arab Republic had voluntarily stayed away for over ten years. It was this arrangement which allowed UNEF to function as a buffer and as a restraint on infiltration. When this arrangement lapsed, United Arab Republic troops moved up to the line, as they had every right to do.

If UNEF had been deployed on both sides of the line, as originally envisaged in pursuance of the General Assembly resolution, its buffer function would not necessarily have ended. However, its presence on the Israeli side of the line has never been permitted. The fact that UNEF was not stationed on the Israeli side of the line was a recognition of the unquestioned sovereign right of Israel to withhold its consent for the stationing of the Force. The acquiescence in the request of the United Arab Republic for the withdrawal of the Force after ten and a half years on United Arab Republic soil was likewise a recognition of the sovereign authority of the United Arab Republic. In no official document relating to UNEF has there been any suggestion of a limitation of this sovereign authority.

Finally, I expressed my deep concern about the threatening circumstances:

I feel that my major task must be to try to gain time in order to lay the basis for a détente. The important immediate fact is that, in view of the conflicting stands taken by the United Arab Republic and Israel, the situation in the Strait of Tiran represents a very serious potential threat to peace. I greatly fear that a clash between the United Arab Republic and Israel over this issue in the present circumstances will inevitably set off a general conflict in the Near East.

Among the possible courses of action I recommended to the Security Council were the resumption of the mixed armistice agreements, which would provide a limited UN presence in the area, and the invoking of Article 40 of the United Nations Charter. Article 40 provides the Council with "supreme powers to put an end to threats to international peace and security and to acts of aggression." In effect, I asked the Council to remind Israel and her Arab neighbors that under an existing resolution, the Council could use any measure, including economic blockade, to suppress any violation of their 1949 armistice. (The Council [on July 15, 1948] for the first time invoked Article 40, ordering Israel and the Arab states to stop fighting the war that had broken out when Israel became a nation in 1948.) The same resolution warned that failure to comply would lead to consideration of the enforcement provisions in Articles 41 and 42 of the Charter. These allow for the use of force, if necessary, with the Council deciding how the force is to be raised. Article 41 allows economic and other measures short of armed force, and Article 42 says that if those measures are not effective or adequate, the Council "may take such action by air, sea or land forces as may be necessary to maintain or restore international peace and security."

My report received a very favorable response from the delegations, from leaders in public life, as well as from the mass media.

Before I deal with the Security Council meetings in which that report was discussed, I wish to put on record a very unpleasant episode that developed between the United Arab Republic and Canada. After the Suez War of 1956, it was Foreign Minister Lester Pearson of Canada who became chiefly responsible for the very concept of the United Nations Emergency Force for the Middle East; he was universally recognized as the father of UNEF, and for this, he was awarded the Nobel Peace Prize in 1957. From the very beginning, however, relations between Canada and Egypt were far from warm. When Secretary General Dag Hammarskjöld negotiated with President Nasser in November 1956 for the stationing of UNEF on Egyptian soil, he proposed Canada among the countries contributing contingents. But because Canada was a member of the British Commonwealth, Nasser did not want Canadians in the force. In *The Cairo Documents*[11] Mohammed Heikal writes:

> Prime Minister Eden had made a statement in which he referred to the Canadians, saying that although the British forces were going to be withdrawn, Her Majesty's troops would still be in Egypt. Nasser said to Hammarskjöld: "I want neither Her Majesty nor her forces from anywhere. . . . the Canadians wear exactly the same uniforms as the British and perhaps our soldiers will mistake them for British soldiers and they will shoot at them and that will create problems. . . . Are they your forces or Her Majesty's?"

At last, Nasser was prevailed upon to accept Canadian troops, along with Indian troops, who are also "Her Majesty's" Commonwealth forces.

The minutes of my meetings at the United Nations on May 17 and 18, 1967, respectively, with representatives of countries contributing contingents to UNEF, leaked outside the meeting chamber before I replied to Nasser's request for the withdrawal of UNEF. The Egyptians were reported to be furious at the news of Canada's vigorous stand against my compliance with Nasser's request. Ambassador El-Kony told me on the evening of May 18 that he feared the worst if Canada decided to stay put while others agreed to leave Egyptian soil. His fears were confirmed. In the course of my talks in Cairo on May 24 with both Foreign Minister Riad and President Nasser, I found them to be highly critical of those countries, particularly Canada, which, in the words of Mr. Riad, "consider UNEF as an occupation force."

Immediately on my return to New York from Cairo on May

---

[11] Op. cit., p. 169.

25, I informed Ambassador George Ignatieff of Canada of my apprehensions about the continued presence of Canadian contingents in UNEF during its final evacuation from the area (which took four weeks, as stated earlier). At 11:25 A.M. on May 27, I received a cable from Foreign Minister Riad requesting me to order the complete withdrawal and departure of Canadian forces within forty-eight hours from the time the cable reached me. The cable accused the Canadian government of resorting to "procrastination and delay" in the departure of its forces and, further, of having sent Canadian destroyers toward the Mediterranean, an act the U.A.R. considered inflammatory.

That same afternoon (May 27), I sent a message to Prime Minister Pearson of Canada requesting the government of Canada to urgently undertake the necessary transportation arrangements to carry out the evacuation.

I immediately informed Ambassador Ignatieff of the substance of the cable, and transmitted the text of Mr. Riad's cable to General Rikhye, with the request to accelerate the evacuation of the Canadian contingent. I then cabled Foreign Minister Riad, informing him that I ordered the UNEF commander to accelerate the evacuation, but warning him that I could not guarantee that it would be fully completed within forty-eight hours.

Due to the very efficient logistic arrangements of the Canadian air force and the full co-operation of the government of the United Arab Republic, the departure of the Canadian contingent from U.A.R. territory, under the able supervision of General Rikhye, was completed within forty-eight hours. I immediately informed Mr. Riad of the completion of the evacuation.

On May 30, I sent a cable to Prime Minister Pearson expressing my deep appreciation for the invaluable contribution Canada had made to UNEF and asking him to convey that appreciation to his government—and especially to all the officers and men of the Canadian contingent.

On June 5, I received a warmly appreciative message from him in which he reaffirmed the full support of the government and people of Canada to me personally and to the United Nations.

In Appendix F, Part IV, I am reproducing, *in extenso*, the texts of my correspondence with Mr. Riad as well as with Mr.

Pearson, in order to highlight the extremely hazardous situation that UNEF would have been in if I had refused to comply with the request of the United Arab Republic to withdraw the force, or had even delayed in my reply to that request. In any event, when the Security Council met on May 29 to consider the report I had submitted on May 26, UNEF (except the Canadian contingent) was still on U.A.R. soil, behind their observation posts, which were already occupied by U.A.R. troops. The Security Council met at 3:00 P.M. on that day.

My report of May 26, in which I called for "a breathing spell," was vigorously endorsed by Ambassador Goldberg as well as by the representatives of China, Argentina, Brazil, Britain, Canada, Ethiopia, and India. To the surprise of everybody, including myself, Ambassador Fedorenko of the Soviet Union did not support my proposal. It was beyond me why the Soviet representative could not endorse the line of action that President Nasser himself had accepted a few days earlier. When I asked him about it at the conclusion of the debate at 7:30 P.M., he merely replied that my report "speaks for itself" and did not require interpretation or elaboration. This reply did not even remotely explain his failure to support the idea of a breathing spell.

That same day (May 29), Alexei Nesterenko told me that the Soviet Union had counseled President Nasser against starting a war. So far, Moscow had avoided taking any public stand on the issue of the U.A.R.'s sovereignty over the Strait of Tiran, but from Nesterenko I got the impression that the Soviet Union did not fully support Nasser's claim to its sovereignty. When I asked him why Fedorenko did not support my recommendation for a breathing spell, he said that Fedorenko most probably had not received any specific guidance on that issue from Moscow. By that time, Washington and London had reacted favorably to President de Gaulle's suggestion (on May 24) of Big-Four talks on the Middle East crisis, but Moscow was still fending off active participation in such a four-power effort. Nesterenko did not know the reason for this attitude of "non-participation," but my assumption was that Nasser was not keen about it because of his suspicion of Washington's and London's motives in the whole affair.

While the Security Council was still in session, disturbing

news reached the United Nations. According to news dispatches, Damascus radio announced on May 29 that Syria and Iraq had signed a military agreement for the co-operation of their armies in case of war with Israel. The broadcast also said that Brigadier General Mahmoud Ereim of Iraq arrived in Damascus on that day with the first Iraqi troops for stationing on the Syrian border facing Israel. On the same day, Iraq and Saudi Arabia announced that they would cut off oil to the West if war were to break out with Israel, a foreshadowing of what came six years later.

At 9:00 P.M. that day (May 29), I got reports from the United Nations office in Cairo of President Nasser's press conference. In effect, the President said that peace in the Middle East was out of the question until the Palestinian Arabs returned to their homeland (part of which is now Israel) and exercised sovereignty there. He stressed (as he had told me five days earlier) his willingness to accept a revival of the Egyptian-Israeli Mixed Armistice Commission, if it were reinstated on the same basis as had been prescribed by the Security Council, but which Israel had declared "dead" after the 1956 war. It should be noted that Ambassador El-Kony's main theme, in his statement in the Security Council on that day, was the reactivation of EIMAC.

The same night, I received reports that Premier Levi Eshkol of Israel had made a moderate radio address to the nation indicating that Israel would continue to negotiate with the major powers to find ways to reopen the Strait of Tiran to Israeli shipping. He said that the Cabinet had decided on "the continuation of political action in the world arena to stimulate international factors to take effective measures to ensure free international passage" in the Strait of Tiran. Diplomatic quarters at the United Nations attributed the calm tone and content of Mr. Eshkol's speech to Abba Eban's report to the Cabinet on his return to Jerusalem after a whirlwind tour of Paris, London, and Washington.

But Israeli newspapers were critical of Eshkol's moderate tone. Voices were heard that the defense portfolio, which the Prime Minister held, should go to "the hero of 1956 war," General Moshe Dayan. (General Dayan became Defense Minister two days later.)

When the Security Council met again at 3:00 P.M. on Tues-

day, May 30, the debate was focused primarily on whether the
U.A.R. had or did not have the right to blockade the Strait of
Tiran. Legal arguments were adduced by both sides in support of
their respective positions. It is interesting to note that Senator J.
William Fulbright, Chairman of the Senate Foreign Relations
Committee, suggested in the course of a press conference, on May
28 in Geneva, that the legal aspects of the blockade should be re-
ferred to the International Court of Justice.

The Security Council again failed to arrive at any agreement.
Mr. George Hakim, Foreign Minister of Lebanon, who arrived in
New York on the previous day, took part in the debate and made
a prophetic statement: "If there were war tomorrow, it would be
because Israel had struck the first blow." The Security Council
was again adjourned at 5:25 P.M. without any decision.

On that day (May 30), very significant developments took
place outside the Security Council. Backed by the United States,
Britain was reported to be taking the initiative in rallying support
for the principle of freedom of passage for all ships through the
Strait of Tiran, which leads into the Gulf of Aqaba. Ralph Bunche
told me that he heard from "a British source" that London was
consulting several maritime nations (including Norway, Sweden,
Liberia, Ghana, Canada, and Japan) on possible moves to assert
the right of passage through the Strait.

In Jerusalem, Foreign Minister Abba Eban, speaking at a
news conference, said that the government of Israel was pursuing
a policy of prying open the Strait of Tiran "alone if we must, with
others if we can." He added, "Now it is clear from the contacts
we've had with the major powers that there are others in the
world who are prepared to make common cause for the restoration of the legal situation in the Gulf of Aqaba."

In Cairo, President Nasser and King Hussein of Jordan, who
arrived at the U.A.R. capital unexpectedly, signed a mutual defense pact binding their governments to "use all means at their
disposal, including the use of armed forces," to repel an attack on
either nation. Only six days earlier, Foreign Minister Riad had
told me in Cairo that the United Arab Republic would never accept Jordanian troops for the defense of his country. The news of
the military alliance between these two nations, avowed enemies

for so long, came as a complete surprise to diplomats at the United Nations. Nasser, who had in the past denounced Hussein for being in league with Israel, addressed the King as "great brother." The King in turn said, "We thank Allah for having guided us and having made us rise to the level of our responsibility." President Nasser also said that he would consider an Israeli attempt to break the blockade of the Gulf as aggression.

Thus, the stage was set for a showdown. The question was: who would strike first? At the end of May, an atmosphere of gloom prevailed in the Security Council. The irony of the Council's proceedings was that almost all members stressed whatever points of my report they considered advantageous to stress, to the neglect of other points. Two draft resolutions were presented on May 31, one by the United States and the other by the United Arab Republic. Both resolutions were based on my report of May 26, but neither of them agreed on any substantive issue! The draft resolution introduced by Ambassador Goldberg called on all parties, as a first step, to comply with my suggestions for gaining a breathing spell. It also proposed that the Council encourage "the immediate pursuit of international diplomacy." The draft resolution introduced by Ambassador El-Kony urged the Council to accept the 1948 armistice agreements and proposed that the Council should order Israel to resume participation in the Mixed Armistice Commission "within two weeks."

When Ambassador El-Kony saw me at 10:45 A.M. on May 31, I asked him why he did not formally accept in the Security Council my proposal of a breathing spell. He replied that his government would not have any objection to a two-week moratorium, but wanted it to be made clear that this arrangement would be "without prejudice to the sovereign rights of the U.A.R." I explained to him that the very concept of a moratorium would involve the temporary suspension of sovereign rights. When he asked me whether Israel had accepted the idea of a moratorium, I told him that it had not, but that I believed the United States was putting pressure on Israel. I asked him why the Soviet Union had not come out with an endorsement of the moratorium. He replied that the Soviet Union agreed with the U.A.R. that it should not prejudice its sovereign rights.

At that meeting, he also told me of the possibility of a visit to Cairo by King Faisal of Saudi Arabia, and said that Morocco had decided to place forty per cent of its armed forces at the disposal of the U.A.R. He said that there was "a very strong feeling" among the Arabs with regard to passage through the Strait of Tiran.

The Security Council did not meet on Thursday, June 1, nor on Friday, June 2, since most members wanted time to consult and to receive instructions from their governments. Meanwhile, the French government was pressing for a four-power conference, to be attended by the United States, the United Kingdom, the Soviet Union, and France. The Soviet Union, however, refused to participate.

On Thursday, June 1, I had a long discussion with Ambassador Hans R. Tabor of Denmark, who assumed the presidency of the Security Council on that date. I stressed the urgency of the Council's taking an action "in one or two days." Failing that, the Big Four should meet immediately, as proposed by General de Gaulle. In my view, I said, war was imminent. He asked me for my candid views on President Nasser's blockade of the Strait of Tiran. I told him that apart from the legal aspects of the case, which could be argued endlessly, that action at this moment, in my view, was President Nasser's "blunder." I also told him that I did not understand the opposition by Israel and the Soviet Union to my suggestion of a breathing spell of two to three weeks, which Nasser had accepted and which Goldberg was now proposing. In reply to his question, I said that EIMAC should be reactivated, as the United Arab Republic had proposed, and that the unilateral disavowal of it by Israel was a clear defiance of UN resolutions.

On Friday, June 2, I saw a report of Foreign Minister Riad's statement in Cairo to the effect that the United Arab Republic would close the Suez Canal to ships of any country that tried to break the blockade of the Strait of Tiran. Reacting to the U.S. declaration of support for the British assertion that the Gulf of Aqaba should be free to ships of all nations, Mr. Riad characterized the move as "nineteenth-century gunboat diplomacy." He warned them of "grave danger if they participate in any aggression against the United Arab Republic."

Another report from Paris said that the U.S. and British ambassadors had presented a joint declaration to the French Foreign Office insisting on their right to freedom of access to the Gulf of Aqaba. The French Cabinet, which met on the same day, issued a declaration (authorized by President de Gaulle) that the French government "is not committed in any way and on any subject on the side of the states involved." The French declaration flatly rejected the idea of a test in the Gulf by Western maritime powers; it continued: "All the states concerned have a right to live, but the worst thing that could happen would be the opening of hostilities." It warned that the country that "used arms first" would have neither French "approval nor, for even stronger reasons, her support."

The French declaration said that, "if the present crisis were followed by a détente, then the problems raised by navigation in the Gulf of Aqaba, the situation of the Palestinian refugees and the conditions of proximity of the states should be resolved at their root by way of international decisions which would have to be preceded by the Big-Four members of the Security Council."

My first reaction was that the French statement would surely arouse resentment in Israel, since it was obviously meant as a warning to that country, whose air force was at that time equipped with French planes and was almost completely dependent on deliveries of French spare parts.

On Sunday, June 4, I went to the office to see the reports from the area, and it was obvious that the situation had greatly deteriorated. Yet the Security Council was still sharply divided on the nature of a resolution. On that day, King Hussein announced the extension, to include Iraq, of his defense pact with the United Arab Republic. He also warned the United States that if it went too far in support of Israel, the friendship it had had with Jordan in the last decade would end. The United States had been circulating a draft declaration by the maritime powers that the Gulf of Aqaba was an international waterway. According to official statements, Britain would endorse that declaration; France and Canada would not. Norway and Japan were still noncommittal, but a few maritime powers were reported to be inclined to favor it. President Nasser, in a broadcast speech on that day, rejected in advance any such declaration. He said any declaration that the Gulf was an international waterway would be considered "a preliminary to an act of war."[12]

I discussed with Ralph Bunche the advisability of a further appeal to President Nasser to agree once again to a breathing spell, as he had done in Cairo on May 24, and to Israel to reconsider its long-standing rejection of EIMAC. We agreed that in view of the statements in the Security Council meetings, there was no likelihood of any such line of action acceptable to the Council, and decided to talk to the two representatives on the next day. We then sent cables to Generals Rikhye and Odd Bull, asking them to keep us informed of the latest developments. By that time, UNEF contingents were no longer in their original observation posts. They were concentrated in the camps behind the line (which had been occupied by U.A.R. forces), awaiting evacuation. Ralph and I left the office at 6:30 P.M.

---

[12] Cable from the United Nations Development Program representative in Cairo, June 4, 1967.

CHAPTER XIII

THE SIX-DAY WAR
AND ITS AFTERMATH

At 3:00 A.M. on Monday, June 5, I was awakened by a phone call. It was Ralph Bunche. His first words were, "U Thant, war has broken out!" The cable office at United Nations headquarters had received a cable from General Rikhye at 2:40 A.M. New York time (8:40 A.M. Middle Eastern time), and, as was the case with all similar urgent cables, the cable officer in charge had immediately phoned Ralph at home. In the past, Ralph would wait until 6:30 A.M. to inform me of important cables, but this time he did not wait. (I am sure his loss of sleep throughout the second half of 1967 accelerated his decline in health.)

The cable read to me on the phone said that at 0800 hours (local time), 2:00 A.M. New York time, two Israeli aircraft violated United Arab Republic airspace over Gaza. One of these aircraft was shot down by antiaircraft fire and fell into the sea. The pilot bailed out and was picked up by a motor launch. Also at 0800 hours, two Israeli aircraft violated United Arab Republic airspace over El-Arish, in Sinai, and were fired upon by antiaircraft guns. The United Arab Republic claimed one Israeli aircraft shot down. UNEF personnel in the Rafah camp reported heavy firing between U.A.R. and Israeli forces across the international frontier south of Rafah, starting at 0800 hours. United Arab Republic authorities in Gaza informed General Rikhye of a large-scale Israeli air raid throughout the U.A.R. including a raid on Cairo. (Israel had denied the raid on Cairo.) U.A.R. authorities also informed General Rikhye that at 0800 hours, Israeli forces had attacked El-Quseima in Sinai.

Ralph Bunche immediately got in touch with Ambassador Hans Tabor of Denmark, president of the Security Council, who had already received reports from the Israeli and U.A.R. representatives. He was also in touch with all members of the Security Council, with a view to holding a Council meeting at 9:00 A.M. I immediately got dressed and left for the United Nations at 3:45 A.M. without, for the first time in my memory, my morning meditation. In the office, cable messages continued to come in.

The Security Council met at nine-thirty, and the president made a short statement quoting the messages he had received from the permanent representatives of Israel and the U.A.R., in which each officially informed him, in his capacity as president of the Security Council, that hostilities had broken out.

I then made my report, based on cables received from General Rikhye. After recounting the sequence of events reported to me by Ralph at 3:00 A.M., I enumerated the developments I had learned about since I arrived in the office. I prefaced my report with this statement: "Of course, . . . United Nations sources have no means of ascertaining how the hostilities were initiated. As usual, reports coming from the parties are conflicting, but all agree that serious military action on land and in the air is taking place at a number of points and is spreading."

In retrospect, I feel that it will serve no useful purpose, nor will it serve the cause of historical accuracy, if I recount what Israel reported or what the United Arab Republic reported on that fateful morning. Immediately after the war, it was well established that Israel had struck first. Apart from the conflicting reports of the two sides at the time, what is really worth repeating now is General Rikhye's report concerning attacks that day on UN personnel, a report I received later in the morning and submitted to the Security Council during that morning session:

> The Commander of UNEF (Rikhye) reported that at 1245 hours local time (6:45 A.M. New York time) Israeli artillery opened fire on two camps of the Indian contingent of UNEF,

which were in the process of being abandoned, and soon thereafter United Arab Republic tanks surrounded one of the camps which still contains one reduced Indian company. Orders have been given for the Indian personnel in both camps to be withdrawn immediately.

General Rikhye also reported that a UNEF convoy immediately south of Khan Yunis, on the road between Gaza and Rafah, was strafed by an Israeli aircraft on the morning of 5 June, although the vehicles, like all UNEF vehicles, are painted white. First reports indicate that three Indian soldiers were killed and an unknown number wounded in this attack. The Commander of UNEF has sent an urgent message through the Chief of Staff of UNTSO (General Odd Bull) to the Chief of Staff of the Israeli Defense Forces urging him again to give orders to Israeli Armed Forces to refrain from firing on UNEF camps, buildings, and vehicles.[1]

The report from General Odd Bull, chief of staff of UNTSO, is also worth repeating. He reported that at 1330 hours local time (7:30 A.M. New York time), approximately one company of Jordanian soldiers occupied the garden of Government House in Jerusalem (headquarters of UNTSO). General Bull protested in person to the commander and asked him to withdraw his troops. He also protested in the strongest terms to the senior Jordanian delegate to the Israel-Jordan Mixed Armistice Commission against the violation of United Nations premises by Jordanian soldiers, whose withdrawal within half an hour he demanded. He also informed the Israeli authorities of these developments and requested them to ensure that Israeli soldiers would not enter the Government House area. By then, an exchange of fire had already begun between the Jordanian soldiers in the Government House garden and Israeli soldiers nearby. General Bull later informed me by an emergency message that Jordanian troops had not withdrawn and were demanding to enter Government House itself, and had demanded that no telephone calls be made from Government House. United Nations headquarters in New York lost radio contact with UNTSO headquarters in Jerusalem at 8:52 A.M. New

---

[1] During the process of evacuation, one Brazilian and fourteen Indian soldiers were killed.

York time. This also meant that United Nations headquarters had
lost direct contact with UNEF headquarters (in Gaza), whose
messages were routed through UNTSO.

At the Security Council meeting, statements were made by the
representatives of India, Israel, and United Arab Republic. Ambassador Parthasarathi of India, who spoke after I did, said:

> My purpose in intervening now is to express our profound
> shock and grief at learning from the Secretary-General that three
> members of the Indian contingent of UNEF have been killed
> and an unknown number wounded in a wanton strafing attack by
> Israel on the withdrawing columns of these forces. Our soldiers
> went to the area ten years ago as sentinels of peace and in the
> service of the international community. That Israeli armed forces
> should have attacked treacherously and brutally these soldiers of
> ours makes them martyrs in the cause of peace. We condemn this
> Israeli action and protest most vigorously against it.

Since any attempt made by me to summarize the statements
made in the Security Council is likely to be interpretive, I shall
avoid doing so. From June 5, 1967, to March 6, 1971, I submitted 1,099 reports to the Security Council pertaining to the war, the
aftermath of the war, cease-fires, breaches of cease-fire, and actions taken by the chief of staff of UNTSO.

On July 14, I submitted the final report on UNEF to the
General Assembly. At that time, only thirty UNEF civilian personnel remained in Gaza to look after United Nations property.
The reports received by me disclosed that at Rafah camp,
members of the UN international and military staff were compelled by an Israeli officer to lie on the ground all night without
food or water. In addition to the Israeli seizure of personal and
office property from Gaza, "all of the United Nations vehicles in
running condition had also been removed by Israeli forces and
were seen in use in the Gaza area." I then stated that in spite of my
several protests to Israel, "continued pilfering, vandalism, organized removal of UNEF property by members of the armed forces,
and continued disorderly conditions within the camp, including
incursions by parties of the local populations, had combined to
make the task for the United Nations representatives extremely
difficult, if not impossible." Ambassador Gideon Rafael informed

me on behalf of his government that all cases of pilfering of UN property had been brought before courts-martial "whenever they came to notice."

In the course of that report, I also made the following points: During its history, UNEF lost eighty-nine personnel killed and many wounded or injured. One Brazilian and fourteen Indian soldiers were killed as a result of Israeli action after June 5. The net cost of the whole UNEF operation to the United Nations was approximately $213 million. This did not include troop salary costs borne by contributing countries.

On the first day of the war (June 5) Prime Minister Pearson of Canada supported President de Gaulle's proposal for a Big-Four meeting. He called on the United States, Britain, France, and the Soviet Union to meet at once in an effort to end the fighting, asserting that the meeting should be on a very high political level; he also said that the responsibility for bringing about a cease-fire rested first with the United Nations Security Council.

On the same day, France suspended deliveries of military equipment and spare parts to the Middle East. The suspension measure applied equally to Israel and the Arab countries, but amounted in effect to an arms embargo against Israel, which alone among the countries involved was largely dependent on French arms. The Israeli air force was equipped almost exclusively with French aircraft, notably Mirage M-C and Super-Mystère interceptors. The suspension of arms deliveries was believed to be President de Gaulle's personal decision.

That same day (June 5), the Middle Eastern oil-producing countries held a conference in Baghdad and decided to take measures to cut off oil supplies to those countries they believed aided Israel. Immediately after the conference, two major producing nations, Kuwait and Iraq, halted all supplies to the United States and Britain. Later, Algeria also announced that it was halting supplies to these two countries (although Algerian oil did not directly go to either country).

On June 6, the United Arab Republic closed the Suez Canal to all shipping and broke all relations with the United States over charges of American support for Israel in the war. Cairo radio asserted that thirty-two United States bombers had left Wheelus Air

Force Base in Libya to fly to Israel on the previous day and had participated in the bombing of Egypt. (Later on, this accusation proved to be false.) On the same day, the United States Embassy in Cairo announced that the U.A.R. Interior Ministry had directed all American nationals and American correspondents to leave the country immediately. Algeria and Syria quickly joined the United Arab Republic in breaking off diplomatic ties with the United States, while Syria also broke with Britain. (The United Arab Republic had broken diplomatic relations with Britain more than a year earlier over the question of Rhodesia.) On the same night, the Sudan severed diplomatic relations with the United States and Britain.

The Security Council meeting was suspended at 11:15 A.M. (June 5) to enable members to discuss the situation privately, and it did not resume until 10:20 P.M. During the recess, I was in almost hourly contact with Generals Rikhye and Odd Bull, and saw, besides, a number of permanent representatives. After meeting late that night for only five minutes, the Council decided to adjourn to study my latest report. It met again at 6:30 P.M. on the next day (June 6). Before the official meeting, members of the Council were in continuous private session, discussing a draft resolution. I also had long private meetings separately with both Goldberg and Fedorenko. The main theme of these discussions was how best to achieve an immediate cease-fire. By 6:00 P.M., agreement was reached on the draft resolution, and the meeting was officially convened thirty minutes later.

Ambassador Hans R. Tabor of Denmark, president of the Council, formally read the draft, which called upon the governments concerned "to take forthwith as a first step all measures for an immediate cease-fire and for a cessation of all military activities in the area," and requested the Secretary General "to keep the Council promptly and currently informed on the situation."

A vote was taken by show of hands, and the draft resolution was adopted unanimously. All members of the Council, in explaining their votes, made fervent appeals to the parties to the conflict to cease hostilities immediately. After the adoption of the resolution, I sent urgent cables to the belligerents conveying its text. It should be noted that this resolution did not end the fighting; a series of resolutions was required to achieve that.

Although Jordan almost immediately announced that it had accepted the Security Council call for a cease-fire, it quickly became apparent that the fighting was not going to end so soon. Jordan, the United Arab Republic, and Syria promptly accused Israel of continuing the attacks despite the Security Council resolution, while Israel said that hostilities continued because the Arab states had not yet observed the cease-fire. Obviously, the Arab states wanted the attacks to end quickly, to save as much territory as they could, while (as the evidence seemed to indicate during the next few days) Israel wanted to achieve certain objectives before ending the fighting.

The continued fighting inevitably led to a series of Security Council meetings that were among the bitterest and most acrimonious in my memory. These meetings were held at any hour, depending on developments in the field. Often they lasted until the small hours of the morning, and one was even convened at 4:00 A.M. Throughout these long and contentious debates, the Arab and Israeli delegates exchanged angry charges, with the Soviet Union's delegate, Nikolay T. Fedorenko, using (in support of the Arabs) the kind of intemperate language—often directed at the United States—seldom heard in the Council chamber. During these meetings, I made innumerable reports to the Council conveying information cabled by General Odd Bull. Because General Bull and his staff had been displaced by the Israelis from UNTSO headquarters in Jerusalem, because there were few observers in the field, and because of the general chaos, these reports were often fragmentary and could do little to dispel the confusion at UN headquarters as to what was actually happening in the war. The reports, however, together with press dispatches, seemed to indicate that Israel continued to press its attacks as, in turn, Jordan, the U.A.R., and Syria accepted the Security Council's calls for a cease-fire.

With fighting continuing on June 7, the Council again met in emergency session and unanimously adopted a second cease-fire resolution, which was proposed by the Soviet Union. It demanded that the governments concerned cease firing as of 2000 hours GMT that day. By that night, Israeli troops, armed and in battle dress, prayed at the foot of the Wailing Wall in Jordanian Jerusalem. They occupied most of the West Bank territory of Jordan and much of the Sinai peninsula. In addition, Israeli tank columns were driving toward the Gulf of Aqaba, while Israeli troops were pushing deeper into Syria.

Although the U.A.R. was now virtually defenseless, it did not accept the Security Council demand for a cease-fire until the next day, June 8. On that day, Israeli forces continued to advance against the U.A.R. and pushed until they reached the Suez Canal and the Red Sea. Also on that day, Israel made clear that it intended to retain permanent control of the Jordanian sector of Jerusalem, an act that would shortly be condemned by almost every member of the UN. And on June 8, news came that Israeli planes had sunk the U.S. naval vessel *Liberty,* mistaking it for an Egyptian ship.

On June 9, Syria announced acceptance of the cease-fire and almost immediately charged in the Security Council that Israel was continuing to advance. In still another emergency session, the Council in a third resolution demanded that "hostilities should cease forthwith"; it instructed me to arrange immediate compliance with the governments of Israel and Syria and report back within two hours. Both governments quickly informed me that they would comply, but Syria soon complained that the Israelis were continuing to attack, an accusation that Israel denied. I repeatedly tried to get accurate information from General Bull but, for the reasons I mentioned earlier, he simply was unable to provide it. I particularly appealed to Israel to restore to General Bull UNTSO's headquarters and wireless facilities, an appeal backed unanimously by the Security Council.

It was nearly eleven o'clock when the Council adjourned, and still there was no cease-fire in Syria. When I went up to my office on the thirty-eighth floor, I found two important press reports. The first, from London, said that Prime Minister Harold Wilson had declared that the Arab states must recognize Israel's right to exist; also that Israel must recognize Arab interests, and particularly that it must contribute to a solution of the problem of the

Arab refugees who had been displaced two decades earlier from what was now Israel. Wilson also said the Big-Four nations must work together toward a lasting settlement of the Middle East crisis, in effect endorsing Charles de Gaulle's proposal made a couple of weeks earlier, a proposal that I had quickly supported.

More dramatic was a report from Cairo that President Nasser had decided to resign, blaming himself for Eygpt's disastrous defeat. Although the National Assembly met later that night and voted not to accept Nasser's resignation, I believed then, and I still believe, that he genuinely wanted to resign. He had gambled, with the genuine conviction of Arab unity and Arab military might, in an attempt "to restore the situation prior to 1956," but he had failed, and failed disastrously. The Gaza Strip and the whole of his Sinai were in Israeli hands. The West Bank of the Jordan and the Jordanian sector of Jerusalem were occupied by his enemy, and Israeli tanks were not far from Damascus. His air force had been almost completely eliminated in the first few hours of June 5, and all his tanks in the Sinai were in the hands of the Israelis. When I saw him on May 24, he had been the personification of confidence. Then, by the second day of the war, he realized that he had been completely knocked out. Nor could Nasser stand the taunts of those Arabs who termed his acceptance of the UN cease-fire "treason" and "surrender."

Nasser was pained when the Soviet Union did not endorse his closing of the Strait of Tiran. In fact, the Soviet Union had not known in advance of the blockade and had not approved it after it had been established. On the other hand, it was the Soviet Union that actively sought a cease-fire and perhaps saved the Arab states from an even worse defeat. On the first day of the war, when the tide of battle turned sharply against the Arabs, the Soviet Union began actively to seek a cease-fire. Indeed, it was later disclosed that Soviet Premier Alexei Kosygin took the initiative on June 5 of using the Washington-Moscow Hot Line to propose a cease-fire.

Driving home to Riverdale shortly before midnight, I had the car radio on. The news was dominated by Nasser's attempt to resign and the intense fighting in Syria—despite the third Security Council cease-fire resolution. As soon as I got home, my daughter

Aye Aye told me that the UN cable office had been trying to reach me. I called back, and the officer on duty told me that two urgent cables had come from the chairman of the Israeli-Syrian Mixed Armistice Commission, messages he had already relayed to Ralph Bunche.

I never did get to bed that night. Ralph and I were in almost continuous touch; at 2:20 A.M., he informed me that the Council would meet in another emergency session at three-thirty at the request of Syria. I hurried back to headquarters, arriving there at 3:15 A.M. to find that Ralph was having a telex conversation with General Bull, who had been given telecommunications facilities in a hotel by Israel.

The Council convened at 4 A.M. Syria accused Israel of advancing on Damascus and of launching air raids against the capital. In response to my urgent requests, General Bull was sending in what information he could obtain, which was very little. Press reports, however, said that Israel was continuing to advance on Damascus. The Israeli delegate flatly denied the reports of the air attacks on Damascus, its airport, or its environs. Shortly thereafter, however, I read to the Council a report from General Bull confirming attacks in the area of the airport and other attacks outside the city.

It was a frantic session, with occasional recesses during which hasty consultations and negotiations were held in and outside the Council chamber. It was also marked by vituperative attacks by Soviet Ambassador Fedorenko against Arthur Goldberg of the United States and Gideon Rafael of Israel—calculated taunts, too personal to befit the Security Council chamber. Fedorenko also announced that the Soviet Union had broken diplomatic relations with Israel.

Just when things seemed very dark, I received another cable from General Bull that I immediately read to the Council. He reported that Israel had requested him to go from Jerusalem to Tel Aviv as quickly as possible to make arrangements with Defense Minister Moshe Dayan for a cease-fire. In a later message, General Bull, who had remained in Jerusalem but had been in touch with Dayan, reported to me that he had proposed "a cease-fire to be effective 1630 hours GMT today, 10 June." "Speed," he added, "is essential." The proposed time was only a couple of hours away.

Both Syria and Israel accepted the proposal, but that evening, at the urgent request of the Soviet Union, the Council met again to consider Syrian charges that Israel had violated the cease-fire. Israel was accused of having taken the important town of Quneitra after the cease-fire. Israel denied the charge, and General Bull was unable to answer my requests for precise information as to whether the cease-fire had been observed. This confused situation continued for a few more days, with the Council, on the night of June 11, adopting unanimously a resolution that called "for the prompt return to the cease-fire positions of any troops which may have moved forward subsequent to 1630 hours GMT on 10 June 1967. . . ." But it soon became apparent that the fighting had ended. The Six-Day War was over.

That same day, June 11, United Press International reported from Jerusalem that Israel's Information Minister, Yisrael Gailille, had said that his country "cannot return to the 1949 armistice agreement and boundaries determined by those agreements." He said that they had been "nullified by the armies, tanks and planes of the United Arab Republic, Jordan, Syria and Iraq." This Israeli decision to hold on to the lands taken from its Arab neighbors sowed the seeds for the war that followed in 1973.

Also that day, the New York *Times* printed two letters, both very relevant to the Security Council discussions, one from Ralph Bunche, which I mentioned earlier, and the other from Dr. Roger Fisher, professor of law at Harvard.

Dr. Fisher's letter contains such a powerful statement on the right of innocent passage that it is worth quoting extensively. He pointed out that while "the Arab states have consistently refused to accept the existence of Israel . . . this does not mean that everything that they do is wrong or that everything Israel does is right." Dr. Fisher asserted that

> the United States press reports about the Gulf of Aqaba situation were grossly one-sided. The United Arab Republic had a good legal case for restricting traffic through the Strait of Tiran.
> First, it is debatable whether international law confers any right of innocent passage through such a waterway. Despite an Is-

raeli request, the International Law Commission in 1956 found no rule which would govern the Strait of Tiran. Although the 1958 Convention on the Territorial Sea does provide for innocent passage through such straits, the United States representative, Arthur Dean, called this "a new rule" and the U.A.R. has not signed the treaty.

There are, of course, good arguments on the Israeli side too, and an impartial international court might well conclude that a right of innocent passage through the Strait of Tiran does exist.

But a right of innocent passage is not a right of free passage for any cargo at any time. In the words of the Convention on the Territorial Sea:

"Passage is innocent so long as it is not prejudicial to the peace, good order or security of the coastal state."

In April Israel conducted a major retaliatory raid on Syria and threatened raids of still greater size. In this situation was Egypt required by international law to continue to allow Israel to bring in oil and other strategic supplies through Egyptian territory— supplies which Israel could use to conduct further military raids? That was the critical question of law.

The U.A.R. would have had a better case if it had announced that the closing was temporary and subject to review by the International Court, but taking the facts as they were I, as an international lawyer, would rather defend before the International Court of Justice the legality of the U.A.R.'s action in closing the Strait of Tiran than to argue the other side of the case, and I would certainly rather do so than to defend the legality of the preventive war which Israel launched this week.

The United States should now demand of Israel the same standards of conduct that it was demanding of the Arab states: Looking ahead one can see that it may be difficult to convince the Arabs that the United States does not decide issues on grounds of race or religion but on the grounds of principle.

Arabs may think that if we hold Egypt to its implied promises to let ships through the Gulf of Aqaba, we should hold Israel to its express promise not to extend its territory.

Arabs may think that if we ask them to accept U.N. troops on their sovereign territory to prevent border raids, we should ask Israel to do the same.

Arabs may think that if we plan to establish some international agency on Egyptian territory to see that the waters of the Jordan

River are available for fair international use, we should plan to establish a similar agency on Israeli territory to see that the waters of the Jordan River are available for fair international use.

Arabs may think that a firm United States guarantee of the borders of the Middle East ought to apply to them as well as to Israel.

Roger Fisher, Professor of Law
Harvard University
Cambridge, Mass., June 9, 1967.

The next day, June 12, Ambassador Kadhim Khalaf of Iraq confided to me that the Arabs were "disillusioned" with the Security Council's ineffectiveness in stopping the war, and that they were considering convening an emergency special session of the General Assembly. But instead, the Security Council met on June 13 at the request of the Soviet Union, and Ambassador Fedorenko introduced a resolution that would condemn Israel in the most vigorous terms, demanding that it withdraw behind the original armistice lines. Arthur Goldberg of the United States argued that a withdrawal was not enough: the proper course included prompt discussions "among the parties concerned, using such third-party or United Nations assistance as they may wish. . . ." But the Council could not agree on either resolution. On the next day, June 14, the Soviet Union draft was rejected, while the United States did not press for a vote on its resolution.

The question, in effect, was being turned over to the General Assembly. Even as I was polling the delegations, however, I had my doubts about the success of any General Assembly action. In the first place, such an important question would require a two-thirds majority, not easy to attain on so controversial an issue. In the second place, whereas the Charter gives the Security Council the authority to take mandatory action, the Assembly can only recommend, not mandate; and although an Assembly resolution passed by a substantial majority has political and even moral influence, it cannot force compliance. Even if the Assembly should adopt a resolution calling for an Israeli withdrawal, Israel would still feel it was under no obligation to accept it—as it had felt in 1956, when Dag Hammarskjöld tried to place the UN emergency force on *both* sides of the border between Israel and

Egypt. For Hammarskjöld's proposal was based on an *Assembly* resolution, not on a *Council* resolution.

To cite a relevant case, the UN force in Cyprus (UNFICYP) was established on the basis of a Security Council resolution, not a General Assembly resolution. If the government of Cyprus were to ask for the withdrawal of UNFICYP from its soil, no Secretary General would be competent to comply with such a request. Only the Security Council could decide whether to withdraw it or not. That is a crucial difference, and that is why I had no choice but to withdraw UNEF when Nasser requested it. There was no mandatory power behind the establishment of UNEF.

But while the Council could not agree on a substantial resolution, it did agree unanimously on a resolution calling on both sides to ensure the safety and welfare of peoples under their authority. It also called on both sides to "scrupulously respect" the 1949 Geneva Convention on the treatment of prisoners of war, and called on Israel to "facilitate the return" of Arab refugees who had fled the areas occupied by Israeli forces in Jordan, Syria, and the Gaza Strip.

By Thursday, June 15, it was apparent that a great majority of UN members favored a special session, even though it was opposed by the United States, which argued that the Security Council had not yet exhausted its possibilities. On that day, it was announced in Moscow that the Soviet delegation of fifty would be headed by no less than Premier Alexei Kosygin, who would stop in Paris the next day to discuss the situation with President de Gaulle. This announcement immediately established the context of the Assembly session, for in rapid succession a host of other world leaders announced their plans to attend. It turned into the most glittering assemblage of my decade as Secretary General. (And ironically, as we shall see, one of the most futile.) Among the heads of state or government were Prime Minister Todor Zhivkov of Bulgaria, Prime Minister Josef Lemart of Czechoslovakia, Prime Minister Jens Otto Krag of Denmark, Prime Minister Jens Fock of Hungary, Prime Minister Aldo Moro of Italy, King Hussein of Jordan, Prime Minister Josef Cyrankiewicz of Poland, Premier Ion Gheorghe Maurer of Romania, and President Nureddin Al-Atassi of Syria. The United Arab Republic was represented by its deputy premier, Mahmoud Fawzi, and among the many Foreign Ministers were such well-known figures as Abba Eban of Israel, George Brown of Britain, and Maurice Couve de Murville of France. And although he did not attend the session, one who was on everyone's mind was President Lyndon B. Johnson. Everyone was wondering whether he and Premier Kosygin would meet and what effect such a meeting might have.

The fifth emergency special session of the General Assembly was called to order at 9:30 A.M., Saturday, June 17, with Ambassador Abdul Rahman Pazhwak of Afghanistan presiding. A half hour before the session opened, Premier Kosygin, accompanied by Foreign Minister Gromyko and Ambassador Fedorenko, visited me in my small office behind the rostrum of the great General Assembly Hall. (My main office was on the thirty-eighth floor of the Secretariat building.) Although he had landed at Kennedy airport less than four hours before, neither he nor Gromyko looked tired; they said they had had some rest on the flight.

I asked Premier Kosygin whether he were planning to meet President Johnson. He said he had no such plans. When I asked what the Soviet response was to President de Gaulle's proposal for Big-Four involvement in seeking peace in the Middle East, he said the proposal was still under study. Since it was a courtesy call and since the session was about to begin, Premier Kosygin left after twenty-five minutes to call briefly on Assembly president Pazhwak, whose little office was next to mine.

Shortly after the session began, Ambassador Goldberg appealed to the delegates to avoid the "hot words, destructive propaganda, diatribes, and disrespect for facts" that had characterized the previous Security Council sessions. To no one's surprise, however, there were many hot words and, because passions were so deep, there was little substantial achievement in the special session; it was adjourned a number of times for consultations and was finally ended on September 18, the day before the regular annual meeting.

Premier Kosygin addressed the Assembly at 10:30 A.M. on Monday, June 19. An hour before he took the rostrum, President Johnson discussed the Middle East before the National Foreign Policy Conference for Educators in Washington. A number of diplomats, including the Assembly president, told me later that the President should have instead used the Assembly as the forum for so important a statement. I agreed. Whether by design or coincidence, President Johnson downgraded the United Nations as a forum for important policy statements.

When Premier Kosygin spoke, he attacked Israel in harsh terms (as expected) and introduced a resolution that would not only condemn Israel and demand that its troops be withdrawn, but also demand restitution for "all the damage inflicted" on the United Arab Republic, Jordan, and Syria. He also proposed that the Big Powers find "a common language" to reach decisions on a lasting peace in the Middle East. Mr. Kosygin read his angry text without a flicker of emotion. His reference to the Big Powers was the first indication of his endorsement of General de Gaulle's proposal.

Foreign Minister Abba Eban of Israel, linguistically nimble, politically able, and personally affable, replied to the Soviet Premier in equally harsh terms. He accused the Soviet Union of feeding an arms race in the Middle East, paralyzing the Security Council, and spreading among the Arabs alarmist reports of Israel's intentions. Reviewing the activities of the United Arab Republic and Syria over the previous ten years, he said that "a hangman's rope" had been woven for Israel. He asserted that "a thousand official statements by the Arabs in the last twenty-four months" announced their intention of destroying Israel.

Then, to my surprise, he criticized me for my agreement, on May 18, to President Nasser's request to withdraw the United Nations Emergency Force from the Israeli-Egyptian frontier. "What is the use of the fire brigade which vanishes from the scene as soon as the first smoke and flames appear?" he asked. I was surprised on two counts. First, his own representative to the United Nations, Ambassador Gideon Rafael, had, as I noted above, officially stated in the Council on June 3, 1967, that the crisis resulted from the U.A.R.'s ultimatum of May 6 demanding the withdrawal of UNEF, and had concluded: The Secretary-General tried to prevent the crisis from getting out of hand. He failed. It was not his fault."

Another reason for my surprise was that when he had seen

me the previous week during the Security Council sessions (and in the presence of Ambassadors Rafael and Ralph Bunche), I had given him a full explanation of why I had to take the decision I took, and he did not react.

So, when the General Assembly met again on Tuesday, June 20, I made a brief reply to him. After stating that I personally welcomed criticism "when it is just, based on fact, and does not obscure or ignore essential facts," I went on:

> I have to say at the outset that I was rather surprised at the breadth and vigor of the Foreign Minister's dissatisfaction with the withdrawal decision, since in a quite recent meeting we had discussed that issue, and at that time I had given a rather full explanation of just why the decision I took had to be taken in the way it was, and I heard no such reaction as Mr. Eban projected to the General Assembly yesterday—nothing like it. I wish now to say that I do not accept as having validity Mr. Eban's strictures on this matter.[2]

I then recounted why UNEF originally had to be stationed *only* on the U.A.R. side of the line: Israel did not permit the United Nations force on its side, "despite the intent of the General Assembly resolution that the United Nations troops should be stationed on both sides of the line." I then went on to say that:

> . . . prior to receiving the U.A.R. request for withdrawal and giving my reply to it, I had raised with the Permanent Representative of Israel to the United Nations the possibility of stationing elements of UNEF on the Israel side of the line. I was told that the idea was completely unacceptable to Israel. Moreover, for all of those ten years, Israel's troops regularly patrolled alongside the line and now and again created provocations by violating it.

In the course of the afternoon session, Mr. Eban replied that though he was certain everything had been done in good faith, "this does not alter the fact that a weakness in the United Nations peace-keeping texture must rank amongst the factors which are universally admitted to have led to the situation we are now discussing."[3]

---

[2] *United Nations General Assembly Verbatim Records,* June 20, 1967.
[3] Ibid.

I had another problem—this time from an unexpected source —in connection with the withdrawal of UNEF. In a six-column headline, the New York *Times* of Monday, June 19, 1967, reported the existence of a "secret" memorandum: "TEXT OF HAMMARSKJÖLD MEMORANDUM ON MIDDLE EAST PEACE FORCE." According to this "secret" memorandum, reportedly written by Dag Hammarskjöld, President Nasser had agreed to limit the use of his sovereign right to repel the United Nations Emergency Force from the United Arab Republic. The memorandum describes a private agreement between President Nasser and Mr. Hammarskjöld, to the effect that the United Nations would not withdraw the forces, and that the government of the United Arab Republic would not order them withdrawn, until both agreed that the troops had completed their tasks. Mr. Hammarskjöld reportedly had given a copy of the memorandum to a friend, Ernest A. Gross, who had agreed to its publication that week. The actual text on this point is reproduced in Appendix G, Part IV.

I telephoned Ralph about 7:30 A.M. on that day (June 19) and asked him if he knew anything about the memorandum. He said he did; he told me that Mr. Gross had mentioned it to him on the day I was to leave for Cairo, and that he had told Gross of his complete ignorance of its existence. Ralph said he believed he had mentioned it to me on the eve of my departure for Cairo on May 22; I did not recollect it.

As soon as I got to the office at 9:00 A.M., I went into a conference with Ralph and Brian Urquhart, both of whom had worked very closely with the late Secretary General on the question of the Middle East. Both of them told me that they had looked for it on the thirty-eighth floor for several days, but could not trace it in official, confidential, or personal files. Brian was then working on a book on Dag Hammarskjöld that was based on all his private papers, but even he was not aware of its existence. Ralph also told me that he had checked with Ambassador El-Kony of the United Arab Republic who, in turn, had checked with his government: nobody in Cairo was aware of its existence, either. We then discussed the motivation for its publication by Mr. Gross on the day Premier Kosygin and Foreign Minister Eban were scheduled to speak. Finally, they started drafting a reply for me to deliver when I went into the General Assembly hall.

While the Assembly session was on, I asked Ambassador El-Kony to see me in my office adjacent to the Assembly hall, and asked him about the memorandum. He said no one in Cairo was aware of its existence, and that his office had issued a disclaimer. He said that if President Nasser had been aware of it, he would never have accepted UNEF on U.A.R. territory. He then gave me a copy of the press release issued by his office. It concluded with the following statement:

> At no time was the Government of Egypt, later the United Arab Republic, aware of the existence of the so-called memorandum by the late Mr. Hammarskjöld of 5 August 1957, and consequently such a paper would have no legal or political binding on the Government of the United Arab Republic.

At lunch, which was attended by Ralph Bunche, Brian Urquhart, C. V. Narasimhan, José Rolz-Bennett, and Constantin Stavropoulos, we discussed the draft reply to the memorandum, and the text in its final form was released to the press after lunch. In the course of my reply, I said, among other things, that the memorandum is not in the official files of the Secretary General's office, was never conveyed to President Nasser, and—if it existed at all—was of a purely private character. I also said that the release of such a paper at this time raised questions of ethics and good faith. The full text of my statement is reproduced in Appendix H, Part IV. (When the Assembly adjourned in September, President Abdul Rahman Pazhwak commented: "It is the general understanding of the entire membership that the good faith of the Secretary-General has not been questioned in this debate.")

As I said earlier, the fifth emergency special session of the Assembly turned out to be futile, despite the glittering assemblage of world leaders. Of the various proposals that were made before the Assembly during the June session, not a single resolution on the substance of the Arab-Israeli conflict received the necessary two-thirds majority. Resolutions sponsored by the Soviet Union and Albania called for a vigorous condemnation of Israel and the withdrawal of Israeli forces from occupied Arab territories, and demanded reparations by Israel for damage inflicted on Arab countries. An American resolution merely called for negotiations based on mutual recognition of territorial integrity and for freedom of innocent maritime passage. A seventeen-power, nonaligned resolution called on Israel to withdraw to positions held prior to June 5, 1967, while a twenty-power Latin-American resolution requested a similar withdrawal and asked the parties to end the state of belligerency. I personally believed that the Latin-American draft was the most evenhanded and realistic. It also called for a full solution of the refugee problem and for the internationalization of Jerusalem, a matter that would be considered at the next regular session. But, as I have indicated, none of these resolutions passed.

Two resolutions, however, were passed overwhelmingly. One was a twenty-six-power "humanitarian" resolution appealing to all governments to assist relief organizations and facilitate transport of assistance supplies. The other was a Pakistani resolution declaring the measures taken by Israel to change the status of Jerusalem invalid and calling on Israel to rescind those measures. This resolution was adopted on July 4 by 99 votes to 0, with 20 abstentions. It also called on the Secretary General to report on its implementation "not later than one week from its adoption."

One of the many disappointments of the fifth emergency session was the meeting between Premier Kosygin and President Johnson at Glassboro on June 23. The news at first buoyed up most delegates, and there was a sense of relief and even ebullience among most diplomats, who expressed the hope that a face-to-face meeting of the two leaders could break the deadlock at the United Nations. The only questions heard in the corridors were: "Where is Glassboro?" and "Why Glassboro—why not New York?" Although the news heartened the delegates, many considered this petty, "halfway, Glassboro business" to be childish. I personally felt that it was unbecoming for two heads of state to resort to a measuring tape on a map to determine a place equidistant from New York and Washington, merely for reasons of prestige. (Glassboro is a small town in New Jersey, about halfway between New York and Washington.) Either New York or Washington would have been much more sensible and certainly much more fitting. In my view, of course, the United Nations would have been the ideal forum.

In any case, on June 23, the focus of world attention shifted from the United Nations to Glassboro, where the two leaders met with their aides for five and a half hours. It was reported that the matters discussed included the Middle East and Vietnam. But nothing came of these well-publicized meetings. During the first meeting of the emerging session, Ambassador Zenon Rossides of Cyprus brought me a note circulated early that morning by Alberto Giovannetti, the permanent observer of the Holy See, calling for an international administration of Jerusalem in order to safeguard free access, by all religious faiths, to the city's holy places. The Vatican proposal was at variance with the plan outlined by Israel for the administration of the holy places. Spanish delegate Manuel Aznar immediately announced that his country was in favor of the internationalization of Jerusalem, on the basis of a 1947 United Nations resolution that said that the whole city should be administered under a regime to be established by the United Nations. After quoting the various United Nations resolutions, the Vatican note said:

> Jerusalem remained divided between Jordan and Israel along the armistice line drawn after the 1947–48 conflict. It should be noted that this was merely an armistice and not peace. The demarcation line was not a frontier, but marked the point at which the belligerents stood when the cease-fire went into effect. The Holy See never modified, much less retreated from, the stand it took when the discussions took place at the U.N. in the years 1947–49. The Holy See remains therefore convinced that the only solution which offers a sufficient guarantee for the protection of Jerusalem and of its holy places is to place that city and its vicinity under an international regime. Only such a regime can properly safeguard the rights of the various religious faiths interested in the safety of and free access to the holy places.[4]

King Hussein addressed the General Assembly on June 26. In a deep and resonant voice he said: "There has been much talk about peace, but there has been little talk about justice. Peace is

---

[4] Reuters News Agency, June 26, 1967.

now claimed by the successful aggressor. But what Jordan and the Arabs want is peace with justice." He appealed to the Assembly not to permit Israel to use captured Arab territory "as a bargaining weapon or for political blackmail." He claimed that Jordanian territory was captured by Israel after his government had accepted the cease-fire. At the conclusion of his speech, the King received the longest and loudest ovation given any speaker thus far.

King Hussein saw me at 2:45 P.M. that day. When I asked him about the prospects for his proposed Arab summit, he was quite optimistic about its taking place. Both in public and private talks, he spoke with a total lack of emotion, or even a flicker of passion or rancor. At my luncheon given in his honor on Friday, June 30, he displayed an equal calm and composure. He not only spoke with a clipped British accent, but used an equally British mode of address, particularly among the military. I was terribly embarrassed when he prefaced every one of his remarks to me with a "sir." Imagine the King of Jordan addressing a former school teacher with a profusion of "sirs"!

When the King left my office, I accompanied him down the elevator and saw his car off, as was the custom adopted by every Secretary General for any head of state. But he seemed to be embarrassed that I followed that custom!

On June 28, Jerusalem was formally reunited. The Arab sector, formally held by Jordan, and some adjacent districts in Jordanian territory, were absorbed by Israel.

On the same day, William Powell, my press spokesman, brought to me a statement issued by the State Department in Washington. It said that "the hasty administrative action taken today cannot be regarded as determining the future of the holy places or the status of Jerusalem. . . . The United States has never recognized such unilateral action by any state in the area as governing the international status of Jerusalem."

Earlier that day, President Johnson had authorized a statement in which the United States took a strong position regarding Jerusalem. In the view of the U.S. government, it said, "There must be adequate recognition of the special interests of three great religions in the holy places of Jerusalem." It continued:

On this principle, [The President] assumes that before any unilateral action is taken on the status of Jerusalem, there will be appropriate consultation with religious leaders and others who are deeply concerned.

Jerusalem is holy to Christians, to Jews and to Moslems. It is one of the great continuing tragedies of history that a city which is so much the center of man's highest values has also been, over and over, a center of conflict. Repeatedly, the passionate beliefs of one element have led to exclusion or unfairness for others.

Men of all religions will agree that we must now do better. The world must find an answer that is fair and recognized to be fair.[5]

On June 29, the news of the annexation of Jerusalem gave rise to sharp reaction in the General Assembly. Both Arab and non-Arab delegates assailed the action. Ambassador Zenon Rossides of Cyprus said that the annexation "clearly denotes an expansionist policy, in violation of the United Nations Charter. Access to Jerusalem must be a matter of right, a world right, and not by permission or tolerance of any state."

On that day, Israeli Foreign Minister Abba Eban gave a press conference and said that the takeover was a step to ensure "peace, sanctity and free access" to the holy places of Jews, Christians and Moslems. "Nothing in Israel's action," he said, "forecloses or was intended to foreclose a discussion of arrangements for ensuring the universal character of the holy places." When asked whether Israel had "annexed" Jerusalem, he said that he preferred to use his own vocabulary. He repeated this reply when asked whether Jerusalem was now a part of Israel. He said:

. . . that word has not occurred in the legislation introduced by the Knesset or in anything I have said, and I therefore prefer to stick to my own definition that we stand for the unity . . . and the protection of holy places with access to all.

I am going to use my own words and to point out that the legislation adopted yesterday didn't deal with that question because it was not a political act at all. It was an act of administrative and municipal union.[6]

---

[5] *USUN Press Release,* June 28, 1967.

[6] United Nations Office of Public Information Minutes, June 29, 1967.

This is an illustration of Mr. Eban's extraordinary adroitness in the choice of words.

Meanwhile, I had been receiving reports from Laurence V. Michelmore, commissioner general of the United Nations Relief and Works Agency, informing me of the increased strain on the resources of the agency due to the newly displaced persons resulting from the Six-Day War; they were estimated at some 100,000 Arabs, in addition to the 1.3 million "old" refugees under its care. On June 30, I informed the General Assembly that I would appoint a high-ranking representative to obtain on-the-spot information on the safety and welfare of civilians in Arab territories occupied by Israel.

Among those who saw me on the morning of Monday, July 3, before the start of the General Assembly, were Soviet Foreign Minister Andrei A. Gromyko, Anatoli Dobrynin, ambassador to Washington, and Ambassador Platon D. Morozov of the Soviet mission to the UN. The fact that it was Dobrynin, not Fedorenko, who accompanied the Soviet Foreign Minister was the first indication to me that Gromyko was aware of the strained relations between myself and the Soviet permanent representative. I had known Mr. Dobrynin when he served as an undersecretary at the United Nations (I was then the permanent representative of Burma). Genial, modest, well-informed, and very relaxed, he is an ideal diplomat and would be an asset to any government he serves.

At 12:00 noon on Wednesday, July 5, Abba Eban saw me. At that meeting, I formally handed him the text of the Assembly resolution calling on Israel to relinquish political control of Jerusalem. He told me that he would transmit the document to his government and that a reply would be forthcoming directly from Tel Aviv. He was pleased with the outcome, or rather the lack of outcome, at the United Nations—and was particularly delighted with the resounding defeat of the Soviet resolution. It is worth noting that Israel voted against the nonaligned draft, abstained on the Latin-American draft, and stayed away when voting took place on the Pakistani draft on Jerusalem. Israel voted, however, for the Swedish draft on humanitarian activities for the area, which also recommended to the governments concerned "the scrupulous respect of the humanitarian principles governing the treatment of prisoners of war and the protection of civilian persons in time of war, contained in the Geneva Convention of 12 August 1949."

In an atmosphere of indecision and depression, the Assembly recessed on Wednesday night (July 5) for one week. Every major political group felt that it had lost out, and almost every diplomat I talked to felt that some new effort must now be made to solve the complex problem of the Middle East.

Three days after the temporary adjournment of the General Assembly, on July 8, serious fighting broke out in the Suez Canal area. As in similar cases, two different versions of the origin of the fighting were given by Israel and the United Arab Republic.

A week earlier, on July 1, a major clash between the two sides, including an outbreak of air and ground fighting, had taken place in the Suez Canal area, and on July 4, I had advised Mahmoud Fawzi and Abba Eban that a United Nations observer force was needed to prevent breaches of the cease-fire. Although they had promised to consult their governments on my proposal, I had received no reply when the new and intensified fighting broke out on July 8.

At the request of both the United Arab Republic and Israel, the Security Council met on the same day (July 8) at 6:00 P.M. I repeated my appeal to both parties to accept the stationing of United Nations observers on both sides of the Suez Canal, as I had advised the two governments on July 4. I stressed the fact that without the presence of such observers on both sides of the Canal, I could not carry out the functions entrusted to me by the Council's cease-fire resolutions.

After several hours of behind-the-scenes negotiations, it was agreed that no formal draft resolution would be presented, but that the president of the Council, Ambassador Makonnen, would read a "consensus." A few minutes after midnight, at 12:20 A.M. Monday, July 10, Mr. Makonnen announced "the consensus of the Council," which was to authorize me to proceed, as I had suggested, with my plan to station UN observers on both sides of the Egyptian-Israeli cease-fire line. It also authorized me "to work out with the governments of the United Arab Republic and Israel, as speedily as possible, the necessary arrangements to station UN military observers in the Suez Canal sector."

At 10:30 A.M., ten hours after the Security Council meeting, Ambassador El-Kony of the United Arab Republic informed me that his government accepted my proposal. Ambassador Rafael of Israel, who saw me an hour later, informed me that his government was seriously considering it. At both meetings, I discussed with both diplomats the countries likely to be acceptable to the U.A.R. and Israel for the purpose of providing military observers. The countries I thought would be acceptable were Sweden, Finland, Burma, and France. I also sent a cable to General Bull mentioning the list, with the request that he get in touch with the military authorities of both Israel and the United Arab Republic to obtain their concurrence.

On Tuesday, July 11, a day before the resumption of the emergency special session of the General Assembly, Israel replied that she agreed to the stationing of United Nations military observers along the cease-fire line on the Suez Canal, provided that observation posts were also established in areas held by the United Arab Republic.

That same day, I received from Ambassador Rafael a letter from Foreign Minister Eban of Israel rejecting the General Assembly resolution that requested the annulment of the unilateral "unification" of Jerusalem. That resolution, presented by Pakistan and adopted on July 4 by 99 votes to 0 with 20 abstentions, expressed the Assembly's deep concern at the situation resulting "from the measures taken by Israel to change the status of Jerusalem." It also considered those measures invalid, and called upon Israel "to rescind all measures already taken and to desist forthwith" from any action altering the status of Jerusalem. At that time, the resolution was cosponsored by Guinea, Iran, Mali, Niger, and Turkey.

Mr. Eban's letter asserted that the city's administrative and municipal "integration" provided the legal basis for protection of the holy places. The letter made it clear that the Israeli government did not consider that the measures taken on June 27 constituted an "annexation" of the Old City of Jerusalem and its religious sites. The letter continued: "The measures adopted relate to the integration of Jerusalem in the administrative and municipal spheres and furnish a legal basis for the protection of the holy places in Jerusalem."

The text of Mr. Eban's letter was released to the press on the same day by the Israeli mission to the UN, and it created a storm in United Nations corridors. Among those who saw me on that day were Ambassador Adnan Pachachi of Iraq, Ambassador José Pinera of Chile, and Ambassador Dimitri S. Bitsios of Greece. All of them believed that for all practical purposes Israel had "annexed" the Old City of Jerusalem. What surprised them more was the lack of any direct reference to the General Assembly resolution in Mr. Eban's reply.

The General Assembly met at 3:00 P.M. on Wednesday, July 12, in an atmosphere of anxiety and anger on the part of most delegates. Again, Ambassador Agha Shahi of Pakistan took the lead in reviving the Jerusalem question. On behalf of his government, he submitted a draft resolution that began by noting "with the deepest regret and concern the non-compliance of Israel" with the earlier resolution. The draft then reiterated the call to rescind all measures already taken and to desist from any action altering the status of the city. The draft finally requested the Security Council to take the necessary measures to ensure its implementation.

In introducing the draft resolution, Mr. Shahi referred to Mr. Eban's letter addressed to me on July 10. He said: "Whatever the euphemisms employed, the fact remains that Israel is attempting to absorb and integrate the Holy City within its territory. There is not a word, not a phrase, not a qualifying clause, in Mr. Eban's letter that suggests that any of the measures taken by Israel in Jerusalem are provisional and subject to a settlement of the Arab-Israel conflict or to a final disposition." He then characterized Mr. Eban's letter as an extraordinary document that "scarcely descends" to refer to the General Assembly resolution.

When the General Assembly met again on July 13, all the speakers were communist, Arab, and Moslem delegates who enthusiastically supported the new Pakistani draft. On that day, several Latin-American delegates met in private caucus to agree on a second draft resolution that would encompass not only the question of Jerusalem but the overall consideration of the Middle East situation. They were searching for a formula that would link the

withdrawal of Israeli forces with the end of the state of belligerency, as they had attempted but failed to do ten days earlier.

The Pakistani draft was put to the vote on Friday, July 14,
and it was adopted without a dissenting vote (100 for, none
against, and 18 abstentions). Israel, as on July 4, did not participate in the voting. Among those who abstained were the United
States, Portugal, South Africa, and some African and Latin-
American countries. Ambassador Goldberg, explaining his abstention, said that peace would not be achieved by resolutions dealing
with only one aspect of the problem. He emphasized, however,
that the United States "does not recognize or accept" the measures taken by Israel, that it regrets them, and regards them as "interim and provisional."

On July 15, Israeli and Egyptian jet fighters clashed over the
Suez Canal in the fiercest fighting since the cease-fire became
effective on June 9. General Odd Bull was able to arrange a new
cease-fire, however, which went into effect at 6:00 P.M. New York
time. Meanwhile, thirty-two officers from Sweden, France, Burma,
and Finland were on their way to establish observation posts.
They were meant to be the eyes and ears of the United Nations,
reporting to me any violations of the cease-fire agreement accepted by Israel and Egypt on June 8, three days after the conflict
began. On July 16, advance contingents of observers established
headquarters in Ismailia on the West Bank and Quantara on the
East Bank. On the next day, they started patrolling in white station wagons that had large blue United Nations flags flying from
their front fenders.

On July 19, Israel made a most important policy statement.
In reply to Mr. Gromyko's letter addressed to the president of the
Security Council, Ambassador Rafael sent a letter to the president
clearly defining the Israeli position. He wrote: "In the view of the
Government of Israel, an integral and inseparable link exists between the withdrawal and disengagement of forces, and the establishment of normal, peaceful and good neighbourly relations between the states of the region.[7] Many delegates noted the absence
of any reference in this statement to the question of the two mil-

---

[7] *United Nations Security Council Document,* July 19, 1967.

lion Arab refugees, just as they had noted, in Arab statements, the absence of any reference to the end of the state of belligerency.

Deadlocked on the formulation of a draft resolution acceptable to both sides, the General Assembly again adjourned on July 21. A significant feature of the last few days of the Assembly was the participation of Anatoli F. Dobrynin, the Soviet ambassador to Washington, rather than Nikolay Fedorenko, in private negotiations between Andrei Gromyko and Arthur Goldberg. It was obvious that Fedorenko was on the way out.

Mr. Gromyko had been working very hard to present a compromise draft resolution, and after several days of discussions with Mr. Dobrynin and Mr. Goldberg, agreement seemed to be in sight.

According to my notes, July 17 to 19 were three momentous days, in that a breakthrough was not only possible but even probable: Gromyko, Goldberg, and Dobrynin even agreed to a draft. Although the actual text was not made available to me, I understood that it contained provisions for the withdrawal of Israeli forces to the positions they had occupied before June 5, and the recognition by the Arabs of the existence of Israel as an independent state. Due credit must be given to all three diplomats for their courage, initiative, and vision at this critical moment. The fact that their private initiative was rejected by both Israel and the Arabs added luster to Goldberg, who himself is a Jew, as well as to Gromyko and Dobrynin, who had a long and stormy session on the night of July 20 with Algeria's Foreign Minister Bouteflika. On July 21, the Assembly ended without a resolution.

In the meantime, Israeli authorities were preparing to tighten their administration of the West Bank of the Jordan River and of the Gaza Strip, in response to growing opposition and civil disobedience in those areas. Ambassador El-Farah of Jordan told me on July 28 that the Israeli authorities were preparing new textbooks for the September opening of Arab schools in the occupied West Bank, and that teachers in Nablus, a major town in the area, were threatening a school strike if their textbooks were replaced by the Israeli Ministry of Education. The government of Israel announced that it would take "appropriate measures" against anyone encouraging incitement to civil disobedience. Unconfirmed reports reaching the United Nations indicated that the Israeli government was split over its policy regarding the West Bank. A minority was reported to favor full annexation of the area. Some Cabinet members were reported to have suggested partial annexation with certain changes in the border, while others had proposed autonomy for the West Bank under defense and economic ties with Israel. Ambassador Rafael, who saw me on July 28, denied any intention on the part of his government of "annexation" of the West Bank.

On August 11, I received a letter from Ambassador El-Farah calling for "more serious steps" by the United Nations against "Israeli acts of lawlessness" in Jerusalem, the Gaza Strip, and occupied areas of the West Bank. It charged Israeli forces in western Jordan with shooting civilians, dynamiting villages, and breaking the cease-fire.

Meanwhile, I was confronted with another delicate problem. During and immediately after the Six-Day War, about 170,000 Arabs had fled from their homes or refugee camps on the West Bank. The Israeli government announced on July 2 that it would readmit these refugees. Thousands returned to their homes unofficially by wading across shallow fords in the Jordan River, and on July 18, the first group of 160 Jordanians returned under the official Israeli repatriation program. Bickering between Israel and Jordan, over procedures and the forms to be filled out by the refugees for Israeli security checks, interrupted the program. Official repatriation, handled through the International Committee of the Red Cross, did not resume until August 18. Israel then announced that it would not permit the return of the refugees after August 31, a deadline Jordan protested.

Meanwhile, I had appointed Ambassador Ernesto A. Thalmann, a former Swiss observer at the UN and a man who was highly respected for his political acumen and impartiality, my personal representative to Jerusalem. On September 8, he submitted to me a lengthy report on the situation in Jerusalem, a document I in turn submitted to the General Assembly.[8] Mr. Thalmann reported that the Arabs of the Old City strongly feared racial

---

[8] United Nations Document No. A/6793, September 8, 1967.

and religious oppression from the Israelis who were now in occupation of the area. He also said that the Israelis showed no willingness to relinquish any of their gains in the June war, as requested by the General Assembly. There was a spirit of resignation rather than of revolt among the Arabs of the Old City, but they were uneasy about the future. Mr. Thalmann gave the Israelis credit for co-operating with him in his mission. Regarding the administration of the Old City, he observed:

> The Israeli authorities stated that they had offered the members of the Municipal Council of the Old City the opportunity to apply for new positions in the framework of the Israel administration, which they refused to do. The Municipal Council of the Old City had been superseded by the Municipal Council of West Jerusalem, which is composed of 21 members, all Israelis, who were elected on 2 November 1965.

Mr. Thalmann noted that the Arabs were willing to co-operate with a regime of military occupation, but that "they were opposed to civil incorporation into the Israel state system." This report was to have been considered by the emergency special session of the General Assembly when it reconvened for a final meeting on September 18, one day before the twenty-second regular session; but when the special session convened at 10:20 A.M. on Monday, September 18, it instead voted unanimously to place the Middle East issue on the agenda of the twenty-second regular session. Thus, the Soviet-sponsored emergency session proved completely abortive, and there was a consensus that the Arab states and their supporters had "missed the bus." The fifth emergency special session of the General Assembly was officially closed only on September 18, 1967, a day before the twenty-second regular session was convened.

A week after the convening of the regular session, Premier Levi Eshkol of Israel, on September 24, made the first announcement of concrete plans for the settlement of territories seized from the Arabs in the Six-Day War. Previously, the government had avoided announcing plans concerning the future of the occupied areas, despite mounting pressure in Israel to keep all that was gained during the war. But a rising wave of violence in the West Bank area was partly responsible for the sudden an-

nouncement of plans for Israeli settlements, which would involve
not only the West Bank but also the Golan Heights, which had
been seized from Syria.

On September 26, the United States State Department said
that the Israeli announcement would conflict with President Johnson's commitment to support the territorial integrity of all states in
the Middle East. Ambassador Goldberg, in his speech to the General Assembly on the day, observed that the cause of peace in the
Middle East could not be served "if military success blinds a
member state to the fact that its neighbors have rights and interests of their own."

In the General Assembly, day after day, most speakers criticized Israel for not making any commitment to withdraw from occupied territories, a step which, they maintained, would generate
other steps toward a peaceful settlement. On October 3, Mr. Eban
made a spirited reply to these criticisms. He said: "Israel will not
return to the political and juridical anarchy or the strategic vulnerability from which she has emerged."[9]

In the general debate, several moderate Arab delegates
stressed the need for a political solution of the problem. On October 16, Fedorenko informed me that the Soviet position still
remained the same: an Israeli withdrawal was a prerequisite to
peace negotiations. I told him that, in retrospect, the Latin-
American draft resolution, which had been rejected by the General Assembly, seemed to be the most balanced and practical basis
for a solution.

But I had a feeling that Fedorenko was no longer authorized
to discuss the Middle East question with me. This feeling was
reinforced when he told me that Vasili V. Kuznetsov, first deputy
foreign minister, would be arriving in New York on that day. The
news cheered me up—just as I had been cheered in those dark
days of the Cuban missile crisis, when the Soviet government, re-
alizing that my relations with Zorin were at a very low ebb, had
sent Kuznetsov as its spokesman.

At 10:30 A.M. on October 17, Kuznetsov saw me—accompanied by Fedorenko! How I wished he were accompanied by

---

[9] *United Nations General Assembly Verbatim Records,* October 3, 1967.

someone else! After an hour-long talk, it was clear that the Soviet Union was once again inclined toward Security Council involvement in the Middle East question, and it was also clear that the Soviet Union was now convinced that a simple formula of condemning Israel and demanding its withdrawal from occupied territories, without reciprocal commitments on the part of the Arabs, would not be adopted by the Security Council. In any case, it was a very pleasant and relaxed meeting, different from my other meetings with Fedorenko.

After Kuznetsov and Fedorenko left, Goldberg saw me, and Ralph Bunche joined us. Goldberg told me that he had had a two-hour talk with Egyptian Foreign Minister Riad the previous day at his Waldorf Towers apartment, and that the United Arab Republic was now agreeable to a Security Council meeting; the idea of a special representative of the Secretary General would also be acceptable to Riad. Goldberg added that Israel was still insisting on the principle of direct negotiations.

On October 20, after my farewell luncheon for Ambassador Rafael (who was posted back to Israel as director general of the Foreign Office), Lord Caradon stayed back and explained to me his government's considered views on the Middle East problem. (These views were the embryo of the famous Security Council Resolution 242, which was adopted on November 22, 1967. It was in many ways a historic resolution, and more will be said about it later.) He asked me if I had anyone in mind for the post of my special representative, if the Security Council were agreeable to such an appointment. I told him that in anticipation of such a Security Council action, I had already approached the government of Sweden (on October 17) regarding the availability of Ambassador Gunnar V. Jarring, who had served as his country's permanent representative to the UN, and who was then Sweden's ambassador to Moscow. Jarring had represented the United Nations in the Kashmir dispute between India and Pakistan, and I had known him at the UN since 1957. Ralph Bunche, who had been dealing with both Kashmir and the Middle East since 1947, had strongly recommended Jarring for the post, and I told Lord Caradon that I was awaiting a reply from Stockholm.

On Monday, October 23, the atmosphere at the United Nations was once again gloomy at the news of the sinking of the Israeli destroyer *Elath* off Port Said on Saturday night, October 21. Ambassador El-Kony, in a letter to the Security Council, said that *"Elath* had been speeding in the United Arab Republic territorial waters" and that Egyptian naval units "were compelled to act in self-defense to stop the advance of the Israeli vessel."

Ambassador Rafael, who could not leave for Israel as originally scheduled because of the impending Security Council meeting, denied that *Elath* had been engaged in offensive operations when she was hit by Egyptian missiles. He contended that "the destroyer was on a normal patrol off the Sinai coast following a routine which has been known to the United Arab Republic for several months." It was the first time, incidentally, that ship-to-ship missiles, apparently under the guidance of homing devices, had been used in combat in the Middle East.

On Tuesday, October 24 (United Nations Day), the Israelis shelled for three hours the Egyptian oil installations in the port city of Suez, and Israel claimed that the United Arab Republic had lost about 80 per cent of its oil refining capacity, as fuel tanks and refineries went up in flames. On the same day the United Arab Republic requested an urgent meeting of the Security Council, which met at 9:00 P.M.

The request for the Council meeting came while I was attending a concert given by the Vienna Symphony Orchestra in the General Assembly Hall, in celebration of United Nations Day. As in the past, I had to make a brief statement during the interval. In the course of my statement, I said:

> At a time when international relations are marked by discord and disharmony, it is a pleasant respite to all of us to listen to the kind of music that we are hearing today. Such music not only pleases the ear, but also elevates our spirits. Besides, it also points to an important lesson.
>
> The functioning of a major orchestra requires co-operation on the part of the performers and leadership from its conductor. . . . In the field of international relations, the performers are the member states. . . . The score is the Charter of the United Nations. If we are to replace the present dissension by harmonious co-operation, we have to be faithful to the score: we have to ob-

serve not only the letter, but the spirit of the Charter in our international relations.[10]

It was when I returned to my seat among the audience that Ralph Bunche came and told me that the United Arab Republic had requested an urgent meeting of the Security Council, and that the president of the Council, Senjin Tsuruoka of Japan, had already started consultations with the members. I immediately left the hall; as soon as I got to my office, I phoned Tsuruoka, who told me that he was still in the process of consultation, and that it seemed the Council might meet at about 9:00 P.M.

When the Council convened that night, and during the ensuing days, there was a flurry of draft resolutions, proposals, and counterproposals. The Soviet Union and the United States, of course, presented sharply conflicting resolutions, the U.S.S.R. calling for a strong condemnation of Israel for its attack on Suez (and compensation for damage), and the United States condemning merely "all violations of the cease-fire." Canada, in its appeal for a cease-fire, also called on the Council to authorize me to dispatch a special representative to the Middle East. (It will be recalled that I had already begun negotiations with the government of Sweden for the release of Ambassador Jarring, and in fact on October 24, Ambassador Astrom of Sweden had informed me that his government would agree to place the services of Mr. Jarring at my disposal.)

Several members also stressed the need to strengthen the UN observer operation in the Suez sector. On October 25, I recommended increasing the number of observers from forty-three to ninety, doubling the number of observation posts from nine to eighteen, and acquiring four small patrol craft and four small helicopters for observers patrolling the canal and adjacent waters.

Also on October 25, the Council unanimously adopted a compromise resolution (which was close to the U.S. proposal) "condemning" violations of the cease-fire and "regretting" the loss of property.

After that date, there were no Security Council meetings on the Middle East until November 9, when the Council met at the

---

[10] *United Nations Press Release SG/SM/841,* October 24, 1967.

request of the United Arab Republic. In the meantime, private consultations revolved on the appointment of a special representative of the Secretary General and his terms of reference. There was no opposition or even reservation to my proposal to appoint Ambassador Gunnar Jarring for that post. Mr. Eban was delighted at my choice, since he had known Mr. Jarring very closely both at the United Nations and at Washington, where the two had been ambassadors of their respective countries. Arab diplomats were equally happy, since, in their view, Sweden had taken a balanced attitude toward the Middle East problem, and since Jarring was highly respected in United Nations circles for his distinguished diplomatic qualities. The Big-Four governments were also enthusiastic about him. The remaining problem was to agree on his terms of reference.

The October 25 compromise resolution on the Suez attack had little effect. Israeli Foreign Minister Eban saw me at 3:30 P.M. on October 30, and reiterated his government's position that direct negotiations between Israel and the Arab states offered the best prospect for a lasting peace. He assured me, however, that his government would "deal with" my special representative if his terms of reference were "not prejudicial to Israel's case." He then delivered to me a note announcing his government's decision to make a special contribution of one million pounds in Israeli currency (about $340,000) to the United Nations Relief and Works Agency in the Middle East, which dealt with the 1.3 million Arab refugees displaced from their homes after the Arab-Israeli war of 1948. The Arab states refused to pay for UNRWA, maintaining that Israel should be made responsible for all such payments.

Meanwhile, the nonpermanent members of the Security Council were meeting daily to bring about an agreed formula. A six-power resolution formulated by India called on Israel to withdraw to positions held on June 4, and on the Arab states to end belligerency; it also coupled Israel's right to use the international waterways to a settlement of the refugee problem. Another resolution by Denmark and Canada made similar proposals. The six-power draft, however, was certain to be vetoed by the United States. Alexei Nesterenko, undersecretary for political and Security Council affairs, told me that the United States was opposed to it. His assumption was that with the elections at hand, the Johnson Administration could not afford to "lose the Jewish vote." The Security Council president for the month, Mamadou Boubacar Kante of Mali announced that night that "the group had not reached agreement on precise proposals to place before the Council." Thus, after twenty days of intense and at times bitter private discussion, the ten nonpermanent members of the Security Council admitted failure. The matter thus went back to the five permanent members, who were similarly divided on the issue.

On Sunday, November 5, King Hussein of Jordan, on the television program "Face the Nation," said for the first time, as part of an overall political settlement in the Middle East, he was prepared to recognize Israel's right to exist in peace and security. He said: "Our offer would mean that we recognize the right of all to live in peace and security in that area, and this represents a very vast and tremendous change from earlier positions." Asked if he meant "all states" in the region, the King replied: "All who live in it, and I think that if we do manage to find the right formula, then it would mean all states." He also said that President Nasser was ready to grant Israel free maritime access to the Suez Canal and the Gulf of Aqaba "if the right conditions were reached" in a general settlement. He also reaffirmed the Arab demand that "there must be a withdrawal" by Israeli forces from occupied Arab territories. The King said that the withdrawal could be linked to other questions, such as Israel's maritime rights and Arab demands for justice for the Palestinian refugees, but that withdrawal was a necessary prerequisite to the solution of all problems. It was the first time that an Arab head of state (except President Bourguiba of Tunisia) publicly stated his willingness to recognize Israel's right to exist in peace and security, as part of an overall political settlement in the Middle East.

Mr. Kuznetsov, who saw me at 12:00 noon on Monday, November 6, said that King Hussein's public views were shared by President Nasser who, for political reasons, could not utter them in public. When I asked him if the United States government was aware of it, he said Washington was fully aware of it. At a luncheon I gave in honor of His Majesty King Mahendra of Nepal on that day, I told Mr. Goldberg what Mr. Kuznetsov had told me earlier. He said that although he had seen Kuznetsov the previous Friday, he had not been informed of it. I wondered whether Moscow or King Hussein himself had directly informed President Johnson of Nasser's new attitude. He had seen Johnson on Friday, November 3. On November 6, King Hussein told the press in Washington that in presenting the Arab position on a Middle East settlement, he was speaking, in effect, for President Nasser. Pressed by reporters to explain whether his recent public statements on the terms of the settlement reflected the Egyptian leader's views, he replied that he had met with Mr. Nasser before coming to the United States, and added: "We have been in extremely close touch. We are very close in regard to our positions. There is no difference."[11]

On November 7, the United Arab Republic called for an urgent session of the Security Council to discuss what it termed the dangerous situation arising from Israel's failure to withdraw its armed forces from the Arab territories it occupied in the June conflict. India, Mali, and Nigeria submitted a draft resolution declaring the occupation or acquisition of territory by conquest inadmissible under the United Nations Charter and calling for an Israeli withdrawal from all occupied territories. The United States followed by making public the text of another draft resolution. This also asked for the withdrawal of Israeli troops, but tied it to action by Arab governments to end their state of belligerency with Israel and to the establishment of "secure and recognized" boundaries in the Middle East. The United States draft was based on "the five great principles for peace" enumerated by President Johnson on June 19, which included respect for the political independence and territorial integrity of all nations in the area, respect for maritime rights, a curb on the arms race, and justice for the Palestinian refugees. On the same day, November 7, the United Arab Republic announced that it would accept President Johnson's five-point formula if Israeli troops withdrew from Arab territory and if the Palestinian refugees were either repatriated or compensated.

The enormous significance of this changed attitude on the

---

[11] The New York *Times*, November 7, 1967.

part of the U.A.R. was not immediately felt at the United Nations. In my view, however, it was the first time that Cairo publicly accepted Washington's formula, including the right of Israel to exist as an independent and sovereign state, and the freedom of innocent passage for Israeli shipping in the Suez Canal and the Gulf of Aqaba. Of course, the withdrawal of Israeli forces from occupied Arab territories and the repatriation or compensation of Palestinian refugees were not spelled out in President Johnson's formula, although it mentioned the "territorial integrity of all nations" and "justice for Palestinian refugees."

On November 8, news dispatches from Cairo reported that Dr. Mohammed H. El-Zayyat, chief spokesman for the Egyptian government (who later became his country's permanent representative to the UN and then Foreign Minister), said at his weekly news conference that the United Arab Republic guaranteed the "right of Israel to exist." Diplomats at the United Nations believed that the declaration was Cairo's strongest public affirmation since the Six-Day War that it considered itself bound not to infringe on Israel's security. Ambassador Vahap Asiroglu of Turkey saw me on that day and said that the Cairo statement could "lead to real peace."

On November 8, India and the United States introduced draft resolutions that seemed, at first, to have good prospects for adoption, but, as it turned out, became bogged down in a procedural wrangle. The Indian resolution affirmed that the acquisition of territory by military conquest is inadmissible, and called for the withdrawal of Israeli forces from those territories; it also affirmed the right of every state to live within secure borders, and called for the settlement of the refugee problem and freedom of navigation in international waterways. The U.S. resolution similarly called for the withdrawal of Israeli forces and a termination of belligerency. Both resolutions, incidentally, requested the Secretary General to send a special representative to the Middle East to initiate negotiations.

But Abba Eban subsequently gave a press conference in which he criticized both the Indian and U.S. draft resolutions on the ground that they did not support Israel's demand for direct negotiations toward a Middle East settlement. He vehemently de-

nounced the Indian draft by saying that the Indian delegation had
written it in consultation with the United Arab Republic on every
point, but had not discussed it with Israel. He considered the
United States draft closer to the Israeli position but emphasized
that none of the proposals gave adequate weight to Israel's
demand for direct negotiations.

When the Security Council met at 3:30 P.M. on Thursday
November 9, Israel refused to participate in the debate for procedural reasons. The list of speakers was read out in the order in
which their names were inscribed, with Israel listed as the seventh
name after the United Arab Republic, India, Nigeria, the Soviet
Union, the United Kingdom, and the United States. Although Mr.
Goldberg argued that the Council should hear the two parties to
the conflict first, and pleaded for Israel to speak immediately after
the United Arab Republic, his attempt to change the procedure
failed. Thus, Israel was scheduled to be the seventh speaker instead of the second, and Mr. Eban withdrew on the ground that
conditions were prejudicial to his position.

Then Foreign Minister Mahmoud Riad of the United Arab
Republic asked the Security Council to consider the use of force
to achieve the withdrawal of Israeli forces from occupied Arab
territories. He said, "We consider that the Security Council has
the authority and indeed the duty to suppress the Israeli aggression and to force the aggressive Israeli forces to return to the positions they held before June 4." But nothing came of Mr. Riad's
proposal. The United Nations was deadlocked once again.

It was at this point that Lord Caradon of Great Britain made
a statement so hopeful and comprehensive in scope that it not
only changed the mood of the Council but resulted in a historic
resolution—and a resolution that *was* adopted unanimously. On
November 15, in the course of a brief statement to the Council,
Lord Caradon said:

> The Arab countries insist that we must direct our special atten-
> tion to the recovery and restoration of their territories. The issue
> of withdrawal is to them of top priority. . . . They seek a just set-
> tlement to end the long and bitter suffering of the refugees.
> The Israelis tell us that withdrawal must never be to the old pre-

carious truce. It must be to a permanent peace, to secure boundaries. . . .

Both are right. The aims of the two sides do not conflict. They
converge. They supplement and they support each other. To imagine that one can be secured without the other is a delusion. They
are of equal validity and equal necessity. The recent consultations
which have been going forward so energetically and continuously
strongly reinforce my conviction that we in this Council now have
a supreme opportunity to serve the interests of all those concerned. Every day it is more clear what should be done. Every day
it is more apparent that we are not dealing with conflicting interests but with complementary interests. Justice and peace are not in
conflict: they are as inseparable as they are indispensable. One
must go hand in hand with the other.

Then he concluded with the words:

I trust that before this week is over, we shall have taken perhaps the most important decision which the United Nations has
ever taken. I trust that by the end of this week we shall have
taken the first essential step to bring the blessings of a just and
peaceful settlement to peoples who have lived in enmity too long.
We must pass a resolution. I hope we can do so unanimously. . . . We want not a victory in New York but a success in
the Middle East.

When the Council met at 4:00 P.M. on November 16, Lord
Caradon, on behalf of his government, introduced a draft resolution that was adopted unanimously, after a lengthy and bitter
debate, on November 22. This historic resolution, popularly
known as Resolution 242, is still the only basis on which a comprehensive solution of the Middle East problem is believed possible.

In reality, the resolution differed little from previous resolutions proposed to the Council. It called for withdrawal of Israeli
forces, an end to belligerency, freedom of navigation, and a settlement of the refugee problem. Like other resolutions, it also called
for the designation of a special representative to proceed to the
Middle East. The full text of Resolution 242 is reproduced in Appendix I, Part IV.

The unanimous vote by the Security Council members in establishing an "evenhanded" framework, as Lord Caradon de-

scribed, for a just and lasting peace between Israel and the Arab states was the first concrete step ever taken by the United Nations to deal with the Middle East problem comprehensively.

My first task was to designate a special representative. The day after the adoption of the resolution, I announced the appointment of Gunnar Jarring, the Swedish ambassador in Moscow, as my special representative.

Mr. Jarring arrived in New York on Sunday, November 26, and he saw me at 11:00 A.M. on Monday to discuss the detailed terms of reference. Ralph Bunche also was present at our meeting. Earlier in the day, Hashim Jawad, former Foreign Minister of Iraq and one-time resident representative of the Development Program in Burma, saw me and expressed concern about Mr. Jarring. He suggested to me that Jarring should be provided with several security aides, citing the case of Count Folke Bernadotte (the United Nations mediator for Palestine, also a Swede, who was assassinated by Israeli terrorists in Jerusalem in September 1948). I mentioned this to Jarring and Bunche, both of whom laughed. First of all, they pointed out, Bernadotte was a mediator and Jarring was not; secondly, Bernadotte had presented specific proposals that Israel categorically rejected. Jarring added that the man responsible for Bernadotte's death was known to his government, that he was still living in Israel, and that action would be taken if he ever set foot on Swedish soil.

While Mr. Jarring had daily meetings, before his departure to the Middle East, with the representatives of Israel, the neighboring Arab states (except Syria, which did not accept Resolution 242), and members of the Security Council individually, I had a different problem to cope with. It was the Soviet Union's challenge to the authority of the Secretary General in increasing the number of United Nations observers in the Suez Canal area. The reader will recall that I had recommended increasing the number of observers from forty-three to ninety. Fedorenko saw me on December 1 and told me that he had had instructions from his government that all such increases, as well as determinations of the nationalities of the observers, should be authorized by the Security Council. I told him that such a procedure would be completely unacceptable to me, since in my view I was competent to increase the number of observers under the existing mandate given to me by the Security Council. If he felt that I was not competent to do so, I suggested that he should call a Security Council meeting and table a draft resolution "authorizing" the Security General to undertake the increases. But if the Security Council were to meet every time General Bull recommended an increase or decrease, it would not only throw the Council into confusion, but would also terminate the long-established tradition under which the Secretary General, in consultation with the force commander, adjusted the size of the UN force in the Congo, the Middle East, or Cyprus.

On the morning of December 8, Fedorenko called for a meeting of the Security Council to discuss the draft resolution he submitted on November 10. This would "authorize" the Secretary General to increase the number of observers in the Suez Canal from forty-three to ninety and to take other measures proposed in the Secretary General's report. "Other measures" referred to my intention to provide additional transport for the observers. But there was no formal meeting. Later in the day, the Council met informally, and Canada and Nigeria played a major role in blunting the Soviet challenge to the powers of the Secretary General. The Security Council agreed by consensus that I could enlarge the United Nations observer force in the Suez Canal zone and provide additional transport for it. The fact that the Soviet Union agreed, without insisting on a formal meeting to consider its own resolution, was taken as an indication that it was primarily interested in making a point for the record. The Soviet doctrine has been, and still is, that the Secretary General's powers of initiative are strictly limited and that the Security Council must explicitly sanction all steps in peace-keeping activities.

On December 21, I received a report from Ambassador Jarring (who had left New York for the Middle East on December 9) saying that he was encouraged by Arab and Israeli willingness to co-operate with him. He wrote from his temporary headquarters in Nicosia, Cyprus, that he had been received "with the utmost courtesy and with expressions of willingness to co-operate with his mission," and that he had discussed the prospects for peace with top officials in Israel, the United Arab Republic, Jordan, and Lebanon.

On January 11, I received two encouraging reports from Mr. Jarring. One was concerned with clearance operations, in the Bitter Lake area of the Suez Canal, to release fifteen ships trapped since the Six-Day War. Mr. Jarring, after a month of commuting between the capitals of the U.A.R. and Israel, laid the groundwork for a working agreement for their clearance. The second report was related to the exchange of prisoners of war between the two countries. At long last, both the United Arab Republic and Israel had agreed to carry out the long-delayed exchange, through the good offices of the International Committee of the Red Cross.

On the same day (January 11), I received another report that was far from encouraging. The Israeli government decided to expropriate 838 acres of the former Jordanian sector of Jerusalem, essentially ensuring Jewish settlement in the Old City. A spokesman for Israeli Finance Minister Pinhas Sapir announced that residences, public institutions, roads, and parks were planned for the area between Mount Scopus (an enclave that had remained in Israeli hands since the 1948 war) and the former armistice line adjacent to the Sanhedrin sector of Israeli Jerusalem. He added that 1,400 housing units were planned, including 400 for Arabs who had been removed from the Old City. French Ambassador Armand Bérard discussed with me on that day the implication of the Israeli action, but there was no move for any UN action, either in the Security Council or the General Assembly.

The long-delayed prisoner exchange began, however, on January 12, across the Suez Canal cease-fire line at Quantara. The process was completed on Tuesday, January 23.

On March 21, 1968, while Mr. Jarring was busy making the rounds of the Middle Eastern capitals and inviting the belligerents to confer with him at his headquarters in Nicosia, a major armed conflict broke out. On that day, an Israeli Army spokesman announced that 15,000 Israeli troops had crossed the Jordan River during the night to attack terrorist bases in Jordan; helicopters, tanks, and other units were engaged in the operation. The attack was the expected retaliation for what Israeli officials had called a mounting wave of sabotage and infiltration launched from Jordanian territory; it differed from previous retaliation raids in that

Israeli forces crossed the river instead of merely using artillery or air strikes to reply to border raids and sabotage.

After a day of bitter fighting, the Israeli units returned across the Jordan River. The thrust had been aimed at a cluster of villages east of Jericho, and a smaller group south of the Dead Sea, that were believed by Israeli authorities to have been centers for terrorists and saboteurs. An Israeli spokesman said that at least 150 saboteurs were killed and that there were some Jordanian army losses; 21 Israeli soldiers were killed and 70 wounded, according to the same spokesman.

The Security Council met at 12:30 P.M. on the same day (March 21), at the urgent request of Jordan. The new Soviet Ambassador, Yakov A. Malik,[12] told the Council that his country was ready to implement sanctions against Israel if she "continued her aggression" in the Middle East. The new Israeli representative, Yosef Tekoah,[13] in his first speech before the Security Council, defended his country's punitive expedition against Jordanian "terrorist bases." But his defense was almost drowned in a chorus of criticism and condemnation in which the United States, usually Israel's strongest supporter, joined. The United States representative, Arthur J. Goldberg, conceded there had been provocation in the form of terrorist raids from Jordan. But the military action taken by Israel, he said, was out of scale to the provocation and "greatly to be deplored."

But on Sunday, March 23, the urgent consultations bore fruit. At that meeting the president of the Security Council, Ousmane Soce Diop of Senegal, read out the draft resolution that was adopted unanimously. The text "condemns" Israel for the military action launched on March 21, and at the same time, "deplores all violent incidents that violate the cease-fire agreement." The latter reference was clearly directed at Jordan for permitting *El-Fatah* commandos to operate out of its territory. The Council also declared that "actions of military reprisals and other grave violations of the cease-fire cannot be tolerated, and [that] the Security

---

[12] He presented his credentials to me on March 13, 1968.
[13] He presented his credentials to me on January 18, 1968.

Council would have to consider further and more effective steps as envisaged in the Charter to ensure against repetition of such acts."

Israel, of course, was critical of the resolution. Premier Levi Eshkol, speaking in Parliament on March 25, said that the United Nations had "once again failed to show full understanding for the state of affairs which had been created by our enemy."[14]

Five days later, on March 29, Israel and Jordan exchanged artillery fire along an eighty-five-mile front in a six-hour clash that included Israeli air strikes. Both Jordan and Israel requested a meeting of the Security Council, which was called at 10:30 A.M. on the next day, March 30. In the absence of Arthur Goldberg, deputy permanent representative William B. Buffum (later U.S. ambassador to Lebanon) and Ambassador Seymour Maxwell Finger saw me at 5:00 P.M. and said that according to their information, the fighting was very serious, involving the loss of at least one Israeli plane.

On March 29, I had announced a twelve-day trip to western European capitals in connection with the meetings of the Administrative Committee on Co-ordination (ACC) in Geneva. Immediately on receipt of the report of renewed fighting, I announced the cancellation of the scheduled trip.

I discussed with William Buffum and Max Finger my long-held position that United Nations observers should be deployed between Israel and Jordan, as was the case in the Suez Canal sector and the Israel-Syria sector. Since the Six-Day War, UNTSO (under General Odd Bull) had been manning the cease-fire lines between Israel and Egypt and Israel and Syria, but no observers had been stationed between Israel and Jordan. Israel had claimed that observers would not be useful in maintaining peace, while Jordan had insisted that there was no acceptable cease-fire line from which the observers could operate. I told the two American diplomats that one practical step to avert frequent clashes between Israel and Jordan (both of which had good relations with the United States) would be to deploy United Nations observers at the scenes of recent clashes between the two countries. When the Council met at 11:00 A.M. on Saturday, March 30, I submitted

---

14 Associated Press news dispatch from Jerusalem, March 4, 1968.

my appeal to the Council to authorize the deployment of observers between Israel and Jordan.

Ambassador Goldberg promptly endorsed my suggestion. Soviet Ambassador Yakov Malik, whose reassignment to the United Nations (after an interval of nearly sixteen years) was a most welcome change after Fedorenko, did not voice disagreement with my suggestion. His speech was confined to his demand that the Council must adopt sanctions against Israel for reprisal raids against Jordan, in violation of the March 24 resolution.

But Ambassador El-Farah of Jordan said that he would have to oppose the deployment of observers between "Jordan and the Israeli-occupied part of Jordan." His government would not like to see "a de facto border," leaving Israel in control of the West Bank of the Jordan River. With Israel also opposed, the Council was unable to take affirmative action on my request.

Meanwhile, Ambassador Jarring had been commuting to Cairo, Jerusalem, and Amman to confer with government leaders. Although all three governments—the United Arab Republic, Israel, and Jordan—had accepted Resolution 242, Syria had not accepted it, partly on the ground that Israel had occupied Syrian territory after the cease-fire of the June war had gone into effect. Syria therefore refused to deal with Ambassador Jarring.

On April 21, 1968, I attended the International Conference on Human Rights in Teheran. Jarring joined me there and reported to me on the progress, or rather the lack of progress, of his efforts. Israel had been insisting on direct face-to-face talks with the Arabs, which the Arabs, in turn, refused. Another impediment to the progress of his mission was the difference in concept of the two sides regarding his mission. Israel wanted to discuss only *procedures* with Mr. Jarring, while the U.A.R. and Jordan wanted to deal with substantive problems. In the view of the Israeli government, his function was primarily to bring about direct talks between the two sides. The Israeli leaders, therefore, refused to discuss with him the question of territories or the nature of a peace agreement.

Thus, despite the tireless, persistent efforts of Ambassador Jarring, the promise of the November resolution had not been fulfilled to any significant degree, and the situation in the Middle East remained much the same as it had been eight months before.

On my return from Teheran on April 23, 1967, I received a report from General Odd Bull indicating that the Israeli government was planning to hold a massive military parade in Jerusalem on May 2, marking the country's twentieth anniversary. Ralph Bunche immediately drafted a message, which went out to the Israeli government the same day, in which I said that the parade would violate the terms of the 1949 armistice agreement covering the level of forces in Jerusalem, as well as the Security Council resolution of July 1967, calling on Israel to refrain from any steps that would change the status of the city. I also said that "the holding of a military parade in this area at the present time might have an adverse effect on the efforts now going forward to find a peaceful settlement of the problems in the area." Israel rejected my protest on the next day.

At the request of Jordan, the Security Council met at 10:30 A.M. on Saturday, April 27. After two long sessions, it voted unanimously to ask Israel to cancel the projected military parade of May 2 through Arab sections of Jerusalem. Israel was bitterly criticized for the project in daylong meetings of the Council. Of the fifteen countries in the Council, only the United States and Brazil did not speak against the parade, although both voted for a resolution tabled by India, Pakistan, and Senegal calling "upon Israel to refrain from holding the military parade scheduled for May 2."[15]

In an emotional speech after the vote, Ambassador Tekoah told the Council that Israel would nevertheless hold the parade and that "behind [it] will march twenty centuries." He also said that the Israeli troops "are free to move, to act, and to parade as they see fit."[16]

On May 2, Israel celebrated her twentieth anniversary with a military parade in Jerusalem that was the biggest in her history. More than a half million spectators lined the five-mile route to watch Israeli soldiers march in defiance of the Security Council

---

[15] *United Nations Security Council Official Records, No. S/1417,* April 27, 1968.
[16] Ibid.

resolution adopted unanimously five days earlier. The parade passed through the Arab and Jewish sectors of the city without incident; the Arabs, however, locked their shops and stayed home. According to General Odd Bull's report, the parade provided the Israeli public with its first look at the American-built Skyhawk fighter-bomber and the Bell helicopter, also built in the United States; scores of both models were included in the aerial display of about three hundred aircraft. The highlight of the parade was a ten-minute review of tanks, artillery weapons, and Russian-built missiles captured in the Six-Day War. I immediately submitted a report to the Security Council, which met at noon, and that night it passed a resolution affirming that it "deeply deplores"[17] Israel's action in defying the Council's unanimously adopted resolution of April 27, 1968.

On May 9, the United States again expressed strong opposition to the unilateral acts of Israel in occupied Jerusalem. Arthur J. Goldberg said that the problem of Jerusalem could not "realistically be solved apart from other aspects of the situation in the Middle East. . . . Unilateral measures, including expropriation of land and legislated administrative action taken by the Government of Israel, cannot be considered other than interim and provisional and cannot affect the present international status of Jerusalem."[18] Mr. Goldberg also urged the Security Council to give "explicit expression of support" to Mr. Jarring's "most difficult mission." By that time, Mr. Jarring had received public acceptances, by the three involved governments, of Resolution 242 and an agreement to meet under his auspices to "devise arrangements to implement" the resolution.

Although private diplomatic talk was centered on the Jarring mission, the Security Council was continuously occupied with the question of Jerusalem. On May 21, the Council voted on a draft resolution, tabled by Pakistan and Senegal, affirming that all measures taken by Israel in Jerusalem, including the expropriation of land and Arab properties, were illegal. The United States and Canada abstained, and the resolution was adopted by thirteen

---

[17] *United Nations Security Council Official Records, No. 1420,* May 2, 1968.
[18] Ibid., *No. 1424,* May 9, 1968.

votes to none. Mr. Goldberg, in explaining his country's abstention, said that the vote would not help the peace-making efforts of
Mr. Jarring and that the Jerusalem problem could not be singled
out for special attention without limiting Mr. Jarring's effectiveness. By that time, Mr. Jarring had made forty visits to Cairo,
Amman, and Jerusalem, without any progress. Israel was still
insisting on direct talks, and it wanted any indirect talks limited to
procedural matters only. The United Arab Republic insisted that
Resolution 242 could be implemented without direct negotiations.
It proposed that Mr. Jarring prepare a timetable that would commit Israel to withdraw from all occupied territories, in return for
peace.

There was to be no peace, however, for the events of the second half of 1968 thwarted both the Jarring mission and the Council's efforts to give effect to Resolution 242.

On August 4, waves of Israeli fighter-bombers pounded a village near the town of Salt, about ten miles east of the Jordan
River. As a result of the three-hour aerial assault, 23 civilians and
5 Jordanian soldiers were killed and 76 civilians and 6 soldiers
were wounded.

The Security Council met at 3:00 P.M. on August 5, and
after almost daily meetings, it adopted (on the night of August
16) a unanimous resolution declaring that the military attacks
launched by Israel against Jordan in recent weeks were a "flagrant
violation of the United Nations Charter and of Security Council
resolutions" dealing with the Middle East. The resolution warned
that if such attacks were to continue, the Council would "duly
take account of the failure to comply with the present resolution."

By far, the most bizarre episode of the summer of 1968 was a
hijacking incident, the consequences of which escalated into a
complex and ominous international crisis. It was bizarre, first, because I was improperly asked to negotiate for the release of some
captured Arab guerrillas in return for the plane—a request I categorically refused—and second, because in the midst of the crisis it
was revealed that the Italian government had been secretly involved in those very negotiations.

Eleven days before the Israeli raid on Salt, on July 23, three
Arab terrorists hijacked an El Al airliner en route from Rome to

Algiers. The plane was on a scheduled flight from Rome to Tel Aviv when the hijacking took place. The official Algerian press agency announced on that day that twenty-one Israeli passengers and crewmen had been detained in Algiers, with the Boeing 707 jet, and that the rest of the passengers (of different nationalities, numbering nineteen) had left for Paris on an Air Algerie plane. In Beirut, an Arab guerrilla organization, the Popular Front for the Liberation of Palestine, declared that it was responsible for the hijacking.

From that day onward, I had to see Israeli and Algerian diplomats almost every day in connection with this detestable crime. On July 24, Algerian Foreign Minister Bouteflika, upon his arrival at Orly airport in Paris, said that "Algeria is not involved either directly or indirectly in this affair of El Al Boeing. It is normal that Algeria should wait until all the circumstances surrounding this affair are known before its position should be determined. Algeria is a sovereign state which respects international morality. It is within the framework of this morality that this affair will end."[19]

On July 26, I addressed a message to President Houari Boumedienne of Algeria in which I commended Mr. Bouteflika's reference to international morality, expressed concern about the obviously serious implications of the hijacking, particularly the adverse effect it would have on Ambassador Jarring's mission, and voiced the hope that his decision would put a speedy end to the problem.

On Sunday, July 28, Ambassador Bouattoura informed me on the phone that his government had released ten Israeli women and children who had been on the hijacked plane, and that they had been flown to Zurich in Switzerland. He said he had not received any reply from his President to my letter sent three days earlier. Of course, neither of us had any means of knowing whether the release of the ten Israeli women and children was the result of my appeal.

Meanwhile, I was in touch with the International Civil Aviation Organization in Montreal, the International Air Transport

---

[19] Agence France press dispatch No. 154 from Paris, July 24, 1968.

Association in Geneva, and the International Federation of Air-line Pilots Associations in London. The last named organization (IFAPA) was contemplating a boycott of Algerian airports if the Algerian government continued to detain the plane, the crew, and the Israeli passengers.

On the evening of August 7, Ambassador Bouattoura gave me an oral reply from his government. Although he was not specific, I got the impression that his government wanted me to exercise my good offices to get the release of the Arab guerrillas captured by the Israelis. In effect, he said that the El Al hijacking was not only a juridicial but also a political problem: the Palestinian Arab refugees had a legitimate grievance, and there must be some gesture on the part of Israel to meet this grievance—in a way that would enable the Algerian government to release the plane, the crew, and the passengers. I made it clear to him that the Secretary General of the United Nations should in no way involve himself in such a negotiation. The hijacking of a commercial plane was a crime, and the detention of its crew and passengers was completely unwarranted. The release of the plane, the crew, and the passengers should not be conditional on the action of any other government. He was dismayed to hear my reaction, but at the same time, did not seem to be clear in his own mind what his government wanted him to convey to me.

Neither he nor I knew at that time that at the request of Israel, the Italian government was actively engaged in negotiating with the Algerian government for the release of the plane and men, in exchange for the release of the Arab guerrillas detained by Israel! As I found out later, Ralph Bunche, as well as José Rolz-Bennett (another undersecretary for special political affairs), were completely in the dark about the Italian involvement. (On August 31, Abba Eban announced, for the first time —after Algeria had released the seven Israeli crew members and the last five Israeli passengers of the hijacked airliner—that he had asked the Italian ambassador in Israel, on July 27, if Rome might undertake a special role of go-between in the case. When it became apparent that it would, the director general of the Israeli Foreign Office, Gideon Rafael, was sent to Rome to confer with the Italian officials.)

My refusal to negotiate with Israel for the release of the guerrillas must have been communicated to Algiers, where there must have been some puzzlement as to why Rome was involved in such a transaction while the Secretary General of the United Nations was not. In any event, on August 13, the International Federation of Airline Pilots Associations announced in London plans to stop commercial flights between Western Europe and Algeria. Two weeks earlier, Captain Ola Forsberg, a Finn who was deputy president of the Federation, and J. J. O'Grady, an Irishman and its principal vice president, had gone to Algiers to try to obtain the release of the seven-man crew. Their efforts yielded no result. Like myself and my senior colleagues at the United Nations, they did not have the faintest idea that the Italian government was involved in a private deal.

On August 15, two days after the boycott decision, I received a message from Foreign Minister Bouteflika, who asserted that the boycott measures were "clearly inspired from the policy of apartheid and racial discrimination and Zionist methods."[20] The message accused the Israelis of having instigated the boycott.

On August 16, I had President Boumedienne's reply to my letter of July 26 expressing the appreciation of the Algerian government for my good offices and stressing that the necessary investigations had not been completed. Political factors, the President said, had also to be taken into consideration. Mr. Bouattoura, who brought me the message, said that "some governments were involved in making some kind of deal" with Israel for the release of the plane and the men; he did not know what governments. I reiterated that I could not be a party to any such deal.

On Monday, August 19, I asked Ambassador Tekoah about the alleged governments involved in negotiating a deal; he said that he was not aware of such an arrangement. In any case, he told me that his government's position was firm: the release must be independent of anything else that might be done, and was not conditional.

Two days earlier, on August 17, I had a meeting with Cap-

---

[20] *United Nations Official Records, UN/SG/MAE44,* August 15, 1968.

tain James O'Grady of IFAPA, who said that in his view the prospects for the release were slim. Neither he nor any of his colleagues was aware of any third-party involvement in the affair. He said that the projected boycott of Algerian airports would go into effect on Sunday, August 18, at midnight.

But for reasons unknown to me, the boycott did not take place. According to Captain Nicolaieff of IFAPA, the Algerian government was playing the French Airline Pilots' Association against the IFAPA. Captain Nicolaieff also felt that a *démarche* by the Secretary General at that time would greatly assist in obtaining the release of the crew and passengers.

Meanwhile, I had been scheduled to attend a session of the Organization for African Unity to be held in Algiers on September 13 or 14. I felt, however, that it would be difficult for me to attend a conference hosted by a government that had defied international public opinion and all norms of morality. So I decided that the best means of demonstrating my protest was to stay away from the conference while the El Al plane and men were still on Algerian soil. Since I did not want to put my feelings on paper, I sent José Rolz-Bennett to Algiers on August 2 to convey my decision to President Boumedienne orally. I did draft a letter to the President in which I did not mention the possibility of my staying away from the conference, but did express my growing concern that the Algerian government had done nothing to release the plane and the men. In it I said:

> It is clearly vital to the preservation of international order and of security in international travel that there be no gain derived from such acts and that governments should act promptly to redress any such incident. Any other course could encourage such acts and lead ultimately to something approaching international anarchy in the skies. There are also other dangerous international implications which require no elaboration here.

Mr. Rolz-Bennett returned from Algiers on August 26. He reported to me that Foreign Minister Bouteflika was very irritated at the mention of my possible absence from the OAU Conference, although President Boumedienne took it calmly. The President assured him of his very early consideration of my letter and promised to send me a reply in a few days. Mr. Rolz-Bennett also gathered from diplomatic sources in Algiers that the Italian government's efforts had also achieved no results.

On August 29, José Rolz-Bennett reported to me that Mr. Mario Franzi, chargé d'affaires of the Italian mission to the United Nations, saw him on that day and gave him copies of the text of a protocol signed by Italy and Israel on August 6, 1968, as well as the text of a letter dated August 25, 1968, and sent by the Italian ambassador in Algiers to the Foreign Minister of Algeria. It was the first time that the government of Italy informed me of its involvement in negotiations between Israel and Algeria. What surprised both Mr. Rolz-Bennett and myself, however, was Mr. Franzi's verbal comments to him. I reproduce below the relevant part of his statement, as reported by Rolz-Bennett:

> Mr. Franzi stated that he had received instructions to inform me that the Italian Government had advised both the Israeli and Algerian Governments that in view of the delay in obtaining final agreement on the release of the hi-jacked aircraft, its crew and the remaining passengers, it declined all responsibility for any failure that may occur regarding the solution of the problem. The Italian Government wished Mr. Franzi to give this message to me as well. I stated that . . . I found it most unusual that this apprehension should also be conveyed through me to the Secretary-General when in fact the Secretary-General had received no information whatsoever from the Italian Government concerning the latter's intervention in the Boeing affair.[21]

Ambassador Tekoah saw me at 3:30 P.M. on August 30 and informed me that the Algerian government had released on that day the seven Israeli crew members and the last five Israeli passengers of the hijacked airliner; he also thanked me on behalf of his government for my role in such an outcome. On the same day, Foreign Minister Abba Eban said in Jerusalem that he expected the release of the plane in a day or two, or as soon as it was airworthy again. (Later, it was disclosed that Israel released and handed back through the Red Cross sixteen Arabs captured before the Six-Day War.) Mr. Eban did not mention the release of

---

[21] Rolz-Bennett's written report to me, dated August 29, 1968.

the detained Arabs, but he said that Israel would honor her commitment to Italy, whose good offices were instrumental in obtaining the release of the airliner, by carrying out a humanitarian gesture."[22] The hijacked plane was flown from Algiers to Rome on Saturday, August 31.

Thus, a deplorable episode came to an end. The role played by the United Nations and its Secretary General was not publicly mentioned by any of the parties. I did not even know whether Algeria had agreed to release the plane and the men in return for the release of sixteen Arabs detained by Israel, or whether my message to the Algerian President about the prospect of my absence from the OAU conference had anything to do with the decision of the Algerian government.

The Security Council was then confronted by a different problem. With effect from September 8, Israel and the United Arab Republic had been fighting an artillery duel across the Suez Canal. Each side accused the other of having started the shelling, which ranged along most of the Canal's hundred-mile length from Port Suez to Quantara. Ten Israeli soldiers had been killed and seventeen had been wounded in the exchange, while Egyptian casualties were five soldiers and six civilians killed and forty-two persons, including twelve soldiers, wounded. The towns of Port Suez and Ismailia had been heavily damaged in the shelling. I had to see the representatives of Israel and the U.A.R. almost every day in an effort to put a stop to the fighting. General Odd Bull rushed to the Canal soon after the shooting began to compile information, and on the morning of September 9, I received his detailed report. According to General Bull, an observation post of the United Nations Truce Supervisory Organization reported that ground-to-ground missiles were used by Israeli forces.[23] I immediately submitted the report to the Security Council, which met on the same day at the request of Israel and the U.A.R.

After several meetings, the Council, on September 18, adopted overwhelmingly a resolution insisting that Israel and the Arab states rigorously respect its cease-fire order, and urging them to co-operate fully with Ambassador Gunnar V. Jarring's efforts

---

[22] United Nations Document UN/SG/MAE/47, September 3, 1968.
[23] *United Nations Security Council Official Records, No. 1449*, September 9, 1968.

for a settlement. Algeria, the only member that abstained, did so on the ground that the resolution failed to get to what it called the root of the problem: the withdrawal of Israeli forces from occupied Arab territories.

On September 23, a development of considerable significance was brought to my attention. Ambassador Karoly-Castorday of Hungary saw me at 6:30 P.M. on that day and told me that he understood the Soviet Union had transmitted a very important compromise peace plan to the United States. According to him, the main features of the plan were:

(1) Israeli's withdrawal to frontiers held before the Six-Day War.
(2) A renewed and greatly strengthened United Nations force in demilitarized areas astride the Israeli and Arab states.
(3) A declaration by the Arab nations ending the state of belligerency with Israel.
(4) A four-power guarantee of borders and peace (by the Soviet Union, the United States, Britain, and France).

It was indeed the most important piece of news since the Six-Day War. The twenty-third session of the General Assembly opened on the next day, and I could not get anybody to confirm the news. A few days later, however, Ambassador William B. Buffum, deputy permanent representative of the United States, confided to me that the Soviet proposal had been conveyed to Israel and that the latter had rejected it. Israel's position all along, of course, had been that it would not withdraw to pre-Six-Day War borders under any circumstances.

On December 26, a dramatic, albeit dastardly, incident took place in Athens, where two Arab gunmen opened fire on a New York-bound El Al jetliner as it prepared to take off from the airport. One of the forty-one passengers was killed, an Israeli air hostess was seriously injured, the plane's engines were wrecked, and the aircraft caught fire. The Greek fire squads were able to put out the fire, however, and the two suspects were caught and disarmed by the Greek police. The news was received with disgust at the United Nations. The general feeling was that the Arabs had once again outraged world public opinion. I told Ambassador Mahmoud Mestiri of Tunisia on that day that it would be highly desirable for responsible Arab governments to publicly condemn this massive crime.

On Saturday, December 28, massive retribution came. On that night, Israeli helicopters landed at Beirut airport and destroyed thirteen aircraft, including at least one Boeing 707, two Caravelles, and a VC-10. The raid was described as an Israeli reprisal for the attack in Athens two days earlier. But the Lebanese government had already denied any responsibility for the Athens attack. Even before the Israeli raid on Beirut airport, the Popular Front for the Liberation of Palestine had issued a statement asserting that the Lebanese authorities had nothing to do with their guerrilla operations. The statement had been made in answer to an Israeli accusation of complicity by the Lebanese government in the Athens attack.

The raid was the third Israeli foray into Arab territory in less than two months. On October 31, Israeli commandos had destroyed two bridges and a power station in the Nile Valley of Upper Egypt, and on December 1, another Israeli commando band had blown up road and railroad bridges thirty-seven miles inside Jordan.

At the request of Lebanon and Israel, the Security Council met urgently on Sunday, December 29. It was the first time since the Six-Day War that Lebanon had directly confronted Israel at the UN.

Ambassador Edouard A. Ghorra of Lebanon described the commando raid as flagrant aggression and said that the damage had been staggering: the destruction of aircraft and installations had involved damages of more than $50 million. He told the Council that condemnation was not enough; he called for sanctions and monetary compensation.

Ambassador Shabtai Rosenne, speaking for Israel in the absence of Yosef Tekoah, said that the Athens raid had been carried out by "a paramilitary organization which operated quite openly in Beirut, with the full knowledge and blessing of the Lebanese Government."[24]

Ambassador J. R. Wiggins of the United States, who had succeeded Ambassador George W. Ball on October 7, 1968, described the Israeli attack as "act of arrogance" that was dispropor-

----

[24] *United Nations Security Council Official Records, No. 1460,* December 29, 1968,

tionate as a reprisal for the attack on the El Al airliner. He said that there is a "difference between the acts of two individual terrorists and those of a sizable official military force operating under Government orders."[25] This was the strongest criticism made by the United States against Israel since the Six-Day War.

Ambassador Yakov A. Malik of the Soviet Union then put the American ambassador on the spot. After describing the Israeli attack as a "premeditated, deliberate decision seeking to undermine the efforts of the United Nations to effect a political settlement," he turned in the direction of the U.S. representative and said: "We understand the difficult situation in which Mr. Wiggins now finds himself. For the first time in the Security Council, a United States representative has seriously condemned an aggressive act by Israel."[26]

The unanimous view of the Council members was that Israel had overreacted. When the Council met again on December 30, Ambassador Tekoah made a spirited defense of his country, but his was a lone voice. The Council severely condemned Israel's attack on the airport; at its meeting on December 31, it unanimously adopted a resolution condemning Israel for its "premeditated military action in violation of its obligations under the Charter and the cease-fire resolutions." It also issued "a solemn warning to Israel that if such acts were to be repeated, the Council would have to consider further steps to give effect to its decisions." The resolution further considered that "Lebanon is entitled to appropriate redress for the destruction it suffered, responsibility for which has been acknowledged by Israel."[27]

It was the strongest resolution yet adopted by the Council on a breach of the peace in the Middle East, though it avoided any suggestion of forcible sanctions under Chapter VII of the UN Charter.

Ambassador Tekoah, speaking after the vote, said in part: "The resolution reflects the moral, political and juridical bankruptcy of the Security Council in respect of the Middle East situation."[28]

---

[25] Ibid.
[26] Ibid.
[27] Ibid., *No. 1462,* December 31, 1968.
[28] Ibid.

CHAPTER XIV

EVENTS LEADING
TO THE ARAB-ISRAELI
WAR OF 1973

On January 2, 1969, I discussed the deteriorating situation on the Israeli-Lebanese border with Foud Boutros of Lebanon and Yosef Tekoah of Israel, separately. There had been reports on New Year's Day of Arab rocket attacks on Israeli settlements and military reinforcements. Mr. Boutros feared that Israel was preparing an attack across the border and said that he was meeting members of the Security Council to consider what appropriate action might be taken. Mr. Tekoah denied any knowledge of his country's preparations for an attack, but he was very critical of "the one-sided decision" of the Security Council in not condemning the Arab terrorist attack on the El Al plane in Athens.

The situation in the Middle East had thus gone from bad to worse. The only hope for a peaceful solution lay in the full implementation of the Security Council Resolution 242, which Israel, the U.A.R., and Jordan had accepted. I now considered that it could be implemented only if the four permanent members of the Security Council—the United States, the Soviet Union, Britain, and France—could back it up. I was fully behind General de Gaulle's long-standing proposal for major-power action within the framework of that resolution. On January 3, Ambassador Malik told me that only the previous day, Ambassador Valerian Zorin had a forty-five-minute discussion with General de Gaulle on the latter's proposal that the four permanent members of the Security Council co-ordinate their policies to facilitate the work of Mr. Jarring.

I then decided to issue a public statement endorsing the French proposal for the active involvement of the Big Four, saying that "the intentions are to seek a solution within Security Council Resolution 242 and are in support of Ambassador Jarring."[1]

It was not the first time that I had endorsed the French proposal of Big-Power involvement, for as early as October 7, 1968, I had written to the Foreign Ministers of the United States, the Soviet Union, Britain, and France proposing that they meet during a General Assembly session and attempt to halt the growing feeling of insecurity in the world.

Meanwhile, on January 10, the Soviets put forward a novel proposal for U.S.-Soviet collaboration. It envisaged (with special U.S.-Soviet guarantees) an initial Israeli withdrawal from all occupied territories, a United Nations buffer force, and—this was the unusual element—the deposit with the United Nations by Israel and the Arab nations a document ending the state of war that had existed since 1948. Then the Security Council would adopt a resolution for the dispatch of UN forces to guarantee, under the Charter, freedom of navigation to the ships of all countries.

That evening, Ralph Bunche told me that he had sounded out Ambassador William Buffum of the United States, who felt that the Soviet proposal was a move in the right direction. Ralph was right in anticipating an Israeli rejection, however. On the same night, Ambassador Yosef Tekoah, in the course of a press interview, said that the Soviet Union's peace proposals "smack of a Moscow plan for a Middle East Munich."[2] On January 12, *El-Fatah,* the Palestinian guerrilla organization, issued this statement in Cairo: "Armed struggle is the only way toward the liberation of our Palestine."[3]

The Johnson Administration now had only eight working

---

[1] United Nations Document, January 3, 1969.
[2] United Nations Files.
[3] Ibid.

days left, and I believed that the President would leave any action on the Middle East to the incoming Nixon Administration. I nevertheless felt that the moment was favorable for Big-Power involvement because international public opinion rightly felt that diplomatic efforts toward a solution had stalled, and would continue to stall without Big-Power backing. (It will be noted that the United States and the Soviet Union did act jointly and promptly when the fourth Arab-Israeli war broke out almost five years later. Their action resulted in the disengagement of Israeli and Egyptian troops in the Suez Canal sector, and for the first time seemed to herald a just and lasting peace in the Middle East.) This was one of the "ifs" of history. If only the United States had responded substantively to the Soviet proposal, as France had done and as Britain would like to have done, the agony, the suspense, and the dark shadow of war that hung over the Middle East for the next five years might have been dispelled. This was one of the cases of missed opportunities; as a result, relative peace came five years too late.

The long-awaited reply by the United States to the Soviet proposal was transmitted to Moscow on January 15, five days before the change of administration in Washington, and the text of the reply was published (and assailed) in Cairo on January 19. In effect, the United States insisted that a Middle East peace settlement should be based on an agreement between the Arabs and Israel, and not imposed by the Big Four or the Big Two.

But two days later, on January 17, France officially proposed that the four permanent members of the Security Council meet to discuss establishing peace. Ambassador Wiggins of the United States told me that afternoon that the United States was not likely to oppose the meeting of the Big Four, and Sir Patrick Dean confirmed my belief that the British government would also favor Big-Four involvement, in order to strengthen the hand of Ambassador Jarring.

President Nixon was inaugurated on January 20, and Charles W. Yost was appointed the new United States ambassador to the United Nations. When he presented his credentials to me on January 23, we discussed the Middle East problem; to my pleasant surprise, he was in favor of concerted action, on the part of the permanent members of the Security Council, to give effect to Resolution 242. Ambassador Jarring arrived in New York on January 27 and started a round of consultations, including talks with the four permanent members. Once again, things looked brighter, and the Big Four (with the backing of the new administration in Washington) seemed determined to break the prevailing stalemate.

While public attention at the United Nations was focused on Big-Four involvement and the Jarring mission, a sensational development took place in Baghdad. On January 26, sixteen persons, including ten Jews, were sentenced to death as spies or saboteurs in the service of Israel.

The question of Iraqi citizens of Jewish faith had been occupying my attention since the Six-Day War. I had been in constant communication with Baghdad on the plight of Jews in Iraq, and I had even sent personal and confidential letters to Ahmed Al-Bakr of Iraq through Omar Abdul,[4] UNDP representative in Baghdad, to facilitate the exit of Jews from the country if they so wished. Although I had no direct means of knowing exactly the conditions of life of the Jewish minority in Iraq, it was clear that they would be better off elsewhere, and that Iraq would also be better off, given the prevailing circumstances, if the departure of those who wished to leave could be sanctioned and arranged, since their continued presence in Iraq would be a source of both internal and international tension. My approach to that problem had been based solely on humanitarian considerations and on my wish for a lessening of tension in the area, since these Jewish people, being citizens of Iraq, were of course under the exclusive jurisdiction of the Iraqi government.

Baghdad radio announced that the sixteen had been publicly hanged on the morning of January 27, and that sixty-five other accused persons were still awaiting trial. I immediately denounced the sentencing and public hanging. Through my spokesman (William Powell), I said, "Mass trials and executions are always to be deplored and are particularly abhorrent and dangerous when they are carried out in such a way as to inflame the emotions of the populace."

---

[4] Formerly permanent representative of the Sudan to the United Nations.

At 5:30 P.M. on that day, Adnan Raouf, chargé d'affaires of Iraq, saw me and protested my statement. He expressed surprise that a matter that was entirely an internal affair of Iraq should have become the subject of a statement by the Secretary General. I explained to him that the reasons behind my statement were humanitarian and asked him to convey my deep concern about those awaiting trial. (On January 13, I had appealed to the Iraqi government not to make the trials and sentencing of fourteen convicted persons a public event.)

On January 28, my office received a cable from the UN Information Center in Cairo saying that my denunciation of the sentencings and hangings in Baghdad had received full coverage in the influential newspaper *Al-Ahram*. There was no means of knowing whether this unexpected display of criticism in the Cairo press against another Arab state had the backing of the U.A.R. government. To my knowledge, President Nasser did not make any public statement on the Baghdad hangings. There was general concern at the United Nations, however, that the cycle of provocative acts and massive retaliations would occur again. Ambassador Yost, who saw me on January 29, told me that Washington had urged Israel not to retaliate against Iraq.

The Big Four now attempted—unsuccessfully—to control the situation in the Middle East. From January 1969 to July of that year, the Foreign Ministers of the four powers held many meetings, but little was accomplished. By midsummer, their efforts finally bogged down and were abandoned. Failure was due chiefly to Israel's continuing insistence on direct talks with the Arabs and to its growing disposition to reject all outside interference with its policies.

Meanwhile, conditions in the Middle East steadily deteriorated. On February 8, Jordan complained to the Security Council that under a proposed Israeli law officially known as the Administrative Registration Law, "all business and professional men must be amalgamated with Israeli counterparts or become Israelis themselves."

On February 12, an Israeli jet brought down a Syrian MIG-21 in a brief aerial encounter over the Golan Heights, and there had been a sharp increase in mortar and rocket attacks from Jordanian territory. After every such attack, Israeli jets were sent to attack sites believed by the Israelis to contain concentrations and headquarters of commando units.

On February 18, four Arab terrorists, including a woman, attacked an Israeli El Al airliner with machine gun fire at Zurich airport as it was taxiing for take off, wounding six persons. An Israeli security guard aboard the plane jumped out and killed one of the attackers with a pistol shot. It was the third action against an El Al plane in recent months.

Immediately after the attack at Zurich airport, the Popular Front for the Liberation of Palestine announced in Amman that it was responsible for the raid. On the same day, I issued a statement vigorously condemning the attack. I then contacted the International Civil Aviation Organization and the International Air Transport Association; I also consulted members of the United Nations especially concerned, with view to finding means to prevent such acts of violence.

On February 20, Ambassador Tekoah handed to me a letter from Mr. Eban, who asked what constructive international action was envisaged to prevent such acts of violence against international civil aviation in the future. He noted that there was deep interest in Israel in my condemnation of the attack, which called for "constructive international action," and said that Israel would like to be informed of all steps taken or planned.

In my reply on February 26, I outlined the steps I had taken with ICAO and IATA as well as with some members of the United Nations, with a view to preventing similar acts of violence. I continued:

> In this connection, improved methods of international police cooperation and regulations of a national as well as an international character may contribute towards the prevention of these acts of terrorism and violence. However, I believe that the only sure way to bring an end to terrorist acts would be some substantial movement toward a peaceful settlement of the major issues underlying the Middle East conflict. In the circumstances, I hope you will agree that, although there may be some scope for positive action by the Secretary-General in a matter of this kind, the most natural and proper recourse, and that which should hold the best promise

for constructive international action, is clearly the Security Council.

It is my firm conviction that the Security Council resolution of 22 November 1967 offers the only practical basis for the promotion of a just and lasting peace in the area. I also remain convinced that progress towards this goal can be made through the dedicated efforts of Ambassador Jarring.

In this connection let me recall what I have stated on another occasion, that "if only all the resolutions and decisions of the principal deliberative organs of the United Nations were heeded by the parties primarily concerned in the area, there would be no Middle East problem today."[5]

Meanwhile, there was a change of leadership in Israel. Premier Levi Eshkol died on February 26, 1969, and the Israeli Labor Party, on March 8, asked former Foreign Minister Golda Meir to be its, and the country's, next leader.

On the same day (March 8), I received reports from General Odd Bull that Israel and the United Arab Republic had staged their biggest battle in four and a half months across the Suez Canal. His report said that the Egyptian oil refineries at Suez City were burning and that since 5:30 P.M. local time, heavy guns had fired across the waterway—for the first time since October 26, 1968. A cease-fire was called for by the United Nations observers, and at 10:40 P.M. local time (after a five-hour battle), the firing stopped.

On March 9, firing was resumed with greater intensity. During the raging artillery duel across the Suez Canal, an Israeli shell killed the chief of staff of the Egyptian armed forces, Lieutenant General Abdel Moreim Riad, who had been inspecting Egyptian positions close to the city of Ismailia.

It seemed that the Middle East would soon be the scene of the fourth Arab-Israeli war. I was in constant contact with the representatives of Israel and the U.A.R. as well as with General Odd Bull, whose UN observers were exerting their utmost to bring about a cease-fire. Four days of incessant firing caused several casualties and considerable damage to living quarters and vehicles. The exact number of casualties was not available. One of the

---

[5] *United Nations Press Release SG/SM/1071*, February 26, 1969.

most regrettable aspects of the artillery battles was the fact that both Egyptians and Israelis tended to keep the UN observation posts between themselves and the enemy. There were ten observation posts on each bank of the hundred-mile-long canal, manned by 96 officers and men. (The breakdown at that time was as follows: 23 Swedes, 19 Finns, 18 Frenchmen, 10 Irishmen, 8 Argentines, 8 Austrians, 6 Burmese, and 4 Chileans.) Under the prevailing procedures, a man who signed up as an observer had to agree to remain at least three months, but was expected to serve a year. Many stayed longer. On March 13, I sent congratulations to the observers for their "great courage and resourcefulness in maintaining the observation operation under fire in spite of risk to themselves and heavy installations, vehicles and equipment."[6]

At this point, discussions among the Big Four were directed mainly at strengthening the hand of Mr. Jarring and providing a stronger UN role in the Middle East. But when Mrs. Golda Meir assumed the office of Premier on March 17, she rejected both a Big-Four involvement in the Middle East problem and a reconstituted and strengthened United Nations force for the area. She said that Israel would continue to insist on direct talks leading to contractual peace with the Arabs. Regarding Israel-United States relations, she implied that certain disagreements had developed with the Nixon Administration.

When I saw Abba Eban at the United Nations on Saturday, March 15, he was very skeptical of Big-Four involvement. He said that he was going to Washington to talk to President Nixon and Secretary of State William Rogers and would attempt to persuade them to abandon Big-Power involvement in a Middle East settlement. His government, he said, would not accept an "imposed" settlement; it would insist on an "agreed" settlement.

In spite of Mr. Eban's plans to abandon a Big-Power initiative, the Nixon Administration went ahead with its decision. On May 24, Mr. Yost told me that the Big-Four permanent representatives would meet the following week and that I would get reports on every meeting held.

On March 30, Israel rejected in advance any Big-Four rec-

---

[6] *United Nations Official Records,* March 13, 1969.

ommendation on the Middle East that would conflict with her vital interests. In a statement issued after a Cabinet meeting, the government said:

> Israel entirely opposes the plan to convene the representatives of states that lie outside the Middle East in order to prepare recommendations concerning the region. Such a procedure undermines the responsibility devolving on the states of the region to attain peace among themselves.[7]

Nevertheless, Big-Four discussions were held on April 3, 8, and 14. The most explicit statement of the Nixon Administration's objectives in the talks was made by Secretary of State William P. Rogers, in the course of a press conference on April 7, in which he said that the four permanent members were seeking agreement on a general formula for a Middle East settlement and were prepared to "use the force of public opinion" to push Israel and the Arab countries into agreement. He said: "If the world community should agree on a certain general formula for the settlement of the Middle East, then I think the Governments in that area would want to think long and hard before they turned it down."

It was at this point that *for the first time,* Israel was offered an explicit public pledge of free navigation through the Suez Canal as part of a six-point settlement. The offer came through King Hussein, who was in Washington speaking with President Nixon with, as he said, the "personal authority" of President Gamal Abdel Nasser. King Hussein listed the following steps the Arabs would act upon:

1. An end of all belligerency.
2. Respect for and acknowledgment of the sovereignty, territorial integrity, and political independence of all states in the area.
3. Recognition of the right of all to live in peace within secure and recognized boundaries, free from threats or acts of war.
4. The guaranteeing for all of freedom of navigation through the Gulf of Aqaba and the Suez Canal.
5. The guaranteeing of the territorial inviolability of all states in the area, through whatever measures necessary, including the establishment of demilitarized zones.
6. The acceptance of a just settlement of the refugee problem.

---

[7] The New York *Times,* March 31, 1969.

In return, King Hussein demanded the withdrawal of Israeli forces "from all territories occupied in the June 1967 war." In presenting this six-point peace proposal to the National Press Club in Washington, the Jordanian King said: "The challenge that these principles present is that Israel may have either peace or territory—but she can never have both."[8]

But on the next day (April 1), the hopes inspired by this dramatic offer were dashed: Israel dismissed as propaganda the six-point peace plan presented by King Hussein. The official comment in Jerusalem was that there was nothing new in the Jordanian King's offer, and that the proposal for an Israeli withdrawal from all occupied Arab territories was unacceptable to Israel.

On his return from Washington, the King stayed for two days in New York, and I offered a luncheon in his honor on April 14. I had a forty-five-minute talk with him (attended by Ralph Bunche) before the luncheon. He said that he was not surprised by the Israeli rejection of his peace plan. Regarding face-to-face talks with Israel, he said that they would be possible after agreement had been reached by all parties to the full implementation of Security Council Resolution 242, including an Israeli withdrawal from occupied territories. He also said that Israel was entitled to territorial adjustments for security purposes, provided that such adjustments did not reflect the right of conquest. He said that adjustments were possible "here and there on a reciprocal basis." The King emphasized the need for success of the Big-Four talks in New York, stressing that the situation in the region was now very grave. As on previous meetings, the King's remarks to me were generously sprinkled with "sir's."

Already, however, a virtual state of war had erupted between Israel and the United Arab Republic, and violent conflicts of increasing intensity were to continue throughout the spring, summer, and fall of 1969. It was evident that neither the Big Four nor the United Nations was having the slightest success in bringing peace to the Middle East. By the end of the year, as I have indicated, the Big Four had suspended their periodic meetings, and there was no doubt that the onus of responsibility had now shifted to the United States and the Soviet Union.

---

[8] United Nations Files, April 10, 1969.

But even the two superpowers were unable to stem the inexorable drift toward war. The sequence of events was as follows.

Since April 8, artillery duels across the Canal had taken place for twelve successive days, and on April 22, I had to report to the Council that the cease-fire ordered two years before "had become almost totally ineffective." I also pointed out that our UN observers were now operating under great danger and difficulty.

As of April 30, there had been three casualties among the UN observers and much material damage, including several caravans and a bus destroyed, and forty-eight vehicles, nine trailers, and some storehouses and residential buildings damaged. UN control centers and observation posts were also damaged on twenty-seven occasions. The reason for this extraordinary damage, in the brief period of two weeks, was the fact that although UN installations and facilities were clearly and unmistakably marked, they were repeatedly fired upon by both sides. My report also reflected, therefore, my serious concern for the safety of nationals of the countries that had contributed observers in the Canal sector. The government of Burma informed me on April 24 that it wanted the Burmese observers to be withdrawn. In spite of my requests to reconsider, Burma's decision was firm, and the six observers were withdrawn before the end of April.

By the middle of May, calm returned to the Suez Canal sector, but on June 15, I received an important report from General Odd Bull. On that day, Israeli authorities evicted the last Arab family living near the Wailing Wall, the west wall of Jerusalem, and began to demolish the area's structures. The action, according to the report, led to several angry scenes and was expected to cause more strife between Arabs and Jews in an area holy to both of them. The Israeli Ministry of Religious Affairs, which had responsibility for the area, said that the eviction and demolition orders followed a finding by Jerusalem engineers that the buildings were a danger to public safety.

Meanwhile, Arab guerrilla activity between Israel and Jordan had increased, and Prime Minister Golda Meir was reported to have warned King Hussein of "an appropriate response" if these activities were not stopped. On June 23, I received a report from General Bull that Israeli commandos had blown up the eighty-five-million-dollar East Ghor Canal, Jordan's most important irrigation project, which was financed mainly by the United States. Completed in 1964 after six years of construction, the fifty-mile canal drew water from the Yarmuk River and served an estimated 60,000 Jordanians in the region.

On the next day (June 24), an oil pipeline leading from the Haifa refinery, one of Israel's major industrial facilities, was blown up, apparently by Arab saboteurs. The fact that a heavily guarded industrial area was chosen as a target of sabotage indicated an intensification of the struggle being waged by Arab guerrillas against Israel.

On the night of June 29, Israeli commandos landed in the Nile valley and sabotaged Egypt's powerline between the Aswan Dam and Cairo. It was one of the most daring raids ever launched by Israeli commandos, since the target was 125 miles west of the Red Sea. The Israelis did not disclose how their forces got to the target, but it was assumed that helicopters were used.

On the same day, Jordanian workers attempting to repair the East Ghor Canal, sabotaged the previous week by Israeli commandos, were prevented from doing so by Israeli gunners.

Thus, the situation had seriously deteriorated. What was worse, the Big Four meetings, which had started on February 6 in an atmosphere of optimism, were now bogged down; there were exchanges of peace proposals between the United States and the Soviet Union, but with no agreement in sight after nearly five months.

On July 1, I received a report from General Bull that Israel's national police headquarters had been moved from Tel Aviv to East Jerusalem, the former Jordanian part of the city. It was the boldest move so far by Israel in the effort to solidify its administrative annexation of the Arab sector. The move came as the Security Council was debating Jordan's complaint that Israel was changing the status of the city. It was significant that in the Council debate on that day, the representative of the United States joined those of the Soviet Union, Britain, and France who reiterated their warning to Israel against actions to absorb the Arab sector of Jerusalem.

On July 3, the Security Council again voted unanimously to

"censure in the strongest terms" actions by Israel in the Arab area of Jerusalem tending to change the city's status. It "urgently [called] once more upon Israel to rescind forthwith all measures taken by it which may tend to change the status of the City of Jerusalem, and in future to refrain from all actions likely to have such an effect."[9] The United States had abstained on a similar resolution approved by the Council in May 1968. The shift from an abstention to support reflected a firmer line taken by the United States, to the effect that Israel should not confiscate or destroy property in occupied Arab Jerusalem. Immediately after the unanimous vote, Yosef Tekoah, Israel's chief delegate, announced that the Council resolution would not affect the annexation of East Jerusalem. He said, "Life cannot stop in Jerusalem; it will continue as it has during the last two years of Jerusalem's rebirth."[10]

Meanwhile, I had received alarming reports from General Bull of the resumption of shelling across the Suez Canal. On July 7, the situation was so serious, and the UN observers were so exposed to the crossfire, that I submitted a special report to the Security Council. I declared that "open warfare has been resumed" by the Israeli and Egyptian forces throughout the Suez Canal cease-fire area. In the month of June, Egyptian forces fired twenty-one times on UN personnel and installations, and Israeli forces five times; two of the ninety-six observers were injured, and most of the time all had to dive under fire into dugouts protected only by sandbags. I told the Council that the observers were serving as "what amounts to defenseless targets in a shooting gallery," and warned of the possibility of withdrawing them if they continued to be fired upon. Two statements from the report show how hopeless the situation seemed to be:

> In fact, never in the history of the United Nations experience with peace-keeping has there been such a complete and sustained disregard for a cease-fire called for by the Security Council and agreed to by the parties.

> I bring this situation once again, and with even greater emphasis

---

[9] *United Nations Security Council Official Records, No. 1485,* July 3, 1969.
[10] Ibid.

and concern, to the attention of the Security Council in full consciousness that I, as Secretary-General, have been and am unable to effect any noticeable improvement in it.[11]

Neither my warning nor General Bull's efforts yielded any result. Two years after the Six-Day War, both sides had raised the
ante along the cease-fire lines, the Arabs to change the situation
and the Israelis to maintain it. Besides the Suez Canal shellings,
Israel and Syria fought air battles between Damascus and El-
Quneitra in the Israeli-held Golan Heights.

The heaviest aerial battle between Israel and the U.A.R. since
the Six-Day War took place over the Suez Canal on July 24. It
seemed the fourth Arab-Israel war was imminent.

On July 27, three months after my warning to the Council expressing grave concern for the safety of UN observers in the
Canal sector, a Swedish observer stationed at Port Taufig on the
Egyptian side was killed during a heavy artillery duel. He was
Major B. Roland Plane and was the first UN observer killed on
the Canal since the observers moved in following the 1967 war.
On the next day, General Bull reported to me that the observer
post near Port Taufig would be closed because water and elec-
tricity had been knocked out in the shelling.

By this time, the Big Four had suspended their periodic meetings, and the matter was left in the hands of the United States and
the Soviet Union. Ambassador Yost told me on July 30 that
Anatoli Dobrynin, the Soviet ambassador in Washington, and either Secretary of State William Rogers or assistant secretary
Joseph Sisco, were in constant contact on the deteriorating situation. Now the main topic of conversation at the United Nations
was whether the two superpowers in concert could stop the
fighting and end the war, as they did in 1956.

On Sunday, August 3, the UN Office of Public Information
sent to my residence a bundle of wire dispatches, as was the case
on every Sunday. The Associated Press had the following item:
"Jerusalem radio announced tonight that Israeli leaders had declared that the nation would retain the Golan Heights, the Gaza

---

[11] Secretary General's Report to the Security Council, (S/7930), July 7,
1969.

Strip and a considerable part of the eastern and southern Sinai Peninsula." The radio quoted the statement of the five-member group, including three Cabinet ministers:

> The Golan Heights and the Gaza Strip shall remain under our rule, and freedom of navigation from Elath southward shall be guaranteed by the independent forces of Israel, which shall rule in the region of the straits. This region, Merhav Shlomo (Region of Solomon), will be linked contiguously with Israel commensurate with security functions and in view of possible attacks in the future.

There was no mention of any decision on the occupied area on the West Bank of the Jordan River. Statements in the past by Israeli leaders indicated, however, that the river would remain the "eastern security border," or one "not to be crossed by foreign armies." The declaration was the first substantial indication of how much of the Sinai Peninsula the Israelis intended to keep. To my knowledge, it was also the first official statement that the Gaza Strip would be retained. By July 1969, the Israeli government had established more than a dozen settlements in the plateau taken from Syria during the Six-Day War. The late Premier Levi Eshkol had once said that the Golan Heights "stick into Israel like a sword in our stomach."

On August 21, an incident of tragic proportions took place in Jerusalem. A fire of undetermined origin destroyed sections of the Mosque of Al-Aksa, one of Islam's most sacred shrines. The fire set off the most bitter outcry and resentment among the Moslem delegates at the United Nations, and on the next day, seven permanent representatives handed to me a letter on behalf of twenty-four Moslem countries. The letter demanded an impartial investigation into the grave event and requested UN action enabling Islamic countries to assess the damage to the shrine and execute plans for its repair. It said, in part:

> The occurrence of this outrage during the time that Jerusalem is under the military occupation of Israeli authorities has filled the population of our countries with profound horror and grief. . . . We therefore emphasize the urgency of . . . action by the United Nations. . . .

On August 23, I sent a reply to Ambassador Roeslan Abdulgani of Indonesia, spokesman for the twenty-four Moslem states, expressing the "hope that the full and verified facts of this most distressing occurrence will be promptly ascertained. This is a matter of serious and sober concern to the United Nations and to all of humanity."[12]

Immediately after the fire, the Israeli government denied any connection with the blaze. Premier Golda Meir visited the mosque in the afternoon of August 21 to express Israel's shock and sorrow to Moslem elders. According to reports from Jerusalem, late in the morning, about two hours after the fire had been brought under control, Israeli troops fired into the air to disperse a crowd of several thousand shouting and stone-throwing Arabs. On the next day (August 22), the Israeli police announced the arrest of a suspect who was identified as an Australian Christian, Michael Dennis William Rohan, a member of the Church of God, an evangelical denomination.[13] But twenty-four Moslem states at the United Nations did not accept the Israeli government's explanation that the Australian had caused the blaze; for two weeks they were busy discussing ways and means of ascertaining the real cause of the Al-Aksa Mosque fire. On September 9, an urgent meeting of the Security Council was called at their request and a group of non-Arab Moslems led by Pakistan offered a resolution that sought to establish an international commission to investigate the blaze, a Moslem commission to restore the Islamic shrine, and a United Nations force to guard Jerusalem's holy places.

The situation continued to deteriorate. All diplomatic moves had stalled; even the two superpowers made no headway. In an attempt to break the deadlock, I gave a working dinner on September 20 for the Foreign Ministers of the United States, the Soviet Union, Britain, and France. At this and subsequent meetings, we tried to create a situation that would make it possible for Arab and Israeli negotiators to establish themselves in more or

---

[12] *United Nations Press Release No. SG/SM/1145*, August 23, 1969.
[13] On December 30, 1969, Dennis Rohan was committed to a mental asylum for an indefinite period. The Israeli court that heard the case ruled that Mr. Rohan was not punishable for his deed because he had acted under an uncontrollable pathological impulse.

less adjacent headquarters and start the process of negotiation—
with Mr. Jarring shuttling back and forth between them. After two
weeks of intensive talks among the four ministers, however, there
was no evidence of any progress.

I was so frustrated with the lack of progress in the diplomatic
search for peace that in the course of my speech to the Navy
League at the Waldorf Astoria Hotel on October 28, I said, "We
may be witnessing in the Middle East something like the early
stages of a new Hundred Years' War."[14]

After appealing for respect of the Security Council's authority
as a means of saving world peace, I deplored the failure of the
Council to enforce some of its past unanimous decisions on important peace-keeping situations. Then I said:

> If the world becomes accustomed to the decisions of the highest
> United Nations organ for peace and security going by default or
> being ignored, we shall have taken a very dangerous step back-
> wards toward anarchy.[15]

During the last two months of 1969, the United States and
the Soviet Union exchanged peace plans. The United States
offered a return to the U.A.R. of all the Sinai Peninsula from Israeli occupation, but stipulated that the future of the Gaza Strip
would be subject to negotiation by Israel and Jordan. It was the
first time that the prewar line in Sinai was unequivocally stipulated
by the United States as the frontier to which the pullback should
take place. Such a plan was sure to be rejected by Israel, however,
and as it turned out, the U.A.R. also rejected it. On November 7,
Ambassador El-Zayyat saw me and said that the latest U.S. proposal was not acceptable to his government.

It was originally agreed that any plan initiated by the U.S. or
the U.S.S.R. must first get the endorsement of both, and then be
presented to Britain and France. After all four powers agreed to
it, the plan would be presented to me for transmission to Mr. Jarring for negotiation with Israel and the Arab states.

On the morning of December 3, the four powers agreed on a

---

14 United Nations Document SG/SM/477, October 28, 1969.
15 Ibid.

"package deal," that is, a settlement incorporating all facets of the Middle East problem.

But the Israeli posture now was to reject any such deal in advance. Earlier in the day, Israeli Foreign Minister Abba Eban told the ambassadors of the United States, Britain, and France in Jerusalem that the Israeli government would not receive Mr. Jarring if he was sent to Israel to negotiate an agreement reached by the Big Four.

On December 9, the most forthright and clear-cut position of the United States was presented by Secretary of State William Rogers in Washington. He asserted that the United States "had supported, and continued to support, the Security Council Resolution of November 22, 1967, as the only framework for a negotiated settlement," and that his government "had committed, and continued to commit, itself to the principle of Israeli withdrawal from territories occupied during the 1967 war in return for Arab acceptance of permanent peace based on binding agreements." Mr. Rogers specifically indicated a return to the Israeli-Egyptian traditional border. He also reiterated the U.S. position on Jerusalem and called for a just settlement of the refugee problem.

On December 12, Foreign Minister Abba Eban, who was on his way to Washington, saw me and said that in the view of his government, Mr. Roger's statement was likely to mar the prospects for peace in the area. He pointed out to me his government's statement issued the previous night, which stressed that "negotiations for peace must be free from prior conditions and external influences and pressures."

The Israeli Cabinet statement referred specifically to Mr. Roger's address on December 9. It said, "The prospects for peace will be seriously marred if states outside the region continue to raise territorial proposals and suggestions on subjects that cannot promote peace and security."[16] I have no record of any Arab reaction to Mr. Roger's statement. My diary for that period indicates only that the Cairo newspaper *Al-Ahram* had commented that the proposals by the American Secretary of State had already been rejected by the United Arab Republic.

---

[16] The New York *Times,* December 11, 1969.

Any hope offered by the recent proposals was thus dashed in a couple of weeks. As it turned out, Mr. Roger's plan was rejected not only by Israel but also by the Soviet Union, which maintained, among other positions, that any Arab government entering into a peace agreement with Israel would be responsible for the prevention of guerrilla attacks. Obviously, Moscow was speaking not for the U.A.R., which had no guerrilla problem, but for Jordan, whose government had very strained relations with the Palestinian guerrillas. Once again, it was a case of missed opportunities; thus the end of 1969 saw no more improvement in diplomatic efforts than the beginning of the year had promised.

By the middle of January 1970, things were as gloomy as they had been a year before. The Big-Four representatives told me that another full-scale war between the Arabs and the Israelis could not be ruled out. Because of the intensity of local passions in Arab-Israeli relations, it was evident that there was not much that any diplomatic initiatives could do to bring peace to the Middle East. At the United Nations, there was practically no support for Israeli's insistence on face-to-face talks with the Arabs, while at the same time, there was a growing feeling that the Arabs must enter into a binding peace agreement with Israel, with borders guaranteed by the Security Council or by the Big Powers.

By February, clashes between the Israelis and the Egyptians became more frequent and intense. On February 11, Cairo claimed that an Egyptian infantry company had carried out a major assault across the Suez Canal and ambushed an armored column. An Egyptian military spokesman said that at least twenty Israeli soldiers were killed or wounded in the ambush and that two were captured. On the same day in Jerusalem, an Israeli spokesman said that Israeli jets had struck at Egyptian positions at the Canal for eighty minutes.

A massive Israeli air raid on the U.A.R. took place on February 12, when Israeli fighter-bombers attacked a scrap-metal processing plant near Cairo, killing over seventy workers and wounding sixty-nine. In Jerusalem, Israeli officials said that one plane might have inadvertently hit a civilian target. Late that day, I received a cable from General Odd Bull informing me that Israeli Defense Minister Moshe Dayan had telephoned him earlier in the day to warn him that one of the bombs dropped was timed to explode after twenty-four hours. Moshe Dayan wanted General Bull to convey this information to Cairo; he had decided to make the request as soon as he had learned that a civilian target had been hit. General Bull informed Cairo accordingly.

The news caused disgust and dismay at the United Nations. In Washington, undersecretary of state Elliot Richardson, acting while the Secretary, William P. Rogers, was on an African tour, issued a statement calling attention also to the Arab terrorist attack at the Munich airport two days earlier, in which an Israeli had been killed. Mr. Richardson said:

> The United States continues to be deeply concerned over the continuation and level of violence taking place between Israel and certain Arab states. We have seen reports of an Israeli air attack on a steel factory at Abu Zabal. We deplore this attack, which apparently has resulted in considerable loss of life and injuries. Neither can we disregard the tragic loss of life and injury to civilians resulting from renewed attacks by terrorists against civilian passengers travelling on international air transports far from the area of conflict.[17]

From all available information, I was deeply concerned that the escalation of the fighting might lead to a new all-out war and might destroy the remaining chances of a diplomatic settlement of the conflict. After discussing this with Ralph Bunche on February 12, I asked General Odd Bull to come to New York the following weekend (February 14–15) for urgent consultations.

General Bull arrived on Sunday, February 15, and I conferred with him (with Ralph Bunche present) for almost two hours on that day. Since I appointed him in 1963 to succeed General von Horn as head of the truce observation team, General Bull had won the respect and affection of both sides. Though tension continued to rise in the area, he managed to break it periodically by arranging prisoner exchanges, and meetings and negotiations on such issues as grazing rights. He is a man of extraordinary charm and dignity, and has the unquenchable optimism of a model mediator. His assessment of the situation was grim. He was

---

[17] *U. S. Department of State Press Release,* February 12, 1970.

optimistic, however, about the future role of the United Nations, both in the diplomatic field and in its observation functions. He reported that the cease-fire had completely broken down in the Suez Canal sector and agreed with me that the Big Powers could play a very important role in restoring it. He feared that Egyptian forays into the east bank of the Canal would prompt massive Israeli reprisals.

While General Bull was still in New York, news reached the United Nations (on February 17) that Israel again carried her bombing raids to the outskirts of Cairo, and warned the Egyptians that there would be no letup in the air attacks until they agreed to abide by the cease-fire ordered by the Security Council in 1967. At my press conference on that day, I said:

> I have studied the three proposals very carefully—the United States proposal, the Soviet proposal and the French proposal—and it seems to me that a common denominator can be found. . . . In my view there are certain basic issues on which the Big Four can come to an agreement leading to the formulation of guidelines to enable Ambassador Jarring to reactivate his mission.[18]

When I said that there was a common denominator on one or two basic issues, I had in mind the U.S. plan of December 9, 1969, involving an Israeli withdrawal to the Israeli-Egyptian international borders and a peace treaty between Israel and her Arab neighbors, with international guarantees of those borders. On these two issues there was general agreement, although opinions differed on the type of treaty to be drawn up. The United States wanted a binding contractual agreement, while the Soviet Union was not explicit on the character of the agreement. In any case, the United States wanted the Arab states to take full responsibility to prevent guerrilla attacks on Israel across the borders, a stipulation to which the Soviet Union did not agree.

In March 1970, another factor complicating the search for peace came into the picture. The Israeli government was reported to have been considering the settlement of Jewish families in occupied territories, although there was strong opposition to the idea

---

[18] *United Nations Press Release No. SG/SM/1211*, February 17, 1970.

within the governing Israeli Labor Party itself. On March 25, however, the government announced the proposed settlement of thirty-one civilian and paramilitary outposts, to be established in the occupied areas for 1970. The largest settlement would be in Hebron, an Arab town of about 38,000 in the occupied part of Jordan. It was proposed to settle 250 Jewish families (about a thousand persons) there. Other settlements included fourteen in the Syrian Golan Heights, seven in the Jordan Valley, and five in northern Sinai and the Gaza Strip. Opponents of the settlement plan argued that Israel was losing all her options for peace by gradually settling the occupied areas in this way.

At the same time, the cease-fire in the Suez Canal sector had completely broken down. Arab guerrilla activity from Lebanese territory against Israeli villages became more frequent, and the growing wave of attacks was always met by massive Israeli reprisals.

At 8:30 A.M. on May 12, 1970, I received a phone call at home from Ralph Bunche. He said that the United Nations cable office had just called to inform him that an Israeli armored attack had been launched in the early hours of that day into Lebanese territory in the general area of Mount Hermon. The report went on to say that according to an Israeli representative, "the present action going on in the El Arkoub area, east of the Habani River, was only aimed at the destruction of Fedayeen commandos and that it was not the intention of the Israeli troops to act against the Lebanese army or population, provided the Lebanese army and population did not support the Fedayeen."[19]

The Security Council met at 11:00 A.M. on that day, and Ambassador Jaime de Pinies of Spain introduced a draft resolution demanding the immediate withdrawal of all Israeli armed forces from Lebanese territory. It was adopted unanimously. The fifteen-member Council voted thirteen to two against a United States amendment intended to soften the resolution by calling for a halt to "all military operations in that area," thus covering also

---

[19] *United Nations Security Council Official Records, No. 1538,* May 12, 1970.

the guerrilla forces that the Israelis said they were attacking. Only
Britain voted with the United States.

On the next day (May 13), the Israeli armored force ended
its thrust into southeast Lebanon and returned to Israeli soil after
a thirty-two-hour operation. Military headquarters in Tel Aviv
said that thirty guerrillas had been killed and fifteen prisoners
brought back across the border. Israeli casualties were given as
eleven soldiers injured, most of them slightly. Beirut radio broadcast on the same day a report by *El-Fatah* saying that thirty to
forty guerrillas had been killed. But the guerrilla forces claimed a
victory over the raiders, including the destruction of several Israeli
tanks, the downing of an Israeli helicopter and its crew, and the
capture of another Israeli soldier.

The Security Council, after meeting in continuous session,
concluded its discussion of the Israeli reprisal raid into Lebanon
and (on May 19) voted a resolution that condemned Israel "for
the premeditated military action" against Lebanon. It also declared that "such armed violations can no longer be tolerated."
The decision of the Council was a clear warning to Israel to desist
from such military actions against the territory of a neighboring
Arab state. The vote was eleven to none, with the United States,
Colombia, Nicaragua and Sierra Leone abstaining. Britain and
France voted for the resolution. This was the eighth occasion
since the 1967 war on which the Security Council had reproved
Israel for breaches of the cease-fire. After the vote, Mr. Tekoah
denounced the resolution as "one-sided."

By June 1970, three years after the Six-Day War, the chances
for peace in the Middle East appeared more remote than ever. I
was still concentrating my efforts on getting a consensus of the Big
Four on two basic issues—withdrawal and a binding peace
agreement. I was in possession of all documents presented by the
four permanent members of the Security Council at their irregular
meetings, and I knew that there was a large area of agreement, as
well as disagreement. Why not single out the agreed formulations,
which could then serve as guidelines for Mr. Jarring? The inclina-
tion of the Big Four at that time, however, was to deal with all issues as a package, and not to pick and choose. I felt strongly that

if such an attitude persisted, the result would be a state of continuing crisis in the area, with no peace in sight.

The United States made one more major effort to break the deadlock. I was in Moscow on June 19, 1970, when I first got a hint of Washington's initiative. At Premier Kosygin's luncheon given for me at the Kremlin, Vladimir Vinogradov, the deputy foreign minister and an expert on Middle East affairs, told me that the United States had sent to Moscow "an interesting plan" on the Middle East. He did not elaborate. On the same afternoon, I left for Minsk, the capital of Byelorussia, in a special plane and returned to Moscow on the next day at 9:00 P.M. At 10:00 P.M., while I was conferring with Mr. Jarring at the guest house in the Lenin Hills where I was staying, an official from the United States Embassy delivered to me a copy of the latest American plan on the Middle East. He said that the plan had been given to the three other Big Powers, as well as to Israel, the U.A.R., and Jordan. The text I received was a letter sent on the previous day (June 19) by Secretary of State William P. Rogers to the U.A.R. Foreign Minister, Mahmoud Riad.

As the Soviets had suggested, the new plan did indeed contain a novel element. This time, the Americans proposed that both Israel and the U.A.R. subscribe to a restoration of the cease-fire for at least a limited period, and that the two parties also subscribe to a statement that would be in the form of a report from Ambassador Jarring to me. The report would say that the U.A.R., Jordan, and Israel agreed to designate representatives to discussions to be held under Mr. Jarring's auspices. The objective of the discussions would be to reach an agreement on peace based on mutual acknowledgement of each country's sovereignty and territorial integrity, and on an Israeli withdrawal to the pre-1967 borders. The full text of the Rogers letter is reproduced in Appendix J, Part IV.

In my view, it was the most balanced and comprehensive plan ever presented by Washington and constituted a real initiative to bridge the East-West differences over the crisis. By then, it was common knowledge at the United Nations, as well as abroad, that I considered agreement by the Big Four, or at least by the two superpowers, essential to ending the crisis in the Middle East.

Mr. Vinogradov also discussed with me a new Soviet plan, the key element of which was Moscow's acceptance, for the first time, of the concept that there must be a formal and binding peace agreement between Israel and her Arab adversaries—not simply an understanding to end belligerency. Now Moscow had come a long way, proposing not only an end to belligerency but also the conclusion of a peace agreement—"preferably in the Security Council chamber where Israeli and Arab representatives would append their signatures in the presence of the fifteen members of the Council." He made it clear, of course, that the prior condition of that legally-binding agreement would be the withdrawal of Israeli forces from *all* occupied territories. After studying the plan, both Mr. Jarring and I felt that the American and Russian views were dramatically closer than they had ever been.

Before I left Moscow for New York on the next day (June 21), I told the Soviet diplomats who came to the airport that we had missed out on two opportunities to restore peace. "This was the third," I said, "and it must not fail."

The American plan actually had no new features except the proposal for a temporary cease-fire of at least ninety days. There was no reference to Syria (since Syria did not accept Resolution 242) and obviously no reference to the Golan Heights. This omission prompted President Nasser to say (in Bengasi, Libya, on June 25):

> I tell you, in the name of your brothers in Egypt, who refuse any compromise for withdrawal, that withdrawal must be from the Golan Heights before Sinai. If we had wanted only withdrawal from Sinai, we could have agreed with the United States on this two years ago. But we have declared more than once that withdrawal must be from Jerusalem, the West Bank of the Jordan, the Golan Heights—and from Sinai later.[20]

The United States plan contained several terms that had been rejected by Israel. These included the acceptance of indirect substantive talks (through Mr. Jarring) without provision for direct negotiations, acceptance of the principle of withdrawal before the bargaining process began, and the idea of a temporary cease-fire.

---

[20] Reuters news dispatch, June 25, 1970.

There was no indication that Israel had shifted its position on any of these items. Israel did not react promptly to the American plan, however, as Nasser did. One reason for its delayed reaction could have been the fact that Israel had been negotiating with Washington for the supply of some planes, for use either as replacements for those that had been lost or as additions to the Israeli air force. At the time that the U.S. plan was made available to the parties, Washington had not decided on Israel's request.

It was only on June 29 that Premier Golda Meir, in a speech to the Israeli Knesset, categorically rejected the concept of a temporary, or conditional, cease-fire with Israel's Arab adversaries, and also rejected suggestions of a full Israeli withdrawal from the Arab territories occupied in the Six-Day War.

At 5:00 P.M. on July 22, Ambassador El-Zayyat informed me that the government of the U.A.R. had told the United States that it was ready to agree to the cease-fire proposed by Washington and based on the Security Council cease-fire resolution. In effect, he said that Cairo had accepted the Rogers plan. In my view, Moscow had played a significant role in getting President Nasser to reverse his previous stand.

On Sunday, July 26, Ralph Bunche phoned me to say that Ambassador El-Farah had informed him that Jordan had also accepted the Rogers plan, and that Amman had so informed Washington. On July 31, the UNTSO Information Office in Jerusalem sent a cable to the UN Office of Public Information saying that the Israeli Cabinet had decided to accept the U.S. formula for a limited cease-fire and the opening of peace talks with the United Arab Republic. The vote in the Cabinet was seventeen to six, and the dissenting ministers—all from the hard-line Gahal faction— were expected to withdraw from the government coalition.[21] On the same day, I sent a cable to Ambassador Jarring requesting him to come to New York for urgent consultations on the reactivation of his mission; he arrived on the night of Sunday, August 2.

Meanwhile, I had to make a very reluctant decision. General Odd Bull of Norway, who had been serving as chief of staff of UNTSO since May 20, 1963, had repeatedly expressed his desire, both to me and to Ralph Bunche, to retire from his post for per-

---

[21] Six ministers of the Gahal Party resigned on August 3, 1970.

sonal reasons. During the seven years that he had been chief of staff, UNTSO had undergone a number of serious crises and, especially since the June 1967 war, had encountered great difficulties. The United Nations had been very fortunate to have had an experienced officer with great diplomatic skill as chief of staff in Jerusalem. In spite of the severe emotion, tension, and controversy characterizing the situation in the Middle East, General Bull had been able to maintain excellent relations with all of the governments concerned. He had certainly fulfilled the duties of chief of staff with skill and devotion.

I complied with his request on July 21, 1970, and on his personal recommendation, appointed his deputy, Major General E. P. H. Sillsavuo of Finland to succeed him. General Sillsavuo had served with UNTSO since October 15, 1967, deputizing for General Bull whenever he was absent, and in the past three months (April to June 1970), had served as acting chief of staff. Like General Bull, he was endowed with qualities of tact, skill, and devotion.

On Monday, August 3, Secretary of State William P. Rogers came to the United Nations to confer with Mr. Jarring and myself. He was accompanied by Joseph J. Sisco, assistant secretary of state for Near Eastern and South Asian affairs, Charles Yost, and William B. Buffum, deputy permanent representative. Ralph Bunche joined us in the talks. In the course of the ninety-minute conference, we discussed procedures for the reactivation of the Jarring mission. It was agreed that the new cease-fire was to be preceded by statements to Mr. Jarring from each party, committing each to take steps under his auspices to carry out Resolution 242.

The acceptance of the Rogers plan by the U.A.R., Jordan, and Israel meant not only the personal triumph of William Rogers and Joseph Sisco, but also a boost for Mr. Jarring. Now there was an air of evident optimism at the United Nations. Although the right-wing Gahal faction withdrew from the Israeli Cabinet in protest over the acceptance of the U.S. initiative, and although Algeria and Iraq strongly objected to Nasser's acceptance of the American plan, the signs were auspicious for the revival of diplomatic efforts. Never since the Six-Day War had the outlook for peace been brighter. I felt that the Middle East would never be the same again; the extremists were being isolated, and the moderates had taken over.

In its formal reply to the United States on August 4, Israel made a public commitment to withdraw its troops from occupied Arab territories, as part of the peace settlement. It was the first time since the Six-Day War that Israel used the word "withdrawal." This was noted with satisfaction in Washington, which had been pressing Mrs. Meir's government for a year to use the word; and in Cairo, which was now under fire from rivals in the militant Arab camp to produce some benefit from its acceptance of the U.S. initiative.

Then things moved fast. On August 6, Mr. Jarring informed me of the willingness of the U.A.R., Jordan, and Israel to designate representatives for peace discussions in accordance with their agreement to carry out Resolution 242. On August 7, I formally reactivated the Jarring mission and reported to the Security Council that Ambassador Jarring "is already intensively at work" and was now expected to capitalize on the momentum, holding the initial talks in New York. On that night (August 7), the cease-fire between the United Arab Republic and Israel went into effect for ninety days, as stipulated in the Rogers plan. It was the fourth Middle Eastern truce in the twenty-two years of Israel's existence.

The same night, I received a letter from Mr. Jarring confirming the truce and, more importantly, the willingness of the parties to participate in discussions:

> The United Arab Republic, Jordan and Israel advise me that they agree:
>
> That having accepted and indicated their willingness to carry out Security Council Resolution 242 (of November 22, 1967) in all its parts, they will designate representatives to discussions to be held under my auspices. . . .
>
> That the purpose of the aforementioned discussions is to reach agreement on the establishment of a just and lasting peace between them based on (1) mutual acknowledgement by the United Arab Republic, Jordan and Israel of each other's sovereignty, ter-

ritorial integrity and political independence, and (2) Israeli withdrawal from territories occupied in the 1967 conflict, both in accordance with Resolution 242.[22]

On August 8, I made a statement announcing Mr. Jarring's letter and declared that the Jarring mission was reactivated. I concluded my statement with these words: "He may rely on my unfailing support and he certainly merits the support of all governments and peoples in the world who believe in peace."

Thus, the first concerted diplomatic effort in more than two decades to bring a formal and binding peace settlement to the Middle East opened at the United Nations on August 25, 1970. Delegates from Israel (Yosef Tekoah), Jordan (Abdul Hamid Sharaf) and the United Arab Republic (Mohammed H. El-Zayyat) began separate discussions on that day with Mr. Jarring.

Our optimism, however, was illusory. The truce was short-lived. Within two days of the cease-fire's going into effect, Israel charged the U.A.R. with violating it by introducing Soviet-made SAM-2 and SAM-3 antiaircraft missiles into the thirty-one-mile-wide military standstill zone in the Canal sector, and recalled Yosef Takoah to Jerusalem "for consultation" from his discussions with Mr. Jarring in New York. The U.A.R. denied the Israeli charges. Mr. El-Zayyat told me that the missiles had already been there when the cease-fire went into effect and that not a single missile had been introduced into the cease-fire zone. He charged that the Israeli objective was to withdraw from the peace exchanges under Mr. Jarring.

Israel had been demanding for two days that the United States, as the sponsor of the cease-fire and the peace initiative, bring about a withdrawal of the missiles before the peace negotiations under Mr. Jarring's auspices could be resumed. Mr. Tekoah was kept in Jerusalem for further consultations. The United States had said that it had no conclusive evidence that the U.A.R. had introduced Soviet-built missiles into the cease-fire zone after the cease-fire had gone into effect. Speaking before executives of the Trade Union Federation (Histadrut) in Tel Aviv on August 31, Mrs. Meir said:

---

[22] *United Nations Official Records*, August 7, 1970.

We are now in the midst of a hard, difficult argument with the United States over Egyptian violations of the cease-fire. The U.S. government has guaranteed that neither side would improve its military position as a result of the cease-fire. But only a few hours had passed when the Egyptians began violating it. We cannot give in on this score. We cannot be weaker should the war along the Suez Canal resume.[23]

On the same day, President Nasser charged that the Israelis had raised the furor as a means of disrupting the Jarring mission. At a meeting with a delegation of the World Peace Council in Cairo, he said:

These missiles had existed long before the cease-fire. It is clear that these missiles were the cause of Israeli Phantoms being shot down.[24]

On September 6, the Israeli government decided to withdraw from the UN peace talks with the United Arab Republic and Jordan until the new missile installations, reportedly introduced in the Suez Canal area, had been removed. The Cabinet decision stressed that Israel would continue to honor the ninety-day cease-fire, would remain committed to the American-sponsored peace-making effort, and would resume the talks as soon as the U.A.R. also honored the commitments she had made to the United States. Ralph Bunche was also assured by the U.S. mission to the United Nations that the Israeli withdrawal meant only a delay and not a final breakdown. Meanwhile, Mr. Tekoah was still in Jerusalem.

The breakdown of the peace talks was exacerbated by a series of hijackings that took place throughout the remainder of September. It turned into a month of violence. On Sunday, September 6, an Arab guerrilla group hijacked four jets bound for New York from European airports—two from Amsterdam, one from Frankfurt, and one from Zurich. The airlines involved were El Al, Trans World, Pan American, and Swissair. The attempt aboard the El Al jet failed, with one of the two hijackers dead and the other, a woman, wounded. The three other jets landed in the Middle East—two in Jordan and one in Cairo. Minutes after landing

---

[23] Associated Press news dispatch, August 31, 1970.
[24] Dispatch from UN Information Office in Cairo, August 31, 1970.

at Cairo airport on the morning of September 7, the Pan Am Boeing 747 was torn by explosions. Reports reaching New York said that all the passengers and crew members, as well as the two Palestinian hijackers, had slid down escape chutes and scrambled away just before the explosion took place. I was shocked with anger and disbelief. As soon as I got to the office on Monday (September 7), I issued a strong denunciation of these acts, once again warning that:

> It is high time that the international community, through the appropriate agencies and organizations, adopt prompt and effective measures to put a stop to this return to the law of the jungle.[25]

The influential Cairo newspaper *Al-Ahram,* in an editorial published on the same day, said that the "attack on international civil aviation does not encourage world feelings of solidarity with the Palestine cause." Such disapproving comment was an indication that extreme elements among the Palestinian Arabs did not have the support of the more reasonable elements in the Arab world.

On September 9, still another airliner, a British BOAC jet, was hijacked by Arab guerrillas over Lebanon on a flight from Bombay to London. The guerrillas ordered the plane flown to Amman, where a Swissair DC-8 and a Trans World Boeing 707 were still held with about 180 passengers as hostages. At the United Nations, the news stirred anger and disgust among the delegates—including the Arabs. The Security Council was immediately called into session at 3:30 P.M., and in one of the shortest sessions ever held (seven minutes), the Council called unanimously for the immediate release of all passengers and crews detained as a result of the hijackings.

On September 10, a government spokesman in Cairo criticized the hijacking of airliners. He said, "We don't support hijacking by any side," and condemned the detention by Israel of two Algerians who had been taken from a British airliner on August 14. The two Algerians, both senior ministerial secretaries, were Major Khatib Jalul and Ali Bazuz. They had been taken from the

---

[25] *United Nations Press Release No. SG/SM/1326,* September 7, 1970.

airliner (a BOAC that had landed at Tel Aviv in transit from Hong Kong to London) by Israeli police. Mr. Jalul's wife had been allowed to continue her journey.

The Algerian government asked me to use my good offices for the release of the two passengers, and I made appeals to the Israeli government both orally (on August 17) and in writing (on August 26) to free the two men. I also offered to send a personal representative to Israel to discuss the case of the two detainees. By September 10, I still had received no reply from the Israeli government, although newspaper reports said that the two men would be treated as prisoners of war (since Algeria had maintained a state of war with Israel). Then, a letter from Ambassador Tekoah acknowledged my appeals but defended the arrest of the Algerians (for interrogation) on security grounds.

On September 12, Arab commandos blew up the three hijacked airliners in the Jordanian desert and announced that they were holding forty passengers as prisoners of war. The remaining three hundred persons originally held were released unhurt. On the next day, September 13, Israeli security forces arrested more than 450 Arab residents of occupied areas in the West Bank of the Jordan and of the Gaza Strip in an apparent attempt to apply pressure on the Arab airline hijackers who still detained forty passengers. The Arabs arrested by the Israeli authorities were reported to include business and professional men and eighty women. They were released six days later, on September 18.

In those days, hijacking was the main topic of conversation at the United Nations. At a dinner on September 14 inaugurating the twenty-fifth anniversary of the United Nations Day Program, I suggested some possible solutions to the problem, warning that we must get to the root of the phenomenon and treat its causes with novel remedies, rather than the usual ones to which it is largely immune. I said:

> Within a civilized and orderly society, a criminal act is judged for its criminal character and not for its political significance. In your country, a Democrat does not applaud a robber because he has robbed a Republican and *vice versa*. But internationally, this is exactly what all too frequently happens. One must start from the premise that . . . air transportation is an international activity

which must be placed under an international rule of law. Airplanes are constructed in one country, owned by another and may be insured in a third country. They travel from one country to another, use facilities all over the world, carry passengers of all nationalities and are often piloted by men of many nationalities. I feel that . . . transit passengers should not be detained under any pretext. Hijacking is of course in a totally different category; it is a crime against an international service affecting a diversity of nations, men, women and interests. This crime must be brought before an international tribunal defending the interests of all peoples and nations and not of any particular people or nation.

It may be of help if all Governments pledge themselves to extradite hijackers, irrespective of their nationality or political affiliation, and bring them before an agreed international tribunal. Hijackers should be prosecuted in the name of the peoples of the world, for the benefit of all travelers and all pilots, irrespective of their nationality, and of all nations, irrespective of their political system.[26]

On September 17, heavy fighting erupted in Jordan between Palestinian guerrillas and King Hussein's army. Battles raged furiously in Amman and several Jordanian towns, resulting in thousands of casualties, and on September 20, Syria was reported to have joined the Palestinians. There were unconfirmed reports that Israel would intervene, and a general feeling at the United Nations that a guerrilla victory in Amman would certainly provoke an Israeli attack. Once again, concerted action by the United States and the Soviet Union was the key factor in easing the Jordanian crisis. Moscow exerted discreet pressures on Syria to refrain from intervention in Jordan, while the United States exerted similar pressure on Israel; thus a wider war was averted.

In the midst of the new crisis in Jordan, on September 28, news reached the United Nations that President Nasser had died in Cairo. I was in a meeting of the Political Committee when the news of the Egyptian President's death was conveyed to me by William Powell of the Information Office. I immediately issued a statement conveying to the government and people of the United Arab Republic

---

[26] *United Nations Press Release SG/SM/1333,* September 14, 1970.

. . . my great sorrow at the incalculable loss which they have sustained. As the leader of the Egyptian people and as an outstanding figure in the Middle East and in the world, President Nasser played an historic part in the events of the last two decades in his area.

On the same day, Cairo radio announced that Anwar Sadat, the Vice President, had become the new interim President of the United Arab Republic.

As to the proposed talks between Israel and the Arab states, the official positions of the parties directly concerned were expressed in categorical terms at the General Assembly. Premier Golda Meir, speaking on the morning of October 21, declared that Israel would not return to the peace talks under Mr. Jarring's auspices "until the situation obtaining at the time when the cease-fire went into effect is restored."

Foreign Minister Andrei A. Gromyko of the Soviet Union said on the same day that there should be an immediate resumption of the Jarring talks "without condition," and described the charges of cease-fire violations as "nothing but a fabrication"; he said Israel was blocking the Jarring talks because she wanted to be "rewarded for her aggression."

The four powers nevertheless continued consultations in an attempt to revive the Jarring mission, and on November 4, the General Assembly, by a vote of fifty-seven to sixteen, called for a three-month extension of the cease-fire and for an unconditional resumption of the Arab-Israeli peace talks under the auspices of Mr. Jarring. The resolution was strenuously opposed by Israel and the United States.

It was the Palestinians who emerged strengthened from the Assembly debate, for the winning resolution stated that their rights must be recognized if a lasting peace were to be reached (although it also recognized the territorial integrity of Israel).

This action in the Assembly produced a three-way split among the Big-Four countries: while the United States voted against the resolution, Britain abstained, and the Soviet Union and France voted in favor of it.

Besides splitting the Big Four, the resolution brought a division in Arab ranks. Seven countries—Algeria, Iraq, Kuwait, Saudi

Arabia, Syria, Yemen, and Southern Yemen—refused to take any part in the vote because they felt that the resolution failed to give satisfaction to "the legitimate aspirations" of the Palestinians.

After the balloting, Foreign Minister Mahmoud Riad told the Assembly that he had been instructed to enter into consultations with Mr. Jarring and said his country would "further observe a cease-fire period of three months." (The prevailing truce was scheduled to expire at 5:00 P.M. New York time on November 5.) After the Assembly session, however, Foreign Minister Abba Eban said that the Assembly action had made resumption of the Jarring talks "less likely than before."

Thus, the year 1970 ended without any perceptible progress toward a peaceful settlement of the Middle East problem. The start of 1971 saw one auspicious development. The Israeli government had finally decided (on December 28, 1970) to resume indirect peace talks with the U.A.R. under Mr. Jarring's auspices, after four months of suspension and indecision, and the talks resumed on January 5, 1971. The resumed talks, however, were only to become bogged down once again over Israeli dissatisfaction with an initiative taken by Mr. Jarring. In fact, it was to be Mr. Jarring's last effort for peace.

After gathering proposals from Israel, the U.A.R., and Jordan in January—proposals both he and I agreed contained no new elements—he took the long-awaited initiative on February 8. In identical letters sent to Israel and the U.A.R., Mr. Jarring asked the two governments for simultaneous prior commitments to a comprehensive peace plan. The letters contained the following provisions:

> Israel would give a commitment to withdraw its forces from occupied UAR territory to the former international boundary between Egypt and the British mandate of Palestine, on the understanding that satisfactory arrangements are made for:
> (a) Establishing demilitarized zones.
> (b) Practical security arrangements in the Sharm-el-Sheikh area for guaranteeing freedom of navigation through the Strait of Tiran and
> (c) Freedom of navigation through the Suez Canal.
> The United Arab Republic would give a commitment to enter

into a peace agreement with Israel and to make explicit therein to
Israel—on a reciprocal basis:

(a) Termination of all claims or states of belligerency.

(b) Respect for and acknowledgement of each other's sovereignty, territorial integrity and political independence.

(c) Respect for and acknowledgement of each other's right to
live in peace within secure and recognized boundaries.

(d) Responsibility to do all in their power to insure that acts
of belligerency or hostility do not originate from, or are
not committed from within the respective territories against
the population, citizens or property of the other party and

(e) Noninterference in each other's domestic affairs.

Mr. Jarring received a positive reply from the government of
the United Arab Republic on February 15. It said that "the UAR
will be ready to enter into a peace agreement with Israel containing all the aforementioned obligations as provided for in Security
Council Resolution 242."

Among other undertakings, the U.A.R. committed itself to
ensure "freedom of navigation in the Suez Canal in accordance
with the 1888 Constantinople Convention," together with ensuring
freedom of navigation in the Strait of Tiran. It also accepted "the
stationing of a United Nations peace-keeping force in Sharm-el-
Sheikh and the establishment of demilitarized zones astride the
borders in equal distances."

But Israel's reply to Mr. Jarring's proposal, which he received
on February 26, was essentially negative. Although Israel "viewed
favorably" the U.A.R.'s readiness to enter into a peace agreement
and said it would withdraw "from the Israel-UAR cease-fire line
to the secure, recognized and agreed boundaries to be established
in the peace agreement," the reply concluded: "Israel will not
withdraw to pre-June 5, 1967 lines."

It was clear from the two replies that the U.A.R., for the first
time in twenty-three years, officially committed itself to enter into
a peace agreement with Israel, while Israel explicitly stated that it
would not withdraw to the pre-June 1967 lines. Thus, Mr. Jarring
was faced with a difficult dilemma. He had asked the two governments to make parallel and simultaneous commitments. The
U.A.R. said that it would. Israel said that it would not.

Even before Israel sent the official reply, it was strongly opposed to the way Mr. Jarring had carried out his role in taking this first initiative in three years. On February 12, Israeli deputy premier Yigal Allon criticized Mr. Jarring, saying that "he is neither an obligatory nor an optional arbitrator."[27]

Among the Big Powers, the United States was the first to defend Mr. Jarring. Assistant secretary of state Joseph Sisco, in his remarks made on February 14 on CBS-TV's "Face the Nation," said, "Mr. Jarring is free to take as little or as much initiative as he desires. He has a very broad mandate. . . . and is acting strictly in accordance with that mandate." He then added, "Painful decisions have to be made and it is now time for those decisions."

Secretary of State William P. Rogers, in a television interview on the night of March 9, said explicitly that the United States was prepared to take part militarily in an international peace force, and said that he felt this was a very adequate guarantee for peace. On the next day, the Israeli Embassy in Washington, in an eight-page policy paper, declared that Israel "will resist all pressures, from whatever the source, be they military or political, that aim at resurrecting Israel's past territorial vulnerability."[28]

Mr. Rogers reiterated the U.S. position in the course of a press conference on March 16, saying that "our policy is that the 1967 boundary should be the boundary between Israel and Egypt."[29] He also appealed to Israel to seek security in a satisfactory political agreement with the U.A.R., guaranteed by an international peace-keeping force, rather than in "acquisition of territory."

On the next day, Premier Golda Meir said, "We cannot trust Rogers' offer, even if it is proposed in good faith. There are certain things beyond which our American friends have to realize we will not go."[30]

It was at this point that Mr. Jarring abandoned his effort. Convinced that the negotiations under his auspices between Israel and the U.A.R. would continue to be deadlocked until Israel

---

[27] The New York *Times,* February 13, 1971.
[28] Ibid., March 11, 1971.
[29] *U. S. Department of State Press Release,* March 17, 1971.
[30] The New York *Times,* March 18, 1971.

agreed to formulate a new position on borders, he decided to resume his post as Swedish ambassador to the Soviet Union and left for Moscow on March 25. He assured me that he intended to resume the talks in New York whenever I considered it appropriate to do so. By that time, my principal adviser on Middle Eastern affairs, Ralph Bunche, was in the hospital with a serious kidney ailment, and I relied on Brian Urquhart, who had been working very closely with Mr. Bunche for twenty-five years. Thus, Mr. Jarring's first diplomatic initiative in three years, made on February 8, 1971, was also his last. It was a strange paradox. The United States, the Soviet Union, Britain, and France had encouraged him to go ahead. In fact, his letter was based on the general area of agreement established by the Big Four in their periodic meetings.

The Big Four reiterated their endorsement of Mr. Jarring's initiative at their meeting of June 24, 1971, held at the Park Avenue apartment of the French delegate, Ambassador Jacques Koscziusko-Morizet, who reported to me on the next day. This fact was officially reported to the Security Council on June 14, 1973, at the request of the U.A.R., by my successor, Kurt Waldheim.[31] It was one of the rare occasions in my experience, however, that a formula that was agreed to by the four permanent members of the Security Council did not go through.

During the rest of 1971, diplomatic efforts for a peaceful settlement of the Middle East problem did not make any headway. I was mainly occupied with reports of the UN Relief and Works Agency for Palestine, the question of Jerusalem, the reopening of the Suez Canal, and the problem of Soviet Jews who wanted to leave the Soviet Union.

Laurence Michelmore, and later Sir John Rennie, the high commissioners for UNRWA based in Beirut, stressed in their periodic reports the paucity of funds, the miserable plight of the refugees, and the further displacements of refugees due to measures taken by the Israeli authorities. In August 1971, I received a report from the high commissioner saying that in the Gaza Strip, several refugee homes had been demolished by the Israeli authori-

---

[31] *United Nations Security Council Official Records, No. 1725,* June 14, 1973.

ties; the report requested me to approach the government of Israel in an attempt to stop the destruction, halt the removal of occupants, and provide adequate housing within the Strip for those already displaced. I acted accordingly in compliance with the report. Israel replied that the destruction had been necessary because the overcrowding and congested layout of the refugee quarters invited terror operations. I was assured that no further demolition would take place unless alternative housing was provided.

The question of Jerusalem was perennially hot: the longest meetings of the Security Council during the year concerned that contested city. One such meeting took place on the night of October 25. After six hours of uninterrupted and sometimes dramatic debate, the Council adopted a resolution urgently calling on Israel to take no further steps to change the character of Jerusalem and to rescind all steps she had taken to that effect. Fourteen members of the Council, including the United States and the Soviet Union, voted for the resolution. No country opposed it, though Syria, which advocated tougher language, abstained.

The Council instructed me to obtain Israel's compliance by any means I saw fit to take, including the dispatch of a representative or a mission, and to report back to the Council within sixty days. But Yosef Tekoah, the Israeli delegate, addressed the Council after the vote and clearly declared Israel's intention to ignore the Council's order. Mr. Tekoah said, "The Council's resolution is an order to stifle Jerusalem. Israel's reaction will be the same as the reaction of other governments would be to an order to stifle Washington, Moscow, London or Paris." He clearly indicated that Israel would continue her policy of refusing to give access to the occupied Arab territories to a United Nations mission of enquiry.

George Bush, the United States delegate, said that the eastern part of Jerusalem was regarded by the United States "as occupied territory and therefore subject to the provisions of international law governing the rights and obligations of an occupying power. We regret Israel's failure to acknowledge its obligations under the fourth Geneva Convention. . . ."[32]

---

[32] Ibid., No. 1582, September 25, 1971.

Although I knew that in view of the very firm position of Israel on this issue, I could not act in any way to comply with the order of the Security Council, I tried to do so. I approached several governments that in my view, would be acceptable to Israel as members of a mission to that country. On October 27, I got the formal acceptance of three governments to my invitation to serve on a commission to go to Jerusalem under the terms of the Council resolution. They were Argentina, Italy, and Sierra Leone. All had diplomatic relations with Israel and were considered to have moderate views on the Middle East problem. But Israel refused to permit the three delegates to enter Jerusalem, since it had publicly "ignored" the resolution. I reported to the Council accordingly.

In September and October, Secretary of State William P. Rogers was in constant touch with me (through George Bush) regarding his efforts to open the blocked Suez Canal to international shipping. Mr. Rogers personally visited the area and proposed that Israel withdraw a few miles from the east bank of the Suez Canal and permit a token Egyptian force across the Canal. If the parties agreed, a United Nations emergency force could be interposed between the two. (It will be noted that this was exactly what Secretary of State Henry A. Kissinger proposed in November 1973, and that both Israel and the U.A.R. agreed to his proposal in January 1974. It is a sad commentary on our times that the war of October 1973 was required to effectuate the agreement.)

On October 12 the Israeli government rejected the points advanced by Mr. Rogers as a basis for an agreement. I was informed by the United States that Israel would not approve a withdrawal of Israeli military forces unless the U.A.R. agreed not to send troops across the Canal. Israel would be agreeable to withdraw a few miles, I was told, only if Egyptian civilians would cross the Canal to make arrangements for clearing and operating it.

Regarding the problem of Soviet Jews, Mr. Tekoah had been in touch with me, on a personal and confidential basis, since the middle of 1969. From time to time, he brought with him dozens of signed petitions from Soviet citizens of the Jewish faith who wanted to leave the Soviet Union. When I first mentioned the matter to Yakov Malik, the Soviet delegate, asking if I could use my good offices to facilitate the exit of Soviet Jews from Russia, he told me that it was a very sensitive matter in his country and advised me not to take any action on the petitions. I tried to convince him that I was fully aware of the juridical aspects of the problem, and that it was an internal affair, but that I wanted to pursue the matter on a purely humanitarian basis. He was insistent that I should not take up the matter with him.

I then decided that I would utilize the good offices of my two Russian aides—Leonid N. Kutakov, undersecretary for political and Security Council affairs, and Victor M. Lessiovski, my special assistant—as channels of communication between myself and Moscow. Whenever I received petitions from Mr. Tekoah, I passed them on to one of them for transmission to Moscow. Even my closest colleagues did not know the procedure I was employing, since I felt that complete discretion alone would bear results.

Later in 1971, Mr. Tekoah informed me that out of over eight hundred petitioners, more than four hundred had already arrived in Israel, and he conveyed his government's appreciation to me for my personal efforts to facilitate the exit of those Soviet Jews. It may be recalled that the Soviets had allowed about ten thousand Russian Jews to go to Israel from 1961 through 1970, an average of only a thousand a year. In 1971, according to reliable reports, about five thousand Soviet Jews had arrived in Israel. Mr. Tekoah asked me what methods I had employed in transmitting the petitions to the Soviet government. I told him that I was sorry that I could not disclose the methods.

I mention this matter because the UN had been accused of indifference to the plight of the Soviet Jews. At the time, my office was receiving a continuous flow of criticism and complaints, some of them violent to the point of irrationality, both from indivduals and organzations, accusing the UN of impotence, apathy, or worse. To stem this tide of uninformed abuse, I outlined, in the course of a speech at the Waldorf Astoria Hotel on September 24, 1971, all the actions the UN had undertaken on behalf of the Soviet Jews.[33]

The last action taken by the General Assembly on the Middle East problem before my retirement was on December 13, 1971. On that day, the Assembly overwhelmingly adopted an Afro-

---

[33] *United Nations Press Release SG/SM/1539*, September 24, 1971.

Asian draft resolution once again calling on Israel to withdraw from the Egyptian territory she had occupied since the Six-Day War. One very important feature of the vote was that every European country—East and West—voted for the resolution.

In addition to its call for an Israeli withdrawal, the resolution asked the Secretary General "to reactivate" the Jarring mission that had been stalemated since February 1971, after Mr. Jarring had taken the diplomatic initiative Israel had rejected.

OBSERVATIONS

Dramatic events have taken place in the Middle East since my retirement from the United Nations' service, and I have been following these events with very close interest. But since I had no personal involvement in these developments, they do not legitimately belong to my memoirs. Nevertheless, I have studied various proposals and plans presented by very knowledgeable and well-intentioned people on the nature of the solution to the problem of the Middle East. I would like here to set forth my concluding observations.

At the time of this writing, hopes for progress toward easing tensions between the Arab states and Israel have centered on the strenuous efforts of Secretary of State Henry A. Kissinger. He may succeed. As we have seen, Ambassador Jarring failed in his effort for a breakthrough because the Big-Four powers—the United States, the Soviet Union, the United Kingdom, and France —did not follow up their private endorsement of his initiative with concrete, practical *action*. Mr. Kissinger does not need any such outside endorsement—although up till now, neither London nor Paris have raised any objection to any of his disengagement plans, and there is even some indication that he has the tacit endorsement of the Soviet Union. I pray that Mr. Kissinger's initiative *will* be followed up with practical action.

Disengagement—the physical separation of contending armed forces—is in itself a major step toward achieving a just and peaceful solution. It is only one of the steps, however. Before peace can be achieved in the Middle East, all the provisions of Security Council Resolution 242 must be implemented.

One may very well object that the language of that resolution, in several places, is vague. (To ensure unanimous support in the Security Council, it was deliberately vague.) My answer is that that was true in November 1967, when the resolution was adopted. In the course of the Big-Four private meetings in 1970, however, an agreed interpretation of most of its provisions had emerged. The United States, the Soviet Union, the United Kingdom, and France had agreed, in general terms, on the nature of an Israeli withdrawal, on the character of a peace treaty, and even on the guarantee of borders by the active participation of the Big Powers, including the United States and the Soviet Union. One major problem the Big Four had not discussed was the border between Israel and Syria. Syria, as we have seen had not accepted Resolution 242 and had refused to co-operate with Mr. Jarring. Now the situation has completely changed: Dr. Henry Kissinger is a most welcome guest in Damascus.

The most serious outstanding problem in the Middle East, however, is that Resolution 242 did not deal adequately with a crucial issue—the Palestinian refugees. For over twenty-five years, these refugees—well over a million of them—have had no homeland, no future, and not even a detectable glimmer of hope on their horizon. For over twenty-five years, the United Nations has not found it possible to take any significant step toward a practical and realistic solution of this great and tragic human issue. The General Assembly has found it possible mainly to discuss, each year, arrangements made through UNRWA for the relief of the refugees in their present plight, without touching upon measures that might achieve a fundamental solution for them.

Of all the humanitarian situations with which the United Nations has been concerned, the plight of the Palestinian refugees should arouse the most active compassion of all the governments and peoples of the United Nations, for we are dealing here with nothing less than the twenty-five-year-old tragedy of a group of people who considerably outnumber the whole population of a number of states that are members of the United Nations.

People may differ on the rights and wrongs of the situation in the Middle East, but one thing is certain: the Palestinian refugees are its innocent and long-suffering victims. I believe the tragedy of the refugees, who three times in twenty-five years have known at first hand the cruel blast of war, demands that the international community, through the United Nations, should live up generously to its humanitarian duty toward them.

Certainly the activities of the more militant Palestinians are not only irresponsible and indefensible but also despicable. No political end, however worthy it may seem to its proponents, can justify means such as the hijacking of commercial passenger aircraft, the kidnapping of diplomats, the blowing up of aircraft and buildings, or terrorism and other barbarous acts against civilians, including women and children. Such acts are not only counterproductive, but have resulted in most cases in massive Israeli reprisals, and hence in more innocent civilian deaths and widescale destruction.

It is now time for this most important feature of the Middle East crisis to be tackled in earnest. It is no longer merely with Egypt or Jordan, or Syria or Lebanon, that Israel must make peace, but with the Palestinians, just as Germany had to make peace with the Jews before she could win reacceptance into the Western community.

Israel's current title derives from the decision made by the United Nations in 1947, when it voted—against the vehement opposition of the Arabs—to partition Palestine into Arab and Jewish states. In other words, the United Nations imposed the state of Israel on the area, despite Arab opposition. The following year, Israel conquered considerably more territory than the United Nations decision had awarded. In any case, according to the UN partition plan, the territories proposed for the Arab and Jewish states were so closely woven with each other that the plan would have been workable only between two peoples that were in very friendly and trustful relations with each other. The Arabs rejected the plan at the time. There are clear indications, however, that responsible Arabs now accept not only the existence of Israel but its territorial integrity, political sovereignty, and security. Egypt's reply to Ambassador Jarring (in February 1971) went so far as to declare that it was prepared to sign a peace treaty with Israel. This attitude is shared by Jordan and Lebanon—if Resolution 242 is fully implemented. I have no doubt that Syria, sooner or later, would follow suit.

So, the creation of a Palestinian Arab state will remain the single most difficult problem. In the creation of that state, the Palestinian refugees must have a say. As I have suggested, the UN partition plan of 1947 will not work for the purpose of the creation of a Palestinian Arab state. Several proposals have been made regarding its location, most of them indicating the West Bank of the Jordan River and the Gaza Strip, with a corridor between the two. At the recent conference of Arab heads of state at Algiers, Yasir Arafat, head of the Palestine Liberation Organization, was recognized by the participants as the sole representative of the Palestinian people. It seems logical, therefore, that he should participate in any discussion regarding the formation of a Palestinian Arab state. In my view, it could be done—with a Big-Power guarantee of the frontiers and the actual presence of Big-Power armed forces on the borders. Once this problem is settled, Israel should have an unfettered right to navigation in the Gulf of Aqaba and the Suez Canal.

I cannot conclude my comments on the situation in the Middle East without making reference to the question of Jerusalem. This problem had been of direct concern to me during my term as Secretary General, not only because it is one of the most complex and difficult in the Middle East conflict, but also because both the General Assembly and the Security Council had charged me with reporting any developments that might tend to change the city's legal status. Before my retirement, there were many reports from the press and other sources concerning a master plan prepared by the Israeli authorities for the construction of housing projects in the Jerusalem area, including the sector controlled by Jordan before June 1967, and the area between the armistice demarcation lines. As soon as I heard of those reports, I sought from the government of Israel detailed information of the reported master plan, but the government did not respond to my request. Thus, I had not been able to fulfill the responsibilities placed upon me by the General Assembly and the Security Council.

At the present moment, international public opinion is focused on two issues regarding the Arab-Israel conflict: that of

Soviet Jewry, a preoccupation of one side, and that of the Palestinian refugees, a preoccupation of the other side. I would like to conclude this chapter with my answer to a question that was asked on this subject at my last press conference, on September 14, 1971:

> In an ideal society, everybody should have the right to leave the country in which he or she does not want to live. At the same time, everybody in an ideal society should have the right to return to his or her own country. That is the essence of the Declaration of Human Rights, which was adopted by the General Assembly in 1948. . . . Therefore, in an ideal society, as I said a moment ago, I think that those Soviet citizens of Jewish faith in the Soviet Union who want to leave the Soviet Union should be permitted to leave, and at the same time, Palestinian refugees who have been refugees for more than twenty years should be permitted to return to their own homes. So there are two aspects to this problem, in terms of the Declaration of Human Rights. But our society is far from ideal, and so we have to keep on trying to fashion the kind of society we want. Only then, of course, shall we be able to implement the Declaration of Human Rights, which, as you all know, is just a declaration and is not mandatory.[34]

---

[34] *United Nations Press Release SF/SM/1530,* September 14, 1971.

PART V

SPHERES
OF
INFLUENCE

CHAPTER XV

THE DOMINICAN CRISIS

INTRODUCTION

One harsh fact of the postwar era was the re-emergence of "spheres of influence" in international politics. The United States staked out its area of special interest with a series of mutual security treaties covering Western Europe, Latin America, South Asia, Southeast Asia, Japan, and South Korea. The Soviet Union, in turn, formed a close-knit Warsaw Pact, which in fact developed into a sphere of dominance.

The ruling circles in Moscow have consistently suppressed all forces of dissent inside the Soviet bloc, while, in the same way, Washington has resisted the introduction into its sphere of any form of political or social system foreign to its own—not only in the Western Hemisphere but also in many other parts of the world.

A close study of postwar developments reveals one indisputable fact: there is an unwritten agreement between Washington and Moscow to respect these vital spheres of interest. In periods of crisis, when Moscow felt that its most vital interests were threatened and as a consequence took prompt and drastic action, the fear of nuclear war has stayed Washington's hand. Similarly, when Washington felt that its security was threatened and took prompt and drastic action, the same fear has given pause to Moscow. The threat, or even the doubtful prospect, of a communist takeover anywhere in the American sphere has usually provoked Washington as much as the threat of a drift away from traditional communist orthodoxy, in its sphere, has provoked Moscow.

This enforced but unwritten agreement between the two

superpowers to respect a line of demarcation beyond which neither of the two dare apply its power is the principal cause of the
impotence of the United Nations in the performance of its primary
function—to preserve peace. For Washington and Moscow—
when their spheres of influence are involved—the United Nations
is decidedly not the agency for maintaining international peace
and security. The Dominican crisis of 1965 and the invasion of
Czechoslovakia in 1968 not only bear out the truth of that unwritten rule, but also bear witness to the profound stirrings for freedom and independence that challenge the two giants within their
realms of influence.

THE CRISIS

There were many occasions in which I had to cancel projected
official visits to member states or interrupt a tour and return to
New York to attend to emergency situations. One such interruption took place on Sunday, May 2, 1965, when the Security
Council was urgently summoned into session to discuss the
crisis in the Dominican Republic that had suddenly erupted a few
days earlier.

After attending meetings of the heads of UN specialized
agencies in Vienna, late in April, I flew to Zurich on Friday, April
30. I was en route to Geneva, where I was scheduled to address
the World Veterans Federation, and had several other engagements, including a meeting with the Foreign Minister of Switzerland. Pierre Spinelli, director of the European office of the
United Nations, met me at Zurich airport and showed me an urgent message from headquarters: the United States government
had informed the Security Council that on April 28, President
Johnson had ordered United States troops ashore in the Dominican Republic "to protect the lives of American citizens" there and
to escort them to safety. The message also said that President
Johnson had requested the Council of the Organization of American States (OAS) to consider the situation in the Dominican
Republic.

As soon as I arrived in Geneva from Zurich, I spoke on the

phone with José Rolz-Bennett, undersecretary for special political affairs. He advised me that the situation was critical, and that the Council of the OAS was considering the U.S. request. I then decided to cancel all engagements in Geneva and return to New York in time for the Security Council meeting (requested by the Soviet Union) scheduled for May 3. I left Geneva on the afternoon of Sunday, May 2. On arrival at Kennedy International Airport in New York, in reply to questions put to me by the press, I said that the situation in the Dominican Republic looked serious. I added that the Security Council had primary responsibility for the maintenance of international peace and security, although I expressed the hope that the OAS could play a useful role.

To understand these developments, something of the historical background of the Dominican Republic should be considered. Beginning in 1822, the history of the country was marked by revolutions and external attacks. Several presidents were overthrown and, in 1916, after the landing of American marines, a United States military government was established. On July 12, 1924, sovereignty was restored to the country. In 1930, Rafael Leonides Trujillo Molina was elected President and remained the controlling factor in Dominican political life until his assassination on May 30, 1961. Under his authoritarian regime, the Dominican Republic achieved some economic progress and administrative stability; but Trujillo suppressed fundamental human rights and exercised a ruthless rule that brooked no internal opposition. At the outbreak of World War II, the Dominican Republic declared war on the Axis powers, rather an empty gesture, and in 1945 became a member of the United Nations.

The assassination of Generalissimo Trujillo initiated a new period of political activity in the Dominican Republic. While President Joaquín Balaguer continued his tenure as head of state, the real governmental power was assumed by Lieutenant General Rafael Trujillo, Jr., who became chief of the combined general staff. All but two of the eight participants in the assassination plot against the dictator were hunted down and killed. Most of the numerous political exiles were prevented from returning to the country, and democratic freedoms continued to be violated.

Meanwhile, however, the underground political movements

that had developed during the Trujillo era began to emerge in the Dominican political scene. Opposition to the Balaguer regime centered mostly on the mildly leftist Dominican Revolutionary Party, headed by Professor Juan Bosch—a poet, historian, and novelist, as well as a political leader, who had long been in exile.

President Balaguer was trying, on the one hand, to prevent another military dictatorship, and on the other, to bar the emergence to power of a popular government with Castroist leanings. But he was frustrated by economic problems, strikes, and street demonstrations. In the face of mounting political unrest, President Balaguer resigned. In December 1962, Professor Bosch was elected President, and on February 27, 1963, inaugurated a constitutional regime.

The Bosch Administration, however, was marked by plots engineered by the military and businessmen who yearned for the privileges they had enjoyed during the Trujillo era and its Balaguer aftermath. President Bosch also found himself under a crossfire from rightist circles, which accused him of Castroist leanings, and the extreme left, which tried to push him into implementing radical socialist reforms. United States pressures were also exercised against Bosch for his vigorous initiatives concerning agrarian reform, as well as for his support of the principle of nonintervention and his reluctance to take any measures against revolutionary Cuba and Cuba's increasing number of sympathizers in the Dominican Republic. Administrative inefficiency was also in evidence, unemployment increased, and a certain degree of popular discontent arose.

On September 25, 1963, after less than seven months in office, President Bosch was overthrown by a military coup headed by General Elías Wessin y Wessin, an air force officer. Evidently one of the reasons for the coup was the attempted deglorification of the military by the Bosch Administration. The military junta declared that the country's problems could not be solved by constitutional means, annulled the Bosch constitution of May 1963, dismissed the National Congress, and installed a civilian triumvirate under Emilio de los Santos. Although foreign reaction to the coup was initially adverse, the United Kingdom recognized the new government in October 1963; this led to recognition by nine other European states and, in December, by the United States.

Changes soon took place in the composition of the Dominican triumvirate: in December, Emilio de los Santos was replaced by Foreign Minister Donald Reid Cabral, who promptly assumed a firm command of the military-supported government.

The Cabral regime, in turn, was marked by widespread popular unrest. Guerrilla warfare increased. Exiled President Bosch, in a comment made in June from Puerto Rico, predicted that there would be "a revolution soon because of . . . corruption in political and military ranks." The Dominican Revolutionary Party called for a "return to constitutionalism without elections"—an objective that appealed not only to supporters of the party but also to a faction of the armed forces. Thus, Bosch became a symbol of democratic hope for change in the country.

On April 24, 1965, a countrywide uprising started, and Dr. José Rafael Molina was installed as Provisional President. But while the rebellion quickly achieved the overthrow of Cabral's regime, it also resulted in a state of civil war that gave rise to serious international repercussions and concern throughout the world.

For only one day after the revolution had started, a divergence of views developed among the rebels. The aim of one faction of army rebels, massively supported by the Democratic Revolutionary Party, was the immediate return of President Bosch. This was firmly opposed by a rightist faction of the armed forces, under the leadership of General Wessin y Wessin, which again wanted to set up a military junta.

While discussions between the two factions were in progress, fighting broke out. It was the escalation of the fighting and the apparent triumph of the leftist rebels that eventually involved the United States. Anti-Wessin (leftist) officers distributed weapons to the people of Santo Domingo, and street mobs took control of the capital city, including its radio station. Several tanks were captured, and Ozama Fortress, an army barracks with more weapons, was seized.

Meanwhile, the national palace and other rebel strongholds were strafed by the air force. The number of dead and wounded in these actions was reported to be in the thousands. President Bosch later accused United States Embassy officials of having ordered this bombing attack to put down the rebellion. After a cease-fire (under the sponsorship of the Papal Nuncio) had provisionally been agreed to on April 30, the rebels appeared to be in control of the central sectors of Santo Domingo, while the opposing forces under General Wessin y Wessin had their headquarters at the vast San Isidro air base, a few miles east of Santo Domingo.

But on April 28, a most important and dramatic event had taken place: United States forces under orders from President Johnson landed in the Dominican Republic. The reason initially given for the armed intervention was the need to protect American lives and property. Later on, as the initial contingents of five hundred marines were built up into a force of several thousand U.S. marines and airborne troops, President Johnson, in formal television statements made on April 30 and May 2, acknowledged American fears that the Dominican Republic might become another Cuba. He said that a total of 14,000 United States troops had been committed in the Dominican Republic to protect American and other foreign residents as well as to "prevent another communist state in this Hemisphere." What had started as a "popular democratic revolution" had been seized by a "band of communist conspirators," according to President Johnson. He appealed to noncommunist rebels to give up their arms and urged all the American nations to support the United States in the defense of "common principles."

In an interview given in Puerto Rico over a United States televison network on May 2, former President Bosch showed great surprise at the charges that communists had taken over control of the Dominican revolt. He said that the Dominican rebellion had been successful until the United States had intervened and changed the situation. Only another twenty-four hours, he added, would have been necessary for the Dominican people to have solved their problems alone. It was reported that United States troops in Santo Domingo became identified with the hard-line, right-wing military elements who opposed the popular demands for the return of President Bosch. Incidents of fire exchanged between the rebel forces and U.S. troops occurred quite often, even after the formal cease-fire agreement had been signed on April 30.

The independent mass media in the United States became increasingly critical of Washington's policies and actions. The New York *Times* of May 21, 1965, said in an editorial:

> The dominating factor which triggered massive American intervention was the fear and threat of a Communist takeover. Had there been a "clear and present danger," the White House reaction would have been understandable. . . . However, there are grave doubts that the threat was nearly so genuine as Washington was so prone to believe.
>
> Linked to the automatic policy of anti-Communism was one expressed by Under Secretary Mann in an interview with the *Times*. United States actions in the Dominican Republic, he said, "are for the purpose of helping to preserve for the people of their nation their right to choose their own government free of outside interference."
>
> But this is exactly what the Dominicans have not been allowed to do. From the beginning, the actions, as well as the effect, of the American intervention were to oppose the pro-Bosch faction and to favor, even militarily, the right-wing junta.
>
> Inferences to be drawn from this Dominican venture are disturbing, so far as they relate to the Caribbean policy of the United States. Every time there is a revolution in Latin America, the Communists will naturally take advantage of it. Is the United States as inevitably to join forces with the governing classes or with those rightist elements who merely announce they are anti-Communist?
>
> The United States had indubitably strengthened Latin-American Communism by its actions. The Dominican Communists are not being killed in Santo Domingo; they have gone underground, or up in the mountains. The democrats, the liberals, the constitutionalists are being killed by troops of a military junta which the United States in effect set up and certainly helped. If this lesson has not been learned, there is reason to despair for the Inter-American System.

On May 3, the day the Security Council met at the United Nations, it was announced that Colonel Francisco Caamaño

Deno, active leader of the rebel forces, had been elected as the country's "Constitutional President" by the reconvened National Congress, and that President Bosch had given up all his rights so that the Congress would be free to elect him. Upon taking the oath as President, Colonel Caamaño declared that he did not want "a direct conflict with North Americans," but he accused the U.S. troops and those of General Wessin of violating the cease-fire. Asked about U.S. government charges regarding the supposed key leadership of communists in the rebel movement, Colonel Caamaño ridiculed the idea, saying that it was impossible that some fifty-odd persons could dominate the whole Dominican nation, which was in arms and demanding the return to constitutionality.

On May 7, a new military-civilian junta headed by General Imbert Barreras was set up. General Imbert asked the OAS to keep an armed force in the Dominican Republic to help maintain peace and charged that the rebel government was communist dominated. The rebel government termed the formation of the civilian-military junta a violation of the cease-fire agreement. They also charged that, through this junta, the United States appeared to be committed to the destruction of the rebel movement. From Puerto Rico, Professor Bosch declared (also on May 7) that he would keep on supporting the Caamaño government, and repeated his determination not to go back to Santo Domingo. He added: "This was a democratic revolution smashed by the leading democracy of the world, the United States. This is why I think my time is over. I belong to a world that has ended politically."

From the very beginning of the Dominican revolt, the implications of President Johnson's actions were never in doubt—that the U.S. sphere of influence should be recognized and accepted. The invasion represented the bold reaffirmation of the Monroe Doctrine. Although Cuba had survived that doctrine, Washington would not permit any other Latin-American or Caribbean country to disturb its political hegemony in the Western Hemisphere.

After the landing of the U.S. troops in the Dominican Republic on April 28, Washington tried very hard to provide a respectable international flag for its forces. By May 6, while the United Nations Security Council was still in session, the United States had succeeded in wrenching from the OAS ambassadors in

Washington an agreement "in principle" to the formation of an Inter-American Peace Force (IAPF). (In this connection, it is worth mentioning that a similar agreement was reached among the Soviet Union, Poland, Hungary, Bulgaria, and East Germany to invade Czechoslovakia in August 1968, with the unconcealed objective of preserving the Soviet Union's sphere of influence. Romania was the only one of the Warsaw Pact countries that refused to participate in this overt aggression.)

The OAS resolution creating IAPF was adopted by a bare majority (two thirds), with fourteen votes in favor, five against (Chile, Ecuador, Mexico, Peru, and Uruguay) and one abstention (Venezuela), which gave an indication of the difficulties that had to be overcome to round up sufficient support for the OAS decision.

In reality, U.S. intervention was severely criticized, both by members of the OAS and by many Latin-American delegates at the UN, especially the representatives of Uruguay and Mexico, who maintained that the United States had directly violated the two articles at the heart of the OAS Charter: the absolute, unconditional bans on intervention by members in one another's affairs, and on occupation of one member's territory by another.

As to the inter-American armed force, only three Central American states—Costa Rica, Honduras, and Nicaragua—had initially agreed to send contingents (which numbered not more than five hundred soldiers who were transported to Dominican territory aboard United States planes). The backbone of the inter-American force in the Dominican Republic was the U.S. 82nd Airborne Division. The United States contributed 22,000 troops to the force at its peak. Latin-American contingents consisted of 21 policemen from Costa Rica, and about 1,600 troops from Brazil, Honduras, and Nicaragua. Thus (as in the Cuba crisis), the United States seemed to have achieved its long-held objective of transforming the OAS into an effective instrument of U.S. policy in Latin America.

The Economist of London, a traditional supporter of U.S. foreign and domestic policies, wrote in its issue of May 29, 1965: ,

> Now that the principle of armed intervention has been established and the shock and outrage gulped down somehow by the Organization of American States, will it be easier for President

Johnson to intervene again, especially if invited in by the government in power? Or are the frustrations of the Dominican entanglement going to discourage the Americans from risking this sort of thing again?

Among the many adverse reactions of political leaders throughout the world, a statement of special significance was made by President de Gaulle of France, who on May 6 criticized the U.S. intervention in Dominican affairs, called for the withdrawal of American troops from that country, and disclosed that France was considering the recognition of Colonel Caamaño's rebel government. Another open criticism of the U.S. action was made at a NATO meeting in London by the Foreign Minister of Norway, Halvard Lange. In response to these criticisms, the U.S. government made public a list of fifty-four "communist and Castroist" leaders who were supposed to have seized control of the rebellion in the Dominican Republic.

Meanwhile, there were widespread reports of illegal arrests, torture, and mass murders in the country. Drew Pearson, in his widely syndicated column of August 13, 1965, had this to say (and there was no subsequent denial from any quarter):

> A gruesome report on Dominican atrocities committed by the government of Gen. Antonio Imbert, U.S. appointed dictator of the Dominican military government, has just been submitted to the Organization of American States. So far it is confidential, but this column has obtained a copy and is able to reveal its shocking contents.
>
> The report shows how the Imbert administration systematically arrested civilians for political reasons, then in transporting them from one jail to another after dark, lined them up and shot them.
>
> Following rumors of these atrocities, the O.A.S. selected a commission of three distinguished criminologists which went to the Dominican Republic, dug up some of the bodies and arrived at the inescapable conclusion that there had been mass murders and that most of the population had been too terrorized to testify. The commission was not able to arrive at the number killed, though one prison, under Gen. Imbert's supervision, once containing 3,000, now has been reduced to 500.
>
> Gen. Imbert was picked by the American Embassy to head the

military junta immediately after the landing of American marines. He has been kept in power only by the marines and by U.S. aid which has been funneled into Santo Domingo to the extent of millions of dollars in food, medicine and actual cash.

When the Security Council began consideration of the situation in the Dominican Republic on May 3, the Soviet representative, Nikolay Fedorenko, urged that the Council condemn the intervention of the United States in the internal affairs of that country as a violation of the UN Charter, and demanded the immediate withdrawal of the U.S. armed forces from Dominican territory. Ambassador Adlai Stevenson, with obvious discomfort at having to defend the intervention, said that the problem was a regional one, and that the OAS should continue to deal with it. He said that the United States would withdraw its troops from the Dominican Republic as soon as the OAS drew up a plan for peace and security in that country.

The Soviet resolution, along with one submitted by Uruguay, failed to get the necessary support in the Council. After a prolonged and bitter debate, especially between the representatives of the Soviet Union and the United States, a new resolution was submitted jointly by the Ivory Coast, Jordan, and Malaysia, and it was unanimously adopted by the Council on May 14. It called for a strict cease-fire and invited the Secretary General to send a representative to the Dominican Republic for the purpose of reporting to the Council on the situation; it also called upon all concerned in the Dominican Republic to co-operate with the representative of the Secretary General in his task.

On the day the Security Council adopted the resolution, I sent an advance party to the Dominican Republic; the party was led by my military adviser, General Indar Jit Rikhye. At the same time, I appointed Mr. José A. Mayobre, executive secretary of the Economic Commission for Latin American, as my representative there; Mr. Mayobre had a record of distinguished service both to his country (Venezuela) and to the United Nations.

When Mr. Mayobre arrived in Santo Domingo on May 17, fighting between the contending parties had flared up, despite a cease-fire agreement that had been effected on May 5 under the auspices of the OAS. On May 21, Mr. Mayobre reported to me that negotiations with the leaders of the two factions for the suspension of hostilities had been successfully concluded, and three days later, he reported that, except for minor incidents, the cease-fire was effective.

Meanwhile, attempts were made in the Security Council by several members (led by France, Jordan, and Uruguay) to enlarge the size of the United Nations team in the Dominican Republic and to strengthen its mandate. These moves received wide support on both sides of the Atlantic. Richard Dudman, a recognized authority on Latin-American affairs, observed in *The New Republic* of June 5, 1965:

> It was the United Nations in the person of José Antonio Mayobre that achieved the first real cease-fire. In entering the picture, the U.N. filled a vacuum left by the ineptness and incompetence of the O.A.S. There is some irony in the situation. The United States intervened because the O.A.S. would have been too slow to act against the Communist threat. The United States then relied on the O.A.S. to make the intervention legal. The O.A.S. stalled and played favourites, largely ignoring Caamaño and dealing with Imbert. The United Nations stepped in, and the Dominican affair became a world rather than a hemispheric problem.

The attempts in the Security Council to give more teeth to the United Nations in the Dominican crisis had a mixed reception in the United States. While national newspapers, including the New York *Times,* welcomed the move, traditional opponents of the United Nations came out against any involvement in this crisis by the World Organization.

Senator Thomas J. Dodd of Connecticut said that the UN mission had done "grave harm" and would have an "unsettling effect." He claimed that it was in competition with the OAS mission and was biased in favor of the Caamaño rebel forces. (It may be recalled that Senator Dodd had been a bitter foe of the United Nations in the Congo.)

After July, there were no further Security Council meetings on the Dominican question. The following year brought the signing of an Act of Reconciliation by the contending factions, the establishment of a provisional government headed by Dr. Héctor

García-Godoy, and, finally, the preparation for a national election on June 1, 1966.

Following the national election—and with the installation on July 1, 1966, of the newly elected government of Joaquín Balaguer and the withdrawal from the Dominican Republic on September 21 of the Inter-American Peace Force—the United Nations mission ended its activities and was withdrawn from the Dominican Republic on October 22, 1966.

It bears mentioning that this was the first time a United Nations peace mission found itself side by side with a regional organization operating in the same country and dealing with the same matters.

The United Nations Charter recognizes the positive value of regional organizations. In Article 52, it recognizes the right of member states to establish regional organizations for dealing with local disputes and other matters relating to the maintenance of international peace and security—provided that those matters are, indeed, appropriate for regional action and that the action itself is consistent with the purposes of the UN. But the same article stipulates that its provisions in no way impair Articles 34 and 35, which give the Security Council the right to investigate any dispute and any member the right to bring a dispute before the Council or the General Assembly. Thus, the Charter encourages the peaceful settlement of local disputes through regional organizations, provided that the primacy and overriding responsibility of the United Nations for international security is fully respected.

In the Dominican crisis, the primacy and overriding responsibility of the United Nations was not acknowledged, much less respected, by the United States. Washington used the OAS as an instrument of its policy in the same way that Moscow used the Warsaw Pact in its invasion of Czechoslovakia three years later. As Ambassador Velazquez of Uruguay had clearly stated, the Charter of the OAS bans the intervention by members in one another's affairs in absolute and unconditional terms. This was exactly what Washington did in the name of the OAS. In the name of hemispheric security, fourteen countries of Latin America were corralled by the United States into the sad farce of giving retroactive legality to the invasion of the Dominican Republic. The

United Nations could play only a marginal role in the crisis—observing and reporting—because Washington wanted it thus far and no further. By arrogating to itself the right to intervene in the affairs of other states, the United States not only ignored the existence of the United Nations, but did precisely what President Johnson accused Russia and China of wanting to do: impose a political regime by force of arms.

One peculiar characteristic of the Dominican episode was the complete reversal of Big-Power attitudes toward the United Nations. The Soviet Union and France, which were very critical of UN activities *in the Congo,* were advocating increased UN participation *in the Dominican Republic,* but were opposed to any OAS involvement in maintaining peace and security. On the other hand, the United States, which had consistently supported UN actions in the Congo, was now bitterly opposed to any United Nations action in the Dominican Republic. Secretary of State Dean Rusk told me that his country would never *permit* UN involvement in the Dominican crisis. Washington was not very happy when most members of the Security Council agreed to authorize the Secretary General to send a small observer mission to that country.

Big-Power attitudes toward the UN role in the Dominican Republic were amusingly summarized by Ambassador Arsene Usher of the Ivory Coast in the course of a debate in the Security Council on May 24, 1965:

> When there was a dispute between two small powers, the dispute eventually disappeared.
> If there was a dispute between a small power and a great power, the small power disappeared.
> And if there was a dispute between two great powers, the Security Council disappeared.

During the Dominican crisis, the Security Council did not disappear, in spite of the bitter dispute between the great powers. Relations between the United Nations and the Organization of American States (under the leadership of the United States) became strained, however. After I sent Mr. Mayobre as my representative to the Dominican Republic on the basis of the Council resolution of May 14, 1965, the OAS decided (on May 20) to send its able Secretary General, Dr. José A. Mora, to that country as the special representative of the inter-American organization. Throughout the crisis, Dr. Mora worked very closely with me, but his relations with Mr. Mayobre became increasingly strained. Mr. Mayobre was convinced that the United Nations should play an effective role in the Dominican crisis, while Dr. Mora felt that the Organization of American States had the only legitimate machinery. Both men are strong-willed, and a clash of personalities ensued.

Washington became increasingly critical of Mr. Mayobre's action. This mood was clearly brought to light on June 25, 1965, when I saw President Johnson at the Opera House in San Francisco on the occasion of the twentieth anniversary celebration of the United Nations. The President reached San Francisco that morning, and he looked very solemn when he arrived at the Opera House after encountering violent antiwar demonstrations on the street. He addressed the gathering at 11:00 A.M. Immediately after his speech, he said that he wanted to talk to me. Led by Governor Pat Brown (of California), the President, his daughter Lynda Bird Johnson, Ambassador Stevenson, and I walked to a small dressing room adjoining the hall. At the door, the President told Stevenson (to the latter's utter surprise) that he wanted to talk to me alone. Stevenson stayed outside with Governor Brown, Ralph Bunche, and others while inside, the President, Miss Johnson, and I took seats on sofas. Someone outside closed the door.

I began the conversation with an expression of thanks for his participation in the celebrations. Although the sixty-minute meeting was mainly concerned with the Vietnam war, the President opened it with remarks on the Dominican crisis. He bluntly said that both Mayobre and Caesar Ortíz-Tinoco (an information officer) were anti-American. I told the President that I did not believe so, and that they were just trying their best to be objective; he did not agree. I reminded the President that Caesar Ortíz was once his pupil in Texas, and to my knowledge always spoke of him with esteem and respect. The President still refused to agree. He said that it was true that Caesar Ortíz was his pupil when he was a teacher in Texas; yet he insisted that the reports he had received from the Dominican Republic "made it clear that he is anti-American."

The President was one of the most complicated and mercurial men in public life. He was at the same time genial and ill tempered, charming and arrogant, friendly and pompous. I am not a good judge of his domestic policies, of which the most laudatory compliments have been uttered and written by knowledgeable people. He was, however, incapable of comprehending the international currents and crosscurrents that the head of the most powerful country in the world should comprehend.

CHAPTER XVI

THE INVASION
OF CZECHOSLOVAKIA

It was Saturday, September 1, 1962, and the sun was shining brightly over historic Prague Castle, where I was received by Antonín Novotný, President of Czechoslovakia. After talks on the prospects for peaceful coexistence and, inevitably, the Congo, I was driven to Czyernin Palace, a huge stone mansion away from everything and everybody. From my living room window, I could not see a single soul; I wondered whether all state guests were accommodated in the same isolated mansion, and thought of the legendary monasteries and temples of Burma, a thousand years before, in which monks and hermits were said to have meditated and led lives of recluses, away from the mundane world.

After a luncheon given by Mr. Martinic, President of the Society for International Relations, I visited Charles University, traditionally one of the greatest seats of learning in Europe. In a most solemn and impressive ceremony, I was presented by the Rector, Jaraslav Procházka, with a medal commemorating the six-hundredth anniversary of the University's foundation. The Rector made a speech welcoming me and explaining his country's program of technical assistance to developing countries, as well as its participation in United Nations technical assistance activities. In conclusion, the Rector said, "Fulfillment of all these tasks requires the maintenance of peace and security, a task in which the United

Nations should play a more active role than it has so far."
Ironically, the United Nations could not play any active role in the
tragic events that took place in Czechoslovakia six years later.

Since that visit, I had received almost every year invitations
from the Czechoslovak government to visit the country again
whenever convenient. On April 26, 1968, Ambassador Milan
Klusak, permanent representative of Czechoslovakia to the United
Nations, conveyed to me the official invitation sent by his Foreign
Minister, Dr. Jiri Hájek, to visit Czechoslovakia in the course of
that year to confer with Czechoslovak leaders and to receive an
honorary degree from Charles University. I accepted the invitation and decided to link the visit to Prague with my projected
visits to Vienna and Geneva. After discussions with the governments concerned, tentative flight schedules were made to leave
New York by Air India on the night of Thursday, August 22, direct to Prague with one short stop in London.

On the day the tentative flight schedule was made (but not
announced), a dramatic event took place at the United Nations.
At that day's press briefing by my spokesman William Powell
(press briefings took place every day at 12:00 noon), Dr. Karel
Kral of the Czechoslovak press agency (which was sponsored by
the government of Czechoslovakia), asked a most unusual question. In effect, he asked whether the Secretary General of the
United Nations could reconcile reported Soviet "pressures" on
Czechoslovakia with a UN resolution, adopted three years earlier
and sponsored by the Soviet Union, barring intervention in the internal affairs of other states. Just before the briefing, Bill Powell
had had a hint that such a question was coming up and had
sought my guidance. Since I had no official information of such
Soviet pressures on Czechoslovakia, I told him to reply simply
that I did not wish to make any comment at present. He answered
Dr. Kral accordingly.

What made his question very dramatic was the fact that a
Czechoslovak government-sponsored correspondent had the courage to publicly ask a question highly critical of alleged "pressures"
exerted by the Soviet Union on Czechoslovakia. Was the question
put under the directive of his government or that of the Czechoslovak ambassador, Mr. Milan Klusak? And was it true that the

Soviet Union was putting pressure on the government of Czechoslovakia under Alexander Dubček? For several months, newspapers had been reporting that Dubček and his colleagues were initiating a series of internal reforms and liberal policies, thus incurring the suspicion and displeasure of the Kremlin leaders. There were also reports that Dubček had invited President Tito of Yugoslavia and Party Leader Nicolae Ceauşescu of Romania to visit Prague to demonstrate their solidarity with the Czechoslovak leaders. The reports also said that the Soviet leaders had meanwhile met in Warsaw with their counterparts from Poland, Hungary, Bulgaria, and East Germany, and that after the meeting, Leonid I. Brezhnev, general secretary of the Soviet Communist Party, had demanded that Alexander Dubček, first secretary of the Czechoslovak party, agree to a meeting on July 19 between the entire ruling bodies of both parties.

On Saturday, July 20, I saw Ambassador Klusak, who said that Dr. Kral's question on the previous day was posed without the knowledge or consent of the Czechoslovak mission. He entirely dissociated himself from the implications of the question and assured me that the situation in his country was in no way likely to disturb international peace and security.

Dr. Kral's question nevertheless caused extraordinary interest among correspondents, although no permanent representative brought up the question of "Soviet pressure" on Czechoslovakia to me even privately in the course of conversations. The fact that there was a serious rift among Czechoslovak nationals in New York was clearly revealed on July 28, when a liberal Czechoslovak weekly in Prague, the *Reporter,* published an article (signed "X.Y.") highly critical of the Czechoslovak mission to the United Nations. It was the first time in my memory that a government-sponsored journal, published in the capital of a member state, openly criticized its own permanent mission accredited to the United Nations. The article accused the Czechoslovak mission in New York of "stereotyped diplomacy," and, in effect, of abetting the campaign against the liberal government under Dubček. By the time this article appeared, Ambassador Klusak had left New York for Prague, and the Czechoslovak mission to the United Nations was run by Jan Muzik, deputy permanent representative.

After the departure of Klusak from New York, news from Czechoslovakia continued to hit the headlines. On July 29, virtually the entire ruling bodies of the Soviet and Czechoslovak Communist parties met in Cierna, Czechoslovakia, a border town close to the Soviet Union. On the Soviet side, nine of the eleven members of the Soviet Politburo, including the party chief, Leonid I. Brezhnev, Premier Alexei Kosygin, and President Nikolay V. Podgorny attended the meeting. All sixteen members of the Czechoslovak Politburo, led by party chief Alexander Dubček, received the Soviet team in a small building that had been a social club for railroad workers. The primary purpose of the Soviet leaders in asking for the meeting was to ask the Czechoslovak leaders to impose necessary controls on the Czechoslovak press and radio, which, in their opinion, was "too free and independent." It was also reported that the Soviet leaders wanted the stationing of Warsaw Pact[1] troops on the West German frontier.

On Thursday, August 1, Tass, the Soviet press agency, issued the text of the joint communiqué, and a copy was sent to me on the same day by the Soviet mission. The communiqué referred to "a broad comradely exchange of opinion on questions interesting both sides," and "an atmosphere of complete frankness, sincerity and mutual understanding."

From the first week of August, Mr. Muzik (who was still in charge of the Czechoslovak mission) used to see me almost every day. He kept me posted on developments in his country, stressing that the winds of change were sweeping all over Czechoslovakia, bringing, among other things, a free Czechoslovak press; "free radio stations," according to him, were mushrooming all over the country. From time to time, he brought with him the texts of statements by party chief Dubček and President Svoboda (the father-in-law of Ambassador Klusak, who had left his United Nations assignment in July). Before he left New York, Mr. Klusak told me that he would probably be assigned to his Foreign Office.

Early in the morning of Tuesday, August 20, I heard on the radio that the Soviet Union and other Warsaw Pact countries had

---

[1] The Soviet Union, Poland, Czechoslovakia, Romania, Bulgaria, and the German Democratic Republic.

massed their troops across the Czechoslovak borders and that an invasion was imminent. I immediately phoned to ask Mr. Muzik and Soviet Ambassador Yakov Malik to see me at my office. Mr. Muzik said that he had no official communication from his government; he had heard the news on the radio that morning. His Foreign Minister, he said, was vacationing in Yugoslavia and he had been trying to contact him the whole morning without success. When I asked what I could and should do in the circumstances, he said that he was unable to offer any advice in the absence of a specific directive from his government. I asked him whether I should go ahead with my planned visit to Prague on August 23. He said that he would try to get instructions from Foreign Minister Hájek, who had officially issued the invitation, and would convey to me any communication he might receive.

Ambassador Malik saw me immediately after Muzik had left. He also had no official word from Moscow and had heard the news of massing of the troops only from the radio. I was convinced that he was not hiding anything from me. I had learned to take Mr. Malik's word in private conversation, as I learned to do in my dealings with Ambassador Goldberg of the United States, Ambassador Roger Seydoux of France, and Lord Caradon of the United Kingdom. All these four seemed to have such confidence in me that I do not remember one single instance in which I doubted their honesty in their dealings with me. I requested Mr. Malik to convey my deepest concern to his government about the impending storm. He agreed to do so.

After Malik left, I had a private meeting with the three undersecretaries, Ralph Bunche, José Rolz-Bennett, and C. V. Narasimhan, to discuss the situation in Czechoslovakia and my planned trip to Europe. Since the Soviet Union was directly involved in the conflict, I did not invite Leonid Kutakov, the Soviet undersecretary general. (For similar reasons, I did not consult Ralph Bunche on the Cuban missile crisis and C. V. Narasimhan on the Indo-Pakistani conflict, although both of them were true international civil servants.) All three felt that there was nothing the Secretary General could do, since the country directly involved—Czechoslovakia—did not seek any United Nations action. Regarding my

projected trip to Europe, they all recommended that I should
cancel it.

Late that night (August 20), the radio news carried the
Soviet government's announcement that its troops had entered
Czechoslovakia early on August 21 (the time difference between
New York and Moscow was eight hours) "at the request of
Czechoslovakia officials" to meet a threat to the socialist system.
The same statement said that Soviet forces, with those of Bulgaria,
Hungary, East Germany, and Poland, had crossed the Czechoslo-
vak borders. It also said that a request for urgent assistance had
been made by leaders of the Communist party and government of
Czechoslovakia. I immediately telephoned José Arujo Castro of
Brazil, that month's president of the Security Council, and
discussed the grim situation. We concluded that in the absence of
any request for a meeting of the Security Council by Czechoslovakia, no immediate action was called for.

On the next day, Soviet Ambassador Malik was the first to
see me. He looked weary, uneasy, and embarrassed. Relevant extracts from my diary are reproduced below:

SECRET
21 August 1968

Ambassador Malik saw me this morning and told me that he
was instructed last night by his Government to see me as soon as
possible and convey to me the statement of the Soviet Government on the Soviet intervention in Czechoslovakia.

I told him that I was very much distressed at the news of the
Soviet action. In my view, his Government's action constitutes a
violation of the Charter and represents a serious set-back to
East/West détente, which has been developing for some time. He
said that his Government had to act at the invitation of the Government and leaders of Czechoslovakia. I told him that I did not
know the real circumstances, since I had to rely on radio and
newspaper reports, but that of one thing I am sure: all public
opinion will be greatly aroused against the Soviet Union and this
action will have serious repercussions on the United Nations. One
immediate result will be felt in the United States: I told him that I
was more than ever convinced that Nixon would be elected President, since anti-Soviet sentiments will be aroused for a long time
to come. I told him that United States public opinion against the

United Nations was already at a low ebb because of its inability to settle the Middle Eastern problem. Now, if the Security Council were to meet, everybody knows that there would be no substantive resolution and United States public opinion particularly would consider it as another sign of United Nations impotence. If such developments take place, it will be very difficult even for me to work. I also told him that I was afraid Washington might not ratify the Non-Nuclear Proliferation Treaty, since the mood in the Congress would be very bitter against Moscow. I told him to please convey my request to his Government to exercise the utmost restraint in its dealings with Czechoslovakia.

Malik said he understood that some members of the Security Council were thinking of a Security Council meeting today, and he said he would oppose such a meeting and also the adoption of any agenda.

I gave Ambassador Malik only the pragmatic arguments that might have influenced the Soviet government, since in such situations, moral arguments would have had very little impact. I mentioned Mr. Nixon in the context of his lifelong record as a hardliner on communism. (It is interesting, however, that it was President Nixon who in 1972 rightly legitimized the communist regimes in Moscow and Peking and tried to close a chapter of East-West confrontation.)

At 11:30 A.M. on the same day, Mr. Muzik brought me a bombshell of a message. He had received news from Yugoslavia that Foreign Minister Hájek (who had officially invited me to visit Czechoslovakia) was still in Yugoslavia and that he (Hájek) did not think that he could go back to his own country! I then decided that there was no point in my attempting to go to Prague the next night, since my official host would not be there and Prague airport was closed to all international flights.

While there was no indication that Czechoslovakia would request a meeting of the Security Council, other member states did seek action by the United Nations, and the Council met on the evening of August 21. Ambassador Malik vigorously opposed the Council's consideration of the question. The onus for the invasion of Czechoslovakia, he said, was on "right-wing extremists" in Prague who were incited by the United States and other "imperialist powers." The Council nevertheless immediately voted to in-

clude the question in the agenda, with only the Soviet Union and
Hungary dissenting.

George W. Ball, the United States representative (who succeeded Arthur J. Goldberg in June 1968), charged that the Soviet
Union had dealt a shattering blow to hopes for a détente between
East and West, and said that the invasion of Czechoslovakia
"casts a shadow across the world."

The highlight of the meeting was, however, Mr. Muzik's
speech. He read into the record two messages received from
Czechoslovakia. The first message, signed by Foreign Minister Jiri
Hájek, instructed the Czechoslovak ambassadors in the Soviet
Union, Poland, Hungary, Bulgaria, and East Germany to issue
"resolute protests" to each of those countries. It also urged that
"the illegal occupation of Czechoslovakia be stopped without
delay" and that "all armed troops be withdrawn from Czechoslovakia." The second message was the declaration of the Presidium
of the National Assembly, protesting "the occupation of Czechoslovakia by armies of the five countries of the Warsaw Treaty."

Mr. Muzik's speech was not at all one-sided. Replying to Mr.
Ball, he said that the Czechoslovaks were not ashamed of the
events of 1948, when the communists supported by the Soviet
Union took power. Mr. Muzik also appeared to support some of
Mr. Malik's charges when he mentioned "imperialist forces" with
designs on the economies of the socialist countries.

Meanwhile, a wave of dismay and anger swept the world.
Many nations reacted to the invasion and occupation of Czechoslovakia with shock and condemnation. Romania, a member of the
Warsaw Pact, was among the first to condemn the Soviet Union
and its Warsaw Pact allies. Addressing a huge crowd in the center
of Bucharest, President Nicolae Ceauşescu reaffirmed Romanian
support for the Czechoslovak people and warned the Soviet Union
and its allies that they would encounter armed resistance if they
tried to invade his country.

President Tito and the top Communist leadership of Yugoslavia, in a party declaration issued on August 22, condemned the
invasion of Czechoslovakia as aggression.

Communist parties throughout Western Europe took the unprecedented step of condemning the Soviet Union in strongly-
worded public statements. From the Communist parties of Italy,

France, and Switzerland came expressions of "surprise and reprobation," "shock," and "grave dissent." Similar statements were issued by party leaders in Britain, Denmark, Austria, and other countries. To my knowledge, no prominent Communist leader in Western Europe went on record in defense of the Soviet move. Of course, many non-Communist leaders also condemned the invasion, notably President de Gaulle, Prime Minister Harold Wilson, Prime Minister Indira Gandhi, and Emperor Haile Selassie.

The strongest condemnation, however, came from Peking. On August 23, two days after the crisis erupted, *Jenmin Jih Pao,* the Communist party's official paper, said that the Soviet press agency's claim that "the Warsaw Pact forces had entered the country at the invitation of Czechoslovak leaders was issued to cover up the Soviet Union's shameless act." As for the Soviet contention that the invasion was intended to safeguard the fruits of socialism, the paper called it "shameless to the extreme." "It reminds one of the experience of the occupation of Czechoslovakia's Sudetenland by Hitler," the article said. "Even today, U.S. imperialists invade Vietnam under the banner of safeguarding peace."

Although Premier Castro of Cuba endorsed the Soviet invasion on political and ideological grounds, he said that it "has absolutely no legal foundation. We believe that there is no doubt that the sovereignty of the Czechoslovak state was violated—to deny this would be a fiction and a lie. . . ."

Against this background of international reaction, the Security Council met again on the morning of August 22. An eight-power draft resolution, introduced by Denmark, would have declared the invasion a violation of the UN Charter and affirmed the right of Czechoslovakia to self-determination; it specifically would have condemned the armed intervention of the Warsaw Pact countries and called upon them to withdraw their forces. After a bitter debate, the session was adjourned till 10:00 P.M. At the night session, Mr. Muzik demanded the immediate end of the Soviet occupation of his country and insisted on the legality of Alexander Dubček's regime. He also told us that Jiri Hájek, the Czechoslovak Foreign Minister, was on his way to attend the session. It was not until the early hours of August 23 that a vote on the resolution was taken. Although it received ten votes in favor and two against, it was rejected because of a Soviet veto.

By this time, President Ludvig Svoboda was on his way to Moscow. Before he left Prague, he had broadcast a statement over Radio Free Prague thanking his countrymen for their support and confidence and urgently asking them to "avoid any action or contacts that would exacerbate the atmosphere in our country and relations with the representatives of foreign armies."

President Svoboda's visit to Moscow was followed with great interest at the United Nations, as rumors had been current for the past three days that Czechoslovak Communist party chief Alexander Dubček, Premier Oldrich Černík, and other leaders had either been executed or were under arrest. In the course of the Security Council debate on August 22, Lord Caradon questioned Ambassador Malik regarding their whereabouts, but Mr. Malik had no answer; most probably he did not know.

In this atmosphere, the Security Council met again on August 23, when the same eight sponsors introduced another draft resolution under which the Security Council would request the Secretary General to dispatch immediately to Prague a special representative who should seek the release and ensure the personal safety of the Czechoslovak leaders under detention and who should report back urgently.

While the Council was still in session, Foreign Minister Jiri Hájek arrived in New York. At the same time, I received a cable from deputy Premier Ota Sik informing me that Dr. Hájek was "authorized to represent Czechoslovakia before the United Nations." But when the Security Council met that night, Dr. Hájek did not participate in the discussions. At nine-thirty, I had a meeting with him and he gave me a vivid and detailed account of the invasion, the mood of the Czechoslovak leadership, and present conditions in his country. I also learned why Dr. Hájek kept silent during the evening debate. Following are extracts from my diary on that meeting.

SECRET

23 August 1968

Dr. Hájek was vacationing on the Adriatic coast in Yugoslavia to prepare himself for my arrival in Czechoslovakia when the Soviet Union and some of its allies invaded his country. He was completely taken by surprise. From Belgrade he was able to contact his President (Svoboda) by phone. Deputy Prime Minister Sik was also with him in Yugoslavia with a few other members of the Government. When Hájek left for New York via Vienna, Sik went to Romania to spend a few days there.

His speech tomorrow in the Security Council would depend on the message he would receive from his President who is at present in Moscow. He thinks the President will be back in Prague tomorrow. He did not want to make any statement in the Council which might not conform to his President's statement.

His President went to Moscow accompanied by six senior members of the Cabinet who are all very competent and recognized leaders. Ambassador Klusak also accompanied the President. He did not know the trend of the discussions in Moscow.

There were at present innumerable clandestine radio stations all over Czechoslovakia and people in Western Europe can listen to many stations any time of the day. The broadcasts are very independent and mostly very critical of the Soviet Union and its allies.

In reply to my question, he said that Mr. Dubček's whereabouts were not known. He could neither confirm nor deny rumours that he had been executed. He also said that Prime Minister Černik's whereabouts were also not known.

The main reason of the Soviet action was the very free press in his country which was very critical of Soviet policies and actions. Some time ago some arms were seized in a hiding place near Kaloroy Vary, but those who were responsible for that arms cache were not apprehended. It is very difficult for his Government to apprehend those responsible for this.

He said that Hungary's participation in the invasion was a complete surprise. Both Janos Kadar and Foreign Minister Péter were very understanding men and had good will towards his country, but he thinks there must be extreme pressure behind them which prompted the action. East German participation in the invasion was "a psychological trauma." The Czechs have very unhappy memories of German uniforms on their soil, and strangely enough East German uniforms looked very much like Nazi uniforms.

There is no confirmation regarding the number of casualties.

Trains are still running out of Prague, but he did not think that the international airport is operating at present. Perhaps some flights are taking place to those Warsaw Pact countries which participated in the invasion.

After the agreement at Bratislava, Dubček tried his best to convince the press that extreme criticism of the Soviet Union would not help the situation. He urged them at length to exercise the utmost restraint. Hájek himself also briefed the press along the same lines before he left for Yugoslavia. He said that nobody could expect an immediate change of tone in the press within one week. (The invasion took place less than one week after the Bratislava agreement.) He thinks the action must have been well planned in complete secrecy. He admitted that newspapers and journals in his country were very frank and by-and-large anti-Russian. That is why the Czech leaders had constantly appealed to the press to exercise restraint.

In reply to my question, he said that the foreign troops on Czech soil at present were estimated at between 170,000 and 200,000. They are very well equipped with the latest armaments.

Dr. Hájek said that Novotný had no chance to return to Prague. Even the Russians had publicly announced that they would not set up Novotný again. He said that David was offered an ambassador's post and he had accepted it. He was on the point of leaving Prague when these developments took place. The new Permanent Representative to the United Nations was to arrive in New York as soon as Klusak left, but he was asked to stay in Czechoslovakia to be there when the Secretary-General arrived.

In reply to my question, he said that the International Geological Conference took place before the current events and he believed that the Conference must have been interrupted. I told him that my brother's son-in-law (Kyaw Nyein) was leading the Burmese delegation to that Conference and that his relatives were worried about him. He said that he was sure no harm would be done to the participants in the Conference.

He said that he wanted to see me again whenever necessary and I told him that I was at his disposal. He reiterated his invitation to visit Czechoslovakia when things return to normal. I told him that I would look forward to an early visit.

On the next day, August 24, Foreign Minister Hájek participated in the Security Council meeting. (Obviously he must have received instructions from Prague.) His speech, though short, was impressive. Although his English was halting, his delivery was calm, dignified, and totally devoid of emotion. He declared that the military occupation of his country "is an act of force that cannot be justified by reason," and rejected the Soviet argument that a military presence was required in Czechoslovakia because the nation was threatened by "external imperialist and internal counter-revolutionary forces." Dr. Hájek described the occupation as a blow "even more cruel because it came from countries from which we had not expected it in the least and from which we did not deserve it in the least." Then, without looking in the direction of Ambassador Malik, he asked the Soviet representative to reveal who, among Czechoslovak leaders, had asked for Russian intervention. Outside the Security Council chamber after the meeting, a diplomat quipped: "During the Dominican crisis, Washington's excuse for invasion was that there were 57 or 58 communists in that country. Now 20,000 or 30,000 Warsaw Pact soldiers are in Czechoslovakia looking for the fellow who had invited them."

While the Security Council was still in session, I received a news agency dispatch from Moscow saying that Czechoslovak party chief Alexander Dubček and Premier Oldrich Černík, who had been seized in Prague on August 21, had been brought to Moscow and were participating in the Kremlin negotiations between the Soviet leaders and the Czechoslovak delegation headed by President Ludvik Svoboda.

It was at this point that we had the first indication of a dramatic reversal in the Czechoslovak position: the government of Czechoslovakia was now requesting that the matter should no longer be considered at the United Nations. For after the Security Council meeting, news reached us that Czechoslovak President Svoboda had announced in Moscow that the Security Council should cease further deliberation. The Czechoslovak mission, however, did not receive any such message from the President. In any case, the Security Council agreed to postpone further debates until Monday (August 26), pending clarification of the news.

Three developments now took place in three separate places. In Moscow, the government newspaper *Izvestia* denounced the Romanian leader Nicolae Ceauşescu for having spoken out against the occupation of Czechoslovakia by troops of the Soviet Union and its Warsaw Pact allies—a denunciation considered significant, especially since it was made while President Svoboda was meeting in the Kremlin with Soviet leaders.

On the same day, President Tito of Yugoslavia and Mr.

Ceauşescu met in the small Yugoslav town of Vrsac, close to the frontier of Romania. The Romanians were reported to have taken defensive measures in the wake of the invasion of Czechoslovakia. Tanyug, the Yugoslav press agency, also distributed to the Yugoslav press a long extract from the attacks on Romania and Yugoslavia by Tass, the Soviet press agency, and Moscow newspapers.

On the same day (August 24), Hsinhua, the Chinese press agency, distributed the text of a speech delivered by Premier Chou En-lai at the Romanian National Day reception in Peking. The Chinese Premier virtually called for a guerrilla resistance movement against the Russians in Czechoslovakia, and advised the Romanians to prepare for one—against the possibility of a Soviet invasion. He promised both countries support. (It is important to note that North Vietnam took the opposite stand, and voiced strong support for the Soviet Union, which was its principal supplier of war material and economic aid.)

On Monday, August 26, the Security Council did not meet as scheduled. Foreign Minister Hájek had not yet received instructions from his President, but rumors were still current that President Svoboda had decided to drop Czechoslovak participation in the Council meetings. On August 27, the expected instructions arrived at the Czechoslovak mission to the United Nations. Mr. Hájek telephoned me at lunchtime asking for an appointment, and I saw him at four-thirty. I reproduce below the relevant part of my diary:

SECRET
26 August 1968

Dr. Hájek told me that he received a message from his President in Moscow last night that negotiations were still going on and it would help him if Hájek were to make an appropriate statement to the effect that Security Council meetings would not contribute towards the peaceful settlement of the problem. He did not know in what manner he should make that statement and asked me for my views. Should he write to the Secretary-General or to the President of the Security Council expressing the attitude of his Government, i.e., that the Security Council meetings would not contribute towards the peaceful settlement of the problem which is under discussion in Moscow? I told him that in my view, the more appropriate manner of expressing such an attitude should be in the form of a press release to be issued by his Mission to the United Nations. He said he agreed with this suggestion. In reply to my question, he said that he did not know when his President and other Czech leaders are coming back to Prague, but he believed that once such a statement is made by him in New York, negotiations would be much easier. He also said that he was asked by his President to come back to Czechoslovakia as early as possible and he had tentatively booked a return flight tomorrow night.

The same afternoon, the Czechoslovak mission issued the following statement at the United Nations:

> Direct top-level negotiations with the aim to end the occupation have been going on in Moscow between the Czechoslovak Socialist Republic and the countries that had occupied the Czechoslovak territory.
>
> In view of this, it is not the opinion of the Government of the Czechoslovak Socialist Republic that the debate in the Security Council could be conducive to the solution of this significant question, and it has asked its delegation not to continue its participation in the debate.

Thus, a tragic episode in modern history came to a close. President Svoboda is still, at this writing, President of Czechoslovakia; Alexander Dubček is reported to be occupied as a self-employed gardener; and Jiri Hájek has a teaching post at Charles University.

The intervention of the United States in the Dominican Republic had been universally criticized, by friends and foes alike. As a result, when the invasion of Czechoslovakia took place three years later, Washington was completely bereft of credentials to condemn Moscow. I agree with the judgment of Senator Eugene McCarthy of Minnesota—that at the height of the Czech crisis, the United States was morally unable even to make a strong protest against the actions of the Soviet Union and its allies. He said that the war in Vietnam and the military interventions in Cuba and the Dominican Republic had made it easier for the Russians to move as they had moved, and harder for the Americans to make serious moral and diplomatic protests.

Without even the moral basis of a condemnation of Moscow

by Washington, the Security Council was once again immobilized, and eight months of liberalization in Czechoslovakia came to an end. The Czechs under Dubček had challenged the most basic tenet of communism as practiced in the Soviet bloc—the dominance of the party in Moscow. In their movement toward fundamental human rights, however, the Czechs also aroused the long-felt fear of Germany in Moscow as well as in all Eastern Europe, except Romania and Yugoslavia. This explains Moscow's swift subjugation of the Czech liberalism. But this subjugation does not refute the basic case for improved East-West relations, nor change the need for what President Nixon called for in his acceptance speech—"an era of negotiation."

The whole sad episode shows that the forces of freedom are growing everywhere, although they can be suppressed by military might. As I said in my Annual Report for 1967–68:

> The action in Czechoslovakia was one of overwhelming military force by one of the two superpowers, assisted by four of its allies, in respect of a small State which was, in fact, a loyal member of its own bloc. The repercussions of this act of sheer military power were felt around the world and have engendered a feeling of dismay, uneasiness and insecurity.
>
> It is, certainly, a frightening commentary on the ominous state of world affairs that one superstate or the other can become exercised to the point of resorting to military action because of a liberalization of a regime in a small country like Czechoslovakia or because of an internal upheaval in another small State, such as the Dominican Republic. In both cases, the action taken was regarded by those who took it as necessary self-protection without any thought of territorial acquisition.
>
> It is, however, a dismal outlook for the small and militarily weak States of the world—as the overwhelming majority of States are—if they can hope to control their own affairs only in so far as they do nothing to displease a powerful neighbour.

Events in Romania, Yugoslavia, and the countries of Asia, Africa, and Latin America are all evidence that change and ferment are at work. All the dangers of what President Nixon called "the era of confrontation" are still present, but these can be reduced only in a spirit of détente, not in the atmosphere of cold war. Above all, the spiraling arms race with its horrible potentialities and astronomical budgets can be arrested and reversed only by Washington and Moscow's working together within the framework of the United Nations, and with due regard to the feelings of the international community, expressed from the forum of the World Organization.

A constructive and most helpful action in these perilous times would be the strengthening of the peace-building and peace-keeping capability of the United Nations system. Conversely, military alliances must gradually give way to a global concept of international security and international progress. This will require an intensified effort to reach the minds and hearts of all men with the irrefutable message that war is not only folly and madness, but that mankind's future depends upon its abolition. There is a need, now more imperative than ever before, for worldwide education towards international understanding and peaceful coexistence.

PART VI

THE
ASIAN
SUBCONTINENT

CHAPTER XVII

THE INDO-PAKISTANI CONFLICT: FIRST PHASE

The year 1965 not only produced the Dominican crisis; it also witnessed hostilities on a large scale between India and Pakistan. Two separate wars broke out. The first was relatively limited, but the second, far more extensive and far more terrifying.

The smaller war was peacefully resolved four years later and is a happy example of how a crisis can be solved by recourse to adjudications by a neutral party. Although no deliberative organ of the United Nations was involved, India and Pakistan successfully arbitrated it with the assistance of the Secretary General. I shall deal with this limited conflict in this section.

Early in 1965, fighting broke out in a desolate and uninhabited salt marsh called the Rann of Kutch, an area about 350 miles northwest of Bombay that forms part of India and borders on Pakistan. India charged that Pakistani armed personnel had intruded into the area. According to letters addressed to the president of the Security Council, India had proposed that a meeting be held between the two governments so that a solution to the problem could be found, but instead (India charged), Pakistan had mounted heavy attacks on two Indian police posts. Pakistan, on the other hand, rejected India's allegations and charged that Indian forces had been making systematic attempts to hinder Pakistani border patrols in their customary movements.

Eventually, the deadlock was broken when the two governments signed a cease-fire agreement. This agreement contained the unique stipulation that the border issue would be submitted to arbitration by a tribunal consisting of three persons, none of whom would be either Indian or Pakistani, and the chairman of which would be nominated by the Secretary General. After obtaining an agreement from the two parties that the tribunal's decision would be binding and not to be questioned "on any ground whatsoever" —the parties also agreed to meet the costs involved in equal proportions—I nominated as chairman Gunnar Karl Lagergren of Sweden, a former judge of the Stockholm Court of Appeal and an able arbitrator of long experience. The tribunal reached its verdict in February 1968, awarding Pakistan about three hundred square miles in the disputed Rann of Kutch.

In India, Prime Minister Indira Gandhi was confronted with a difficult, even critical, situation. There were bitter outcries aganst the verdict and even an attempt to march into the Rann to stop its demarcation. With a show of extraordinary courage and moral commitment, the Prime Minister stood her ground and, in an address, reminded the nation that India had agreed in advance to accept the tribunal's verdict without conditions. In July 1969, India and Pakistan signed a series of maps delineating the border between them in the long-disputed area. Thus a conflict was resolved by the method of mediation alone, with a prior agreement that the arbitrator's decision would be binding.

CHAPTER XVIII

THE LARGER WAR

While the dispute over the Rann of Kutch (which erupted in April 1965) was peacefully resolved four years later, a second conflict—this time in the region of Kashmir—broke out between India and Pakistan the following August and had no such happy conclusion.

The Indo-Pakistani dispute over Kashmir had been before the United Nations since 1948. At the risk of over-simplification, it may be said that India had maintained that Kashmir was a part of India, while Pakistan had maintained that the people of Kashmir must exercise the right of self-determination, in accordance with various Security Council resolutions. Since the beginning of 1965, there had been a sharp increase in the number of violations by both sides of the 1949 cease-fire line in Kashmir, including a serious one in May, when Indian troops in battalion strength attacked and captured Pakistani positions. Despite the presence in the area of a UN military observer group (UNMOGIP), which was under the command of General Robert H. Nimmo of Australia, armed men, frequently not in uniform, crossed the cease-fire line from the Pakistani side, and there was periodic but heavy artillery fire across the line from both sides. From August 5, 1965, onward, tension was heightened and large-scale hostilities occurred. It was apparent that the cease-fire agreement of July 29, 1949, had completely broken down.

From the beginning of this crisis to its end, practically every attempt I made to mediate it was frustrated by the recalcitrance of either or both parties. (In the end, as it turned out, it was the Soviet Union rather than the United Nations that produced an agreement between India and Pakistan.) Because of Pakistani objections, I was unable even to make a public appeal to both sides to withdraw to the pre-August positions. Ambassador Amjad Ali of Pakistan said that such an appeal would create the impression that the UN wanted to maintain the status quo, which in his view favored India. And when I decided to send Dr. Ralph Bunche, undersecretary for special political affairs, on an urgent mission to India and Pakistan to meet with the heads of government, both sides imposed conditions, so that we had to abandon the mission. Meanwhile, the fighting intensified, and the newspapers of both India and Pakistan criticized General Nimmo and myself—for completely contrary reasons.

As the situation further deteriorated, on September 1, I addressed urgent parallel messages to Prime Minister Lal Bahadur Shastri of India and President Mohammed Ayub Khan of Pakistan, appealing for a military pull-back by both parties to the 1949 cease-fire line.

On the same day (September 1), resourceful and energetic Ambassador Arthur J. Goldberg of the United States (who happened to be president of the Security Council for that month) endorsed my appeal, and on September 3, I had a series of meetings with him and all other members of the Security Council, which then included Ambassador Platon Morozov of the U.S.S.R., Lord Caradon of the United Kingdom, and Ambassador Roger Seydoux of France. I explained to them the critical situation developing in Kashmir and impressed on them the urgent need for a Security Council meeting to consider the crisis.

On the next morning (September 4), Ambassador Goldberg called a meeting of the Council. The result was that the Council unanimously adopted a resolution calling for a cease-fire and for both sides to co-operate with the UN observer group. Subsequently, however, General Nimmo's reports to me indicated that

fighting continued on both sides of the line. There was no doubt
that the conflict was broadening. On September 6, I sent an urgent
report of these developments to the Council, as a result of which it
convened again.

It was this meeting of the Security Council that shifted the responsibility for stopping the fratricidal war to me and initiated my
urgent mission of that month to India and Pakistan. For, in a
mood of near desperation, the Council again adopted a resolution
that not only called on the two sides to stop hostilities "immediately and promptly," but also requested the Secretary General to
"exert every possible effort" to gain those ends. In introducing the
resolution, Ambassador Ramani of Malaysia said: "[This] throws,
we realize, on the shoulders of the Secretary-General, burdened
and bent as he is with the numerous problems of a strife-prone
world, the additional burden of bringing some calm to this dis-
tracted area . . . which has continuously lived under the shadows
of war and conflict for eighteen long years. I am sure, as we all
are, that he will find the means to give prompt effect to our draft
resolution. If there is anyone who can find such means, he alone
can—and, if I may say so, I am confident he alone will."[1]

I immediately accepted the responsibility entrusted to me by
the Council, a decision that was received with great enthusiasm,
and discussed with Ambassador Goldberg and Ralph Bunche the
modalities of my flight schedule to the two countries.

Later, Ambassador Goldberg told me that President Johnson
had offered his presidential plane for my use, if I so desired, for
the flight to Karachi. I thanked him and the President for such
generosity and thoughtfulness, but said that I had better not take
advantage of the President's offer, since I could take a commercial
airline up to Karachi. (I told Ralph that I would be terribly un-
comfortable in the presidential plane, which would be far too lux-
urious for me; with only five passengers, the huge Boeing 707
would be almost empty.) My office had made tentative bookings
for my flight; the problem was how to get to India from Pakistan.
General Nimmo's official plane could not fly over the Indo-Paki-

---

[1] *United Nations Security Council Official Records, No. 1238,* September
6, 1965.

stani border, which was then the scene of extremely violent
fighting. Ambassador Goldberg suggested that I should take advantage of a small United States plane in Teheran for the purpose.
I accepted his kind offer and requested him to inform Washington
accordingly.

By the time I left New York on the evening of September 7,
news reached United Nations headquarters that fighting had
spread far beyond the Kashmir cease-fire lines. In August, the
original military initiative had been taken by the Pakistanis in
disputed Kashmir; after a month of fighting across the cease-fire
line, India was now launching a massive thrust into the Punjab,
away from Kashmir. The swiftness of the Indian attack in that unexpected area came as a shock and caught Pakistan off balance.
Indian tank units were heading toward Lahore, the official capital
of West Pakistan.

The Pakistanis were employing American-made Sherman and
Patton tanks, while in the air they had F-66 Sabres and supersonic
F-104 Starfighters, provided by the United States under the terms
of mutual defense arrangements. The Indian air force at the time
did not have an all-weather interceptor capability; for the most
part, it comprised subsonic fighters bought from Britain and
France. India had recently bought some Russian MIG-21s, however, and there were reports that they were being assembled at
Ambala, an air base in northern India.

The attack by the Indians into the Punjab came at a time
when Pakistani forces were pressing hard on the Kashmir front
about 150 miles to the north of the Lahore-Amritsar sector. Obviously, the Pakistanis had not calculated that India would strike
overland with her 1st Armored Division. But twenty-four hours
after the Indian push toward Lahore, Pakistani paratroopers
landed near Patiala and Ambala, two towns about 150 miles north
of New Delhi. General Nimmo's assessment was that the Indian
troops on all fronts had a ratio of three to two against the Pakistanis. But this numerically superior Indian force was up against
heavier Pakistani fire-power and more modern weapons.

Against this background, I left New York at 8:00 P.M. on
Tuesday, September 7, 1965, on a BOAC flight, accompanied by
Brian Urquhart, Ramses Nassif (a press aide), Donald Thomas,

and Lucien Lemieux, both of my office. At Kennedy International Airport, I made a brief statement to the press corps assembled there, which I concluded with the following words:

> I have accepted this responsibility without hesitation because of the enormity of the threat to the peace of the world in this raging conflict between two of the great countries and peoples of Asia. I have no illusions about this mission: the issues are infinitely complicated and difficult and the situation out there is extremely grave. Kashmir has posed a baffling problem for the United Nations for seventeen years. I need say only that I will do my very best and hope that my mission will prove helpful. On its completion, I will, of course, report to the Security Council, and will have nothing to say about it until then.

Most of that overnight flight was occupied with discussions with Brian on the method of approach to the problem, both in Rawalpindi and New Delhi. In any case, I could never sleep well in flight. About four hours after takeoff, I tried to get some sleep, but visions of Kashmir appeared in my mind. I had been there before, in October 1951, when I was the guest of Sheikh Abdullah, then Prime Minister of Kashmir. I remembered the serenity of life in Kashmir, the unspoiled beauty of the landscape—and Sheikh Abdullah himself, a giant of a man known there as The Lion of Kashmir. I recalled that it was his dream to make Kashmir a model state.

After brief stopovers at London, Geneva, and Beirut, the plane arrived in Teheran a few minutes after midnight. There we got reports that Karachi airport had been bombed by Indian planes only a few minutes earlier. Since it was uncertain whether our Pakistani plane would proceed to Karachi, I took advantage of the U.S. offer of one of its embassy planes. After a few hours' rest, we flew to Karachi and landed there at 7:20 A.M. on September 9.

I immediately proceeded to Rawalpindi, where I was to meet President Ayub Khan. The press corps surrounded me as soon as I alighted from the plane, but I declined to discuss the substance of my mission. I noticed that the airport was ringed by antiaircraft guns, and that armed sentries were on guard near the control tower. Ali Bhutto, the Foreign Minister of Pakistan, and Agha

Shahi of the Foreign Office, among others, greeted me, and after an hour's preliminary discussion, we drove to the President's palace.

President Ayub Khan, who carried his six-foot, three-inch frame with dignity and elegance, impressed me as a strong and imperious leader. He had seized power in 1958, and with military precision had instituted a sweeping land reform program, reorganized the government, and taken drastic measures against corruption. A perfect soldier, he had ruled with an iron hand, and he had only contempt for intellectuals. President Khan spoke with a clipped British accent; he had a tough and no-nonsense air about him. All this, together with his magnificent physique and brush mustache, gave one the feeling of what an ideal field marshal should be. He was the De Gaulle of Asia.

At our meeting, the President stressed that India had embarked on a course of aggression across the cease-fire line because it could not suppress the "freedom fighters" in the "occupied territory of Jammu and Kashmir," and that Pakistanis who crossed the line could not be blamed for going to their assistance.

I explained to him my mandate, defined by the September Security Council resolutions, which gave me no authority to discuss the overall question of Kashmir. My only mandate was to achieve a prompt and effective cease-fire; without that, the threat to world peace in Kashmir was in reality greater than that in Vietnam. I had in mind the potential role of Peking (which had backed Pakistan) and Moscow (which had backed India). He insisted, however, that the Security Council ought to concern itself with the fundamental problem, which was to get a territorial settlement that would stick. Obviously, there was no meeting of minds, and we moved to the dining room for the luncheon the President gave me.

On the next day, September 10, after my visit to the UN-MOGIP office in Rawalpindi, I met with Foreign Minister Ali Bhutto, who immediately impressed me as articulate, well-informed, and impassioned. Lawyer, scholar, and politician blended in him when he talked. He had studied at the University of California and then at Christ Church, Oxford, where he had been one of the most brilliant students of Dr. Sarvepalli Radhakrishnan, then professor of comparative religions. Although Radhakrishnan was now the President of India, Mr. Bhutto, in line with the Asian tradition that a student must show respect to his teacher, wanted me to convey his regards to his old professor when I saw him in New Delhi. The President of India was deeply touched when I conveyed Mr. Bhutto's message to him.

Mr. Bhutto told me that massive tank battles were raging in all fronts. Like President Ayub Khan, he reiterated Pakistan's conviction that a cease-fire alone would not stick. Without the settlement of the whole Kashmir issue, the sore was certain to fester and erupt periodically, inflaming the entire area.

One of my life's ambitions was to visit Taxila, seat of the oldest Buddhist university in the world; I mentioned this to Mr. Bhutto at our first meeting on September 9. He kindly arranged that visit for the next day, and after lunch, took me in his car to the ruined city, which is about an hour's drive from Rawalpindi.

The sacred ruins of Taxila are beyond description. Sandstone statues of the Buddha in various poses were exhibited in the museum, which was well kept, and I saw from its door vast stretches of the ruins of a once-flourishing Buddhist seat of learning. Mr. Bhutto must have noticed that I was speechless with awe and veneration at the spectacle. He told me that the Archeological Department of Pakistan was still supervising excavations. The same evening, he invited me to his house and presented me with an exquisite standing statue of the Buddha, from his personal collection. It still remains one of my most prized possessions.

When I saw President Ayub Khan again before leaving Pakistan, he was not at all receptive to the idea of a cease-fire, though he assured me that he would accept a cease-fire if it could lead to an overall solution of the Kashmir problem. (India's position was that the Kashmir Assembly had approved the accession to India in 1953, and that the Security Council could not reverse the decision.) In reply to my question, the President said he would be agreeable to Big-Four involvement in the "whole problem of Kashmir." As darkness set in, all the lights inside the palace were turned off, and he explained to me that a blackout had been in force since the outbreak of hostilities. I told him that I had noticed it the previous night, when the housekeepers in the guest house had put heavy shades on the bedroom lights. The President laughed and said, "So long as the Secretary General is in Rawalpindi, a blackout is certainly not necessary." We both laughed. It was getting dark, and since I knew that the President had urgent duties to attend to, I took leave of him. At the guest house, I went over cables sent to me from my New York office; among them were several messages from heads of state or government. It was obvious that there was very serious concern on the part of the international community over the intensification of the war.

We left Rawalpindi on September 11 in the same U.S. plane that had brought us from Teheran and, after a complicated flight —we were told that we had to avoid flying over Pakistani naval units—landed at New Delhi airport on Sunday, September 12, after a stop at Bombay.

At the airport, I was met by officials of the Indian Foreign Office, the Burmese ambassador to India, and various other officials, including General Nimmo. I was driven straight to the President's palace (Rashtrapati Bhavan), a massive architectural masterpiece, once the official residence of the British viceroys. At 12:30 P.M., I called on the President Sarvepalli Radhakrishnan, the eminent scholar and philosopher, and the author of several profound works on philosophy and Eastern religions. In my view, his greatest contribution to modern thought is his profound philosophy of the religion of the spirit. This, coupled with his deep religious conviction, leads him to the conclusion that the essence of all religions is the same. "Religion," he says, "is not a creed or code, but an insight into reality." Dr. Radhakrishnan thus takes religion out of the realm of conflict and dogma. For me, meeting him meant more than meeting the president of the most populous democracy in the world, for before me was a great philosopher and a teacher. It was a spiritual experience. We discussed the *Dhammapada,* perhaps the best-known and most influential book of the Buddhist canonical literature (which he translated into English from the Sanskrit). He was deeply touched, as I have already mentioned, when I conveyed Mr. Bhutto's regards to him. Then he gave me a copy of his broadcast message, delivered the previous night from All-India Radio, and asked me to read it at my leisure.

Although the broadcast text spoke of avoiding "any form of hatred of the people of Pakistan, who are our kith and kin," and recommended a spirit of sacrifice and compassion, it also stressed the need for an Indian victory, and blamed Pakistan for taking "the law into its own hands." It was Dr. Radhakrishnan the head of state, not the philosopher, who spoke in these terms. The tone was that of a politician.

After our conversation, he gave me lunch. There were just the two of us, and how delicious the vegetable dishes were—simple but nourishing; I think I could live on them day in and day out. At the lunch, he also made some observations on the *Dhammapada*.

Later, I called on Prime Minister Shastri at his modest home. In physical terms, he was the direct antithesis of President Ayub Khan. The Prime Minister was a short man with a simple demeanor—quite unlike a formidable field marshal. An English writer once wrote a witty essay on honorifics. After recalling examples like "His Excellency the Ambassador" and "His Majesty the King," he suggested with tongue in cheek that a new system of honorifics should be considered: "His Ferocity the Field Marshal," "His Velocity the Air Marshal," and so on. Prime Minister Shastri reminded me of that witticism: it occurred to me that the most appropriate title in his case would be "His Simplicity the Prime Minister."

But Prime Minister Shastri forcefully expressed his distress that the Security Council had failed to act promptly when "thousands of armed infiltrators equipped with Pakistani arms and ammunition" launched a massive attack "on India" on August 5, 1965. I explained to him the purpose of my mission, which was confined to implementing the Security Council resolutions of September 4 and 6. I told the Prime Minister that it was my intention to address identical appeals to both governments for a cease-fire, specifying time and date. Later, I drafted the appeal and sent it (in code) to the President of Pakistan through the UNMOGIP office in Rawalpindi, to be delivered at 2000 hours Rawalpindi time, on Sunday, September 12. Simultaneously, an identical message was delivered to Prime Minister Shastri at 2030 hours New Delhi time on the same day.[2]

The appeal called for an unconditional cease-fire on September 14 and a withdrawal of all armed personnel on both sides to positions held before August 5.

This appeal, as it turned out, was not only unsuccessful, but was the first of a series of equally unsuccessful appeals and negotiations, the failure of which necessitated my going before the Security Council, in the end, to proclaim my helplessness. For while each side expressed a desire for a cessation of hostilities, each side also imposed conditions and qualifications on the proposed cease-fire. India, on its side, promptly accepted the cease-fire—but only with respect to its armed forces in uniform; it reserved the right to deal with infiltrators who had crossed into Kashmir from the Pakistani side. Pakistan also accepted—but demanded that the cease-fire provide for an overall political settlement of the entire dispute. These qualifications resulted in a second set of identical messages, this time asking for a cease-fire on September 16. Prime Minister Shastri of India accepted this appeal without conditions. But not President Khan. He stuck by his position that the cease-fire should provide "effective machinery that would lead to a final settlement." A third set of messages was sent on September 15. In this one, I offered to meet once again with the two heads of state and reminded them that they had had offers from a number of world leaders who were willing to be available for conciliatory assistance.

Just after sending the third appeal, I left New Delhi for Bombay (on September 15) and the next day, left Bombay by Air India for New York.

The plane landed at Kennedy airport at 3:15 P.M. Among those who met me were the president of the Security Council (Ambassador Goldberg) and all the members of the Council! On their behalf, Mr. Goldberg thanked me for my efforts for a cease-fire. I was overwhelmed and at a loss for words. Never in the history of the United Nations had a Secretary General been met at the New York airport by all the members of the Security Council,

---

[2] There is a time difference of half an hour between New Delhi and Rawalpindi.

and there was no doubt that Mr. Goldberg's initiative was responsible for this unprecedented show of support. I drove straight to my office, where I found President Ayub Khan's reply to my third message.

The President's third reply was as negative as his other two had been. I had now played all my cards. There was nothing more I could do than to report to the Council that the situation was deadlocked. In my second report (of September 16), I gave a brief account of my own observations on the prevailing situation. In this tragic war, two closely associated nations found themselves locked in a destructive struggle that was crippling and potentially disastrous for both. Each nation felt that it had been abused by the other, and each was convinced that the other had committed aggression. In common, they had a feeling of having been let down to some extent by their allies and by the United Nations. At the same time, the United Nations watched in bewilderment and anxiety the spectacle of two sister states, with both of which many countries have close links, engaged in a fratricidal struggle.

After describing the mood of the leaders in both countries, I observed that "these are the factors which also make it difficult for the leaders on both sides to respond to the unconditional cease-fire appeals of the Security Council." I pointed out that the recent crisis had inevitably served to harden even further the previous positions taken by the two governments, since each had the feeling that only outside support had made it possible for the other to commit what it believed to be aggression. And so we had not only a deadlock but a paradox:

> The Security Council is thus faced with a paradoxical situation. It has passed urgently and unanimously two resolutions requiring an immediate cessation of hostilities. It has authorized me to exert every possible effort to give effect to these resolutions. Before and during my mission, I have received messages of support and offers of assistance from leaders in all parts of the world. Both sides have expressed their desire for a cease-fire and a cessation of hostilities in the entire area of the current conflict. Nevertheless, up to now, I have not succeeded in securing an effective practical measure of compliance by the two sides with the Security Council's resolutions.

But my report also offered the Council some positive suggestions. Pursuant to Article 40 of the Charter, it could *order* the two governments to cease hostilities, warning them that failure to comply would incur sanctions under Article 39. It could also request the two heads of state to meet and try to resolve the dispute; in addition, it could create and make available to them a committee to assist in such talks.

When the Council met on September 17 and 18, fighting on all fronts was reported to be intensified. Indeed, the war had now taken on a new dimension, for on the eighteenth, the Indian representative, M. C. Chagla, interrupted the proceedings with a dramatic announcement: Chinese troops were massing on the Indian border. "At four points," he said, "they have indulged in probing actions and are poised for an invasion in a serious attack."

Even though the consensus in the Council was to act on the basis of my suggestions in the report, it found itself deadlocked and unable to produce a draft resolution acceptable to both India and Pakistan. The mood of the members was one of utter gloom. Finally, after a day of private consultations, the Council met once more at fifty-five minutes after midnight on September 19, when Ambassador J. G. de Bens of the Netherlands introduced a draft that proved acceptable; it was passed by a vote of fourteen in favor and one abstention. In this resolution, the Council demanded that a cease-fire should take effect on September 22, with a withdrawal of all armed personnel to positions held before August 5, 1965; it also stipulated that the Council would consider what steps could be taken to assist in a settlement of the political problem underlying the conflict. At 2:50 A.M. on September 20, I transmitted the resolution to the two governments via UN cable facilities, and that afternoon, sent identical messages to both governments asking them to inform me that cease-fire orders had been issued. On the same night (September 20), Prime Minister Shastri informed me that he would order a cease-fire on September 22. That night, word also reached us that Mr. Ali Bhutto, Pakistan's Foreign Minister, was on his way to New York with a message from his President. He arrived on the night of the twenty-first, and at 2:30 A.M. the Council convened. Mr. Bhutto took the floor. In an emotion-charged speech, after stressing the imperative need of self-determination for the people of Jammu and Kashmir, he informed us that President Khan had ordered his armed forces to "stop fighting as of 1205 hours . . . today."

Subsequently, I set up two separate observer units to supervise the cease-fire: the India-Pakistan Observation Mission (UNIPOM), on the border between India and West Pakistan, and UNMOGIP, which had similar functions on the old cease-fire line in Kashmir.

But the cease-fire ordered by the Security Council did not materialize: fighting continued in several areas both inside and outside Kashmir. General Nimmo, chief military observer of UN-MOGIP (who was also asked to take charge of UNIPOM pending the arrival of its chief officer, Major General MacDonald) reported to me that Pakistani troops at Punch (in Kashmir) had been observed firing with rifles and light machine guns toward the Uri-Punch road from dominating positions west of the road.

On the same day (September 24), UN military observers at Lahore (in Pakistan) reported that, in the area between the two armies, both sides had opened fire with field artillery, medium tanks, recoilless rifles, and light and medium machine guns. General Nimmo and his deputy contacted the commands on both sides by phone to get the firing stopped. I immediately submitted a report to the Security Council.[3]

Such breaches of the cease-fire were a daily occurrence, and every time I received reports from General Nimmo, I immediately informed the Security Council of such breaches. Meanwhile, a section of the international press criticized both UNMOGIP and UNIPOM for being "passive," particularly in the Lahore sector. Such criticisms, of course, were based on a misunderstanding of the functions of the UN military observers, whose primary duty was to observe and report, directly to me, on the area of conflict outside of Kashmir and beyond the Kashmir cease-fire line. The observers in the field were to do all they reasonably could to persuade local commanders to restore the cease-fire in cases in which firing had occurred, but they had no authority to order an end to firing.

---

[3] Security Council Report No. S/6710, September 25, 1965.

By the middle of October, the situation had not improved and had actually worsened. On October 13, I sent messages to the Prime Minister of India and the President of Pakistan renewing my appeal for steps to be taken to bring about the withdrawal of armed personnel to the positions of August 5.

On October 22, Pakistan asked for an urgent meeting of the Security Council to consider the grave and rapidly deteriorating situation. Pakistan charged that India was planning a new offensive in the Rajasthan sector (outside Kashmir) and was also planning a new offensive in Kashmir. India argued that Pakistan's effort to have the Security Council discuss the "so-called grave political developments" within the territory of Jammu and Kashmir was an attempt to compromise the internal sovereignty of India.

The debate continued until November 5. During these meetings, the organization of the UN observation mission was discussed, and the actions taken by the Secretary General were challenged. At the Security Council meeting of October 25, 1965, Ambassador Nikolay Fedorenko of the Soviet Union asserted that I had exceeded my prerogatives in giving effect to the Council resolutions. He claimed that "only the Security Council was competent to take the necessary decisions on all specific matters connected with UN observers, namely, their functions, number, command, the financing of their activities, and so on."

Ambassador Goldberg immediately came to my defense, as did the representatives of Jordan, the United Kingdom, China, the Ivory Coast, and several other countries. They were satisfied that I had acted in complete accord with the clear mandates given to me by the Council.

In an earlier chapter, I have dealt with my own conception of the role of the Secretary General, and it will not be necessary to elaborate on it. I will only say that almost all members of the Security Council at that time supported the Secretary General's actions and his competence. France, while not challenging the urgent measures I might have to take, considered that in setting up any peace-keeping operation, the Security Council itself should decide on matters such as the main characteristics of the operation, its command, financing, and duration. This has been, and still is, the position of France regarding the functions of the Secretary General vis-à-vis the Security Council. It was the Soviet Union that from time to time questioned the actions and competence of the Secretary General in areas other members considered to be his legitimate domain.

Meanwhile, reports from the field indicated in general an overall tendency toward improvement in the observance of the cease-fire.

On November 5, the Security Council held its last meeting of 1965 on the India-Pakistan question; it adopted a resolution under which the Council demanded the prompt and unconditional execution of the proposal for a meeting of the representatives of India and Pakistan with a representative of the Secretary General for the formulation of a plan and schedule of withdrawals by both parties.

After consultations with both parties, I appointed Brigadier General Tulio Marambio of Chile as my representative for the purpose of formulating a plan for withdrawals.

Under the chairmanship of General Marambio, a series of joint military meetings were convened during January at UN operation headquarters in Lahore and Amritsar. On January 29, 1966, an agreement was reached by both parties and by General Marambio. It provided for the disengagement and withdrawal of armed personnel, in two stages, by February 25.

On January 31, 1966, the military observer group (UN-MOGIP) and the observation mission (UNIPOM) reported that the first phase of the disengagement and withdrawal plan had been completed in all sectors without incident. Later reports stated that the second phase (removal of defense works) had been completed on February 20. On February 26, 1966, I reported to the Security Council that the withdrawal of troops by India and Pakistan had been completed on schedule. The withdrawal provisions of the Security Council's resolutions had thus been fulfilled by the two parties.

In my last report on my efforts to give effect to the resolutions, I indicated that I intended to have the observation mission cease all functions as of March 1, and thereafter to disband not later than March 22, 1966.

From the above narrative, no conclusion should be drawn

that the Security Council, or for that matter the United Nations, was mainly responsible for achieving the cease-fire and withdrawal. Of course, the Security Council resolutions and the massive opinion of the international community, as reflected in the Council debates, were contributing factors in the final outcome. The main credit for achieving the cease-fire and withdrawal, however, must be given to Soviet Premier Alexei Kosygin for having produced the historic "Tashkent Declaration" signed by the two heads of government.

On December 8, 1965, it was announced that the Prime Minister of India and the President of Pakistan, acting at the invitation of the government of the U.S.S.R., had agreed to meet at Tashkent, on January 4, 1966, to discuss the long-standing dispute.

At the conclusion of the Tashkent meetings, which were mediated by Premier Kosygin, Prime Minister Shastri of India and President Ayub Khan of Pakistan signed (on January 10, 1966) a declaration in which they asserted their firm resolve to restore normal and peaceful relations between their two countries and to reaffirm their obligation under the UN Charter to settle their differences through peaceful means. It was at this meeting that the February 25 deadline for a phased disengagement was agreed upon. The declaration also expressed agreement on the repatriation of prisoners of war, the restoration of economic and trade relations, and the normal functioning of diplomatic missions of both countries.

On the day the two leaders of India and Pakistan met with Premier Kosygin at Tashkent (January 4), I got the sad news of the death of General Robert H. Nimmo in Rawalpindi. And on the day the declaration was signed (January 10), I was informed of the sudden death of Prime Minister Lal Bahadur Shastri at Tashkent. Statements I issued on those dates expressed my heartfelt admiration for both men, and there followed cables to Premier Kosygin, President Ayub Khan, and Foreign Minister Sardar Swaran Singh of India expressing my deep satisfaction with the measures agreed upon at the Tashkent meeting.

The Tashkent Declaration propelled Mr. Kosygin into the world scene as a supernegotiator. I had met the Soviet Premier

several times and talked with him on various issues. I have yet to
meet a world statesman whose quiet dignity and courteous manners can match Mr. Kosygin's. Like Mr. Shastri, he is simple,
modest, and serene but, at the same time, firm. By patching up a
truce between India and Pakistan, he not only proved himself to
be an able and persistent mediator; he also demonstrated that the
Soviet Union can play a significant role in South and Southeast
Asia. No doubt Mr. Kosygin had the added advantage of the silent support of the Big Powers (except China). In fact, the common hostility of the United States and the Soviet Union toward
China strengthened Mr. Kosygin's hands in the restoration of stability to the subcontinent. President Ayub Khan also showed extraordinary courage and statesmanship in signing the declaration,
reaffirming his commitment under the United Nations Charter not
to settle his disputes with India by force. For this, he became the
target of a violent and relentless attack in his own country. He
even offered to attend Mr. Shastri's funeral in New Delhi, but did
not do so, for security reasons, only at the request of the Indian
authorities. As later events unfolded, this courage was a factor in
his own downfall.

CHAPTER XIX

INTERLUDE: PILGRIMAGES, 1967

In 1967, I made another trip to the Asian subcontinent that covered five countries: Ceylon (now Sri Lanka), India, Nepal, Afghanistan, and Pakistan.

Before flying to New Delhi, I stayed two days in Ceylon as a guest of the government. The highlight of my visit to that country was the special exposition of the Sacred Tooth Relic of the Buddha, at Kandy on April 9. The exposition included an impressive and moving ceremony conducted by the Diyawardene Nilame, head of the Temple of the Sacred Tooth. According to Buddhist chronicles, a tooth of Lord Buddha was once secretly smuggled out of India to Ceylon by some Buddhist monks, and was deposited in the temple, enclosed within heavy iron walls. Special expositions are made only on the occasions of visits to the temple by prominent Buddhists, for the purpose of worship.

Another very memorable experience during that trip occurred on April 11, when I visisted Sanchi (near Bhopal) in India. The great Buddhist Emperor Asoka built innumerable religious edifices and monuments all over the subcontinent (they are at any rate attributed to Asoka). Known in India as *stupas* or *topes,* one of the most revered in the Buddhist world is the *tope* in Sanchi. Excavations in Sanchi were first made in 1822 and again in 1851. At the second excavation, one of the smaller *topes* was found to contain part of the ashes from the funeral pyres of Sariputta and Moggallana, two of the Buddha's closest disciples.[1] Indira Gandhi, who was now Prime Minister, kindly arranged for my pilgrimage to Sanchi by providing a special plane.

In New Delhi, Prime Minister Gandhi presented me with an exquisite bronze head of the Buddha (probably of the fourth or fifth century A.D.) which, along with the sandstone statue of the Buddha given to me by Mr. Bhutto two years earlier, is one of my two most precious possessions. On April 12, I received the first Jawaharlal Nehru Award for International Understanding, presented by President Sarvepalli Radhakrishnan on behalf of the Nehru Memorial Award Committee.[2]

One of the most important days of my life was April 14, 1967, when His Majesty King Mahendra of Nepal sent me to Lumbini, the birthplace of Lord Buddha, in his helicopter. Lumbini, the capital of Nepal, is a very sacred place for Buddhists all over the world; it stands on an equal footing with the greatest shrines of other world religions.

I was struck by the isolation of the site and its comparative inaccessibility to ordinary pilgrims and tourists. A twenty-one-kilometer bullock cart track, impassable in the rainy season, is the only link between the nearest airport, Bhairawa, and the sacred site. In spite of this, however, thousands of pilgrims visit Lumbini every year, in reverence of the spiritual and moral values that the Buddha prescribed as a basis for achieving inner tranquillity, tolerance, and compassion. In the Buddha's time (he was born in 623 B.C.), Lumbini was described as a beautiful garden. Today, it bears little resemblance to its appearance at the time of the Buddha's birth. The sacred garden itself has become little more than an open field on which is a collection of buildings of no great importance—with the sole exception of the Asoka Pillar. The inscription on the Pillar tells us that Emperor Asoka, the greatest propagator of Buddhism in history, came in person in 249 B.C. to pay homage at the birthplace of the Buddha.

---

[1] Rhys Davids, *Buddhist India* (New York: Putnam, 1903), pp. 287–88.
[2] The award was accompanied by a check for 100,000 rupees ($13,230), which I donated to the United Nations International School, New York.

Visible monuments are few. In addition to the Pillar, there is the modern temple of Maya Devi (mother of the Buddha), which was no doubt built over the foundations of more than one earlier temple. It contains a poorly preserved stone relief depicting the birth scene. Archaeological excavations undertaken in 1933–34 revealed the brick foundations of a monastery, some small votive *stupas,* and large plinths.

I felt very strongly that the site *must* be developed. On returning to Katmandu, I discussed with the King and members of his government how best to develop it. The King assured me of the co-operation of his government in any action that the international community might take. Immediately on my return to New York, I got in touch with Paul Hoffman, administrator of the United Nations Development Program, and René Maheu, director general of UNESCO in Paris. With the active co-operation of both, the project was initiated, and later that year (1967), the government of Nepal made a formal request to the United Nations for technical assistance. Since then, several preliminary steps have been taken toward the realization of my dream. As a result of the co-ordinated work of the United Nations, the UN Development Program, and the United Nations Educational, Scientific, and Cultural Organization (UNESCO), a master plan for the development of Lumbini has emerged. At UN headquarters, an international committee has been formed with the permanent representative of Nepal as chairman, for the purpose of giving effect to the project. At the time of this writing, the preliminary estimate of the total cost of the project, which is to be financed by voluntary contributions, is in the neighborhood of $5,660,000.

From Katmandu, I left for Kabul, Afghanistan, where, for the first time during my tour, regional political problems were discussed. The Afghan leaders complained of Pakistan's "obstinacy" in regard to the problem of the Pathan tribesmen, a minority group living in the northern part of Pakistan that borders on Afghanistan. The Pathans, ethnically similar to the Afghans, were clamoring for autonomy. His Majesty King Mohammed Zhir Shah gave me a memorable banquet at Gulkhana Palace on the evening before I left Kabul.

On the morning of April 18, I flew to Rawalpindi, Pakistan.

From the plane, I could see the famous Khyber Pass, the scene of historic battles between the British and the "natives" in the early days of British colonialism; we also flew over the sprawling military airport near Peshwar, from which Francis Gary Power's U-2 plane took off before it was shot down over the Soviet Union; Dr. Henry Kissinger also secretly took off from Peshwar for Peking in 1970, thus heralding a new epoch in Sino-American relations.

In India, M. C. Chagla was now the Foreign Minister, and S. S. Pirzada was the Foreign Minister in Pakistan. Mr. Bhutto, who had disagreements with President Ayub Khan, particularly over the latter's signing of the Tashkent Declaration, had resigned, and was courageously building a political force of his own. My meetings with President Ayub Khan and Foreign Minister Pirzada were devoted to Vietnam, Indo-Pakistani relations, and the nuclear nonproliferation treaty. For the first time, I learned that Pakistani leaders were not happy with the manner in which the Tashkent Declaration was implemented—or rather, not implemented. Although a cease-fire and a withdrawal to the positions of August 5, 1965, had been achieved, they told me that high-level talks between the two heads of state never materialized.

In the view of the government of Pakistan, the question of Jammu and Kashmir was still a "matter of direct concern to both sides," but India had closed the door on this question, on the ground that the Kashmir Assembly had "confirmed the accession to India." The Pakistanis maintained that the Assembly was not representative of the people, since its members "were hand-picked" by India. It was obvious that although the Kashmir question was closed as far as India was concerned, it was very much open in the eyes of Pakistani leaders.

After attending the President's luncheon, he suggested that I should see Islamabad, the projected capital of Pakistan. Modern buildings were still in the process of construction when I visited the new city at 4:00 P.M. It reminded me of Brasilia, the new capital of Brazil, an architectural dream city that defies description.

CHAPTER XX

THE BIRTH
OF BANGLA DESH

Although the Tashkent Declaration closed a chapter of the Indo-Pakistani conflict, its underlying causes were still simmering four years after my trip to the Asian subcontinent. At the close of 1970, barely five years after the Tashkent meeting, these currents erupted in East Pakistan, leading to the cesarean birth of Bangla Desh.

In February 1971, an Indian Airlines aircraft was hijacked, under mysterious circumstances, from Srinigar (Kashmir) to Lahore (West Pakistan). At Lahore airport, the hijackers blew up the plane, and the Indian government banned all flights of Pakistan's civilian aircraft over India. Pakistan accused India of having engineered the hijacking of the plane through its agents to provide an excuse for the overflight ban, thus "further [increasing] difficulties and tensions between the two wings of Pakistan."

Like many others, I watched with a growing sense of horror as the long-smoldering political tension between West Pakistan and East Pakistan developed, in March 1971, into mob violence, slaughter, and massacre. On March 26, the Office of Public Information at the United Nations sent me the following news dispatch from Calcutta:

> Sheikh Mujibur Rahman, President of the Awami League, proclaimed this Friday the independence of East Pakistan, which becomes the "Popular Republic of Bangla Desh."
>
> This news is reported by the Indian News Agency which monitored it from the Voice of the Free Bangla Desh Radio. Violent fighting is also reported.

The next few days brought sensational reports of "massive massacres" of Bengalis and of other atrocities committed by the Pakistani army against the people of East Pakistan.

The conflict had its root in the deep split between the Punjabis of West Pakistan and the Bengalis of the more populous East Pakistan. (East and West Pakistan were separated by about a thousand miles of Indian territory.) Its immediate cause was the election of December 1970, the first of its kind in the nation's history.

Pakistan, which (with India) became independent of Britain in 1947, had never had a popularly elected government. During most of her history, she had been under military rule. Before the election, President Mohammed Yahya Khan[1] attempted to introduce real democracy in Pakistan by adopting the principle of "one man, one vote," which ensured, however, a permanent majority for East Pakistan (with a population of 75 million), as against West Pakistan (with a population of 50 million). The results of the election reflected the deep political and economic gulf between the Punjabis and the Bengalis. Nearly all the seats in the future National Assembly allocated to East Pakistan were won by the Awami League, a group of secessionists under the leadership of Sheikh Mujibur Rahman. The runner-up was the Pakistan People's Party (under Mr. Bhutto, the former Foreign Minister), which won all the seats in West Pakistan. Thus, the Awami League became the majority party of *all* Pakistan.

The Constituent Assembly was due to meet in March to frame a constitution and to arrange for the transfer of power to the newly elected National Assembly. As a result of a disagreement between the two parties on certain basic issues concern-

---

[1] President Ayub Khan relinquished his office on March 24, 1969, calling upon General Yahya Khan, commander-in-chief of the army, to succeed him and preserve the integrity of Pakistan.

ing the constitution to be drafted, President Khan decided to postpone the Assembly in order to give them time to reach agreement.
The Awami League, however, did not agree to the postponement;
it began to take control of the civilian administration in East
Pakistan. Sheikh Rahman then demanded full autonomy for East
Pakistan, with a separate currency and control over revenue raising, foreign trade, and foreign aid. The West Pakistani leaders
were not prepared to accept Sheikh Rahman's demands.

Meanwhile, in many parts of East Pakistan, more militant
members of the League urged complete independence from Pakistan, and in some towns, Pakistan's flag was burned, and photographs of Mohammed Ali Jinnah, "the Father of Pakistan," were
trampled upon. There was no doubt that the overwhelming majority of the people of East Pakistan were for complete independence.

Against this background, President Yahya Khan was convinced that what the Awami League wanted was not autonomy,
but secession and the "mutilation" of Pakistan. On the night of
March 25, the President called in the army "to maintain law and
order." He also banned all political activities and issued new mar-
tial law regulations.

From then on, as a result of press censorship, very little au-
thoritative news came out of East Pakistan, although it became
known that the Pakistani army had taken ruthless measures
against the Bengalis. Reports of the killing of unarmed civilians
aroused world concern. By the end of March, hundreds of thousands of terrified refugees from East Pakistan had fled across the
frontier to India, thus imposing a tremendous burden on the Indian government. Meanwhile, Pakistan accused India of having
incited the Bengalis to rise up against Pakistan and alleged that
Bengali "freedom fighters" were receiving military training on Indian soil.

The problem was compounded by the extraordinary apathy
of the Security Council, which was due to the fact that neither
India nor Pakistan wanted action by the United Nations. Because
each party insisted that the conflict was an internal affair, none of
the permanent members of the Council would support a call for a
meeting.

Some people have argued that I should have invoked Article

99 of the Charter, under which a Secretary General may bring to the attention of the Council any matter he considers a threat to world peace. But given the negative attitudes of India and Pakistan, I doubted that a majority of the Council members would have agreed even to hold a meeting; and even if they did, no agenda could have been adopted because Pakistan would have argued that international peace was not involved—that is, that the dispute was purely a matter between Pakistan and the Awami League. If I had then been accused of having invoked Article 99 on a "false" premise, my utility as a prospective mediator would have been seriously jeopardized. I was, however, in almost daily contact not only with India and Pakistan, but also with individual members of the Council, most of whom refused even to discuss the situation.

After four months of this futile exercise, I distributed a confidential memorandum (on July 20) to the Council members, warning them that the conflict could all too easily expand, erupting the entire subcontinent in fratricidal strife, and that the United Nations must now attempt to mitigate the tragedy. In August, I made the memorandum public, and it was in fact an implied invocation of Article 99. Yet it was not until December 4, over four months after my warning, that the Security Council met, and even then, the Council was unable to act: there was not even the shadow of a consensus whether the dispute involved India and Pakistan, or West Pakistan and East Pakistan, or India, Pakistan, and "Bangla Desh." I therefore had to confine myself to the humanitarian aspects of the problem, and in May, I organized an international aid program for the refugees in India, designating Prince Sadruddin Agha Khan as its high commissioner.

Meanwhile, the press carried reports that the Awami League, whose leader, Sheikh Mujibur Rahman, was presumed to have been captured by Pakistani troops, declared itself "The Government of the People's Republic of Bangla Desh." As the tragedy intensified, Big-Power involvement became a real possibility. The Soviet Union sought to delay recognition of East Pakistan by India, while the People's Republic of China warned India that it would support Pakistan against any Indian expansionist move.

By June, the number of Pakistani refugees flooding into India was reported to be near five million! Cholera broke out in Calcutta, the population of which had now swollen to over twelve million. Understandably, a mood of indignation and disgust swept over India.

Yet the Security Council was immobilized. The Big Powers did not agree; they did not even discuss the problem privately. As a result of this inaction, the United Nations was criticized. At a luncheon given to me in June by the UN Correspondents Association, an angry Indian reporter asked me why the UN had not come to grips with the real problem of Bangla Desh, but instead had dealt "only with peripheral humanitarian problems." I acknowledged that the entire episode was "a very terrible blot on the page of human history," but did not answer the correspondent directly.

I could not answer the correspondent because several weeks earlier, I had taken unusual (and secret) steps to try to bring about a political understanding between President Khan and the Awami League, and I could not disclose what I had done. It was something no other organ of the United Nations could have done. In April, I had written a secret letter to His Excellency Tunku Abdul Rahman, the former Prime Minister of Malaysia and a man of immense personal prestige in the Islamic world. Tunku was a friend of the late Jawaharlal Nehru as well as President Yahya Khan; a devout Moslem, Tunku was at that time the Secretary General of the Islamic Conference of Foreign Ministers. Thus, he would be a most qualified negotiator in the conflict, and I wrote to ask him if he would exercise his good offices to bring about a viable political settlement.

On May 3, Tunku replied that he would undertake the task "in the name of God and in the cause of humanity." My letter and Tunku's answer are reproduced in Appendixes A and B, Part VI.

Tunku and I agreed that if and when he contacted President Khan, he would not disclose that I had approached him; since he had previously been approached by many Moslem organizations, including the Islamic Conference, we believed that this would provide him with sufficient grounds for undertaking the mission. On July 17, he succeeded in contacting President Khan and informed me that his talks with the President were "satisfactory." He was proceeding to East Pakistan to make an on-the-spot study of the situation.

On July 23, I received another letter from Tunku (sent from

Jeddah, Saudi Arabia) outlining his plans to get the two leaders—President Yahya Khan and Prime Minister Indira Gandhi—together. He added, "Both . . . leaders, I think, are amenable to reason but both are inclined to be harassed by the prevailing mood of the nations."

After that, I followed his activities through news dispatches, and it became apparent that India would not receive a delegation of the Islamic Conference, although it had high regard for Tunku. My worst fears were confirmed when I received a lengthy report from him, marked "secret" and dated September 7. His covering letter said, in part, "We are unable to visit West Bengal in India because of India's objection to the inclusion of the representatives of the Islamic Conference." It concluded, "I have also sent an appeal to President Yahya Khan to exercise clemency if Mujibur Rahman is found guilty of the offence for which he is charged."

Since Tunku wrote this report on behalf of the Islamic Conference, and not as my representative, and since I have no authority to reproduce or quote from it, I shall refrain from doing so. In any case, it was clear that Tunku was not going to be able to bring about a meeting between President Khan and Prime Minister Gandhi. The episode of a private mission had come to a close.

As I indicated earlier, the leader of the separatist Awami League, Sheikh Mujibur Rahman, had reportedly been captured in Dacca by Pakistani troops in March. For three months, nobody knew whether Mujibur was dead or alive, and if alive, where he was detained. President Yahya Khan was reported to have been furious whenever anyone, including friendly diplomats, asked him about Sheikh Mujibur. But it was obvious that a political solution could be found only with the co-operation of Mujibur, since his execution would put an end to all conciliation efforts. His fate was therefore a matter of extraordinary interest among the representatives at the UN.

Against this background, I decided to make a personal appeal to the President and sent him a confidential letter under my personal seal in August. He did not reply to my appeal, nor did he comment on various other approaches made privately by several governments. His views on Sheikh Mujibur and the Bengalis were charged with emotion, bitterness and, at the same time, a certain callousness. The following excerpt from an interview by Pierre

Bois of *Le Figaro* is most revealing of the President's insensitivity on this issue.

QUESTION: But you speak of [Mujibur] in the past? What has become of him?

ANSWER: He is in prison.

QUESTION: Where?

ANSWER: I have no idea. Does your President in France know where all the criminals are?

QUESTION: But he is all the same your main enemy. . . .

ANSWER: He is not my personal enemy. He is that of the Pakistani people. Don't worry, everyone in Pakistan knows where he is. But it is useless to ask them, they will not tell you.

QUESTION: But international opinion?

ANSWER: I have had enough of justifying myself. I said that he was alive, one has only to take my word for it.

QUESTION: One spoke of the army atrocities concerning the tragic night of March 25.

ANSWER: One has forgotten to speak of the atrocities of the Awami League. On March 2 in . . . Chittagong, the Awami League grabbed the non-Bengalis, Biharis, Punjabis, and others, and bled them to death. A slaughter.

QUESTION: But your army?

ANSWER: My army is a professional army and well trained. I myself was trained in the Indian Army. If my soldiers kill, they kill in a clean way.

QUESTION: You have denied that there were 250,000 dead.

ANSWER: This is very exaggerated, but of course there were some deaths. What happened in Dacca was not a football match. When one fights, one does not throw flowers.[2]

I later learned that Sheikh Mujibur's trial had begun on August 11, but it was not disclosed where it was being held, and the proceedings were secret. On August 20, the world heard the news that he was charged with "waging war against Pakistan," and that he was being defended by an eminent Pakistani jurist. After that, nothing more was heard about the trial.

Now the international community became the passive ob-

---

[2] The New York *Times,* September 29, 1971.

server of a grim spectacle. On the one hand, India and Pakistan were moving inexorably toward an all-out war, and on the other hand, the United Nations was standing by helplessly, watching conditions steadily deteriorate. Peace talks were firmly ruled out by both sides, although President Khan asked for the posting of UN observers to the area and a withdrawal by both sides to "peacetime positions," implying for the first time that India and Pakistan were in a state of war. (India, incidentally, rejected the proposal.) Late in October, news from Karachi reported that Pakistani forces had killed 501 "enemy troops," defined as "Indians and Indian agents," in heavy fighting in East Pakistan. As to the Security Council, even a meeting was out of the question, since the Soviet Union was strongly opposed to it, maintaining that the problem was an internal one between Pakistan and the Awami League. India's problems, meanwhile, were compounded by natural disasters that hit the State of Orissa in the form of a cyclone and tidal waves; the number of dead was put at about 10,000, with hundreds of thousands homeless and untold damage to crops.

On November 23 President Khan declared a national emergency and put the whole country on a war footing.

At that time, I was in a hospital with a recurrence of a stomach ulcer I had had for seven years, and Roberto Guyer and Brian Urquhart kept me posted on developments. I was discharged November 27, and the first to see me at home on November 29 was Ambassador Samar Sen of India, who told me that the fighting in the border areas had intensified; his Prime Minister, he added, was concerned about my health.

As soon as Mr. Sen left my residence, I went over the papers sent over from my office. Among them was a news agency dispatch from Calcutta saying that the "Cabinet of the Bangla Desh Government" had dropped out of sight. It continued, "Unconfirmed but widely believed reports indicate that the Cabinet flew to New Delhi on Tuesday (November 23) in a special plane to confer with the Indian Government. One rumour is that Prime Minister Indira Gandhi called them to the capital to tell them that she is going to grant formal recognition to the Bangla Desh Government."

On Tuesday, November 30, among those who saw me at

home was Ambassador Yakov Malik of the Soviet Union. He said
that the basic problem in South Asia was the implementation of
self-determination in East Pakistan and the transfer of power to
the Awami League. He saw no other alternative. When I asked
him what he thought of Security Council action, he replied that
if the Security Council were to meet, the only "sensible thing" for
it to do would be to deal with the basic political issue of East
Pakistan.

By December 2, the Indians were reported to have seven divisions poised around East Pakistan, while Pakistan had assembled a force of about 10,000 irregular troops in Jammu and
Kashmir.

The war started on December 3 with air battles: Pakistani
planes carried out repeated raids on eleven Indian air bases and
two other military targets, while Indian bombers attacked targets
in Karachi, and air raid sirens wailed in Rawalpindi and other
West Pakistani cities.

The Security Council, at long last, met in emergency session
at 5:00 P.M. on that day. There was an air of pessimism in the
Council chamber, and with good reason, for in a series of meetings over the next few days, resolution after resolution was introduced, debated, and put to the vote—only to be vetoed by the
Soviet Union or otherwise fail to get the necessary votes for adoption. This time, the situation was far more complex than it had
been in 1965, when an easing of tensions culminating in the
Tashkent agreement was accomplished. There was a general feeling that India had a legitimate grievance against Pakistan, which
had abrogated the results of a free election, thus opening the flood-
gates to unmanageable millions of refugees, who were now on Indian soil. On the other hand, there was the feeling that India had
damaged its case and forfeited much of the good will it had enjoyed by deliberately exploiting the crisis with a massive war in
order to dismember Pakistan.

From the start, it was clear that India would not agree to a
cease-fire and withdrawal. There were acrimonious exchanges between the ambassadors of India and Pakistan, the Indian charging
Pakistan with genocide, and the Pakistani charging open, "classi-
cal" aggression on the part of India. There was a bitter clash between the Soviet Union and the People's Republic of China over

whether to invite representatives of secessionist Bangla Desh to address the Council. Even a Soviet resolution—which did not ask for a cease-fire, but merely requested Pakistan to "cease all acts of violence by Pakistani forces in East Pakistan"—failed to pass. Meanwhile, fighting in the area became more intense, and I had to ask the governments of India and Pakistan for a cessation of all military activities in, around, and over Dacca, the capital of East Pakistan, which was then under siege, for the purpose of evacuating United Nations and other personnel.

On December 6, India recognized The People's Republic of Bangla Desh. When the Security Council met for the third consecutive day, it finally acknowledged its incapacity to deal with the conflict. Ambassador A. A. Farah of Somalia, who played a prominent role in the debates, moved (under the "Uniting for Peace" resolution) that the question of Bangla Desh be referred to the twenty-sixth session of the General Assembly. That resolution, adopted in 1950 in regard to the Korean question, provides that if the Council fails to exercise its primary responsibility for the maintenance of international peace, the General Assembly shall consider the matter immediately with a view to making recommendations for collective measures, including the use of armed force when necessary, to restore peace.

There were several instances in the past in which the Security Council referred a question to the General Assembly: in October 1956, the Suez Canal crisis was referred to the Assembly; the question of Hungary was similarly referred in November 1956; and in 1958, the question of Lebanon was again referred to the Assembly. The resolution provides that an emergency meeting for this purpose is to be called, if requested by any nine or more of the fifteen Council members or by the majority of the members of the United Nations. Thus, no Security Council veto is permitted.

When the vote was taken at about 11:00 P.M. on that day, eleven voted in favor and none voted against; France, Poland, the Soviet Union, and the United Kingdom abstained. The main reason for the abstentions of France and the United Kingdom was their doubt about the wisdom of passing the issue to the Assembly, which has no power of enforcement under the Charter (as the Security Council has). The very fact that the Security Council decided to refer the question to the General Assembly was in itself a

political and diplomatic defeat for India. In the Assembly, much
to the distress of those who sympathized with the Indian case, her
defeat was more humiliating. On the night of December 7, the Assembly approved a resolution urging India and Pakistan to stop
fighting and pull back their troops. It was essentially the same as
the resolution vetoed in the Security Council by the Soviet Union.
The vote was 104 in favor, 11 against, and 10 abstentions, India,
the Soviet Union, and other East European countries voting
against it. Thus, the overwhelming majority emphasized the isolation of India and the Soviet Union, as the conviction grew among
the members that the United Nations must immediately take some
sort of action.

Just before the General Assembly met, I received a report
from Prince Sadruddin Agha Khan in Geneva that war conditions
had forced the suspension of United Nations food shipments to
East Pakistani refugees in India. The government of India had
closed Calcutta airport to international flights, resulting in the suspension of shipments of blankets, which constituted a large part of
the relief program. The harbor at Calcutta was also closed, and
fourteen ships heading for Calcutta with tens of thousands of tons
of food from Rangoon and Bangkok would not be able to unload.

In addition, the International Committee of the Red Cross informed Paul-Marc Henry, my representative in Dacca, that the intensity of fighting and widespread killings impeded humanitarian
efforts. I took the occasion of the General Assembly meeting,
before the vote took place, to appeal to all parties to the conflict,
no matter what their allegiance, to take every possible measure to
spare the lives of the innocent civilian population that was
afflicted by the hostilities.

Meanwhile, changes had taken place in the government of
Pakistan. On December 7, President Yahya Khan called on the
seventy-seven-year-old Bengali politician Nurul Amin to become
Pakistan's first Prime Minister since 1958. Zulfikar Ali Bhutto
became deputy prime minister and Foreign Minister. (Amin and
Bhutto had been political foes; Bhutto called his appointment "a
bitter pill.")

The war did not end with the adoption of the General Assembly resolution. There were intensive informal discussions among
several delegates to bring the question back to the Security Coun-

cil, but the grim truth emerged again that the Council, which is the principal organ to deal with matters threatening international peace and security, is unable to take effective action when there is conflict among the Big Powers. Immediately after the adoption of the resolution, for instance, an Indian government spokesman said in New Delhi that India did not feel bound by it. "The good thing about a General Assembly resolution," he added, "is that it is recommendatory, not mandatory. It is one thing to vote, but another to grapple with a complex situation."

Nevertheless, on December 9, Pakistan decided to accept the General Assembly's call for a cease-fire, although the acceptance message made no mention of the ten million refugees who had streamed from East Pakistan into India.

Critics of Pakistan had long contended that it would be impossible to get the refugees to go home unless the Pakistani government reached some sort of accord with the elected representatives of East Pakistan, particularly with their leader, Sheikh Mujibur Rahman.

No reply was received from the government of India on that day, but the Associated Press reported that Prime Minister Indira Gandhi had rejected the General Assembly's call for a cease-fire and withdrawal, saying that India would "take all steps" to achieve the independence of East Pakistan.

Meanwhile, Indian troops had closed in on Dacca. Based on the reports received from my representative there, I proposed to both India and Pakistan the establishment of neutral enclaves in Dacca for foreigners (who numbered over five hundred) and forty-six UN employees awaiting evacuation by air from the besieged city. The zone, comprising the headquarters of the UN relief operations, together with a hotel and a hospital, was to serve as an assembly area for the UN staff and foreigners before they were taken to the airport to be flown out. On the morning of December 9, the Indian government promised a truce in the air, and arrangements were made to attempt the evacuation from Dacca in two British and two Canadian C-130 transports.

Also on December 9, the commander of India's eastern forces said that the retreat of the Pakistanis in East Pakistan had become a rout, as Indian troops pushed the foe into an ever-shrinking circle whose center was Dacca. In Rawalpindi, the

Pakistani government continued to insist that its troops were holding fast in East Pakistan. But reports began to multiply that Pakistani troops were killing Bengali civilians as they retreated, and
that Bengalis were killing non-Bengali Pakistanis and those who
collaborated with them. On December 10, a Pakistani military
spokesman in Rawalpindi conceded that Indian troops outnumbered the Pakistanis by six to one, and that Indian troops were reported to have crossed the wide Meghina River and to be heading
toward Dacca.

For me, the immediate problem was the evacuation of the
United Nations personnel and the foreigners stranded there. My
only contact with the situation in Dacca was through my representative, Paul-Marc Henry, who reported to me daily. Since
Dacca's airport had been smashed beyond repair by Indian
bombs, it seemed unlikely that the UN employees or other foreign
personnel could be evacuated before the Indians took Dacca.

On December 11, a Canadian air force plane from Calcutta
—one of the four C-130 transports brought to the Indian city
under United Nations auspices—got within thirty miles of Dacca
and asked for permission to land. It was ordered away by the control tower. According to the pilot, the control tower radioed, "We
don't give a damn about UN auspices. No plane that has landed
in India can come down here." The plane returned to India.
Since India was insisting that all planes meant for the airlift from
Dacca must stop in Calcutta on the way in and out, there was no
alternative route to take. The Indian authorities said that determining the routes of the planes in this manner was the only way
their safety could be guaranteed. But the real reason, in my view,
was that India wanted to make sure that no Pakistani officials,
military or civilian, escaped on the planes.

Ralph Bunche died of a prolonged and acute kidney ailment
on December 9. After attending funeral services on December 11,
I returned to the United Nations to meet with seventeen ambassadors collectively on humanitarian aid for the refugees. Then I met
separately with India's Foreign Minister Sadar Swaran Singh and
Pakistan's Ambassador Agha Shahi on the airlift question; both
assured me of co-operation. As soon as they left, I got a report
that a Canadian air force plane (bearing a United Nations symbol) finally gave up the attempt to reach Dacca and flew back to

its base in Bangkok. The plane, coming in from Bangkok over the Bay of Bengal, had been rocked by antiaircraft fire from a ship. Three British planes, with similar United Nations emblems, stayed in Calcutta in the hope that a new airlift could be organized on the next day, December 12.

It was the third time the airlift had fizzled. While the Dacca evacuation was going badly, I later got reports that the evacuation of foreigners from Karachi in West Pakistan (to Teheran) had been completed in British planes. It was not until December 12 that the Pakistani authorities in Dacca permitted the airlift of foreigners and UN personnel from Dacca. Three British Royal Air Force C-130 Hercules transports made a total of four trips to and from Dacca. Most of the non-UN evacuees flew to Singapore, where the planes were based, after an inspection stop in Calcutta.

On December 12, as news reached the United Nations that Indian troops advancing on Dacca had reached a small town twenty-two miles from the provincial capital, the United States requested the immediate convening of the Security Council. The Council met at 4:00 P.M., and Ambassador George Bush immediately tabled a draft resolution calling upon India to accept forthwith a cease-fire and a mutual withdrawal in the Indian-Pakistani war. Mr. Bush castigated India for having intervened militarily in East Pakistan and placed in jeopardy "the territorial integrity and political independence of its neighbor, Pakistan." He wanted to know India's further intentions. "For example," he asked, "does India intend to use the present situation to destroy the Pakistani army in the West? Does India intend to annex territory in West Pakistan . . . [or in] Pakistan-controlled Kashmir? [If not] . . . then a prompt disavowal is required."

When the resolution was put to the vote on the next day, the Soviet Union killed it with a veto. During the debate, Ambassador Yakov Malik explained that he had to veto the U.S. draft mainly because it did not include a call for a political settlement. It was obvious that there was no prospect of any agreement on the nature of the solution. And, indeed, at the next meeting, there were unmistakable signs that the Council was visibly shifting its focus to political issues. The main reason for the change was the latest news that reached the United Nations: the civilian regional government in Dacca, formed by the Pakistani military authorities, had resigned. As Indian bombers were attacking Dacca, destroying several buildings (including the official residence of the Governor of East Pakistan) the entire regional government resigned, dissociating itself from the central administration of President Yahya Khan.

Now a new British-French draft resolution clearly implied that power had to be handed over to the local representatives in East Pakistan. When the Council met again on December 15, there were several draft resolutions before it besides the British-French draft. By then the fall of Dacca was imminent, and the Council's shift to the political consideration of the problem was more evident than ever. For the first time, the majority of the Council members appeared to agree with Ambassador Yakov Malik when he said: "the Council should recognize that, simultaneously with the cease-fire, power in East Pakistan must be transferred to the representatives of the majority party, elected in December 1970."

No vote on any of the resolutions was taken at that meeting, which was adjourned after midnight. When the meeting was resumed at 10:30 A.M. on December 16, Foreign Minister Swaran Singh of India made a dramatic announcement: India, having accomplished its objectives, had ordered a cease-fire! Singh quoted this statement by his Prime Minister:

> Now as the Pakistani armed forces have surrendered in Bangla Desh and Bangla Desh is free, it is pointless in our view to continue the present conflict. Therefore, in order to stop further bloodshed and unnecessary loss of life, we have ordered our armed forces to cease fire everywhere on the western front with effect from 2000 hours repeat 2000 hours IST (Indian standard time) on Friday the 17th, repeat 17th December 1971. It is our earnest hope that there will be a corresponding immediate response from the Government of Pakistan.

Then things moved fast. On December 17, President Yahya Khan responded by ordering a cease-fire in the West. The last meeting of the Security Council on the Indo-Pakistani conflict took place on December 21. It was now possible, of course, to reach agreement on an acceptable draft resolution, and one was promptly passed.

To a considerable extent, the resolution represented a compromise of several drafts that had been presented to the Council in the past. It also took account of the realities of the prevailing situation. Among other things, it demanded a durable cease-fire and a cessation of hostilities in all areas of conflict, and called for international assistance in the relief of the suffering of refugees; it also called for their rehabilitation and for their return in safety and dignity to their homes.

Meanwhile, on December 19, Zulfikar Ali Bhutto left New York for Rawalpindi, as he was asked by President Yahya Khan to form a new government, and on December 21, he took over the functions of the President from Yahya Khan. Immediately after his assumption of office, he announced his intention to undertake a fundamental overhaul of Pakistan's internal and foreign policies, including the imminent release of Sheikh Mujibur Rahman.

The Indian conquest of East Pakistan was complete and the new nation of Bangla Desh was born.

The events of 1972 and 1973 in the subcontinent did not directly involve me; since I had retired, I was no longer in official contact with the governments concerned, but could follow developments only from the news media. It is therefore difficult to conclude the story of Bangla Desh with a complete analysis.

Some fundamental questions need to be posed, however. While there is absolutely no doubt about the brutal character of Pakistan's military suppression of the Bengalis from March 25, 1971, onward—the savagery of the atrocities committed have few parallels in history—there is considerable doubt about India's role in this grim episode. What was the effect of India's response—in terms of international law, in human terms, and in the context of the doctrine of noninterference in the internal affairs of another state? Some of the answers are suggested by two distinguished Indians, both Hindus. Dr. Jagat Narain, professor of law at Queen's University of Belfast in Northern Ireland, maintains that while India's action in East Pakistan was a clear breach of international law, "yet this very act is bound to highlight the ineffectiveness of international law in coping with the worst man-made disaster in human history. If India is held guilty under the law, it provides no answer to what she should have done. . . . It seems strange that international law should expect an already poor neighbouring state to bear the burden of sustaining 10 million aliens, but that no similar obligation should be placed on other, richer states according to their resources. Can all this be justified in the name of non-intervention?"[3]

On the other hand, Dr. Nirad Chaudhuri, a well-known Bengali author, takes a dim view of India's motivations:

> These troubles would not have taken the extreme form they finally took unless India had been a factor in the situation. To my thinking, a settlement between the Bengali Muslims and Pakistan would have been arrived at even after the military suppression if India had not helped the Bengali insurgents to organize attacks on East Bengal from her territory. By showing an obvious desire to profit by the troubles, India stiffened the back of the Pakistan government.
>
> I am also unable to credit the Government of India with any genuine sympathy for the suppressed Muslims in East Bengal, because I know what they feel for the Bengalis in West Bengal. The resentment of Hindu Bengalis against Delhi is not less burning than the Bengali Muslim's against Rawalpindi.[4]

No matter how history judges the motivations of India or Pakistan, their conflict had a tragic result for the international community: a major victim of the war was the United Nations and the principle of international co-operation that it embodies. The World Organization received one more serious blow, and in my view, with some justification. For throughout the struggle, the United Nations had made no move to act; my pleas and warnings to the Security Council, both privately and publicly, fell on deaf ears. The Council was immobilized, both by the refusal of the parties directly involved (India and Pakistan) and by the major powers, to face up to their obligations under the Charter to confront the issues forthrightly.

As a friend to both India and Pakistan, and as one who was brought up to admire and absorb the cultural heritage of both countries, I felt a sharp pang of distress at the tragic turn of events. India, which had a legitimate grievance, as narrated above, took two contradictory positions. On the one hand, it argued that the repression in East Pakistan was a threat to its security. On the other hand, it insisted that the problems of Pakistan were strictly an internal affair, not subject to UN intervention.

---

[3] *The London Times,* December 8, 1971.
[4] Ibid., December 21, 1971.

Pakistan, on its side, went through the motions of inviting UN intervention, but on terms prejudicial to the interests of the repressed Bengalis and their Indian sympathizers. From the point of view of Pakistan (West Pakistan), the Awami League was a nonparty and Sheikh Mujibur Rahman a nonperson; the only issue was Kashmir.

During the General Assembly debates on the Bangla Desh question in December, I became increasingly worried about another matter that directly affected me. On January 23, 1970, I had announced publicly that I would not serve another term "under any circumstances whatsoever."

Ten months after that announcement, the Security Council had still made no effort to consider the question of my successor, and it was the Council's responsibility to recommend a candidate to the General Assembly for appointment. Several governments had come out with the names of candidates, but although private consultations had been going on, no serious attempts had been made by the Council to agree on one.

Since my discharge from the hospital, I had reiterated my decision in very categorical terms to several delegates, particularly the permanent members of the Security Council, who have the veto power to reject any candidate. It was, therefore, with a great sense of relief that I learned of the first secret meeting of the representatives of the United States, China, the Soviet Union, France, and Britain on December 7; it was the first breakthrough in the long-neglected question of "the search for a successor." Much to my distress, however, the first meeting was an abortive one. Although it was "secret," news reached me in the evening that the Big Powers had vetoed each other's candidates. For example, China first proposed Dr. Felip Herrera, a distinguished Chilean banker and educator. The United States opposed the nomination. Again, China proposed another Chilean, Dr. Gabriel Valdés, the former Foreign Minister of Chile. Again, the United States opposed the nomination, saying that it would oppose any Chilean. China then proposed Ambassador Carlos Ortíz De Rozas, permanent representative of Argentina to the United Nations. Now it was the turn of the Soviet Union to oppose the nomination. Thus, any candidate proposed by one was opposed by the other, and there was no sign of agreement on any candidate. I wondered whether there would be any agreement eventually. The indications were ominous, and I felt terribly sick.

Against this background, the Security Council met on December 17 to consider a candidate. Seven names were proposed at that meeting, but only one—Ambassador Kurt Waldheim of Austria—got ten affirmative votes (the necessary minimum vote is nine). But the United Kingdom and China vetoed the nomination. At its second meeting on December 20, the Council again was unable to recommend any candidate. Out of ten names proposed, only three received the required votes: Ambassador Waldheim, Ambassador Ortíz De Rozas of Argentina, and Ambassador Max Jacobson of Finland. All three, however, were vetoed—Kurt Waldheim by China, Ortíz De Rozas by the Soviet Union, and Max Jacobson again by the Soviet Union. At its third and last meeting on December 21, six names were proposed, and three got the required votes: Ortíz De Rozas (12), Kurt Waldheim (11) and Max Jacobson (9). Both Ortíz De Rozas and Max Jacobson were vetoed by the Soviet Union, however. Ambassador Kurt Waldheim therefore emerged as the successful candidate.

Thus, December 21 was a memorable day on two counts: the last meeting of the Security Council on Bangla Desh took place on that day, and the Council recommended that the General Assembly appoint Ambassador Waldheim to succeed me. I was so relieved and elated at the news of the Council's agreement on my successor that I immediately phoned my wife and daughter about my "liberation," asking them to inform our friends of the extraordinary news.

On the next day, Mr. Waldheim received the unanimous approval of the General Assembly. I closed my eyes and meditated. I prayed for the success of Mr. Waldheim and the United Nations.

PART VII

GLOBAL CHALLENGES

The foregoing survey of the bitter and frequently bloody disputes of the 1960s tragically illustrates the consequences of that pre-atomic, nation-oriented mentality I discussed in the opening pages of this book. As I pointed out then, the realities of the present-day world call for a new quality of planetary imagination; they call for a *global* mentality that takes account of the nature of interdependence and the imperative need to change. In this section, I should like to assess what I see as the realities of the present world situation.

For the past fifteen years and more, I have never tired of saying that the issue facing mankind is not primarily the contest between communism and democracy. The more essential issue is the division of the world into the prosperous and the abject poor, the weak and the strong, the ruler and the ruled, the master race and the subhuman. Even before I was appointed Secretary General of the United Nations, I had been convinced that the most serious source of tension in the world is the division of the world into rich nations and poor nations. I had stressed my conviction that this division of the world is more real, more lasting, and ultimately more explosive even than that between the communists and non-communists.

While there is no doubt that political ideologies still constitute the basis of the most serious tension in the world, one can see that the rigid concepts of capitalism and communism are gradually giving way to a more eclectic approach. Capitalist countries have accepted several socialist ideas, such as planned economic growth, full employment, and equality of opportunity, and have adopted several measures in the field of social security that would have been considered revolutionary at the beginning of this century. Communist countries, in an effort to improve their production and to satisfy the needs of their people, are, on the other hand, using methods developed in capitalist systems, such as incentives. In many Eastern European countries, economists have become aware that the growing complexity of the economic systems in their countries calls for a certain measure of decentralization of the decision-making process. I do not regard these developments as implying any weaknesses on the part of either capitalism or communism. They are only signs that, as a result of their effort to be efficient and to promote the greatest good of the greatest number —which, after all, is a common goal of all political systems—the sharp distinctions between the two systems are beginning to lose their edge. Even such fundamental freedoms as freedom of speech, freedom of conscience, and freedom of association, which were absent in communist societies for so long, are emerging in varying degrees in communist countries. The rate of such emergence will be related to the willingness of these societies to open up to the outside world. In any event, political and ideological tensions will continue to be a feature of our time.

While the ideological conflict that developed after World War II resulted in a division of the world into East and West, the gap between rich and poor countries has led to a kind of North-South division of the world. By the time I was appointed Secretary General, statistics showed that two thirds of the world's population living in the less developed regions of the world still shared less than one sixth of the world's income. In 1962, the annual per capita income in these regions averaged $136, while that of the population of the economically advanced North America and Western Europe averaged $2,845 and $1,033, respectively.

These abstract figures do little to convey the realities that underlie the gaps in income. In spite of dramatic improvements in the prevention of disease (which over the preceding decade had added ten to twenty years to the expectation of life in the developing countries) the average life expectancy in these countries still fell far behind that in the North Atlantic countries. In particular, the tragic death of small children weighed far more heavily upon the developing lands. In the most highly developed countries, the mortality rate of children up to five years of age varied from 4.5 to 6.3 per 1,000. Yet in Latin America, the rates were five to ten times higher, and in Africa, higher still.

One reason for the contrast in mortality rates lies in the disparities in medical services—in medical personnel, hospital beds, drugs, and preventive medicine. In North America, Western Europe, and the Soviet Union, for instance, there is generally one doctor for fewer than 1,000 inhabitants, compared with one for 6,000 in India, 32,000 in Afghanistan, 39,000 in Mali and approximately 96,000 in Ethiopia. Failure to invest adequately in the control of disease and the promotion of health has led, in many parts of the world, to a deterioration of standards of health and sanitation.

Another reason for the difference in mortality rates certainly lies in disparities in diet. Men and women in North America and Western Europe eat, on the average, about 3,000 calories and 80 to 90 grams of protein a day. In Latin America (outside Argentina), the average falls to 2,400 calories and some 70 grams of protein; in Asia, to 2,100 calories and 50 grams—a level still below pre-war standards; in Africa, the protein consumption is lower still. But these abstractions give no true sense of the nutritional disparity—between the steaks and chocolates, the salads and fruits in the diets of the developed countries, and the bowl of rice, with little variety beyond a change of sauce that makes up, day in and day out, the food of most Asians. In Burma, there is a persistent belief that the more rice one eats, the more healthy one will be!

These inadequacies in diet and medical care are made more intolerable, for about a billion people, by the desperate standards of housing they are forced to endure. The major cities of the developing continents all have their densely crowded shanty towns, in which 20 to 30 per cent of the city's inhabitants may be living—without water, without sewers, without roads. And out in the countryside, the shacks of laborers, of untouchables, and of the rural unemployed only seem a little less miserable because of their larger ratios of light and air.

The misery of much of the developing world is a progressive misery. In the early sixties, it threatened to grow worse if the international community neglected to take prompt and vigorous action. In 1961, economists and social scientists estimated that the numbers of unemployed men and women suffering from hunger and malnutrition would be markedly greater in 1971 than a decade earlier. For it is in the poor countries that the highest growth rate of population is found. In the early sixties, there was simply no prospect of growth in agricultural production sufficient to accommodate that rising flood of people.

Thus the postwar world witnessed two revolts—the revolt for political freedom and, at the same time, the revolt of the have-nots. Over the centuries, black- and brown-skinned humanity had accepted "the white man's burden," and at the same time, had been willing to accept poverty as a fact of life. The fifteen years that elapsed between the end of World War II and the beginning of the sixties were marked by a categorical rejection of this concept.

I felt very strongly when I assumed the duties of Secretary General that it is no longer either morally acceptable or politically expedient for the more advanced nations to ignore the backwardness and poverty of the others. In the development of democratic nations, the tax system is a tacit recognition of the responsibility of a society for all its members, of the more fortunate for the less fortunate. I also felt deeply that, in the society of nations, there is the need to recognize the *general* responsibility for alleviating poverty and misfortune among two thirds of humanity.

This view of the human situation was widely shared by member states, both large and small. When President Kennedy, in the course of his address to the General Assembly in September 1961, proposed that the 1960s be designated as the United Nations Development Decade, the reception was one of undivided enthusiasm.

The postwar revolution in world communications and the

flowering of independence for many underdeveloped countries had already had a tremendous impact on the aspirations of poorer peoples all over the world. Almost overnight, the ideals of economic progress, of longer life, and of a better life through improved nutrition, health, shelter, and education reached the poor countries that had remained so far outside the mainstream of the industrial revolution. It had taken that revolution over a century to spread from Europe to North America and to Japan, but within a few short years the revolution of rising expectations swept over other countries. Economic and social progress became the overriding priority for all the newly-independent nations. A deep scrutiny of and a bold challenge to traditional international economic relations took place. Every possible pressure was exerted by the new countries to obtain greater international economic justice and a better lot for their peoples. The world suddenly woke up to the fact that probably never before in history had such enormous differences prevailed in the fates of human beings living at the same time on the same planet.

The revolution of economic development, a major feature of our time, looked for every possible avenue of expression; it knocked at the hearts and at the purses of peoples, in an effort to create a worldwide consciousness and response to its impatient and rightful demands. It was not good enough to tell the developing countries that they had to do the job themselves and that the fate of their peoples was their own concern. They pointed—often, angrily—at the exploitation to which they had been subjected for so long, and which continues to this day in the form of low prices for their raw materials and agricultural products and high prices for their imports of manufactured goods and industrial equipment. No wonder that the United Nations became the major forum and battleground in which the developing countries denounced current injustices, appealed for worldwide help and solidarity, put forth proposals for international action, and established economic and social development as the overriding priority for the world community.

With the launching of the Development Decade by the General Assembly at the end of 1961, all member states and their peoples were to intensify their efforts during the 1960s to halt and reverse the increasing gap in per capita incomes between the rich and the poor. The objective was to attain, in each developing country, a minimum annual growth rate of 5 per cent in aggregate national income by the end of the decade. Our vision was that of a world community in which the wealth created in it is so divided that the vast majority of people have the education, the skills, the environment, and the kind of income needed to lead a satisfying life.

The men and women who wrote the UN Charter had perceptive vision when they singled out economic and social development as one of the main factors of peace. In their global view of the postwar period, they saw the gulf between the rich and the poor as one of the gravest new threats to world peace and understanding.

The Economic and Social Council was established as one of the principal organs of the Charter and was entrusted with the task of dealing with the profound challenge of meeting human needs in the vital areas of food, clothing, shelter, health, education, human rights, and so on. Together with the specialized agencies, the United Nations, for the first time in history, provided mankind with mechanisms that would seek to improve the life of every man, woman, and child on earth. This was a goal perhaps more revolutionary than any political revolution in history.

With the help of my colleagues from the specialized agencies, I presented my proposals for action to the Economic and Social Council at its summer session in 1962. They dealt with new approaches to development planning, the mobilization of human resources, international trade, development financing, technical co-operation, and other aids to development. The Council endorsed my suggestions[1] and later gave full support to the Freedom from Hunger Campaign, the new World Food Program, and to a planned conference on the application of science and technology to the problems of the less developed areas. The Council also established a thirteen-member committee to keep under review activities and progress during the decade.

By 1965, however, I concluded that the results had been dis-

---

[1] Contained in *The United Nations Development Decade: Proposals for Action,* publication sales no. 62.11.B.2.

appointing. In a report I submitted on the decade at midpoint, I observed that many indicators of economic advance showed that the rate of improvement between the 1950s and 1960s *had declined*. The gap between the per capita incomes of the rich and poor countries had *widened* by 1965. I pointed out that the objectives of the decade were not likely to be achieved by 1970, unless governments of both developed and developing countries were willing to give a massive new impetus to development. Well-meaning declarations of intent had to be followed by actual implementation of programs, many of which would involve some sacrifice. Otherwise, the aspirations embodied in the Development Decade would remain mere pious hopes.

The First Development Decade has been called by some a modest success, by others, a disappointment and a failure. If the results are measured in terms of growth and assistance alone, then the decade was a dismal failure. By 1970, the average rate of growth of national income in the developing countries as a whole had virtually touched 5 per cent. Despite that modest advance, the scale of contributions for aid from the major donors was shrinking in relation to their growing resources. The net flow of financial aid to developing countries declined from .79 per cent of the gross national product in 1960 to about .66 per cent in 1969, though this still represented a rise in absolute amounts.

Some of the reasons for failure were that the resources made available to meet the major requirements of the developing countries were far from satisfactory. The flow of funds to those countries since 1961 had leveled off. Words were spoken, gestures were made, but the sense of clear commitment seemed to be absent. In addition, the richer nations of the West tended to approach the whole problem of development with an unrealistic time scale in mind. In their view, the young economies should have been well on their way to self-sustaining growth within a decade if resources were mobilized and considerable aid were channeled. But the plain fact is that even the most successful of the developed nations—the United States—took eighty years to reach industrial maturity. Even the most ingenious—Japan—took at least forty for its first revolution and, since the war, fifteen for its second. The nations that seek to develop their economies today face all the dilemmas of rapid transition—how to modernize static farming, how to choose industries that actually produce a surplus, and how to finance the new skills needed to produce more capital. But they face even tougher problems as well—the population explosion, uncontrolled urbanization, unfavorable trade patterns, and inefficient technology.

At the end of the ten-year period, according to the United Nations Statistical Office, the developing countries had achieved an annual average increase of about 4.6 per cent in their total gross domestic product, but because of population growth, this meant only a 2 per cent increase in their per capita gross product. Moreover, while some countries had made rapid progress, in others the rate was very moderate.

But there was also a bright side to the Development Decade. Priorities for development were more clearly defined than before. In particular, international economic co-operation and the United Nations itself were greatly strengthened during the decade.

Looking back over my ten years of office, if I feel that peace and justice have been desperately slow in coming to humanity, I have at least the satisfaction of knowing that some significant progress has been achieved in other fields. Very remarkable progress, for instance, was made in freeing mankind from the scourge of malaria, which had been considered the world's greatest single cause of disablement. During the decade, it was possible to extend antimalaria measures to large areas. As a result, over a billion people are now living in areas in which this disease has been completely eradicated. By preventing incapacity and death due to malaria, the antimalaria campaign has broken the vicious circle of poverty and disease in many areas of the world. Specifically, it has contributed to a greater rice production in some countries by increasing the work output of the labor force. This achievement, unparalleled in the annals of public health, would not have been possible without the efforts of national governments, assisted by the World Health Organization and other UN agencies.

At the time of my retirement, dramatic progress had been made in eradicating smallpox, as a result of the global campaign launched by the World Health Organization in 1966. Now there are clear signs that this disease will be eliminated from the face of the earth before the end of the seventies.

An important feature of the First Development Decade had been the creation of the World Food Program, an undertaking of the Food and Agriculture Organization of the United Nations, for multilateral food aid to developing countries. From the beginning of 1963 to the close of 1971, the World Food Program had committed more than $1 billion in food aid to a total of almost 500 development projects in some 83 countries.

The success of the efforts by FAO and some private foundations in developing and cultivating high-yield cereals has dramatically improved the food supply in a number of areas in which the food situation in past years stood at the very edge of disaster. This "green revolution" has proved conclusively that the scientific and technological bases for increased agricultural productivity and, therefore, an abundant world food supply are indeed available. This multilateral effort had grown sevenfold during the First Development Decade. When the Second Development Decade was launched in 1971, with the aim of doubling world food production before 1981, there was a mood of optimism at the United Nations, an optimism based on the success of the First Development Decade in this particular field. I am confident that the momentum thus gained by the World Food Program as an instrument of international assistance to development will not be lost in the next few years.

The decade also witnessed a thorough reorientation of the International Labor Organization. Comprehensive long-term programs were initiated in the areas of human resources, conditions of work and life, and the development of social institutions and research. Important developments in the field of human rights included the adoption of the declaration concerning the policy of *apartheid* of the Republic of South Africa, the formulation of a program for the elimination of *apartheid* in labor matters in that country, and the launching of an intensive program of action with a view to promoting equality of opportunity and treatment in employment.

The past decade also saw the establishment of the United Nations Industrial Development Organization on January 1, 1967, with its headquarters in Vienna. During the decade, there was an unprecedented expansion of world trade, and total exports have tripled since 1961; developing countries have also been able to rely increasingly on the financial institutions of the United Nations system for development assistance. The International Monetary Fund played a very significant role in facilitating this assistance. During the close of the decade, the International Bank for Reconstruction and Development (the World Bank) also greatly expanded and accelerated its activities. For the first time in its history, the Bank financed projects in public health, education, and other fields that have great social as well as economic impact. The decade also witnessed the emergence of new regional development banks. They have already shown their capacity for assisting the economic development of their respective regions.

The period from 1961 to 1971 witnessed amazing scientific and technological developments. Artificial earth satellites now serve as meteorological observing platforms, and high-speed electronic computers permit weather prediction. The World Weather Watch, operated by the World Meteorological Organization since 1967, is an outstanding example of a highly useful and successful international endeavor on a truly global scale.

During the past decade, enthusiasm for the potential benefits of modern scientific and technological advances had been tempered by a growing realization that these wondrous tools are also increasing man's capacity to destroy the human and natural resources of the earth. It has become quite clear that a unified global endeavor to control and preserve man and his environment is urgently required. One specialized agency of the United Nations, the Inter-Governmental Maritime Consultative Organization, was already helping, before the end of the decade, to prevent pollution of the sea by oil, and its activities are now being extended to cover other shipborne pollutants. Marine pollution was only one of many topics included in the agenda of the historic United Nations Conference on the Human Environment, held in Stockholm in June 1972.

The preservation of mankind's cultural heritage is another of the many areas in which international action has proved feasible and successful during recent years. The international campaigns sponsored by the United Nations Educational, Scientific, and Cultural Organization to protect endangered art monuments indicate that peoples and nations are capable of pooling their resources and ingenuity in an effort to save the glories of human civilization for future civilizations.

Outside the scope of the First Development Decade, the United Nations was involved in several other activities that have a direct bearing on the fashioning of a better society and a more livable world. Discussions on the feasibility of a United Nations university, continuing consideration to promote the peaceful use of nuclear energy by the International Atomic Energy Agency, the proposed creation of a global automatic telephone network by the International Telecommunication Union, and the planning of major air navigation surveys by the International Civil Aviation Organization are some of the instances that tell the other part of the United Nations story, which is one of the most successful and at the same time the least known.

No one will ever be able to evaluate the impact and historical effects of these efforts. It means little to say that each year the UN employs an average of 8,000 international experts, provides more than 5,000 fellowships, supplies $30 million of equipment, supports 1,200 major preinvestment projects and 2,500 smaller-scale development projects; or that during the first Development Decade, $3,400 million were estimated to have been invested as a direct or indirect result of fundings of UN-aided projects.

Some of the results are: clean water running in villages, children freed from hunger and early death, employment of more people, greater access to consumer goods, sewers in cities, and better crops, schools, universities, hospitals, and roads in developing countries.

When I travelled in the poorer continents, I heard everywhere expressions of thanks for this splendid co-operation between the rich and the poor peoples of the world. It will stand out as a fact of prime historic importance that the emergence of a global society during the 1960s was accompanied by the building of this bridge between the North and the South, between the rich and the poor. In my view, this bridge is growing stronger with the passage of time. It is a sign of hope for mankind—a sign I saw when visiting the developing countries—that part of the struggle for economic and social betterment is waged under the common flag of the United Nations. For international solidarity is an ingredient of the daily life in those countries; their nationhood and development have unfolded in the context of an interdependent and concerned world. The United Nations has a moral meaning for the children of developing countries, for they have received the imprints of love from fellow human beings at a time when the mind and the heart are very receptive. Seeds of future understanding and solidarity have thus been sown in the impoverished and more populated two thirds of the world, at the time of transition into the global age. Perhaps some day this slow and patient building of a better economic order will be recognized as one of the most lasting contributions of the United Nations, during a period when many of the deeper realities of our global society were still blurred by political disputes and turmoil.

At the end of the Development Decade in 1970, the United Nations Development Program (the result of the merger of UN technical assistance and the preinvestment fund) had total yearly resources of $260 million, donated by 128 governments.

Such sums will of course appear modest to those who are familiar with the magnitude and poignancy of the problem of poverty in two thirds of the world. They look even less impressive when compared with the huge resources wasted on armaments (more than $1 trillion from 1963 to 1969). During my mandate, I never ceased to underline their inadequacy in the face of the senseless spending on potential forces of destruction and death, instead of construction and life. My appeals, alas, were of little avail. The armaments and defense budgets of the world continue to mount, and in 1968 the more advanced countries spent approximately $173 billion on armaments, this being about fourteen times as much as they contributed for aid. I feel very strongly that the substantial savings resulting from disarmament can rapidly accelerate the raising of economic and social standards of the less-developed countries. It is well to remember, however, that the strategy enunciated in the launching of the First Development Decade had only political and moral force; it did not bind the governments to a legal commitment. I can only hope that the Second Development Decade, launched in 1970, will be more successful than the first.

Humanity has reached the point of no return. Acceptance of the community of interest has become a requirement of human survival on this planet. It can no longer be dismissed as an idealistic concept, unrelated to realities. The traditional sovereign state is no longer a viable guarantee of a nation's security or economic prosperity, nor even a guarantee of national survival. More and more men of science and scholarship, as well as business leaders and public administrators, have come to grasp this underlying fact of interdependence today.

The World Organization that I tried to serve for over a decade is not merely a hallowed name, to be lauded or by-passed as national policies dictate. It is a realistic and indispensable framework of world management, within which all national statesmen must view their responsibilities today. From now on, they must adapt and adjust their national ethos and institutions to those principles and purposes of the Charter that have been accepted by "We, the Peoples" as a working basis of their common life. It is a sad fact, however, that most member states use the machinery of the United Nations only when they feel that their own interests will be served by such use, or when all unilateral efforts at a solution have failed. In most cases, the United Nations has been by-passed in the settlement of international disputes, particularly by the Big Powers, when those disputes were within their own spheres of influence. The invasions of the Dominican Republic in 1965 and of Czechoslovakia in 1968 are cases in point.

In the introductory pages of this book I mentioned another basic belief of mine—a belief that has run like a current through these chapters. It relates to the attitude of the individual citizen. For it is not only the sovereign state that must adopt the global view; the individual person should also recognize the imperative demands of interdependence. I go so far as to suggest the need for a new concept of citizenship.

A new quality of planetary imagination is demanded from all of us as the price of human survival. I am not decrying that form of nationalism that prompts the individual citizen to appreciate and praise the achievements and values that his native land has contributed to the well-being and happiness of the whole human race. Nor am I calling for international homogenization, for I rejoice in cultural and national uniqueness. But I am making a plea—a plea based on these ten years of looking at the human condition from my unique vantage point—for a dual allegiance. This implies an open acceptance of belonging—as in fact we all do—to the human race as well as to our local community or nation. I even believe that the mark of the truly educated and imaginative person facing the twenty-first century is that he feels himself to be a planetary citizen.

Perhaps my own Buddhist upbringing has helped me more than anything else to realize and to express in my speeches and writings this concept of world citizenship.

In this book, I offer that concept as part of my own contribution to building the future World Community.

APPENDIXES

APPENDIXES

PART II

APPENDIX A

Aide-Mémoire to the Governments of the United States, North Vietnam, and South Vietnam, and to the National Liberation Front

On many occasions in the past, the Secretary-General of the United Nations has expressed his very great concern about the conflict in Viet-Nam. That concern is intensified by the growing fury of the war, resulting in the increasing loss of lives, indescribable suffering and misery of the people, appalling devastation of the country, uprooting of society, astronomical sums spent on the war, and last, but not least, his deepening anxiety over the increasing threat to the peace of the world. For these reasons, in the past three years or so, he submitted ideas and proposals to the parties primarily involved in the war, with a view to creating conditions congenial to negotiations, which, unhappily, have not been accepted by the parties. The prospects for peace seem to be more distant today than ever before.

Nevertheless, the Secretary-General reasserts his conviction that a cessation of the bombing of North Viet-Nam continues to be a vital need, for moral and humanitarian reasons and, also, because it is the step which could lead the way to meaningful talks to end the war.

The situation being as it is today, the Secretary-General has now in mind proposals envisaging three steps:

(a) A general stand-still truce

(b) Preliminary talks

(c) Reconvening of the Geneva Conference

In the view of the Secretary-General, a halt to all military activities by all sides is a practical necessity if useful negotiations are to be undertaken. Since the Secretary-General's three-point plan has not been accepted by the parties, he believes that a general stand-still truce by all parties to the conflict is now the only course which could lead to fruitful negotiations. It must be conceded that a truce without effective supervision is apt to be breached from time to time by one side or another, but an effective supervision of a truce, at least for the moment, seems difficult to envisage as a practical possibility. If the parties directly involved in the conflict are genuinely motivated by considerations of peace and justice, it is only to be expected that earnest efforts will be exerted to enforce the truce to the best of their ability. Should a public appeal by the Secretary-General in his personal capacity facilitate the observance of such a truce, he would gladly be prepared to do so. Appeals to that effect by a group of countries would also be worthy of consideration.

Once the appeal has been made and a general stand-still truce comes into effect, the parties directly involved in the conflict should take the next step of entering into preliminary talks. While these talks are in progress, it is clearly desirable that the general stand-still truce should continue to be observed. In the view of the Secretary-General, these talks can take any of the following forms:

(1) Direct talks between the United States of America and the Democratic Republic of Viet-Nam.

(2) Direct talks between the two governments mentioned in (1) above, with the participation of the two Co-Chairmen of the Geneva Conference of 1954.

(3) Direct talks between the two governments mentioned in (1) above with the participation of the members of the International Control Commission.

(4) Direct talks between the two governments mentioned in (1) above, with the participation of the two Co-Chairmen of the Geneva Conference of 1954 and of the members of the International Control Commission.

The Secretary-General believes that these preliminary talks should aim at reaching an agreement on the modalities for the reconvening of the Geneva Conference, with the sole purpose of returning to the essentials of that agreement as repeatedly expressed by all parties to the conflict. These preliminary talks should seek to reach an agreement on the timing, place, agenda and participants in the subsequent formal meeting—the reconvening of the Geneva Conference. The Secretary-General deems it necessary to stress that the question of participants in the formal negotiations should not obstruct the way to a settlement. It is a question which could be solved only by agreeing that no fruitful discussions on ending the war in Viet-Nam could take place without involving all those who are actually fighting. Since the Government in Saigon, as well as the National Liberation Front of South Viet-Nam, are actually engaged in military operations, it is the view of the Secretary-General that a future formal conference could not usefully discuss the effective termination of all military activities and the new political situation that would result in South Viet-Nam, without the participation of representatives of the Government in Saigon and representatives of the National Liberation Front of South Viet-Nam.

In transmitting these proposals to the parties directly concerned, the Secretary-General believes that he is acting within the limits of his good offices purely in his private capacity. He hopes that the divergent positions held by the parties both on the nature of the conflict and the ultimate political objectives will not prevent them from giving their very serious attention to these proposals. Indeed, he takes this opportunity to appeal to them to give their urgent consideration to his proposals.[1]

---

[1] *United Nations Press Release SG/SM/682,* March 28, 1967.

PART III

Identical Messages from the Secretary General to President Kennedy and Chairman Khrushchev, October 24, 1962

I have been asked by the Permanent Representatives of a large number of Member Governments of the United Nations to address an urgent appeal to you in the present critical situation. These Representatives feel that in the interest of international peace and security, all concerned should refrain from any action which may aggravate the situation and bring with it the risk of war. In their view it is important that time should be given to enable the parties concerned to get together with a view to resolving the present crisis peacefully and normalizing the situation in the Caribbean. This involves on the one hand the voluntary suspension of all arms shipments to Cuba, and also the voluntary suspension of the quarantine measures involving the searching of ships bound for Cuba. I believe that such voluntary suspension for a period of two to three weeks will greatly ease the situation and give time to the parties concerned to meet and discuss with a view to finding a peaceful solution of the problem. In this context I shall gladly make myself available to all parties for whatever services I may be able to perform. I urgently appeal to Your Excellency to give immediate consideration to this message.[2]

---

[2] *United Nations Security Council Official Records, No. 1024,* October 24, 1962.

APPENDIX B

Message to President Kennedy

I have today sent a further message to Chairman Khrushchev expressing my grave concern that Soviet ships already on their way to Cuba
might challenge the quarantine imposed by your government and produce a confrontation at sea between Soviet ships and United States
vessels, which could lead to an aggravation of the situation. I have also
stated that what concerns me most is the fact that such a confrontation
and consequent aggravation of the situation would destroy any possibility of the discussions that I have suggested as a prelude to negotiations on a peaceful settlement. I have accordingly expressed to him my
earnest hope that Soviet ships already on their way to Cuba might be
instructed to stay away from the interception area for a limited time
only, in order to permit discussions of the modalities of a possible
agreement which could settle the problem peacefully in line with the
Charter of the United Nations. In continuation of my message of yesterday and my speech before the Security Council, I would now like to
appeal to Your Excellency that instructions may be issued to United
States vessels in the Caribbean to do everything possible to avoid direct confrontation with Soviet ships in the next few days in order to
minimize the risk of any untoward incident. If I could be informed of
the action taken by your government on the basis of this appeal, I
could inform Chairman Khrushchev that I have assurances from your
side of your cooperation in avoiding all risk of an untoward incident. I
would express the further hope that such cooperation could be the
prelude to a quick agreement in principle on the basis of which the
quarantine measures themselves could be called off as soon as possible.[3]

APPENDIX C

Message from President Kennedy

I have your further message of today and I continue to understand and
welcome your efforts for a satisfactory solution. I appreciate and share

---

[3] *United Nations Press Release SG/1358,* October 26, 1962.

your concern that great caution be exercised pending the inauguration of discussions.

If the Soviet Government accepts and abides by your request "that Soviet ships already on their way to Cuba . . . stay away from the interception area" for the limited time required for preliminary discussion, you may be assured that this government will accept and abide by your request that our vessels in the Caribbean "do everything possible to avoid direct confrontation with Soviet ships in the next ten days in order to minimize the risk of any untoward incident." I must inform you, however, that this is a matter of great urgency in view of the fact that certain Soviet ships are still proceeding toward Cuba and the interception area.

I share your hope that Chairman Khrushchev will also heed your appeal and that we can then proceed urgently to meet the requirements that these offensive military systems in Cuba be withdrawn, in order to end their threat to peace. I must point out to you that present work on these systems is still continuing.[4]

APPENDIX D

Message to Chairman Khrushchev

In continuation of my message of yesterday and my statement before the Security Council, I would like to bring to Your Excellency's attention my grave concern that Soviet ships already on their way to Cuba might challenge the quarantine imposed by the United States and produce a confrontation at sea between Soviet ships and United States vessels, which could lead to an aggravation of the situation. What concerns me most is that such a confrontation and consequent aggravation of the situation would destroy any possibility of the discussions I have suggested as a prelude to negotiations on a peaceful settlement. In the circumstances I earnestly hope that Your Excellency may find it possible to instruct the Soviet ships already on their way to Cuba to stay away from the interception area for a limited time only, in order to permit discussions of the modalities of a possible agreement which could settle the problem peacefully in line with the Charter of the United Nations.

I am confident that, if such instructions could be issued by Your

---

4 Ibid.

Excellency, the United States authorities will take action to ensure that a direct confrontation between their ships and Soviet ships is avoided during the same period in order to minimize the risk of any untoward incident taking place.

If I could be informed of the action taken by Your Government on the basis of this appeal, I could inform President Kennedy that I have assurances from your side of your cooperation in avoiding all risk of an untoward incident.

I am at the same time addressing the enclosed appeal to President Kennedy.[5]

APPENDIX E

Message from Chairman Khrushchev

Dear U Thant,

I have received and studied your telegram of 25 October. I understand your anxiety for the preservation of peace, and I appreciate highly your efforts to avert military conflict.

Indeed, if any conflict should arise on the approaches to Cuba—and this may become unavoidable as a result of the piratical measures taken by the United States—this would beyond question seriously complicate the endeavours to initiate contacts in order to put an end, on a basis of negotiation, to the critical situation that has now been thrust on the world by the aggressive actions of the United States.

We therefore accept your proposal, and have ordered the masters of Soviet vessels bound for Cuba but not yet within the area of the American warships' piratical activities to stay out of the interception area, as you recommend.

But we have given this order in the hope that the other side will understand that such a situation, in which we keep vessels immobilized on the high seas, must be a purely temporary one; the period cannot under any circumstances be of long duration.

I thank you for your efforts and wish you success in your noble task. Your efforts to ensure peace will always meet with understanding and support on our part.

The Soviet Government has consistently striven, and is striving, to

---

[5] *United Nations Press Release SG/1357,* October 26, 1962.

strengthen the United Nations—that international Organization which constitutes a forum for all countries of the world, regardless of their socio-political structure, in order that disputes arising may be settled not through war but through negotiations.

Accept, Sir, the assurances of my highest consideration.

N. KHRUSHCHEV[6]

APPENDIX F

Message to Prime Minister Fidel Castro of the Revolutionary Government of Cuba

I hope that Ambassador García Incháustegui has conveyed to Your Excellency the appeal that I addressed to you and to President Dorticós through him in the course of the statement I made before the Security Council on 24 October. I then recalled the following words of President Dorticós, uttered from the rostum of the General Assembly on 8 October:

"Were the United States able to give us proof, by word and deed, that it would not carry out aggression against our country, then, we declare solemnly before you here and now, our weapons would be unnecessary and our army redundant."

As Ambassador García may have reported to you, I have received fairly encouraging responses to my appeal for negotiations and a peaceful solution of the problem from the President of the United States and from the Chairman of the Council of Ministers of the U.S.S.R. Your Excellency can make a significant contribution to the peace of the world at this present critical juncture by directing that the construction and development of major military facilities and installations in Cuba, and especially installations designed to launch medium range and intermediate range ballistic missiles, be suspended during the period of negotiations which are now under way.

It would encourage me greatly to have an affirmative reply to this appeal very urgently.[7]

---

[6] Ibid.

[7] *United Nations Press Release SG/1359,* October 26, 1962.

APPENDIX G

Message from Prime Minister Fidel Castro

Your Excellency,

I have received your message dated 26 October, and express my appreciation of your noble concern.

Cuba is prepared to discuss as fully as may be necessary, its differences with the United States and to do everything in its power, in co-operation with the United Nations, to resolve the present crisis. However, it flatly rejects the violation of the sovereignty of our country involved in the naval blockade, an act of force and war committed by the United States against Cuba. In addition, it flatly rejects the presumption of the United States to determine what actions we are entitled to take within our country, what kind of arms we consider appropriate for our defence, what relations we are to have with the U.S.S.R., and what international policy steps we are entitled to take, within the rules and laws governing relations between the peoples of the world and the principles governing the United Nations, in order to guarantee our own security and sovereignty.

Cuba is victimizing no-one; it has violated no international law; on the contrary, it is the victim of the aggressive acts of the United States, such as the naval blockade, and its rights have been outraged.

The Revolutionary Government of Cuba would be prepared to accept the compromises that you request as efforts in favour of peace, provided that at the same time, while negotiations are in progress, the United States Government desists from threats and aggressive actions against Cuba, including the naval blockade of our country.

At the same time I express to you our willingness to consider attentively any new suggestions you may put forward; furthermore, should you consider it useful to the cause of peace, our Government would be glad to receive you in our country, as Secretary-General of the United Nations, with a view to direct discussions on the present crisis, prompted by our common purpose of freeing mankind from dangers of war.

Unreserved respect for the sovereignty of Cuba is the essential prerequisite if Cuba is to contribute with the greatest sincerity and goodwill, grudging no step towards the solution of the present problem, and joining forces with all those peoples who are struggling to save peace at this dramatic moment in the life of mankind; Cuba can do whatever is asked of it, except undertake to be a victim and to renounce the rights which belong to every sovereign state.

I reiterate the assurances of my highest consideration.

MAJOR FIDEL CASTRO RUZ
Prime Minister of the Revolutionary Government of Cuba[8]

APPENDIX H

Letter of October 25, 1962, to Earl Bertrand Russell

Dear Earl Russell,

Thank you for your kind letter of 18 October. I share your feeling regarding the gravity of the international situation. Since you wrote, the Cuban situation has also contributed to an increase in tension.

In the circumstances I wish I could give an affirmative or encouraging reply to your enquiry regarding your addressing the General Assembly of the United Nations. Unfortunately, under the rules, only delegations of Member Governments can participate in the General Assembly debate. Apart from Member Governments, visiting Heads of State or Heads of Government may be invited to address it. I am so sorry that the rules do not permit any other personage, however eminent, to address the General Assembly. I hope you will understand my difficulty in this regard.

With warmest regards,

Yours sincerely,
U THANT
Acting Secretary-General[9]

APPENDIX I

Letter of October 27, 1962, from Adlai E. Stevenson Defining Interception Area Around Cuba

Excellency:

My Government has instructed me to inform you that the "inter-

---

[8] Ibid.
[9] United Nations Files.

ception area" referred to in your letter of October 25 to the President
of the United States and in his reply of October 26, comprises:

(a). the area included within a circle with its center at Havana
and a radius of 500 nautical miles, and,

(b). the area included within a circle with its center at Cape
Maysi (Maisi), located at the eastern tip of the island of Cuba, and a
radius of 500 nautical miles.

You may wish to pass the above information to Chairman
Khrushchev, so that he can proceed in accordance with his October 26
letter to you, in which he stated that he had ordered the masters of
Soviet vessels bound for Cuba, but not yet within the interception area,
to stay out of the area.

Accept, Excellency, the renewed assurances of my highest consideration.

ADLAI E. STEVENSON

APPENDIX J

*Confidential Working Paper of November 12 Given to Adlai E.
Stevenson*

There will be established a United Nations Observation Group operating from the headquarters of the United Nations in New York. The
Group will consist of eminent personalities and military observers
from non-aligned countries.

The main purpose of the Observation Group will be to help nor-
malize the situation in the Caribbean. For this purpose the countries
in the Caribbean and in Central America will agree to receive the
United Nations Observer Group and guarantee them freedom of
movement in their respective territories.

One of the primary tasks of this Group will be to verify on the
ground the dismantling of missile bases capable of launching medium
range and intermediate range ballistic missiles in Cuba, and their return to the U.S.S.R. Included in its terms of reference will be the responsibility to investigate any complaint or suspicion that, in any part
of the Caribbean or in Central America, nuclear weapons or missiles
are being introduced or missile sites established for offensive purposes.

The Group will also have authority to investigate complaints that
offensive preparations are being made in any part of the Caribbean or

Central America with a view to launching an invasion against the territory of any other country in the Caribbean or in Central America.

After the situation in the Caribbean has been normalized the
terms of reference of the Group may be enlarged by agreement among
the parties.

These are the proposed terms of reference of the Observer Group.
If the proposal is accepted in principle by Cuba and the U.S.A. in the
first instance, then consultations will be undertaken with all the parties
concerned with a view to securing the widest possible acceptance of
this proposal. Thereafter negotiations will be undertaken in order to
work out the detailed arrangements for the Observer Group.[10]

APPENDIX K

U. S. Draft Declaration on the Settlement of the Missile Crisis

CONFIDENTIAL
EYES ONLY STEVENSON

In letters of President Kennedy on October 27 and of Premier
Khrushchev and President Kennedy on October 28, 1962, firm undertakings were made regarding the settlement of the Cuban crisis.

These undertakings were stated in President Kennedy's letter of October 27 and quoted in the Acting Secretary General's letter of October 28 along the following lines:

(1) The U.S.S.R. would agree to remove from Cuba, under appropriate United Nations observation and supervision, all weapons systems capable of offensive use and would undertake, with suitable safeguards, to halt the further introduction of such weapons systems into
Cuba.

(2) The United States would agree—upon the establishment of
adequate arrangements through the United Nations to ensure the carrying out and continuation of these commitments—(a) to remove
promptly the quarantine measures now in effect, and (b) to give assurances against an invasion of Cuba. The President also expressed his
confidence that other nations of the Western Hemisphere would be
prepared to do likewise.

The United States notes the statement made by the Soviet Union
that all medium and intermediate range missiles, all nuclear weapons
and components have been removed from Cuba, that all IL-28 bomber

10 United Nations Files.

aircraft will be removed by December 20, and that all sites for medium range and intermediate range missiles have been dismantled. It notes also that the U.S.S.R. has stated its intention to withdraw all military units and personnel placed there for the servicing or guarding of these weapons systems. The United States notes further the statement of the U.S.S.R. that no weapons capable of offensive use will be introduced into Cuba in the future. We welcome these statements and assurances.

The undertakings in the President's letter of October 27 that the United Nations would be enabled to verify the removal of missiles and bombers and the destruction of sites, and that United Nations safeguards would be agreed upon to ensure against further introduction into Cuba of weapons systems capable of offensive use, have not been fulfilled. A minimum inspection procedure was, however, arranged in cooperation with the U.S.S.R., under which the United States naval vessels have received substantial verification that Soviet vessels leaving Cuba have carried out the number of missiles which the U.S.S.R. had certified to the United States as having been in Cuba. The Soviet Union has also agreed to a similar form of verification of the impending withdrawal of all IL-28 bomber aircraft introduced into Cuba.

In view of the steps that have been taken by the Soviet Union to date: the United States on its part, as of November 20, 1962, lifted the quarantine instituted on October 23, 1962; and the United States further gives assurance that, provided no nuclear weapons or other weapons capable of offensive use are present in or reintroduced into Cuba, and provided Cuba does not take action to threaten the peace and security of the Western Hemisphere, it does not intend, as the President made clear at his press conference on November 20, to invade Cuba or support an invasion of Cuba.

This statement is made on the understanding that by reason of the refusal of Cuba to permit arrangements contemplated to assure the carrying out and continuation of the commitments in regard to the maintenance and introduction of such weapons systems in Cuba, the United States will, until such time as such arrangements can be effected, continue to employ such other means of observation and verification as may be necessary.

The undertakings stated herein do not alter or impair the rights and obligations contained in the United Nations Charter or the Inter-American Treaty for Reciprocal Assistance, to both of which the United States is a party.[11]

---

[11] United Nations Files.

APPENDIX L

Text of Statement by U Thant Broadcast by Radio Moscow, August, 30, 1962

Today I am concluding my five-day visit to the Soviet Union, and my heart is filled with thankfulness to the people and the Government of this great country under Chairman Khrushchev for having made this visit possible.

I am no stranger to this country, since I visited it in 1955, though in a different capacity. In Moscow, in Yalta and in Kiev I saw very striking changes. Innumerable new buildings have arisen in seven years; streets are cleaner and the people look happier. There was even a festive air in some of the places I visited. As usual, warmth and friendliness were in evidence all around.

The leaders of the Soviet Union with whom I had the opportunity to exchange views on some of the major problems facing the world today impress me with their desire for peace and their keenness to do away with the vestiges of the last war. But fear and suspicion, which for so long have characterized international relations, are still in evidence here as in the West.

Let me be candid. When Soviet foreign policy concerned itself with what was happening in the rest of the world—for instance in the Congo—it did so out of fear and suspicion of what it regarded as "imperialists."

And I beg to be excused for saying that the Russian people do not fully understand the true character of the Congo problem. This lack of understanding is probably due to the absence of presentation of the other side of the coin, and I am sure that if only they have the means of knowing all the facets of the problem they will certainly revise their opinion of the nature of the United Nations involvement in the Congo and decide to shoulder their share of the heavy responsibilities now being undertaken by the World Organization in seeking a peaceful solution of the Congo problem.

I am saying all this with a heavy heart, because diplomacy demands honeyed words. I am not a believer in honeyed words, since they will not help the great and courageous people of the Soviet Union to arrive at a balanced appraisal of the situation.

I am particularly grateful to the President of the Presidium of the Supreme Soviet of the U.S.S.R., Mr. Leonid Ilyich Brezhnev, for having graciously granted me an audience; to Chairman Khrushchev, who received me as a member of his family and who gave me an illuminating exposition of the Soviet approach to major problems; to Mr. Kosygin, First Deputy Premier; to Mr. Gromyko, Foreign Minister, and to other Soviet leaders for the opportunity provided to me for a most friendly and useful exchange of views.

I shall certainly cherish the happiest memories of my present visit to this great country for years to come and I very sincerely wish the people of the Soviet Union peace and prosperity, and friendship with all peoples which they desire.

I also want to take this opportunity of offering my grateful thanks to the people and Government of the Ukrainian S.S.R. for the very warm hospitality accorded to me during my brief stay in Kiev.

PART IV

APPENDIX A

The Composition of UNEF Before the Six-Day War

The numerical strength and composition of UNEF on May 15, 1967 was as follows[12]:

Brazil	433
Canada	795
Denmark	2
India	978
Norway	61
Sweden	530
Yugoslavia	579

UNEF total 3,378

APPENDIX B

Aide-Mémoire of May 17, 1967, to Ambassador El-Kony, Permanent Representative of the U.A.R.

1. The Secretary-General of the United Nations requests the Permanent Representative of the United Arab Republic to the United Nations to convey to his Government the Secretary-General's most serious concern over the situation that has arisen with regard to the

---

[12] United Nations Document A/6669/Add.2., June 19, 1967.

United Nations Emergency Force in the past twenty-four hours as a result of the demands upon it made by United Arab Republic military authorities and of certain actions of United Arab Republic troops in the area.

2. Before engaging in detail, the Secretary-General wishes to make the following general points entirely clear:

(a) He does not in any sense question the authority of the Government of the United Arab Republic to deploy its troops as it sees fit in United Arab Republic territory or territory under the control of the United Arab Republic.

(b) In the sectors of Gaza and Sinai, however, it must be recognized that the deployment of troops of the United Arab Republic in areas in which UNEF troops are stationed and carrying out their functions may have very serious implications for UNEF, its functioning and its continued presence in the area.

(c) The Commander of UNEF cannot comply with any requests affecting the disposition of UNEF troops emanating from any source other than United Nations Headquarters, and the orders delivered to General Rikhye on 16 May by military officers of the United Arab Republic were not right procedurally and quite rightly were disregarded by General Rikhye.

(d) UNEF has been deployed in Gaza and Sinai for more than ten years for the purpose of maintaining quiet along the Armistice Demarcation Line and the International Frontier. It has served this purpose with much distinction. It went into the area and has remained there with the full consent of the Government of the United Arab Republic. If that consent should be withdrawn or so qualified as to make it impossible for the Force to function effectively, the Force, of course, will be withdrawn.

3. The following is the sequence of events which have given rise to the present crisis:

(a) At 2200 hours (Local Time) on 16 May Brigadier Eiz-El-Din Mokhtar handed to General Rikhye, the Commander of UNEF, the following letter:

"For your information, I gave my instructions to all UAR Armed Forces to be ready for action against Israel the moment it might carry out any aggressive action against any Arab country. Due to these instructions our troops are already concentrated in Sinai on our eastern borders. For the sake of complete security of all UN troops which install OPs along our borders, I request that you issue your orders to withdraw all these troops immediately. I have given my instructions to our Commander of the eastern zone concerning this subject. Inform back the fulfilment of this request. Yours, Farik Awal: (M. Fawzy) COS of UAR Armed Forces."

(b) The Commander of UNEF replied that he had noted the contents of General Fawzy's letter and would report immediately to the Secretary-General for instructions, since he had no authority to withdraw any troops of UNEF, or in any other way to redeploy UNEF troops except on instructions from the Secretary-General.

(c) On learning of the substance of General Fawzy's letter to General Rikhye, the Secretary-General asked the Permanent Representative of the United Arab Republic to the United Nations to see him immediately. The Permanent Representative of the United Arab Republic came to the Secretary-General's office at 1845 hours on 16 May. The Secretary-General requested him to communicate with his Government with the utmost urgency and to transmit to them his views, of which the following is a summary:

(i) The letter addressed to the Commander of UNEF was not right procedurally since the Commander of UNEF could not take orders affecting his command from a source other than the Secretary-General. General Rikhye was therefore correct in his insistence on taking no action until he received instructions from the Secretary-General.

(ii) The exact intent of General Fawzy's letter needed clarification. If it meant the temporary withdrawal of UNEF troops from the Line or from parts of it, it would be unacceptable because the purpose of the United Nations Force in Gaza and Sinai is to prevent a recurrence of fighting, and it cannot be asked to stand aside in order to enable the two sides to resume fighting. If it was intended to mean a general withdrawal of UNEF from Gaza and Sinai, the communication should have been addressed to the Secretary-General from the Government of the United Arab Republic and not to the Commander of UNEF from the Chief of Staff of the Armed Forces of the United Arab Republic.

(iii) If it was the intention of the Government of the United Arab Republic to withdraw the consent which it gave in 1956 for the stationing of UNEF on the territory of the United Arab Republic and in Gaza, it was, of course, entitled to do so. Since, however, the basis for the presence of UNEF was an agreement made directly between President Nassar and Dag Hammarskjöld as Secretary-General of the United Nations, any request for withdrawal of UNEF must come directly to the Secretary-General from the Government of the United Arab Republic. On receipt of such a request, the Secretary-General would order the withdrawal of all UNEF troops from Gaza and Sinai, simultaneously informing the General Assembly of what he was doing and why.

(iv) A request by the United Arab Republic authorities for a temporary withdrawal of UNEF from the Armistice Demarcation Line and the International Frontier, or from any parts of them, would be considered by the Secretary-General as tantamount to a request for the complete withdrawal of UNEF from Gaza and Sinai, since this would reduce UNEF to ineffectiveness.

(d) The Secretary-General informed the Commander of UNEF of the position as outlined above, as explained to the Permanent Representative of the United Arab Republic, and instructed him to do all that he reasonably could to maintain all UNEF positions pending further instructions.

(e) At 0800 hours GMT on 17 May, the Commander of UNEF reported that on the morning of 17 May, 30 soldiers of the Army of the United Arab Republic had occupied El Sabha in Sinai and that their troops were deployed in the immediate vicinity of the UNEF Observation Post there. Three armoured cars of the United Arab Republic were located near the Yugoslav UNEF camp at El Sabha and detachments of 15 soldiers each had taken up positions north and south of the Yugoslav camp at El Amr. All UNEF Observation Posts along the Armistice Demarcation Line and International Frontier were manned as usual.

(f) At 1030 hours GMT on 17 May, the Commander of UNEF reported that troops of the United Arab Republic had occupied the UNEF Observation Post on El Sabha and that the Yugoslav UNEF camps at El Queseima and El Sabha were now behind the positions of the Army of the United Arab Republic. The Commander of UNEF informed the Chief of the United Arab Republic Liaison Service of these developments, expressing serious concern at them. The Chief of the United Arab Republic Liaison Service agreed to request the immediate vacation of the Observation Post at El Sabha by troops of the United Arab Republic and shortly thereafter reported that orders to this effect had been given by the United Arab Republic military authorities. He requested, however, that to avoid any future misunderstandings, the Yugoslav Observation Post at El Sabha should be immediately withdrawn to El Queseima camp. The Commander replied that any such withdrawal would require the authorization of the Secretary-General.

(g) At 1200 hours GMT, the Chief of the United Arab Republic Liaison Service conveyed to the Commander of UNEF a request from General Mahmoud Fawzy, Chief of Staff of the Armed Forces of the United Arab Republic, for the withdrawal of UNEF Yugoslav detachments in the Sinai within twenty-four hours. He added that the Commander of UNEF might take forty-eight hours or so to withdraw the UNEF detachment from Sharm-el-Sheikh.

(h) At 1330 hours GMT, The Commander of UNEF reported that a sizable detachment of troops of the United Arab Republic was moving into the UNEF area at El Kuntilla.

4. The Secretary-General is obliged to state that UNEF cannot remain in the field under the conditions described in the foregoing paragraphs. The function of UNEF has been to assist in maintaining quiet along the Line by acting as a deterrent to infiltration and as a buffer between the opposing forces. It can discharge neither of these functions if it is removed from the Line and finds itself stationed behind forces of the United Arab Republic. In other words, UNEF, which has contributed so greatly to the relative quiet which has prevailed in the area in which it has been deployed for more than ten years, cannot now be asked to stand aside in order to become a silent and helpless witness to an armed confrontation between the parties. If, therefore, the orders to the troops of the United Arab Republic referred to above are maintained, the Secretary-General will have no choice but to order the withdrawal of UNEF from Gaza and Sinai as expeditiously as possible.

5. The Secretary-General wishes also to inform the Permanent Representative of the United Arab Republic that as of now, on the basis of the fully reliable reports received from the Chief of Staff of the United Nations Truce Supervision Organization in Palestine, there have been no recent indications of troop movements or concentrations along any of the Lines which should give rise to undue concern.

6. The Secretary-General requests the Permanent Representative of the United Arab Republic to transmit the contents of this *aide-mémoire* with utmost urgency to his Government.

APPENDIX C

Text of Statement by President Nasser on the Withdrawal of UNEF

On May 13 we received information that Israel was concentrating on the Syrian border huge armed forces of about 11 to 13 brigades. These forces were divided into two fronts, one south of Lake Tiberias and the other north of the Lake. The decision made by Israel at this time was to carry out an aggression against Syria as of May 17. On May 14 we took our measures, discussed the matter and contacted our Syrian brothers. The Syrians also had this information.

On this basis, Lieut-General Mahmud Fawzi left for Syria to co-ordinate matters. We told them that we had decided that if Syria was attacked, Egypt would enter the battle from the first minute. This was the situation on May 14. The forces began to move in the direction of Sinai to take up normal positions. News agencies reported yesterday that these military movements must have been the result of a previously well-laid plan. And I say that the sequence of events deter-mined the plan. We had no plan before May 13, because we believed that Israel will not dare attack any Arab country and that Israel would not have dared to make such an impertinent statement.

On May 16 we requested the withdrawal of the United Nations Emergency Force (UNEF) in a letter from Lieut-General Mah-mud Fawzi. We then requested the complete withdrawal of UNEF. A big world-wide campaign, led by the United States, Britain and Canada, began opposing the withdrawal of UNEF from Egypt. Thus we felt that there were attempts to turn UNEF into a force serving neo-imperialism. It is obvious that UNEF is in Egypt with our approval and therefore cannot continue to stay in Egypt except with our approval. Until yesterday, a great deal was said about UNEF.

A campaign is also being mounted against the United Nations Secretary-General because he made a faithful and honest decision and could not surrender to the pressure brought to bear upon him by the United States, Britain and Canada to make UNEF an instrument for implementing imperialism's plans. It is quite natural—and I say this quite frankly—that had UNEF ignored its basic mission and turned to achieving the aims of imperialism we would have regarded it as a hostile force and forcibly disarmed it. We are definitely capable of doing such a job.

I say this now not to discredit the UNEF but to those who have neo-imperialist ideas and who want the United Nations to achieve their aims. There is not a single nation which truly respects itself and enjoys full sovereignty which could accept these methods in any form. At the same time I say that the UNEF has honourably and faithfully carried out its duties. And the United Nations Secretary-General re-fused to succumb to pressure. Thus he issued immediate orders to the UNEF to withdraw. Consequently, we laud the UNEF which stayed ten years in our country serving peace. And when they left—at a time when we found that the neo-imperialist forces wanted to divert them from their basic aim—we gave them a cheerful send-off and saluted them. . . .

The United Nations adopted a number of resolutions in favour of the Palestinian people. Israel implemented none of these resolutions. This brought no reaction from the United States. Today U. S. Senators, members of the House of Representatives, the press and the entire world speak in favour of Israel, of the Jews. But nothing is said in favour of the Arabs. The U.N. resolutions which are in favour of the Arabs were not implemented. What does this mean? No one is speaking in the Arab's favour. How does the United Nations stand with regard to the Palestinian people? How does it stand with regard to the tragedy which has continued since 1958? The peace talk is heard only when Israel is in danger. But when the Arab rights and the rights of the Palestinian people are lost, no one speaks about peace, rights or anything.

Yesterday and the day before yesterday the entire world was speaking about Sharm-el-Sheikh, navigation in the Gulf of Aqaba, and the Elath port. This morning I heard the B.B.C. say that in 1956 Abdel Nasser pledged to open the Gulf of Aqaba. Of course this is not true. It was copied from a British paper called *The Daily Mail*. No such thing happened. Abdel Nasser would never forfeit any UAR right. As I said, we would never give away a grain of sand from our soil or our country.

The armed forces' responsibility is now yours. The armed forces yesterday occupied Sharm-el-Sheikh. What is the meaning of the armed forces' occupation of Sharm-el-Sheikh? It is an affirmation of our rights and our sovereignty over the Aqaba Gulf. The Aqaba Gulf constitutes our Egyptian territorial waters. Under no circumstances will we allow the Israeli flag to pass through the Aqaba Gulf.

APPENDIX D

General Rikhye's Minutes of the Meeting of May 24, 1967, Between the Foreign Minister of the U.A.R. and the Secretary General

1. The meeting opened at 9:45 hours on Wednesday, 24 May 1967 at the Ministry of Foreign Affairs Office, Giza. The SG started

the conversation by recounting developments which had led to his ordering the withdrawal of UNEF. He said that he had consulted the UNEF Advisory Committee and representatives of governments contributing contingents to UNEF before the final action was taken. Brazil, Canada, Denmark, and Norway were not in favour of SG's compliance with UAR request for withdrawal. Sweden also did not seem to approve of the action of withdrawal. Only India, Pakistan, and Yugoslavia fully supported his action. Outside these consultations, French attitude seemed to be favourable. UK and US were opposed to withdrawal, and the Soviet Union wanted the Secretary-General to comply with UAR request for withdrawal. SG also added that the UNEF Advisory Committee could have taken steps for the convening of a special session of the General Assembly under the relevant resolution, but no member state indicated any desire to take such an initiative.

2. SG then discussed Ambassador Goldberg's letter given to him and gave a copy to FM for his personal information. This letter, dated March 15, 1957, stresses US policy regarding UNEF. FM said he was well aware of it and it was old story.

3. FM, in a lengthy discourse, gave details of events which led to UAR's request for withdrawal of UNEF from Sinai and Gaza Strip. He said a few days ago the area was peaceful. There had, however, been an escalation of aggression by Israel against Arabs, especially against Jordan and Syria. There had been attacks against Jordan water projects, many incidents involving increasing the use of weapons, i.e., exchange of fire, guns, tanks, and the latest use of air force was most serious. The Israelis had the upper hand here because other Arab countries did not possess comparable air forces. Israel followed the pattern of boasting after 1956. Recently Eban and Rabin threatened to invade Syria and take Damascus.

4. UAR had made no move before receiving reports of Israeli concentrations. They had received information of a plan of invasion by Israel against Syria. Only on 15 May US Chargé d'Affaires in a meeting with FM, when referring to the situation in Syria, had said, "We take it most seriously."

5. "Strangely," the FM continued, "after we had decided to move against Israel, US Chargé told us that there were no concentrations but would not give us any guarantees. We were back in a similar situation as existed in 1956 when the US Ambassador gave us similar information, and yet we were attacked.

6. "We understand that Israel does not intend to annex Syria, and Damascus is not part of their plan. Their plans are confined, however,

to south of Syria where bulk of Syrian Army is deployed, which they wish to destroy, as well as the military and economic installations. Israel could achieve this with its Air Force and invade South Syria. By the time Security Council would meet, it would be possible for them to have inflicted serious punishment on Syria. Israel then, supported by its friends, would agree to having a new UNEF on Israel-Syrian frontier.

7. "Israel's positions on the Syrian border are weak. Syria holds dominant positions and can open fire on a number of settlements in north Israel. Israel is determined to alter this situation. UAR had a parallel experience in 1956 with the difference that it did not have any large installations in the Sinai. Therefore, when US Chargé told me that they are against aggression, it means little to us. I told US Chargé that they were supporting and encouraging Israel. US will share responsibility of any attack. UAR had no choice but to move into the Sinai for we had no time to make any moves. Our deterrent action would make Israel think twice before they attack now."

8. FM said that he agreed with SG on total withdrawal of UNEF without leaving one single soldier. Withdrawal of consent to placing peace-keeping forces must be the last word according to the agreement between his government and the late SG. "I told the Canadian Ambassador that if there was any delay in the withdrawal of Canadian Contingent, we would send them away by force. The SG had saved the UN flag and the idea of peace-keeping."

9. SG said that US still maintains that we were wrong in withdrawing UNEF. FM stated that for political reasons often personal ambition has led many in US to lose their balance on the question of Israel.

10. FM, continuing with his discourse, said that "when UNEF withdrew, we moved into Sinai, including Sharm-el-Sheikh. We had decided to restore conditions as they were before 1956. Israeli propaganda before 1956 had stated that Gulf of Aqaba was not important to them, but after 1956 Israel claimed that they had succeeded by opening the Gulf. By re-establishing UAR positions in Sharm-el-Sheikh and closing the Gulf of Aqaba, the UAR has pulled the last curtain on the Israeli aggression of 1956. Israel will not profit from that aggression anymore."

11. FM stated that Eilat was not too important economically. "The question is of prestige with Israel as it is with us. We realize that Israel considered question of Sharm-el-Sheikh a serious one. It had posed as a powerful country, but our recent actions would affect their interests. Israel is losing prestige inside and outside that country, which would affect their future financial support and rate of immigration.

12. "Our move was important from our point of view. We are defensive in posture; we had no plans to attack Israel. We realize that any attack by us would create a great international crisis. If US intends to support Israel and exploit the situation, we are ready. The extent of such support is open to question."

13. The SG inquired whether the US Ambassador had told the FM of its past commitments to Israel concerning the Gulf of Aqaba. The FM replied that the US Ambassador had only said, "We are against aggression."

14. FM then informed the SG regarding developments in the Arab World. He said that they had received offers of co-operation from all the Arabs but had refused any aid from Jordan and Saudi Arabia. Tunisia was too unimportant to even consider.

15. The SG said that Israeli delegation had told him that they attached the greatest importance to the Strait of Tiran and that they would be prepared to go to war. Before President Nasser's statement of 22 May, Ambassador Goldberg and the Canadian Ambassador George Ignatieff had advised him of similar Israeli reaction. According to a cable from New York, there may be a Security Council meeting today. The SG had to submit a report after his visit to Cairo. Some delegations had suggested that he invoke Article 99, but he declined to do so for several reasons including the position of USSR and France and some members of the Security Council. Hammarskjöld had done it only once, during the Congo crisis. At that time the entire membership supported his initiative. SG stated that the UAR case had to be presented in the light of Big-Power play. Ambassador Fedorenko had told him that he was sure that the UAR would not do anything to precipitate a crisis over the Gulf of Aqaba. SG requested FM not to take any precipitate action.

16. FM said that their stand on the Gulf of Aqaba was firm. They had anticipated all possible moves, including possibility of war with Israel. Only yesterday he was present at talks with the President and with the FM and COS (Chief of Staff) of Syria. They had agreed to be firm. If the US attacked the UAR, what could they do? "UAR is a small power. When President Nasser makes a statement he does so after a great deal of deliberation. He cannot withdraw from that position." The prestige of the UAR and all Arabs was involved. This point had not been discussed by the FM with the US Ambassador. If the US wished to avoid war, they should consider making a balance. In the case of Gulf of Aqaba, US alleges that UAR has violated international law. These were legal arguments, and the UAR was prepared to discuss them.

17. FM further said that there was the question of the GAA

(General Armistice Agreement). Israel would not accept to implement and return to the GAA. If US was serious, they should help in this respect. Implementation of GAA means to Israel (a) no permanent border (b) that Israel does not yet exist as a state (c) there exists a state of belligerency (d) reinstatement of El Auja situation prior to 1955. Although Israel had violated GAA in respect of El Auja, UAR had agreed to continue relations with EIMAC (Egypt-Israel Mixed Armistice Commission) to indicate its willingness to cooperate with UN. US had talked about presence of UN in the area. FM had asked new US Ambassador for clear proposals. FM had said that UN was already present with the GAA. SG remarked that Israel's position was clear on EIMAC. FM agreed because Israel had said "EIMAC is dead and buried." Israel was also not cooperating with ISMAC (Israel-Syria Mixed Armistice Commission). FM said that expansion of EIMAC would be discussed if Israel accepted GAA. Israel's policy was to occupy Demilitarized Zone area. That is why they were after DZ on Syria. If MAC attempted to prevent cultivation of DZ on Syrian border, Israel would not agree. UAR had patiently waited, but then Israel's attack on Gaza on 28 February 1955 had been the turning point.

18. SG inquired about UAR's attitude on question of repatriation and compensation of Palestine refugees. FM indicated that since this arose out of a GA resolution, they would not raise it at this point.

19. SG informed FM that Ambassador Goldberg had told Bunche of US advice to Israel not to send ships through Gulf of Aqaba during the period of negotiations, but Israel's reaction was negative.

20. SG asked UAR position on Security Council meeting being called today. FM replied that he had no complaint. He would not object if Ambassador El-Kony were called to participate in the meeting.

21. SG sounded FM as to possible UAR reaction if he made an appeal to freeze the situation in the Gulf along lines during Cuban crisis. SG mentioned moratorium for two to three weeks to give him time for consultations and discussions. FM replied that his Government did not wish to show any weakness to its people, and especially the Army. If Security Council attempted to pass a resolution against UAR action in Gulf of Aqaba, it would surely be vetoed by Soviet Union. The question might then perhaps go to GA, which would not be able to do much.

22. The SG said that we all should look for a solution to calm down the present crisis. He would appeal to Israel not to send ships

through Gulf of Aqaba for a certain period, for if a ship were sent and the UAR acted against it, the situation would explode.

23. The SG asked FM's reaction to possibility of SG's appointing a personal representative in the area who could base himself in Gaza and have access to Israel and UAR. The FM wanted clarification on his functions. The SG said these could be discussed at the meeting with the President.

24. The SG informed FM regarding his own, and later, Canadian initiative to persuade Israel to accept UNEF on their side. He asked FM's reaction, and latter replied that it would be all right from their point of view, if Israel agreed. However, UAR would not agree to re-establishment of UNEF on its territory.

25. SG then raised matters relating to EIMAC and asked if UAR would agree to their patrolling and establishing OP's (Observer Posts) in Gaza Strip and Sinai. FM replied situation relating to EIMAC as existed before 17 May 1967. They would not permit UNMO's (UN Military Observers) to enter the Sinai.

26. The SG inquired whether UAR would object to construction of a barbed wire along ADL (Armistice Demarcation Line). FM said that this was an old question, unacceptable to the UAR. However, if Israel wished to construct wire on their side and away from the ditch, they would not object. UAR was against sign-posting or any permanent marking which would indicate that the present armistice lines had changed into an international frontier.

27. The SG then discussed some broad aspects of disposal and dumping of UNEF property. He informed FM that it was UN's intention to transfer some equipment to Pisa and Jerusalem for use by UN peace-keeping operations, present and future. Some of the surplus equipment would be disposed of locally. FM said that their Army had everything but like every other army were always greedy to obtain more. He understood the SG's position.

28. The SG, in taking leave of the FM, reiterated his main lines of approach to resolve the present crisis: firstly, a moratorium for a two to three week period to allow time for discussions; secondly, to attempt to obtain Israel's agreement to reactivate GAA, for which he would seek US support. Lastly, to discuss with the President the possibility of his recommending to the Security Council the appointment of a special representative to this area.

29. The FM agreed to consider these questions and also to arrange for the SG to discuss with the President at dinner.

30. The meeting closed at 1230 hours.

APPENDIX E

General Rikhye's Minutes of the Meeting of May 24, 1967, Between President Nasser and the Secretary General

1. The President received the SG at his residence for dinner and discussion at 2000 hours on 24 May 1967. The SG opened the conversation by saying that he was required to make a report to the Security Council on his visit to Cairo. He would therefore like to have the President's reaction to his proposal on declaring a moratorium in the Gulf of Aqaba. SG also told the President that on his way to Cairo, he got information at Paris airport regarding the closing of the Gulf of Aqaba. To be frank, he was very much surprised, since in his view war was inevitable, for that action.

2. The President briefly stated the position of the UAR along the same lines as the Foreign Minister during SG's meeting with him earlier in the day. Regarding the closing of the Gulf of Aqaba, President said that the decision had been made some time earlier. The question was the timing of the announcement of the decision. If the announcement were to be made after SG's visit to Cairo, it would be widely interpreted that SG had been snubbed. So it was decided to announce it before SG's arrival. President said that already two ships entering the Gulf had been searched by the UAR; however, he wished to help the UN in restoring peace, especially when it was threatened by the attitude of Israel which had given every indication of invading Sharm-el-Sheikh. UAR forces were prepared to defend themselves. President would, however, accept SG's proposal for a moratorium for a period of two weeks. It was no longer possible for him to physically withdraw his blockade but he would issue orders that his people in the Gulf would be "good boys" as long as Israel on its part complied with SG's request.

3. SG stated that he would cable Bunche tonight if possible to carry out consultations to persuade Israel not to send shipping through the Gulf for some time and to refrain from sending strategic materials to Eilat as required by the UAR.

4. The question of UN supervising compliance of this agreement during the two-week moratorium period was considered and rejected by the President on the grounds of breach of armed forces' security involved with any UN presence.

5. The President said that UAR had achieved its goal by return-

ing to pre-1956 position, with one difference: that they were now in a position to defend their country and their rights. He had accepted offer of troops from Algeria, Kuwait, and Iraq. UAR did not require military assistance from any other Arab country, but it was important to agree to accept token contributions in the interest of the morale of the Arab world. The populace of these countries had received a great fillip in their morale, and many volunteers were offering themselves for the fight with Israel if UAR is attacked. President assured SG that UAR would not be the first to attack.

6. President covered the position of the major Powers and blocs on the question of the Gulf blockade. He said that the US had always supported Israel. The Russians have declared their support for the UAR. France was neutral, and the UK followed the US line. The line-up was typical of the present division amongst the major Powers. UAR relations with US have deteriorated over the years because of a clash of mutual interests. US had applied economic pressure and stopped assistance last year. UAR had to reduce its industrial production and to limit importation of raw material to provide sufficient hard currency to buy food. The economic position had improved for this year. The President had declined, however, any offers of new assistance from US, UK and West Germany. His position also was that if credits were made available, interest on past loans would have to be paid. He had therefore refused to pay interest on loans to US, UK and West Germany. The International Monetary Fund had also applied some pressures as had the World Bank. But his position was, if no more credits, no payment of past dues and interest. France and Italy had renegotiated medium loans to long-term loans. UAR had also been able to obtain some credit elsewhere, and the UAR economic position had somewhat improved. He concluded by stating UAR's determination to retain its independence of action and to defend its sovereignty and its rights.

7. The SG asked President's comments on the possibility of an appointment of a special representative of SG to the area with possible location at Gaza. The President said that US and Canada had in 1957 attempted to place Gaza Strip under UNEF administration. This was unacceptable to UAR then, as would be any appointment which might indicate international presence after withdrawal of UNEF by anyone other than EIMAC. The President offered, however, to accept any UN diplomatic presence in Cairo and assured the SG of his fullest cooperation. SG said he would discuss with Israeli representative on his return to New York.

8. During a discussion on possible developments during the Security Council meeting, FM said that the item inscribed was the Middle East. There were lots of trouble spots in the Middle East besides the Gulf of Aqaba, and it would appear that a free-for-all discussion would take place in the Security Council. The SG said that the Security Council would be involved first of all in a procedural wrangle and would probably spend a few days on it. The President said that he had already instructed the FM to open the UN files on the failure on the part of Israel to comply with UN resolutions. On the other hand, Egypt had always supported and cooperated with the UN and would continue to do so.

9. The President then raised the question of removal and disposal of UNEF property. He said that their armed forces would be prepared to buy any items for disposal.

10. Rikhye informed President of the arrangements already made that certain items, including vehicles, radio sets, and other military type equipment, would be transferred to Pisa and Jerusalem as required. Other items for disposal were being sorted out, and UAR would be informed about availability.

11. The SG confirmed arrangements, especially about the transfer of certain items to Pisa and Jerusalem. The President expressed his acceptance of such an arrangement and promised his fullest cooperation. He said that if any difficulties arose, these should be brought to the notice of the armed forces authorities who had his instructions to cooperate with UN.

12. The President then offered to the SG the highest UAR military decoration for UNEF. At first this was misunderstood. SG and Rikhye thought the offer was for individual officers and men. The President, however, clarified the point by saying that he was offering a decoration for UNEF as a whole along the customary military lines when a whole unit or a formation is decorated. The SG said that he would like to give further consideration to this generous offer of the President and would send him a reply from New York.

13. The President stated his gratitude to UNEF and to UN for helping the UAR in 1956 and since then till now. He conveyed his great appreciation for the assistance rendered by UNEF in keeping and maintaining peace in the area. He asked Rikhye to convey his personal thanks to all ranks for the services rendered to the UAR and for keeping peace in the area.

APPENDIX F

Texts of Cables from the Secretary General and the Governments of the U.A.R. and Canada Regarding the Withdrawal of the Canadian Contingent to UNEF

Mahmoud Riad, Foreign Minister of the U.A.R., to the Secretary General

I have the honour to bring to your attention a serious and grave situation resulting from the regrettable attitude of the Government of Canada, in connection with the United Nations Forces, to the withdrawal of which you have agreed upon the request of the United Arab Republic Government. From the beginning, the Canadian Government has persistently resorted to procrastination and delay in the departure of these forces. We noted from the outset that Canadian Government took unfriendly position towards my Government.

Furthermore, the Government of Canada took certain military measures on which we have received definite information that some Canadian destroyers have already sailed towards the Mediterranean, an act which inflamed the public opinion in my country, to an extent that I fear that it already reached the point of hatred against Canada.

In view of these serious acts and in the light of the present situation in the Middle East, and desirous to prevent any probable reaction from the people of the United Arab Republic against the Canadian Forces in UNEF, which may have undesirable reflection on the United Nations forces as a whole, I urge you to order the complete withdrawal and departure of the Canadian forces immediately, and not later than forty-eight hours from the time my cable reaches you.

I hasten to inform you that our forces are ready to provide all the necessary facilities for the transportation of the Canadian Forces to the nearest possible place, namely Cyprus.

The Secretary General to Mahmoud Riad

Excellency, I have the honour to acknowledge receipt of your cable of 27 May 1967 in which you urge me to order the complete withdrawal and departure of the Canadian contingent in UNEF immediately and not later than forty-eight hours from the time of the receipt of your cable. As you know, the Commander of UNEF and United Nations Headquarters have been working on plans for the expeditious evacuation of UNEF, and these plans, of course, included the speedy withdrawal of the Canadian contingent. I deeply regret the circumstances which have led to the request for the immediate withdrawal of the Canadian contingent as stated in your cable. To avoid any further aggravation of the situation, I have immediately instructed the Commander of UNEF to accelerate the evacuation of the Canadian contingent. I am sure you will understand that, while the Canadian Government and the Commander of UNEF will cooperate in implementing this evacuation as quickly as possible, it cannot be absolutely guaranteed that it will be fully completed within forty-eight hours of the receipt of your cable, although all concerned are agreed that the Canadian contingent shall be evacuated with the minimum delay possible. I note with appreciation your offer to provide transportation facilities if necessary to take the Canadian contingent to Cyprus. I do not believe, however, that Cyprus would be an appropriate destination for the Canadian contingent, and we are therefore arranging to evacuate it elsewhere. May I request you, Excellency, to take all possible measures to ensure that, for the very short period of time in which the Canadian contingent of UNEF remains on UAR territory, their status as members of UNEF will be fully respected and any unnecessary friction or unpleasantness avoided.

The Secretary General to Prime Minister Lester Pearson of Canada

In view of circumstances which have developed in relation to the Canadian Contingent of UNEF, the possibility of accelerating the withdrawal of the Canadian Contingent from the area was discussed with the Permanent Representative of Canada on 26 May 1967. On the morning of 27 May I received a message from Mr. Mahmoud Riad, the Minister of Foreign Affairs of the United Arab Republic, on this same subject, the substance of which has already been communicated to you by the Permanent Representative of Canada. In the light of these developments and after consultations with the Permanent Representatives of Canada, I have now given instructions to the Commander of UNEF that the Canadian Contingent of UNEF should be evacuated from United Arab Republic territory as quickly as possible. I therefore request the Government of Canada to undertake urgently the necessary transportation arrangements to carry out this evacuation. I have made it clear in my reply to the message of the Minister of Foreign Affairs of the United Arab Republic that, while all possible efforts will be made to evacuate the Canadian Contingent as soon as possible, it cannot be absolutely guaranteed that the evacuation can be completed within forty-eight hours. I have also asked him to take all possible measures to ensure that, for the short period of time in which the Canadian Contingent of UNEF remains on UAR territory, their status as members of UNEF will be fully respected and any unnecessary friction and unpleasantness avoided. (May 27, 1967.)

Now that the Canadian forces serving with the United Nations Emergency Force (UNEF) in Gaza are leaving the area in which UNEF has been operating for ten and a half years, I wish to express to you personally, and through you to the Government and people of Canada, and particularly to the great number of officers and men who have served in UNEF over the years, my deep appreciation of the invaluable contribution which Canada has made to UNEF.

You yourself, Mr. Prime Minister, were the prime mover in proposing the original idea of UNEF to the General Assembly. Your plan for a truly international peace and police force was, at that time, a pioneering innovation in international affairs which provided a means of overcoming a most threatening and dangerous crisis. Your imaginative plan was eagerly accepted by the General Assembly and put into operation with great skill and dispatch by my predecessor, Dag Hammarskjöld. . . .

The armed forces of Canada have played a most distinguished part in UNEF throughout its period of operations, as indeed, they have in other United Nations peace-keeping efforts. Lieut. General E. L. M. Burns of Canada was the first Commander of the Force and gave magnificent service in overcoming the many and extraordinary problems of this completely novel operation. . . .

Irrespective of the circumstances of the withdrawal of UNEF and the consequences of that withdrawal, ten and a half years' successful service to peace is a historic achievement. Canada's large role in that achievement and your Government's unfailing understanding of the requirements of United Nations peace-keeping operations are widely recognized and appreciated here. I would be grateful if you would express that appreciation to your Government and especially to all the officers and men of the Canadian Armed Forces who have served at one time or another with UNEF. (May 30, 1967.)

Prime Minister Pearson to the Secretary General

Thank you for the warm message you sent me expressing appreciation to the Government and people of Canada, and particularly to the Canadian officers and men who served in the United Nations Emergency Force, for the contribution Canada has made over the years to that peacekeeping force.

Successive Canadian Governments, the people of Canada and Canada's armed forces have been proud to be closely associated from the very beginning with this historic United Nations undertaking which for over ten years has made such a vital contribution to the maintenance of peace in the Middle East.

Despite current difficulties faced by the United Nations in the peacekeeping field, I am hopeful that it will be possible to profit from the experience gained in UNEF and to use the lessons learned to develop in due course, within the framework of the United Nations, more effective machinery "to save succeeding generations from the scourge of war," in the words of the Charter. In the continuing effort that must be carried on to plan for United Nations peacekeeping forces, organized and established in a way which will avoid the disturbing experience we have just gone through in the disbanding of UNEF, the United Nations can count on our full support. Recent events show that the work of the United Nations in the field of peacekeeping is not less, but more important than ever and that this work must include advance planning so that United Nations peacekeeping forces in the future will have a clear and strong basis on which to operate.

I greatly appreciate the generous references in your message to the role I was privileged to share with others in the establishment of UNEF. I should like to take this opportunity to associate myself with your references to the great contribution made by your predecessor, Dag Hammarskjöld. Without his selfless devotion to the United Nations and to the cause of world peace and his unrivalled diplomatic skill, United Nations peacekeeping would never have developed as it did. You, Mr. Secretary-General, have carried on the tradition which he established and have guided the Organization with untiring energy and selfless sincerity through what has been a most difficult period of the United Nations' history. The Government and people of Canada are deeply appreciative of the very heavy responsibilities you are bearing and, on their behalf, I wish to reaffirm full support to you personally and to the Organization over which you preside. With warm personal regards.

APPENDIX G

Text of "Secret" Memorandum by Dag Hammarskjöld Concerning the Withdrawal of UNEF

The most desirable thing of course, would have been to tie Egypt by an agreement in which they declared that withdrawal should take place only if so decided by the General Assembly. But in this naked form, however, the problem could never have been settled. I felt that the same was true of an agreement to the effect that withdrawal should take place upon "agreement on withdrawal" between the U.N. and the Egyptian Government. However, I found it worthwhile to try a line, very close to the second one, according to which Egypt would declare to the United Nations that it would exert all its sovereign rights with regard to the troops on the basis of a good faith interpretation of the tasks of the force. The United Nations should make a reciprocal commitment to maintain the force as long as the task was not completed. If such a dual statement was introduced in an agreement between the parties, it would be obvious that the procedure in case of a request from Egypt for the withdrawal of UNEF would be as follows. The matter would at once be brought before the General Assembly. If the General Assembly found that the task was completed, everything would be alright. If they found that the task was not completed and Egypt, all the same, maintained its stand and enforced the withdrawal, Egypt would break the agreement with the United Nations. Of course Egypt's freedom of action could under no circumstances be limited but by some kind of agreement. The device I used meant only that instead of limiting their rights by a basic understanding requesting an agreement *directly concerning withdrawal*, we created an obligation to reach agreement on the fact that the tasks were completed, and thus, *the conditions for a withdrawal established.*

APPENDIX H

Text of U Thant's Statement to the Press on the "Secret Memorandum"

1. It is not an official document, is not in the official files of the Secretary-General's office, and its existence has never been reported in

any way to any organ of the United Nations, including the UNEF Advisory Committee. It was thus of a purely private character and although supposedly secret in nature, is said to have been given by him to one or more of Mr. Hammarskjöld's friends. To say the least, the release of such a paper at this time would seem to raise some question of ethics and good faith.

2. It can be said with full confidence that this paper was never conveyed to President Nasser or to the Government of the United Arab Republic; that Government knew nothing about it and was in no way bound by it.

3. I, however, had been made aware of the substance of the paper before my visit to Cairo to talk with President Nasser.

4. The crux of the matters dwelled upon in the Hammarskjöld paper is the understanding between Mr. Hammarskjöld and President Nasser which sometimes has been referred to as the "good faith" accord. There is, in fact, nothing new about this. In my special report to the General Assembly of 18 May (A/6669, paragraph 7), I gave the text of an *aide-mémoire* which I had immediately sent to the Government of the United Arab Republic on the "good faith" accord. No response to it was received.

5. It is puzzling to me, however, that those who attempt to read so much into the Hammarskjöld paper, and particularly into the "good faith" accord, do not see—or do not choose to see—the clear fact that the "good faith" accord, having been reached in November 1956, had a more limited scope and could not possibly have envisaged or have had any relevance to the later function defined for UNEF by the General Assembly in February 1957. In the OPI (Office of Public Information) background release EMF/449 of 3 June 1967, entitled "Notes on Withdrawal of United Nations Emergency Force (UNEF)," this point was clearly stated in paragraph 17 of that paper in the following words:

"It has been asserted that the so-called 'good faith' accord (see document A/6669 of 18 May 1967, paragraph 7) implied that Egypt's acceptance of General Assembly Resolution 1000 (ES-I) of 5 November 1956 would oblige Egypt to continue to accept the presence of UNEF until the task of the Force was completed. Such a view . . . also ignores the fact that this understanding was reached in mid-November 1956 and therefore could relate only to General Assembly Resolution 1000 (ES-I) of 5 November 1956, which defined the task of UNEF in very general terms as being 'to secure and supervise the cessation of hostilities.' At that early stage the purpose of the Force in reality was to replace the withdrawing forces of France, Israel and the United Kingdom, and to be, in fact, the condition for the withdrawal of those forces. Hostilities ceased, automatically in fact, once UNEF was deployed and thus its task at that time was completed. It was not until its resolution of 2 February 1957 that the General Assembly broadened the function of UNEF in its Resolution 1125 (XI) by stating that:

> the scrupulous maintenance of the Armistice Agreement requires the placing of the United Nations Emergency Force on the Egyptian-Israeli armistice demarcation line and the implementation of other measures as proposed in the Secretary-General's report. . . .

That broader task, clearly, is not completed, and it would be impossible to say at present when it will or can be completed. The Armistice has already endured for over 18 years. But this was not the task envisaged or defined for UNEF when Secretary-General Hammarskjöld and President Nasser reached the "good faith" understanding.

APPENDIX I

Text of Resolution 242

The Security Council,
Expressing its continuing concern with the grave situation in the Middle East,
Emphasizing the inadmissibility of the acquisition of territory by war and the need to work for a just and lasting peace in which every State in the area can live in security,
Emphasizing further that all Member States in their acceptance of the Charter of the United Nations have undertaken a commitment to act in accordance with Article 2 of the Charter,
1. Affirms that the fulfilment of Charter principles requires the establishment of a just and lasting peace in the Middle East which should include the application of both the following principles:
(i) Withdrawal of Israeli armed forces from territories occupied in the recent conflict;
(ii) Termination of all claims or states of belligerency and respect for and acknowledgement of the sovereignty, territorial integrity and political independence of every State in the area and their right to live in peace within secure and recognized boundaries free from threats or acts of force;

2. Affirms further the necessity

(a) For guaranteeing freedom of navigation through international waterways in the area;

(b) For achieving a just settlement of the refugee problem;

(c) For guaranteeing the territorial inviolability and political independence of every State in the area, through measures including the establishment of demilitarized zones;

3. Requests the Secretary-General to designate a Special Representative to proceed to the Middle East to establish and maintain contacts with the States concerned in order to promote agreement and assist efforts to achieve a peaceful and accepted settlement in accordance with the provisions and principles in this resolution;

4. Requests the Secretary-General to report to the Security Council on the progress of the efforts of the Special Representative as soon as possible.[13]

APPENDIX J

Text of William P. Rogers' Letter to the Foreign Minister of the U.A.R.

With the above thoughts in mind, the United States puts forward the following proposal for consideration of the United Arab Republic.

A. That both Israel and the U.A.R. subscribe to a restoration of the cease-fire for at least a limited period;

B. That Israel and the U.A.R. (as well as Israel and Jordan) subscribe to the following statement which would be in the form of a report from Ambassador Jarring to the Secretary-General, U Thant:

"The U.A.R. (Jordan) and Israel advise me that they agree:

A. That having accepted and indicated the willingness to carry out Resolution 242 in all its parts, they will designate representatives to discussions to be held under my auspices, according to such procedure [and] at such places and times as I may recommend, taking into account as appropriate each side's preference [as] to method of procedure and previous experience between the parties:

B. That the purpose of the aforementioned discussions is to reach agreement on the establishment of a just and lasting peace between

---

[13] *United Nations Security Council Official Records,* No. 1379, November 16, 1967.

them based on (1) mutual acknowledgement by the U.A.R. (Jordan) and Israel of each other's sovereignty, territorial integrity and political independence, and (2) Israeli withdrawal from territories occupied in the 1967 conflict, both in accordance with Resolution 242.

C. That, to facilitate my task of promoting agreement as set forth in Resolution 242, the parties will strictly observe, effective July 1 until at least Oct. 1, the ceasefire resolutions of the Security Council."

We hope the U.A.R. will find this proposal acceptable: we are also seeking Israeli acceptance. In the meantime, I am sure you will share my conviction that everything be done to hold these proposals in confidence so as not to prejudice the prospects for their acceptance.

I am sending a similar message to Foreign Minister Rifai (of Jordan). I look forward to your early reply.

WILLIAM P. ROGERS

PART VI

APPENDIX A

Letter from U Thant to His Excellency Tunku Abdul Rahman

23 April 1971

Dear Tunku,

It is with considerable hesitation that I write to you now but I hope that you will feel that in the circumstances this unusual approach to you is justified.

I am sure that Your Excellency must have followed with as much concern as the rest of the world, recent events in East Pakistan. Since we had a fairly large United Nations Development Programme there (which has been temporarily suspended) I have received some authentic information, including information from the United Nations personnel stationed in East Pakistan, about the happenings there, which deepen my concern. While the military operations may appear to be successful, and a measure of peace may return to East Pakistan, I find it difficult to believe that normal life can proceed unless there is some political understanding between the leaders of West Pakistan and East Pakistan. I also believe that a massive international humanitarian effort may be needed if the civilian population is to avoid acute suffering and hardship in the difficult days ahead. This is a matter which I have already taken up with President Yahya Khan.

It is with this predominantly humanitarian concern in mind that I now write to you to ask if you feel you could take some personal interest in the matter. Your Excellency, as the former Head of Government of a Moslem State and even more in your present capacity, [you] have a special interest in resolving this tragic conflict between brother Moslems. I feel that the exercise of your personal good offices might help to bring about, in time, a more viable political settlement than would be possible under present conditions.

I shall be most grateful if you could indicate to me your personal reaction in this matter. I feel that time is of the essence and that quick action is needed.

With assurances of my highest consideration,

Yours sincerely,
U THANT

APPENDIX B

Message from Tunku Abdul Rahman to U Thant

Thank you for the message which was redirected to me in London. I would consider it a privilege to undertake a task in the name of God and in the cause of humanity and will be happy to serve as requested by you. Before I make the move I would be happy to receive authentic information available to you or in your possession so as to enable me to be fully informed if and when I meet the President and officials of Pakistan. I have been approached by many Muslim organizations previously, but have been cautious because Pakistan Government does not welcome outside help. On the other hand the President is well disposed and indicated that I could come to Pakistan any time. Will be back Jeddah on May 2nd and await your reply.

INDEX

Paris, France, Vietnam peace talks in, 77–78, 79, 80, 83, 84
Parker, W. Gibson, 233
Pate, Maurice, 24
Pathan tribesmen, 418
Pauling, Linus, 169
Pazhwak, Abdul Rahman, 267, 271
Peace (peacemaking), UN and, 22–23 (*see also* specific agencies, aspects, countries, crises, developments, individuals, events); economic and social development and, 446, 448; role of Secretary General and, 30, 31, 33
Pearson, Lester, 55, 243–44, 245–46, 257, 448–90
Peru, 202
Phenomenon of Man, The, 25
Philippines, the, 27, 52, 203
Philosophy of Civilization, 24–25
Pinera, José, 279
Pinies, Jaime de, 333
Pire, Dominique Georges, 22–23, 230–31
Pirzada, S. S., 419
Plane, B. Roland, 325
Plan of National Reconciliation (Congo), Thant and, 141–42
Podgorny, Nikolay V., 380
Pogue, George, 96
Poland, 64–65, 74
Popular Front for the Liberation of Palestine, 303ff., 317–18
Population growth, 444, 448
Portugal, 45, 87, 285
Poverty (underdevelopment), Thant on need for United Nations and change in, 38–39, 441ff.
Powell, William, 274, 315, 344, 378
Prague, 381; Thant in, 377–78
Procházka, Jaraslav, 377–78
Punjab (Punjabis), 402, 421

Quaison-Sackey, Alex, 8
Quantara, 280, 296, 308
Quijano, Raul, 130

Rabin, Yitzhak, 236, 479
Radhakrishnan, Sarvepalli, 23, 405, 406–7, 417
Rafael, Gideon, 9, 14, 223, 239, 256–57, 262, 268–69, 278, 280–81, 282, 285, 286, 304
Rafah camp, UNEF, 253, 256
Rahman, Sheikh Mujibur, 421–22, 423, 425–26, 431, 435, 437
Rahman, Tunku Abdul, 424–25, 486–87
Ramani, Radahkrishna, 401
Ramati, Shaul, 198
Rangoon, Burma, 66, 70, 71, 72, 73–76; first Asian Socialist Conference (1951), 198
Rann of Kutch, India, 397–98, 399
Raouf, Adnan, 316

Rawalpindi, Pakistan, 403, 404–5, 406, 418–19, 428, 431–32, 435
Red Cross: and Congo crisis, 125–26; International Committee (IRCC), 53, 54, 138, 180, 183, 185, 190, 282, 296, 430
Rennie, Sir John, 349
Resolution 242 (UN Security Council), and Middle East conflict, 285, 293–94, 299–300, 302, 312–13, 321, 329, 336, 339–40, 347, 353–54, 355–56, 493–95; text of, 493–94
Reston, James, 232–33
"Reverence for life" ethic, 24–25
Rhodes, 206, 232
Rhodesia, 112. See also Rhodesia and Nyasaland; Southern Rhodesia
Rhodesia and Nyasaland, 132–34
Riad, Mahmoud, 222, 224, 235–36, 237, 241, 244, 245–46, 248, 250, 285, 292, 335, 346, 487–88; killed, 318
Rice production and use, 443, 448
Richardson, Elliot, 331
Rikhye, Indar Jit, 114, 121–22, 123, 142, 155, 161, 178–79, 181, 182, 185–86, 188, 371; and Middle East conflict, 220, 222, 223, 234, 235, 237–38, 242, 245, 252, 253–55, 258, 473, 474, 478–86
Roa, Raúl, 181, 182
Rodinson, Maxine, 240
Rogers, William P., 319, 320, 325, 329–30, 331, 335, 337, 338, 339, 348, 351, 494–95
Rohan, Michael Dennis William, 327
Rolz-Bennett, José, 271, 304, 306–7, 363, 381–82
Romania, 369, 379, 384, 389–90, 392
Roosevelt, Mrs. Eleanor, 200
Roosevelt, Franklin D., 31
Rosenne, Shabtai, 310
Rossides, Zenon, 273, 275
Rouleau, Eric, 232
Rowan, Carl T., 109
Rubin, Morris H., 231
Rusk, Dean, 63, 69, 70, 78, 80, 374
Russell, Bertrand, 169–72, 466

Sadat, Anwar, 345
Sadruddin Aga Khan, Prince, 423, 430
"San Antonio formula," Johnson's, 78
Sandstrom, Emil, 130
San Francisco, Calif., 67, 69; UN twentieth anniversary celebration in, 67, 69
Santos, Emilio de los, 364–65
San Yu, General, 73
Sapir, Joseph, 199
Sapir, Pinhas, 296
Sarawak, 51–52
Saud, King, 49
Saudi Arabia, 27, 49, 247, 250, 345–46
Scali, John, 191
Schramme, Jean, 97
Schweitzer, Albert, 24–25